Dedication

This book is dedicated to the many patients, family members, and caregivers, including nurses, physicians, chaplains, firefighters, and police officers, who so generously shared their beliefs and experiences in the hope of clarifying the importance of spirituality in nursing. Some have crossed over to a new life; others continue to live courageously, finding meaning and hope in the experience of illness or in ministering to those who are ill. Their words, quoted extensively in the following pages, are their legacy. I am privileged to be the storyteller.

God called to Moses out of the bush: "Remove the sandals from your feet, for the place on which you are standing is holy ground."

Exodus 3:4–5

The nurse's smile warmly embraces the cancer patient arriving for a chemotherapy treatment.
> *This is holy ground.*

The nurse watches solicitously over the pre-op child who tearfully whispers, "I'm scared."
> *This is holy ground.*

The nurse gently diffuses the anxieties of the ventilator-dependent patient in the ICU.
> *This is holy ground.*

The nurse tenderly takes the hand of the frail elder struggling to accept life in the nursing home.
> *This is holy ground.*

> *The nurse*
>> *reverently touches and is touched by*
>>> *the patient's heart,*
>>>> *the dwelling place of the living God.*

> *This is spirituality in nursing,*
>> *this is the ground of the practice of nursing,*
>>> *this is holy ground!*

Custom Sixth Edition

Spirituality
in Nursing

STANDING ON HOLY GROUND

MARY ELIZABETH O'BRIEN,
PhD, RN, MSW, MTS, FAAN

Professor Emeritus
School of Nursing
The Catholic University of America
Washington, DC

JONES & BARTLETT
LEARNING

World Headquarters
Jones & Bartlett Learning
5 Wall Street
Burlington, MA 01803
978-443-5000
info@jblearning.com
www.jblearning.com

Jones & Bartlett Learning books and products are available through most bookstores and online booksellers. To contact Jones & Bartlett Learning directly, call 800-832-0034, fax 978-443-8000, or visit our website, www.jblearning.com.

Substantial discounts on bulk quantities of Jones & Bartlett Learning publications are available to corporations, professional associations, and other qualified organizations. For details and specific discount information, contact the special sales department at Jones & Bartlett Learning via the above contact information or send an email to specialsales@jblearning.com.

Production Credits

VP, Executive Publisher: David D. Cella
Executive Editor: Amanda Martin
Associate Acquisitions Editor: Rebecca Stephenson
Editorial Assistant: Christina Freitas
Vendor Manager: Sara Kelly
Senior Marketing Manager: Jennifer Scherzay
Product Fulfillment Manager: Wendy Kilborn
Composition and Project Management: S4Carlisle Publishing Services

Cover Design: Kristin E. Parker
Rights & Media Specialist: Wes DeShano
Media Development Editor: Troy Liston
Cover Image: © Cyril Leclerc/EyeEm/Getty
Chapter opener image: © Herzlinde Vancura/Dreamstime.com
Printing and Binding: LSC Communications
Cover Printing: LSC Communications

To order this product, use ISBN: 978-1-284-15771-0

Library of Congress Cataloging-in-Publication Data

Names: O'Brien, Mary Elizabeth, author.
Title: Spirituality in nursing : standing on holy ground / Mary Elizabeth O'Brien.
Description: Sixth edition. | Burlington, Massachusetts : Jones & Bartlett Learning, [2018] | Includes bibliographical references and index.
Identifiers: LCCN 2016047291 | ISBN 9781284121001
Subjects: | MESH: Spirituality | Nurse-Patient Relations | Religion and Medicine | Christianity | Nursing Care—ethics | Philosophy, Nursing
Classification: LCC RT85.2 | NLM WY 87 | DDC 610.7301—dc23 LC record available at https://lccn.loc.gov/2016047291

6048

Printed in the United States of America
22 21 20 19 18   10 9 8 7 6 5 4 3

Contents

Acknowledgments

The author's loving thanks is extended to the many patients and caregivers, both professional and family, who graciously and generously shared their thoughts and experiences, included in the text, in the hope of helping others who may one day tread a similar path.

Much appreciation must also be expressed to the editorial and production staff of Jones & Bartlett Learning, who have continued to support the work of preparing the revised and updated editions of *Spirituality in Nursing: Standing on Holy Ground*.

And, finally, my deepest and most abiding gratitude is to God, the source of my strength and the center of my life; to the Father who provides me with the courage and energy to write, to His Divine Son, Jesus Christ, whose care for the ill and infirm provides the model for ministry to the sick and to the Holy Spirit, without whose inspiration and guidance these pages would never have been completed.

CHAPTER 1

Spirituality in Nursing: Standing on Holy Ground

God called to Moses out of the bush: "Moses, Moses!" And he said, "Here I am." "Come no closer," God said. "Remove the sandals from your feet, for the place on which you are standing is holy ground."

Exodus 3:4–5

> Nursing is really about being intuitive and spiritual. . . . When you see nursing as a calling, you go to this higher level which is the vocation level, which has a spiritual dimension to the profession. . . . I think that whenever there is another human being involved, you see yourself as in a vocation, you really understand . . ."I can make it better. That is the ministry way of looking at nursing; that is the spiritual way of looking at it.

Anne, Supervisor of a Critical Care Unit

Perhaps no scriptural theme so well models the spiritual posture of nursing practice as the Old Testament depiction of Moses and the burning bush. In the biblical narrative, God reminded Moses that, when he stood before his Lord, the ground beneath his feet was holy. When the nurse clinician, nurse educator, nurse administrator, or nurse researcher stands before a patient, a student, a staff member, or a study participant, God is also present, and the ground on which the nurse is standing is holy. For it is here, in the act of serving a brother or sister in need, that the nurse truly encounters God. God is present in the nurse's practice of caring just as surely as He was present in the blessed meeting with Moses so many centuries ago. In an editorial in the *Journal of Christian Nursing*, Judy Shelly (2003) reminded us that "the holy ground we as nurses are called to enter may be . . . difficult . . . we face pain, suffering, fear, communication barriers, cultural and ethnic prejudice, injustice, impossible working conditions and constant obstacles" (p. 3). However, Shelly added, although we may at times "feel inadequate and defeated . . . God is with us. He offers us his peace" (p. 3). This, I believe, is the gift and the grace of our nursing vocation of "standing on holy ground." This is the blessing; the precious knowledge that, however great or small our nursing task may be, God is with us and will give us His peace.

This introductory chapter addresses the nurse's spiritual posture, "standing on holy ground," while also offering a historical perspective on the spiritual ministry of nursing. The overall relationship between spirituality and nursing practice is explored; the concepts of spirituality—as distinguished from religiosity or religious practice—and nursing are defined with a view to understanding their meaning for the contemporary nurse. Nursing practice is examined in relation to the nurse's spiritual stance in caring for patients, the nurse's participation in the provision of holistic care, and the nurse's role as healer. Finally, a practice model, labeled a "Nursing Theology of Caring," is described.

The empirical data on the spiritual concerns and needs of the ill in the present chapter, as well as those in the following chapters, are derived from nursing research with persons suffering from a multiplicity of illness conditions in a variety of settings. The author conducted both formal and informal interviewing and observation with these patients, their family members, and their nurse caregivers. The interview and observational data are supplemented by materials excerpted from journals maintained during the conduct of the research and also during a hospital chaplaincy experience.

▶ The Spiritual Ministry of Nursing: A Historical Perspective

In a small but classic volume, *The Nurse: Handmaid of the Divine Physician*, written in the early 1940s, Franciscan Sister Mary Berenice Beck articulated what a great number of nurses of her era, especially those of the Judeo-Christian tradition, understood as the spirituality of their practice. Historically, nursing was viewed in large part as a vocation of service, incorporating a clearly accepted element of ministry to those for whom the nurse cared. A nurse's mission was considered to be driven by altruism and empathy for the sick, especially the sick poor. The practicing nurse of the early and middle 20th century did not expect much in terms of worldly rewards for her efforts. She envisioned her caregiving as commissioned and supported by God; to Him alone were the thanks and the glory to be given. This vision of nursing as a spiritual ministry is reflected in Sr. Mary Berenice's nurse's prayer:

> I am Thine Own, great Healer, help Thou me to serve Thy sick in humble charity;
>
> I ask not thanks nor praise, but only light to care for them in every way aright.
>
> My charges, sick and well, they all are Thine. (Beck, 1945, p. xvii)

Other nursing authors of the time also supported the concept of nursing as a calling, with a decidedly spiritual element undergirding its practice. As nurse historian Minnie Goodnow (1916) asserted, "Nursing is not merely an occupation, temporary and superficial in scope; it is a great vocation" (p. 17). She added, "It [nursing] is so well known to be difficult that it is seldom undertaken by a woman who has not, in the depths of her consciousness, an earnest purpose to serve humanity" (p. 17). And, in the introduction to an early fundamentals of nursing textbook, *The Art, Science and Spirit of Nursing* (1954), author Alice Price observed, "Nursing is possessed of a spiritual quality, in that its primary aim is to serve humanity, not only by giving curative care to the bodies of the sick and injured, but by serving the needs of the mind and spirit as well" (p. 3). For the Christian nurse, the frequently quoted scriptural text supporting practice was that of Matthew 25:35–40, "For I was . . . sick and you took care of me. . . . I tell you, just as you did it to one of the least of these . . . you did for me."

A condition that kept the original spiritual ministry of nursing alive in this country was the fact that many early to mid-20th century nurses received their education in nursing schools affiliated with one of the predominant religious denominations. Prior to the development of contemporary undergraduate and graduate programs in nursing, the three-year diploma schools that were the norm were generally not associated with academic institutions. Rather they were sponsored by individual hospitals, many of which were religiously affiliated. These schools tended to be small and insular in character, taking on the spiritual élan of the hospital with which they were connected. This was evident in the rituals of passage such as "capping" and graduation that were often conducted in places of worship with the blessing of a cleric included as part of the ceremony.

In the latter half of the 20th century, however, although some U.S. nursing schools did retain a strong spiritual milieu as a characteristic feature, many of the newer university and college-affiliated programs began to focus on the professional character of nursing. Nursing publications and conferences described the characteristics of a profession, and much debate centered around how nursing incorporated specified professional criteria, particularly the criterion of autonomy of practice. These discussions were appropriate, as advanced health-care technology and burgeoning knowledge generated by the behavioral sciences resulted in the practicing nurse requiring and receiving ever more sophisticated education related to patient care. For a time, at least, the proverbial pendulum appeared to swing toward the science, rather than the art, of nursing. This represented a concerted effort to bring nursing practice up to standard alongside medical practice and that of other caregiving professions.

During the 1970s and 1980s, however, despite the fact that curricula in baccalaureate and newly emerging master's and doctoral programs in nursing were becoming increasingly more complex in terms of the biologic and behavioral sciences, many were beginning to acknowledge the need for holistic health care. With the advent of the concept of holism, came a reawakening of the importance of the ill person's spiritual nature and a heightened concern for spiritual needs. In identifying a model for holistic nursing, nurse clinician and researcher Cathie Guzzetta (1988) described holistic concepts as incorporating "a sensitive balance between art and science, analytic and intuitive skills, and the ability and knowledge to choose from a wide variety of treatment modalities to promote balance and interconnectedness of body, mind and spirit" (p. 117). Thus, in the holistic nursing model, patients' spiritual nature and needs are brought into equal focus with their cognitive and physiologic needs.

Nursing literature, both professional and lay, now began to address the spiritual component of the human person. Books and articles abounded relating to such topics as prayer, spiritual counseling, "near-death" experiences, interactions with angels, and volunteer activities undertaken for spiritual motives. Many individuals in our society were seeking to find transcendent meaning in their lives. It was not surprising, then, that nurses, now more solidly entrenched in their professional identities, should follow suit. As theorist Barbara Barnum (1994) pointed out, whereas nursing's focus in the past was on the "biopsychosocial" model of care, more recently nurse scholars have demonstrated a renewed interest in the spiritual dimension of caregiving (p. 114). Barnum's assertion was reflected in an increase in the nursing literature in conceptual and research-based articles related to the association between spirituality and health/illness. One example was the work of Jean Watson (1995) who observed, "At its most basic level nursing is a human-caring, relational profession. It exists by virtue of an ethical-moral ideal, and commitment to provide care for others" (p. 67). Watson's comment reflected a newer understanding of the spiritual ministry of nursing practice.

▶ Spirituality and Nursing Practice

In order to provide some basis for beginning a discussion of spirituality and contemporary nursing practice, there must be a common understanding of the concepts of spirituality and nursing. Spirituality, as a personal concept, is generally understood in terms of an individual's attitudes and beliefs related to transcendence (God) or to the nonmaterial forces of life and of nature. Religious practice or religiosity, however, relates to a person's beliefs and behaviors associated with a specific religious tradition or denomination. Nurses need to have a clear understanding of this distinction or they may neglect spiritual needs in focusing only on a patient's religious practice (Emblen, 1992, p. 41).

The latter point is strongly supported by nurse practitioner Patricia Alpert (2010) in the article "Spirituality Goes beyond Religiosity: A Much Needed Practice in Nursing." In the article Alpert asserts, as noted previously, that "religion and spirituality are not synonymous" and points out that religiosity may only be "a partial expression of one's spirituality" and that "in health care, spiritual care may be viewed as religious care" (p. 140). Alpert defines *spiritual care* as "any act that nourishes the soul or spirit" (p. 141) and describes spiritual care as "fundamental to nursing practice" (p. 141).

Reinert and Koenig (2013) propose "defining spirituality in the context of religious involvement when conducting research, while using a broader definition of spirituality when providing spiritual care" (p. 2622). As noted by scholar Barbara Pesut (2013), spirituality, as well as religion "will likely continue to play an enduring role in providing fundamental meaning for nursing work" (p. 5).

Spirituality

Spirituality, as related to holistic nursing, has been described by Dossey (1989) as "a broad concept that encompasses values, meaning, and purpose; one turns inward to the human traits of honesty, love, caring, wisdom, imagination, and compassion; existence of a quality of a higher authority, guiding spirit or transcendence that is mystical; a flowing, dynamic balance that allows and creates healing of body-mind-spirit; and may or may not involve organized religion" (p. 24). Pamela Reed (1992) presented a paradigm with which to explore spirituality in nursing by defining *spirituality* as "an expression of the developmental capacity for self-transcendence" (p. 350). Nurse anthropologist Madeleine Leininger (1997, p. 104) identified spirituality as a relationship with a supreme being that directs one's beliefs and practices.

Spirituality viewed as a human need has been described as "that dimension of a person that is concerned with ultimate ends and values. . . . Spirituality is that which inspires in one the desire to transcend the realm of the material"

(O'Brien, 1982, p. 88). For many individuals, especially those adhering to the Western religious traditions of Judaism, Christianity, and Islam, the concept of transcendence incorporates belief in God. This is reflected explicitly in the conceptualization of spirituality articulated by nurse Ruth Stoll (1989) who asserted, "Through my spirituality I give and receive love; I respond to and appreciate God, other people, a sunset, a symphony and spring" (p. 6). Prayers as indicating a meaning in life have been identified as indications of spirituality (Meraviglia, 1999); spirituality may thrive, however, outside the sphere of organized religion (Kendrick & Robinson, 2000).

Three characteristics of spirituality posited by Margaret Burkhardt (1989) include "unfolding mystery," related to one's attempt to understand the meaning and purpose of life; "harmonious interconnectedness," or an individual's relationship to other persons and/or to God; and "inner strength," which relates to one's personal spiritual resources and "sense of the sacred" (p. 72). Spirituality was proposed as a "cornerstone" of holistic nursing by Nagai-Jacobson and Burkhardt (1989) who suggested that questions appropriate to exploring a patient's spirituality might include how the individual understands God and what things give meaning and joy to life (p. 23). Each nurse needs to understand his or her own spirituality, keeping in mind that this personal belief system may differ significantly from that of a patient and family.

The nursing literature offers no one clear definition of *spirituality*. As pointed out by Verna Benner Carson in the *Journal of Christian Nursing* (1993), "Definitions of spirituality represent a variety of worldviews and the opinions of people from divergent walks of life" (p. 25). Common to most descriptions of spirituality, as reflected in the early and later nursing literature, are the elements of love; compassion; caring; transcendence; relationship with God; and the connection of body, mind, and spirit.

Nurse educator Janice Clarke presents a critical view of nursing's definition of *spirituality* by suggesting that theology may provide needed insight into the concept. Clarke (2009) concludes that the broad explanations of spirituality existing in some of the nursing literature has led to "definitions which have the tendency to result in a type of spiritual care which is indistinguishable for psychosocial care, hard to explain to patients and difficult to put into practice" (p. 1666).

In an article on the "range and diversity of definitions" of spirituality within the nursing literature, however, Swinton and Pattison (2010) argue that "It is in fact the vagueness of the concept that is its strength and value" (p. 226). These authors feel that a "thin" definition of spirituality will increase the usefulness of the concept in practical situations (p. 232). Other authors agree that the concept of spirituality in nursing is appropriately "open to interpretation" (Noble & Jones, 2010, p. 565); that "the concept (of spirituality in nursing) and its application have been the subject of much debate" (Pike, 2011, p. 743); and that "spirituality in nursing is a subject that is not easily defined, interpreted or understood" (Ellis & Narayanasamy, 2009, p. 886).

This diversity in the definitions of spirituality in nursing literature, accepted by Swinton and Pattison, is also supported by Bruce, Shields, and Molzahn in the paper "Language and the (Im)possibilities of Articulating Spirituality" (2011). The authors assert that incompleteness or differences in definitions of spirituality are "perhaps necessary and to be welcomed" (p. 44). They conclude that "lack of agreement [of definitions of *spirituality*] may suggest a way to protect profound human experiences" from being too cavalierly dismissed and/or the differences in definition may simply reflect "the impossibility of solidifying in language what is too fluid and experiential" (p. 50).

Ultimately the meaning of spiritualty in nursing practice will be guided by the spirituality and spiritual attitudes of those providing care; attitudes and behaviors such as presence and patient centeredness (Ramezani, Ahmadi, Mohammadi, & Kazemnejad, 2014, p. 11); kindness, compassion, and tenderness (Meehan, 2012, p. 990); and empathy and humility (Narayanasamy, 2015, p. 246).

Nursing

Writing in the early 1950s, Alice Price (1954), offered a definition of *nursing* that incorporated not only the concept of the patient's spiritual nature, but the altruistic vocation of the nurse as well. She described nursing as neither pure science nor true art, but as a combination of both. "Nursing, as a profession, will embrace more than an art and a science; it will be a blending of three factors: of art and science, and the spirit of unselfish devotion to a cause primarily concerned with helping those who are physically, mentally or spiritually ill" (p. 2). Price ultimately defined *nursing* as "a service to the individual which helps him to regain, or to keep, a normal state of body and mind; when it cannot accomplish this, it helps him gain relief from physical pain, mental anxiety or spiritual discomfort" (p. 3). Although Price was writing some 25 to 30 years prior to the widespread acceptance of the term *holistic nursing,* her vision of the professional nurse's role clearly included attention to the needs of a patient's spirit, as well as to the needs of the body and the mind.

In their book *Introduction to Nursing,* written 40 years after publication of Price's 1954 text, coauthors Lindberg, Hunter, and Kruszewski (1994) argued that, because of the continual growth and development of the profession, no single definition of nursing can be accepted (p. 7). The authors presented excerpts of nursing definitions articulated by a cadre of theorists from Florence Nightingale in 1859 to Martha Rogers in 1970 but, ultimately, suggested that each practicing nurse develop a definition of his or her own. Lindberg and colleagues did, however, express the hope that, whatever one's definition, it will contain an emphasis on caring or nurturing as a motivating factor for choosing nursing (p. 7).

Following the suggestions of Price in 1954 and Lindberg, Hunter, and Kruszewski in 1994, a potential working definition of nursing follows:

> Nursing is a sacred ministry of health care or health promotion provided to persons both sick and well, who require caregiving, support, or education to assist them in achieving, regaining, or maintaining a state of wholeness, including wellness of body, mind, and spirit. The nurse also serves those in need of comfort and care to strengthen them in coping with the trajectory of a chronic or terminal illness, or with experiencing the dying process.

The spiritual dimensions of the definition relate to two concepts: first, the sacred ministry of caring on the part of the nurse; and second, the ultimate goal of the patient's achievement of a state of wholeness, including the wellness of body, mind, and spirit. These concepts are next explored in terms of the nurse's spiritual posture, the patient's spiritual wholeness, and the nurse–patient spiritual interaction.

Later nursing authors also focused on the importance of spirituality in nursing. Some examples included a discussion of spirituality as a key concept in the nursing models of Betty Neuman, Margaret Newman, Rosemary Parse, and Jean Watson (Young & Koopsen, 2011, p. 7); a critique of nursing's definitions of spirituality (Clarke, 2009); an analysis of the current debate about spirituality in nursing

(Gray, 2009); identification of philosophical approaches to the study of spirituality in nursing (Tinley & Kinney, 2007); and literature reviews on spirituality and nursing and health outcomes (Como, 2007; Pesut, 2008).

▶ The Nurse's Spiritual Posture: Standing on Holy Ground

Spiritual writer Sister Macrina Wiederkehr (1991) advised, "If you should ever hear God speaking to you from a burning bush, and it happens more often than most of us realize, take off your shoes for the ground on which you stand is holy" (p. 2). How appropriate, it seems, to envision practicing nurses, who must come together with their patients in caring and compassion, as standing on holy ground. God frequently speaks to us from a "burning bush," in the fretful whimper of a feverish child, in the anxious questions of a preoperative surgical patient, and in the frail moans of a fragile elder. If we "take off our shoes," we will be able to realize that the place where we stand is holy ground; we will respond to our patients as we would wish to respond to God in the burning bush.

But what does it really mean to "take off one's shoes"? Sister Macrina asserted that it means stripping away "whatever prevents us from experiencing the holy" (1991, p. 3). She added that God speaks to us in many "burning bushes of today" and that "the message is still one of holy ground"; it is a message that is often missed "because of [our] unnecessary shoes" (p. 3). In the contemporary conduct of nursing practice, nursing education, nursing administration, and nursing research, some of us may admit to having a number of unnecessary pairs of shoes littering our professional closets. First, there are running shoes, which many of us wear as we rush pell-mell from task to task in order to manage the day. As we fly about, feet barely touching the ground, it is easy to forget, in the busyness, that where we are standing is a holy place. Another often relied on pair of shoes are sturdy walking brogues, which provide protection against unwanted intrusions. Unfortunately, their insulated soles, which keep us safe and secure, may also prevent our feet from feeling the holy ground on which we walk. And then there are old, favorite loafers, well-worn and cozy. When we are wearing these shoes, we can so rest in their comfort that we need not be troubled by any disturbing bumps in the holy ground. We nurses probably have, I am sure, many more unnecessary pairs of shoes that prevent our feet from experiencing holy ground. But recollections of times past when, literally or figuratively, we have been able to take off our shoes, even if only briefly, well validate the Old Testament message.

▶ Holistic Nursing: The Body, Mind, and Spirit Connection

At times we hear an individual described as being truly healthy. The assumption underlying such a remark may relate not so much to the physical health or well-being of the person as to the fact that he or she is perceived as solidly grounded spiritually. One can be possessed of a healthy attitude toward life, even if suffering from a terminal illness. In order to achieve such a spiritual grounding in the face of physical or psychological deficit, the individual must be closely attuned to the body, mind, and spirit connection; one must understand and accept the value of the spiritual dimension in the overall paradigm of holistic health.

As our society advanced scientifically during the past half century, it became increasingly more difficult for some in the health-care community to give credence to the importance of the spiritual nature of the human person, especially in relation to health/illness issues. Ultimately, however, caregivers began recognizing that sensitivity to a patient's spiritual needs was critical if they were to provide truly "holistic" health care. Nurse and minister Ann Robinson (1995) believed that nurses must "embrace the spirituality of the human community" in order to support their patients' holistic health behaviors (p. 3).

Authors Dossey and Keegan (1989) defined the concept of holism, which undergirds holistic health and holistic nursing care, including the body, mind, and spirit connection, as "the view that an integrated whole has a reality independent of and greater than the sum of its parts" (p. 4). They described holism as consisting of a philosophy of positive, interactionally based attitudes and behaviors that can exist not only in one who is well but also in one who is seriously or terminally ill (p. 5). Nurses practicing care supportive of such holism need to envision the spiritual needs of a patient as deserving of attention equal to that provided in response to physical and psychosocial concerns.

Overall, holistic nursing is supported by and alternately supports the intimate connection of body, mind, and spirit. Nursing of the whole person requires attention to the individuality and uniqueness of each dimension, as well as to the interrelatedness of the three. In *The Wholeness Handbook*, Emeth and Greenhut (1991) described the body, mind, and spirit elements: The body is the physical substance of a person that can be perceived in empirical reality; the mind is that dimension of an individual that conceptualizes; and the spirit is the life principle that is shared with all humanity and with God. "It is the dimension of personhood that drives us to create, love, question, contemplate and transcend" (pp. 27–28). Those practicing holistic nursing today truly "appreciate the need to integrate the body, mind and spirit within the delivery of health care" (Boswell, Cannon, & Miller, 2013, p. 329).

For the nurse seeking to provide holistic health care, then, the spiritual dimension and needs of the person must be carefully assessed and considered in all therapeutic planning. Spiritual care cannot be separated from physical, social, and psychological care (Lo & Brown, 1999; O'Connor, 2001). Often it is uniquely the nurse, standing either literally or figuratively at the bedside, who has the opportunity and the entreé to interact with patients on that spiritual level where they strive to create, love, question, contemplate, and transcend. Here, truly, the nurse is standing on holy ground.

▶ The Nurse as Healer

The nurse, standing as he or she does on the holy ground of caring for the sick, is well situated to be the instrument of God's healing. In the sacred interaction between nurse and patient, the spiritual healing dimension of holistic health care is exemplified and refined. The nurse stands as God's surrogate and as a vehicle for His words and His touch of compassionate care.

Healing has been described variously as facilitating openness to the "communication of the Holy Spirit, whose message is always wholeness" (Johnson, 1992, p. 21); "the process or act of curing or restoring to health or wholeness, the body, the mind and the spirit" (Haggard, 1983, p. 235); and "to make whole" (Burke, 1993, p. 37). The concept of the nurse as healer incorporates the characteristics of all three definitions; that is, the nurse healer must listen to the voice of God; desire to restore health either of body or of spirit; and attempt to assist the patient in achieving wholeness and integrity of body, mind, and spirit. For the nurse of the Judeo-Christian tradition, spiritually oriented scriptural models of healing abound in both the Old and the New Testaments.

Yahweh's healing power is reflected in Old Testament Scripture in such narratives as Elijah's healing of the widow's son (1 Kings 17:17–23) and Elisha's cleansing of Naaman's leprosy (2 Kings 5:1–14). In the New Testament account of the ministry of Jesus, 41 healings are identified (Kelsey, 1988, p. 43). Jesus healed by word and by touch, sometimes even using physical materials such as mud and saliva. Always, Jesus' healings were accompanied by love and compassion for the ill persons or their families, as in the case of Jairus' young daughter, who her parents thought to be dead. Jesus comforted Jairus with the words, "The child is not dead but sleeping" (Mark 5:39). And then, "He took her by the hand and said to her, 'Talitha cum,' which means 'Little girl, get up!' And immediately the girl got up and began to walk about" (Mark 5:41).

In her doctoral dissertation entitled "Biblical Roots of Healing in Nursing," Maria Homberg (1980) posited that an established biblical tradition reflecting the healing power of such concepts as respect for human dignity and positive interpersonal relationships has parallels in contemporary nursing (p. 2). Homberg suggested that the biblical history of healing can be used by nurse educators to support the importance of these concepts. Dossey (1988) identified the characteristics of a nurse healer as having an awareness that "being present" to the patient is as essential as technical skills, respecting and loving all clients regardless of background or personal characteristics, listening actively, being nonjudgmental, and viewing time with clients as times of sharing and serving (p. 42). These characteristics reflect the spiritual nature of healing described in the Old and the New Testament Scriptures. Finally, nurse educator Brenda Lohri-Posey (2005) says that to become a "compassionate healer" a nurse must "recognize the ability to be a healer" and understand that "healing occasions are unique for each patient" and that "the healing occasion" may change a nurse's "beliefs about pain and suffering" (p. 37).

The Nurse as Wounded Healer

When a nurse is described as a healer, one tends to focus on his or her ability to relieve suffering. The label "healer" evokes the concept of a strong and gifted individual whose ministry is directed by care and compassion; this is an appropriate image. What may be forgotten in such a description is the fact that sometimes the gift of healing has emerged from, and indeed has been honed by, the healer's own experiences of suffering and pain. In exploring the nurse's healing role as an "anonymous minister," a gerontologic nurse practitioner, Sharon, describes using her own pain in counseling patients: "I may not talk about my pain . . . [but] I understand where they're coming from if they're hurting." Sharon, who imagined this experience as being "united in suffering" with those she cared for, reflected Henri Nouwen's (1979) classic conceptualization of the wounded healer. Nouwen described the wounded healer as one who must look after personal wounds while at the same time having the ability to heal others. The wounded healer concept is derived from a Talmudic identification of the awaited Messiah:

> He is sitting among the poor covered with wounds. The others unbind all their wounds at the same time and bind them up again, but he unbinds one at a time and binds it up again, saying to himself: "Perhaps I shall be needed; if so, I must always be ready so as not to delay for a moment." (Tractate Sandhedren, as cited in Nouwen, 1979, p. 82)

The nurse, as any person who undertakes ministry, brings into the interaction personal and unique wounds. Rather than hindering the therapeutic process, the caregiver's wounds, when not unbound all at once, can become a source of strength, understanding, and empathy when addressing the suffering of others. The nurse as a wounded healer caring for a wounded patient can relate his or her own painful experiences to those of the ill person, thus providing a common ground of experience on which to base the initiation of spiritual care.

Two discussions that validate the meaning and importance of the "wounded healer" concept in nursing and health care are those presented by Niven on the meaning of the wounded healer concept for nurses (2008) and teaching the concept of the wounded healer Graves (2008).

▶ A Nursing Theology of Caring

In the previous pages the nurse is described as having the opportunity to heal and to facilitate wholeness, and in the process, to be in the posture of standing on holy ground. But what is it that initiates and supports such nursing practice? What theological or spiritual understanding and beliefs guide the nursing activities of contemporary practitioners? Perhaps these questions can best be answered in the exploration of a nursing theology of caring. The theology of caring encompasses the concepts of being, listening, and touching and was derived from the author's clinical practice with a variety of acutely and chronically ill patients. The nursing theology of caring is supported by the Christian parable of the Good Samaritan:

> A man was going down from Jerusalem to Jericho, and fell into the hands of robbers who stripped him, beat him and went away leaving him half dead. . . . But a Samaritan, while traveling . . . saw him and was moved to pity. He went to him and bandaged his wounds, having poured oil and wine on them. Then he put him on his own animal, brought him to an Inn, and took care of him. (Luke 10:30, 33–34)

The Gospel relates Jesus' parable of the Good Samaritan, told in response to a question posed by a scholar of the law who asked, "Teacher," he said, "what must I do to inherit eternal life?" (Luke 10:25). Jesus said to him, "What is written in the Law?" In response to Jesus' question, the scholar replied, "You shall love the Lord your God with all your heart . . . and your neighbor as yourself" (Luke 10:27). To justify himself, however, the scholar added, "And who is my neighbor?" (Luke 10:29). Jesus related the parable of the Good Samaritan in reply. At the conclusion of the parable, Jesus asked the scholar, of all those who had seen the beaten man, which one was truly a neighbor. The scholar replied, "The one who showed him mercy." Jesus said to him, "Go and do likewise" (Luke 10:36–37).

In a commentary on the parable of the Good Samaritan, Kodell (1989) noted that Jesus' story was intended to challenge a prevailing but discriminating attitude in the society of the time—the fact that a Samaritan, a member of an ethnic group despised by some, could behave so lovingly. The parable, Kodell pointed out, exemplified the love commandment: while the lawyer suggests that not all persons are his neighbors, Jesus' reply indicates that one must consider everyone a neighbor regardless of nationality or religious heritage and affiliation (p. 62). This Gospel narrative provides nurses with a model of unequivocal concern and nondiscrimination in providing care to those in need; it reflects the conceptual framework to support a nursing theology of caring.

Prior to discussing a theology of caring, on which nursing practice may be based, the key concepts of theology and caring will be explored briefly.

Theology

The term *theology* comes originally from the Greek words *theos* meaning "God," and *logos* or "science." The contemporary meaning of theology is "an intellectual discipline, i.e., an ordered body of knowledge about God" (Hill, 1990, p. 1011). The study of theology is often described according to Anselm of Canterbury's conceptualization as "faith seeking understanding." In this context, faith is viewed as "a stance of the whole person towards God, characterized by radical trust, hope, love and commitment" (Fehr, 1990, p. 1027). Each nurse's personal understanding of theology will be informed by myriad factors: religious or denominational heritage, formal and informal religious education, religious and spiritual experience, and current faith practices.

Caring

James Nelson (1976), in his exploration *Rediscovering the Person in Medical Care*, reported that "Underneath . . . important assumptions about the unity of the person and the individual's and community's participation in the healing process lies a fundamental truth: the importance of caring" (p. 62). Nelson added that in health-care facilities (clinics, hospitals, nursing homes) staff have a primary interest in "curing" certain disease and illness conditions. Ministers and nurses must, however, remember the importance of their vocational call to care (p. 62). Nelson defined caring as "an active attitude which genuinely conveys to the other person that he or she does really matter. . . . It is grounded in the sense of uniqueness and worth which, by the grace of God, the other has" (p. 63).

One of the earliest nursing theorists of caring is Madeleine Leininger (1978), who defined the concept as referring to "direct (or indirect) nurturant and skillful activities, processes and decisions related to assisting people in such a manner that reflects behavior attributes which are empathetic, supportive, compassionate, protective, succorant, educational and otherwise dependent upon the needs, problems, values and goals of the individual or group being assisted" (p. 489). In her later writings, Leininger described caring as the central focus or dimension of nursing practice (Leininger, 1980, 1988, 1991). Nurse authors Eriksson (1992); Montgomery (1992); and Benner, Tanner, and Chesla (1996) also identified caring as a central concept of nursing, as did Simone Roach (1992), who postulated five attributes of the concept: "compassion, competence, confidence, conscience, and commitment" (p. 1). In their practice, nurses have always embraced the concept of caring as integral to the essence of the profession (Picard, 1995; Pinch, 1996). And ultimately, through the manifestation of caring nursing practice, nurses engender the kind of trust and confidence in their patients that leads to the promotion of good health (Bishop & Scudder, 1996, p. 41).

Finally, seven characteristics of caring were identified in a study of 200 nurses' stories describing patient care; these were "caring, compassion, spirituality, community outreach, providing comfort, crisis intervention, and going the extra distance" (Hudacek, 2008, p. 124).

The following section, "Dimensions of Caring," encompasses the characteristics of caring as identified in the theological and health-care literature and the goal of a healing outcome as understood in the clinical practice of nursing. Patient examples are drawn from the author's journal chronicling a chaplaincy experience at a research medical center.

▶ Dimensions of Caring

For the nurse practicing spiritual caring, three key activities may serve as vehicles for the carrying out of the theological mandate to serve the sick: being with patients in their experiences of pain, suffering, or other problems or needs; listening to patients verbally express anxieties or emotions, such as fear, anger, loneliness, depression, or sorrow, which may be hindering the achievement of wellness; and touching patients either physically, emotionally, or spiritually to assure them of their connectedness with others in the family of God.

In and of themselves the acts of being with, listening to, or touching a patient may not constitute spiritual care. These behaviors, however, grounded in a nurse's spiritual philosophy of life such as that articulated in the parable of the Good Samaritan, take on the element of ministry; they constitute the nurse's theology of caring.

Being

Being with a sick person without judgment creates space for meaning to emerge and for the holy to be revealed.

—**E. Emeth and J. Greenhut**, 1991, p. 65

The concept of "being" indicates the idea of a nurse's presence or of simply being with a patient or family member during a time of need. Often, after the therapeutic procedures have been completed, the medications have been given, and the formal nursing interventions have been carried out, ill persons and/or family members long for a nurse to just be with them for a few minutes; to be a caring presence, not listening for they may be too fatigued to talk; not touching for they may be in too much pain for physical contact. But just to be there, to be present during their time of loneliness and suffering.

The association between spirituality and nursing presence was highlighted in an article describing a unique clinical experience for nursing students during which the students worked with the poor and homeless, taking on an advocacy posture for their clients. The students affirmed that the clinical practicum provided "an experience of self-discovery and maturation in understanding spirituality and nursing presence in nursing practice" (Rankin & DeLashmutt, 2010, p. 282).

In fact, a nurse's presence is viewed as such a well-accepted nursing activity that two nurse theorists have developed a "mid-range theory of nursing presence" (McMahon & Christopher, 2011). In the theory, professional nursing presence is described as "dependent upon the combination of five variables: individual nurse characteristics, individual client characteristics, shared characteristics within the nurse-client dyad, and environment conducive to relational work, and the nurse's intentional decisions within the practice domain" (p. 71). This theory, the authors believe, contributes to an understanding of the "relational aspects of nursing practice within the contemporary healthcare environment" (p. 71).

A description from the author's journal of an experience with a young cancer patient reflects the importance of being present with a patient in need.

> This morning a young man, Michael, who was facing mutilating surgery in hope of slowing the progress of advanced rhabdomyosarcoma, asked to talk to me; he said, "I need you to help me understand why this is happening. I need you to help me deal with it." I sought consultation both in prayer and from my own spiritual mentor before the meeting. I entered Michael's room, however, with much trepidation; how could I possibly help him "understand why" God seemed to be allowing his illness. As it turned out, Michael was the one who helped me. As soon as I sat down, he said, "There are some things I've been thinking about that I need to tell you," and the conversation continued with Michael sharing much about his own faith and his attempt to understand God's will in his life. As I prepared to leave, Michael got up, hugged me, and said, "Our talk has helped a lot"; we prayed together for the coming surgery. Simply being with Michael as he struggled with the diagnosis of cancer in light of his own spirituality constituted the caring. I did not have, nor did I need, any right words; I only needed to be a caring presence in Michael's life.

Emeth and Greenhut (1991), in their discussion of understanding illness, described the importance of being with patients and families, especially when, as with Michael, they need to ask questions for which there are no answers. "We cannot answer the question, 'Where is God in this experience?' for anyone else; rather, we must be willing to be with others in their experience as they live with the questions and wait for their personal answers to emerge. This 'being with' is at the heart of health care" (p. 65).

Listening

Many people are looking for an ear that will listen... He who no longer listens to his brother will soon no longer be listening to God either... One who cannot listen long and patiently will presently be talking beside the point and never really speaking to others, albeit he be not conscious of it.

—Dietrich Bonhoeffer, 1959, p. 11

The concept of listening is an integral part of being with a person, as was learned from the interaction with Michael. However, as his illness progressed, there were also times when being with Michael in silence was a significant dimension of caring. In some situations, however, active listening, with responsive and sensitive feedback to the person speaking, is important in providing spiritual care.

Ministering to Philip, a young man diagnosed with anaplastic astrocytoma, revealed the importance of such listening. Philip, because of his neurologic condition, had difficulty explaining his thoughts, especially in regard to spiritual matters, yet he very much wanted to talk. Philip described himself as a born-again Christian, a fact of which he was very proud.

> On my first visit Philip showed me a well-worn Bible in which he had written comments on favorite Scripture passages. As our meetings continued, I began to realize that if I opened the Bible and focused on a particular passage, Philip's speech was helped by looking at the words. I tried to listen carefully, to follow and comprehend Philip's thoughts on the Scripture and its meaning in his life. Our sharing was validated one day when Philip reached out and took my hand and said, "I'm glad you're here; I really like our talking about God together."

In a discussion of spirituality and the nursing process, Verna Carson (1989) recognized the importance of such listening. "The ability to listen is both an art and a learned skill. It requires that the nurse completely attend to the client with open ears, eyes and mind" (p. 165). And, in a poignant case study entitled "A Lesson Learned by Listening," palliative care nurse Katie Jantzi affirmed the importance of listening to a dying patient, reminding us that patients are our "best teachers" (2005, p. 41).

Touching

And there was a leper who came to Him, and knelt before Him saying: "Lord, if you choose you can make me clean." He stretched out His hand and touched him saying: "I choose. Be made clean." Immediately his leprosy was cleansed.

—**Matthew** 8:2–3

The Christian Gospel message teaches us compellingly that touch was important to Jesus; it was frequently used in healing and caring interactions with His followers. Loving, empathetic, compassionate touch is perhaps the most vital dimension of a nursing theology of caring. At times the touch may be physical: the laying on of hands, taking of one's hand, holding, or gently stroking a forehead. At other times a nurse's touch may be verbal: a kind and caring greeting or a word of comfort and support. Physical touch has been described in the nursing literature as encompassing five dimensions of caring: physical comfort, emotional comfort, mind–body comfort, social interaction, and spiritual sharing (Chang, 2001).

Perhaps one of the most rewarding experiences with the use of caring touch occurred during an interaction with Erin, a nine-year-old newly diagnosed with acute lymphocytic leukemia.

> Erin was about to begin chemotherapy and was terrified at the thought of having IVs started; the staff asked if I would try to help calm her during the initiation of treatment. One of the pediatric oncology nurses pulled up a stool for me next to Erin so that I could hold and comfort her during the needle insertion. After the procedure was finished and I was preparing to leave, Erin trudged across the room dragging her IV pole, wrapped her arms around me, and said, "Thank you for helping me to get through that!"

It is not surprising that Carson (1989) identified touch, associated with being with a patient, as critical to the provision of spiritual caring. She suggested that the nurse's "presence and ability to touch another both physically and spiritually" is perhaps his or her most important gift (p. 164). And, in describing the power of "compassionate touch," Minister Victor Parachin asserts, "Whenever we reach out with love and compassion to touch another life, our contact makes the burden a little lighter and the pain more bearable.... By reaching out and touching someone through deed or word, we provide the extra push that person needs to carry on, rather than give up" (2003, p. 9). "The human touch," Parachin concludes, "can make the difference between life and death" (p. 9).

Ultimately the activities of being, listening, and touching, as exemplified in Jesus' parable of the Good Samaritan and in a nursing theology of caring, will be employed in a variety of ways as needed in the clinical setting. This is what constitutes the creativity of nursing practice; this is what constitutes the art of the profession of nursing.

▶ Nursing as a Vocation: Called to Serve

Nursing, as a profession, has developed significantly during the past half century. The vocation or spiritual calling to care for the sick, addressed earlier in the chapter, somewhat diminished during nursing's heightened concern with professionalism, is experiencing a reawakening among contemporary nurses. This may be related to the interest in spiritual and religious issues manifested in the larger society. Taking a historical perspective, Nightingale scholar JoAnn Wiederquist pointed out that Florence Nightingale did, from the inception of the nursing profession, consider nursing a spiritual vocation. Wiederquist cited founder of nursing Nightingale's assertion, "A new art and science (nursing) has been created since and within the last 40 years and with it a new profession, so they say; we say *calling*" (Nightingale, as cited in Wiederquist, 1995, p. 6).

A number of nursing articles have addressed the topic of nursing as a "vocation" or "calling" to serve the sick. A variety of nurse authors have sought to explain why 21st-century professional nursing may be also appropriately described as an altruistic or spiritual vocation of service. In the book *The Nurse Apprentice 1860–1977*, British nurse educator Ann Bradshaw supports the concept of nursing as a vocation (2002). While admitting the importance of current nursing education, Bradshaw laments the fact that some professional nurses have lost their initial sense of vocation or calling (2002). In a 2010 article on the understanding of the nursing "vocation," Bradshaw observed that "whether the historical ideal of vocation remains important, negatively or positively, to the attitudes, values and motivations of the clinical nurse and the quality of patient care, is a relevant and significant issue" (p. 3465).

Theologian Mikael Lundmark provided an analysis of nursing as a vocation, commenting on the work of both Bradshaw and Eriksson; their writings, he concluded, both explicitly and implicitly advocated "a vocational understanding of nursing" (2007, p. 778). And, in exploring the concept of professional nursing from an ethical perspective, Karolyn White observed that "nursing is best understood as a vocational occupation" (2002, p. 279). White's argument was based on Blum's model of vocations, which identifies a vocation as a calling in which workers identify with "traditions, norms and meanings" (p. 279).

Finally, anecdotal nursing journal articles abound describing a nurse's personal identification with nursing as a vocation of service, including "Answering God's Call"

(Schmidt, 1997); "Hearing the Call to Nursing" (Jeffries, 1998); "Childhood Interest in Nursing Has Become Lifelong Vocation" (King, 2003); "Responding to God's Call" (McKoy, 2004); and "God's Call" (Folta, 2005).

Nursing, as both a vocation and a profession, encompasses a unique commitment to provide both care and compassion for those one serves. The subject of spirituality in nursing practice includes concern not only with the personal spiritual and religious needs of the patient and nurse, but with the spiritual dimension of the nurse–patient interaction as well.

▶ References

Alpert, P. T. (2010). Spirituality goes beyond religiosity: A much needed practice in nursing. *Home Health Care Management & Practice, 22*(2), 140–143.

Barnum, B. S. (1994). *Nursing theory: Analysis, application, evaluation*. Philadelphia, PA: J. B. Lippincott.

Beck, M. B. (1945). *The nurse: Handmaid of the divine physician*. Philadelphia, PA: J. B. Lippincott.

Benner, P., Tanner, C. A., & Chesla, C. A. (1996). *Expertise in nursing practice: Caring, clinical judgment and ethics*. New York, NY: Springer.

Bishop, A. H., & Scudder, J. R. (1996). *Nursing ethics: Therapeutic caring presence*. Sudbury, MA: Jones & Bartlett Learning.

Bonhoeffer, D. (1959). *Life together*. New York, NY: Harper & Brothers.

Boswell, C., Cannon, S. B., & Miller, J. (2013). Students' perceptions of holistic nursing care. *Nursing Education Perspectives, 34*(5), 329–333.

Bradshaw, A. (2002). *The nurse apprentice 1860–1977*. Aldershot, UK: Ashgate.

Bradshaw, A. (2010). An historical perspective on the treatment of vocation in the Briggs Report (1972). *Journal of Clinical Nursing, 19*(23–24), 3459–3467.

Burke, B. H. (1993, September). Wellness in the healing ministry. *Health Progress, 74*(7), 33–39.

Burkhardt, M. A. (1989). Spirituality: An analysis of the concept. *Holistic Nursing Practice, 3*(3), 69–77.

Bruce, A., Shields, L., & Molzahn, A. (2011). Language and the (im)possibilities of articulating spirituality. *Journal of Holistic Nursing, 29*(1), 44–52.

Carson, V. B. (1993, Winter). Spirituality: Generic or Christian. *Journal of Christian Nursing, 10*(1), 24–27.

Carson, V. B. (Ed.). (1989). Spirituality and the nursing process. In *Spiritual dimensions of nursing practice* (pp. 150–179). Philadelphia, PA: W. B. Saunders.

Chang, S. O. (2001). The conceptual structure of physical touch in caring. *Journal of Advanced Nursing, 33*(6), 820–827.

Clarke, J. (2009). A critical view of how nursing has defined spirituality. *Journal of Clinical Nursing, 18*(1), 1666–1673.

Como, J. M. (2007). Spiritual practice: A literature review related to spiritual health and health outcomes. *Holistic Nursing Practice, 21*(5), 224–236.

Dossey, B. M. (1988). Nurse as healer: Toward an inward journey. In B. M. Dossey, L. Keegan, C. E. Guzzetta, & L. G. Kolkmeier (Eds.), *Holistic nursing: A handbook for practice* (pp. 39–54). Rockville, MD: Aspen.

Dossey, B. M. (1989). The transpersonal self and states of consciousness. In B. M. Dossey, L. Keegan, L. G. Kolkmeier, & C. E. Guzzetta (Eds.), *Holistic health promotion: A guide for practice* (pp. 23–35). Rockville, MD: Aspen.

Dossey, B. M., & Keegan, L. (1989). Holism and the circle of human potential. In B. M. Dossey, L. Keegan, L. G. Kolkmeier, & C. E. Guzzetta (Eds.), *Holistic health promotion: A guide for practice* (pp. 3–21). Rockville, MD: Aspen.

Ellis, H. K., & Narayanasamy, A. (2009). An investigation into the role of spirituality in nursing. *British Journal of Nursing, 18*(14), 886–890.

Emblen, J. D. (1992). Religion and spirituality defined according to current use in nursing literature. *Journal of Professional Nursing, 8*(1), 41–47.

Emeth, E. V., & Greenhut, J. H. (1991). *The wholeness handbook: Care of body, mind and spirit for optimal health.* New York, NY: Continuum.

Eriksson, K. (1992). Nursing: The caring practice, "Being There." In D. A. Gaut (Ed.), *The presence of caring in nursing* (pp. 201–210). New York, NY: National League for Nursing Press.

Fehr, W. L. (1990). The history of theology. In J. A. Komonchak, M. Collins, & D. A. Lane (Eds.), *The new dictionary of theology* (pp. 1027–1035). Collegeville, MN: The Liturgical Press.

Folta, R. (2005). God's call. *Christian Nurse International, 11*(1), 7.

Goodnow, M. (1916). *Outlines of nursing history.* Philadelphia, PA: W. B. Saunders.

Graves, L. (2008). Teaching the wounded healer. *Medical Teacher, 30*, 217–219.

Gray, J. (2009). Debate on spirituality needed. *Nursing Standard, 23*(23), 10.

Guzzetta, C. E. (1988). Nursing process and standards of care. In B. M. Dossey, L. Keegan, C. E. Guzzetta, & L. G. Kolkmeier (Eds.), *Holistic nursing: A handbook for practice* (pp. 101–126). Rockville, MD: Aspen.

Haggard, P. (1983, fall). Healing and health care of the whole person. *Journal of Religion and Health, 22*(3), 234–240.

Hill, W. J. (1990). Theology. In J. A. Komonchak, M. Collins, & D. A. Lane (Eds.), *The new dictionary of theology* (pp. 1011–1027). Collegeville, MN: The Liturgical Press.

Homberg, M. (1980). *Biblical roots of healing in nursing* (Unpublished doctoral dissertation). Teacher's College, Columbia University, New York, NY.

Hudacek, S. S. (2008). Dimensions of caring: A qualitative analysis of nurses' stories. *Journal of Nursing Education, 47*(3), 124–129.

Jantzi, K. (2005). A lesson learned by listening. *Journal of Christian Nursing, 22*(1), 41.

Jeffries, E. (1998). Hearing the call to nursing. *Nursing, 3*(2), 71–72.

Johnson, R. P. (1992). *Body, mind, spirit: Tapping the healing power within you.* Liguori, MO: Liguori.

Kelsey, M. T. (1988). *Psychology, medicine and Christian healing.* San Francisco, CA: Harper & Row.

Kendrick, K. D., & Robinson, S. (2000). Spirituality: Its relevance and purpose for clinical nursing in a new millennium. *Journal of Clinical Nursing, 9*(5), 701–705.

King, J. (2003, January). Childhood interest in nursing has become lifelong vocation. *The Catholic Herald, 16*, 6.

Kodell, J. (1989). *The gospel according to Luke.* Collegeville, MN: The Liturgical Press.

Leininger, M. M. (1978). *Trans-cultural nursing: Concepts, theories and practice.* New York, NY: John Wiley & Sons.

Leininger, M. M. (1980). Caring: A central focus of nursing and health care services. *Nursing and Health Care, 1*(3), 135–143.

Leininger, M. M. (1988). *Care: The essence of nursing and health.* Detroit, MI: Wayne State University Press.

Leininger, M. M. (1991). Foreword. In D. A. Gaut & M. M. Leininger (Eds.), *Caring: The compassionate healer.* New York, NY: National League for Nursing Press.

Leininger, M. M. (1997). Transcultural spirituality: A comparative care and health focus. In M. S. Roach (Ed.), *Caring from the heart: The convergence of caring and spirituality* (pp. 99–118). New York, NY: Paulist Press.

Lindberg, J. B., Hunter, M. L., & Kruszewski, A. Z. (1994). *Introduction to nursing: Concepts, issues, and opportunities.* Philadelphia, PA: J. B. Lippincott.

Lo, R., & Brown, R. (1999). Holistic care and spirituality: Potential for increasing spiritual dimensions of nursing. *Australian Journal of Holistic Nursing, 6*(2), 4–9.

Lohri-Posey, B. (2005). Becoming a compassionate healer. *Journal of Christian Nursing, 22*(4), 34–37.

Lundmark, M. (2007). Vocation in theology-based nursing theories. *Nursing Ethics, 14*(6), 767–780.

McKoy, Y. D. (2004). Responding to God's call. *Journal of Christian Nursing, 21*(2), 35–37.

McMahon, M., & Christopher, K. (2011). Toward a mid-range theory of nursing presence. *Nursing Forum, 46*(2), 71–82.

Meehan, T. C. (2012). Spirituality and spiritual care from a careful nursing perspective. *Journal of Nursing Management, 20*(8), 990–1001.

Meraviglia, M. G. (1999). Critical analysis of spirituality and its empirical indicators: Prayers and meaning in life. *Journal of Holistic Nursing, 17*(1), 18–33.

Montgomery, C. L. (1992). The spiritual connection: Nurses' perceptions of the experience of caring. In D. A. Gaut (Ed.), *The presence of caring in nursing* (pp. 39–52). New York, NY: National League for Nursing Press.

Nagai-Jacobson, M. G., & Burkhardt, M. A. (1989). Spirituality: Cornerstone of holistic nursing practice. *Holistic Nursing Practice, 3*(3), 18–26.

Narayanasamy, A. (2015). Reflexive account of unintended outcomes from spiritual care qualitative research. *Journal of Research in Nursing, 20*(3), 234–248.

Nelson, J. B. (1976). *Rediscovering the person in medical care*. Minneapolis, MN: Augsburg.

Niven, E. (2008). The wounded healer: What has the concept to offer nursing? *Nursing Ethics, 15*(3), 287–288.

Noble, A., & Jones, C. (2010). Getting it right: Oncology nurses understanding of spirituality. *International Journal of Palliative Care Nursing, 16*(11), 565–569.

Nouwen, H. J. (1979). *The wounded healer*. Garden City, NY: Image Books.

O'Brien, M. E. (1982). The need for spiritual integrity. In H. Yura & M. Walsh (Eds.), *Human needs and the nursing process* (Vol. 2, pp. 82–115). Norwalk, CT: Appleton-Century-Crofts.

O'Connor, C. I. (2001). Characteristics of spirituality, assessment and prayer in holistic nursing. *Nursing Clinics of North America, 36*(1), 33–46.

Parachin, V. M. (2003). The power of compassionate touch. *Journal of Christian Nursing, 20*(2), 8–9.

Pesut, B. (2008). A conversation on diverse perspectives of spirituality in nursing literature. *Nursing Philosophy, 9*, 98–109.

Pesut, B. (2013). Nursings' need for the idea of spirituality. *Nursing Inquiry, 20*(1), 5–10.

Picard, C. (1995). Images of caring in nursing and dance. *Journal of Holistic Nursing, 13*(4), 323–331.

Pike, J. (2011). Spirituality in nursing: A systematic review of the literature from 2006–2010. *British Journal of Nursing, 20*(12), 743–749.

Pinch, W. J. (1996). Is caring a moral trap? *Nursing Outlook, 44*(2), 84–88.

Price, A. L. (1954). *The art, science and spirit of nursing*. Philadelphia, PA: W. B. Saunders.

Ramezani, M., Ahmadi, F., Mohammadi, E., & Kazemnejad, A. (2014). Spiritual care in nursing: A concept analysis. *International Nursing Review, 61*(2), 211–219.

Rankin, E., & DeLashmutt, M. (2010). Finding spirituality in nursing presence: The student's challenge. *Journal of Holistic Nursing, 24*(4), 282–288.

Reed, P. G. (1992). An emerging paradigm for the investigation of spirituality in nursing. *Research in Nursing and Health, 15*, 349–357.

Reinert, K. G., & Koenig, H. G. (2013). Re-examining definitions of spirituality in nursing research. *Journal of Advanced Nursing, 69*(12), 2622–2634.

Roach, S. (1992). *The human act of caring*. Ottawa, Canada: Canadian Hospital Association.

Robinson, A. (1995). Spirituality and risk: Toward an understanding. *Holistic Nursing Practice, 8*(2), 1–7.

Schmidt, K. (1997). Answering God's call. *Journal of Christian Nursing, 14*(1), 11.

Shelly, J. A. (2003). Walking on holy ground. *Journal of Christian Nursing, 20*(3), 3.

Stoll, R. I. (1989). The essence of spirituality. In V. B. Carson (Ed.), *Spiritual dimensions of nursing practice* (pp. 4–23). Philadelphia, PA: W. B. Saunders.

Swinton, J., & Pattison, S. (2010). Moving beyond clarity: Towards a thin, vague and useful understanding of spirituality in nursing care. *Nursing Philosophy, 11*, 226–237.

Tinley, S. T., & Kinney, A. Y. (2007). Three philosophical approaches to the study of spirituality. *Advances in Nursing Science, 30*(1), 71–80.

Watson, J. (1995, July). Nursing's caring-healing paradigm as exemplar for alternative medicine. *Alternative Therapies, 1*(30), 64–69.

White, K. (2002). Nursing as vocation. *Nursing Ethics, 9*(3), 279–290.

Wiederkehr, Sr. M. (1991). *Seasons of your heart*. New York, NY: HarperCollins.

Wiederquist, J. (1995). Called to serve. *Christian Nurse International, 11*(1), 4–6.

Young, C., & Koopsen, C. (2011). *Spirituality, health and healing: An integrative approach* (2nd ed.). Sudbury, MA: Jones & Bartlett Learning.

CHAPTER 2

Nursing Assessment of Spiritual Needs

The healer has to keep striving for . . . the space . . . in which healer and patient can reach out to each other as travelers sharing the same broken human condition.

Henri J. M. Nouwen, *Reaching Out*, 1986, p. 93

When you view nursing as a vocation, it helps you to assess the patient as a whole. You know, to really think about what their needs are physically, mentally, and spiritually. You see the whole person and are able to help them better by doing that; by assessing everything that's going on.

Terri, Team Leader on a Pediatric Unit

The first step in planning spiritual care for one who is ill is conducting a needs assessment; this may be done formally in the context of nursing research, or informally through interaction with the patient and family. The ill individual's level of spiritual development and religious tradition and practice are important variables to be explored. In this chapter, tools to assess spiritual and religious beliefs and needs are presented; these tools were developed through nursing research with persons living with a variety of illness conditions. Nursing diagnoses related to alterations in spirituality, derived from patient assessment, are examined, and selected nursing studies in which patients' spiritual and religious beliefs and needs were identified are described.

▶ Nursing Assessment

During the past few decades, nursing assessment of hospitalized patients' problems and needs has become increasingly more sophisticated. Assessment tools vary depending on the care setting, for example, intensive care versus a general care unit; nevertheless, today's nursing assessment instruments are much more detailed than the medical model–oriented database forms of the past. Recently nurses' comfort level in conducting assessment of patients' spiritual needs has also received significant attention (Taylor, 2013, p. 178). Although it is admitted that some nurses may feel uncomfortable or unprepared to discuss spiritual or religious topics with patients (Ameling & Povilonis, 2001; Brush & Daly, 2000), a systematic approach to assessing spiritual well-being (SWB) is recommended (Govier, 2000). In addition to assessing physiologic parameters, caregivers also assess psychological and sociological factors that may impact patients' illness conditions. A significant weakness, however, among many contemporary nursing assessment tools is the lack of evaluation of a patient's spiritual needs. Frequently, the spiritual assessment is reflected in a single question asking the religious affiliation of the individual. The assumption is that the patient's spiritual care can then be turned over to a hospital chaplain assigned to minister to persons of that religious tradition.

Although the important role of the hospital chaplain is in no way devalued, the nurse, if he or she is to provide holistic care, should have first-hand knowledge of the spiritual practices and needs of a patient. If no detailed spiritual assessment is carried out, such information, even if revealed during a chaplain's visit, might never be communicated to the nursing staff. A patient may, however, reveal a spiritual problem or concern in some depth to the primary nurse during an assessment at the bedside. In health-care facilities with well-functioning departments of spiritual ministry, excellent communication often takes place between pastoral caregivers and nursing staff. This is the ideal. In such situations, chaplains attend nursing care conferences and share in holistic health planning for patients. If the nursing staff has performed a spiritual assessment, this information, combined with the chaplain's insight and advice, can serve to round out the spiritual dimension of the holistic health-care plan.

In the contemporary era of home health care, assessment of a patient's spiritual beliefs and needs is also critical to developing a holistic home nursing care plan. Frequently the home care patient experiencing or recuperating from illness is isolated from sources of spiritual support such as attendance at worship services and interaction with other members of a church or faith group. In such a case, the home health-care nurse may be able to assist the patient in verbalizing his or her spiritual or religious needs; the nurse can then offer creative strategies for meeting those needs. The nurse may also provide a bridge between the patient and family and their church, recommending counseling from an ordained pastoral caregiver if this seems warranted.

Nursing authors continue to discuss the importance of assessing patients' spiritual needs (Young & Koopsen, 2011, pp. 149–152), as well as the value of continuing to develop spiritual assessment tools (Power, 2006). The need for spiritual assessment is identified specifically for such populations as intensive care unit (ICU) and coronary care unit (CCU) patients (Timmins & Kelly, 2008) and families of those who are ill (Tanyi, 2006). Assessment of the spiritual needs of terminally ill patients is a current concern for palliative care nurses (Smyth & Allen, 2011).

In light of current understanding of the need to evaluate patients' spiritual concerns, a number of recently developed spiritual assessment tools, appropriate for nurses' use with patient populations, are currently being proposed and tested. Some of these include: the "Hope Tool" (Blaber, Jones, & Willis, 2015); the "Spiritual Health Scale" (Hsiao, Chiang, Lee, & Han, 2013); the "FACIT-SP Spiritual Well-Being Scale" (Haugen, 2014); and the "Two Stage Spiritual Assessment in Health Care Settings" instrument (Hodge, 2015).

▶ The Joint Commission Mandate on Assessment of Spiritual Needs

During the past several decades, The Joint Commission (formerly the Joint Commission for Accreditation of Healthcare Organizations) has recognized the importance of spiritual and religious beliefs and traditions for persons who are ill or disabled. This concern is reflected in The Joint Commission's standards relating to spiritual assessment and spiritual care both for those who are hospitalized (Standard R1.1.3.5) and those living in nursing homes (Standard PE1.1.5.1) (The Joint Commission, 2003). The Joint Commission's standards "reflect the need to recognize and meet the spiritual needs of patients" (Sanders, 2002, p. 107).

The Joint Commission has "acknowledged that patients' psychosocial, spiritual and cultural values affect how they respond to care and has addressed spirituality and emotional well-being as aspects of patient care" (Clark, Drain, & Malone, 2003, p. 659). Standards refer to both spiritual services and pastoral care for health-care patients (p. 659). Care of patients' spiritual needs is now considered central to care provided in health-care organizations, which The Joint Commission recommends "(1) acknowledge patients' rights to spiritual care and (2) provide for these needs through pastoral care and a diversity of services that may be offered by certified, ordained or lay individuals" (La Pierre, 2003, p. 219).

The Joint Commission website suggests that assessment of patients' spiritual needs should be carried out not only to determine religious denomination, but also to identify spiritual and religious beliefs and practices, especially as related to coping with illness or disability. Some questions to be included in a spiritual assessment include: "Who or what provides the patient with strength and hope?"; "Does the patient use prayer in (his/her) life?"; "What type of spiritual/religious support does the patient desire?"; "What does dying mean to the patient?"; "Is there a role of church/synagogue in the patient's life?"; and "How does faith help the patient cope with illness?" (The Joint Commission, 2008).

The importance of the identified Joint Commission standard for the patient's spiritual assessment continues to be supported in contemporary health care–related chapters and articles (Hodge, 2006; Young & Koopsen, 2011). It is now understood that nurses must be involved in patients' spiritual care in the United States as "the Joint Commission (formerly JCAHO) requires spiritual assessment as part of health care" (Pesut, Fowler, Reimer-Kirkham, Taylor, & Sawatzky, 2009, p. 342).

▶ HIPAA Regulations and Spiritual Assessment

As noted, The Joint Commission, which accredits health-care organizations, has essentially mandated that nurses pay attention to patients' spiritual needs. Staff nurses, as members of the health-care team, have access to records for the patients under their care, and thus it seems that the confidentiality dimension (privacy standards) of the Health Insurance Portability and Accountability Act (HIPAA) should not be a concern. The HIPAA regulations may, however, impact patients' spiritual needs/care indirectly by limiting access to patients' personal clergy person or pastoral care provider.

In an article published in the newsletter of the Lutheran Services in America (2004), one pastor complained that since the advent of HIPAA his access to general information about hospitalized parishioners has been limited. He observed that before HIPAA he was "able to provide better pastoral care when [he] could see the entire patient list" (p. 1).

The situation appears to be somewhat different for the minister who is a hospital chaplain. In a series of three articles in consecutive issues of the *Association of Professional Chaplains (APC) News*, the authors raised the topic of HIPAA's impact on hospital chaplains and their clinical pastoral education (CPE) students (White, 2003; White & Pierce, 2002a, 2002b). The conclusion seemed to be that patient records would be available and accessible to these pastoral care providers as they were, in fact, clinically trained members of the health-care team with responsibility for patients' spiritual care. A distinction in title was suggested by the president and CEO of the National Association of Catholic Chaplains (NACC) as follows: "The chaplain is a health care professional; the clergyperson is a religious leader; the chaplain tends to the spiritual needs of all the patients; the clergyperson tends to the religious needs of his or her congregants" (Driscoll, 2003, p. 4). Thus, it seems that a pastoral care provider's role description might significantly impact his or her access to patient records as controlled by HIPAA regulations.

Spiritual Development

Central to assessing a patient's spirituality is a basic knowledge of the spiritual development of the human person. A number of theories attempt to track spiritual development; significant among these is James Fowler's (1981) paradigm set forth in his book *Stages of Faith Development*. Fowler's theory, encompassing seven stages of faith development, emerged from data generated from research with persons across the life span from 3.5 to 84 years of age.

Fowler (1981) described faith as "not always religious in its content or context" (p. 4). He explained that faith has to do with one's finding coherence in life, with seeing oneself in relation to others "against a background of shared meaning and purpose" (p. 4). Faith is viewed as deeper and more personal than organized religion, as relating to one's transcendent values and relationship with a higher power, or God. Although Fowler admitted that more research needs to be done, his work demonstrated a preliminary pattern of relationships between the stages of faith development and chronological age. Fowler's seven faith stages and their approximate corresponding age categories are as follows:

1. Undifferentiated Faith is a "prestage" (infancy) in which the seeds of trust, courage, hope, and love are joined to combat such issues as possible "inconsistency and abandonment in the infant's environment" (p. 121). This faith stage has particular relevance for the maternal–infant nurse concerned with issues of parental–infant bonding.

2. Intuitive–Projective Faith (3–6 years) is an imitative "fantasy-filled" period in which a young child is strongly influenced by "examples, moods, actions and stories of the visible faith of primarily related adults" (p. 133). Pediatric nurses, especially those working with chronically or terminally ill children, will find guidance for dealing with the child's spiritual and emotional needs from Fowler's conceptualization of this stage.

3. Mythic–Literal Faith (7–12 years) is described as the time when the child begins to internalize "stories, beliefs and observances that symbolize belonging to his or her own faith community" (p. 149). In working with slightly older pediatric patients, the concept of mythic–literal faith can help the nurse to support the child's participation in rites, rituals, and/or worship services of his or her tradition, which may provide support and comfort in illness.

4. Synthetic–Conventional Faith (13–20 years) describes the adolescent's experiences outside the family unit: at school, at work, with peers, and from the media and religion. Faith provides a "basis for identity and outlook" (p. 172). Fowler's definition of this faith stage provides an understanding of how the ill adolescent may relate to both internal (family) and external (peer) support and interaction during a crisis situation.

5. Individuative–Reflective Faith (21–30 years) identifies a period during which the young adult begins to claim a faith identity no longer defined by "the composite of one's roles or meanings to others" (p. 182). This is a time of personal creativity and individualism that has important implications for the nurse, including patient autonomy in planning care for the ill young adult patient.

6. Conjunctive Faith (31–40 years) is a time of opening to the voices of one's "deeper self" and the development of one's social conscience (p. 198). Nurses caring for patients in this faith stage must be sensitive to the adult's more mature spirituality, especially in relation to finding meaning in his or her illness.

7. Universalizing Faith (40 years and above) is described by Fowler as a culmination of the work of all of the previous faith stages, a time of relating to the "imperatives of absolute love and justice" toward all humankind (p. 200). Nurses need to be aware that patients may vary significantly in terms of degree of accomplishing the imperatives of this final stage. Assessing approximately where the mature adult patient is, related to such faith, will help in understanding both the patient's response to an illness condition and his or her need for external support in coping with the crisis.

Although a nurse may not be able to identify every patient's stage of faith development chronologically, Fowler's theory with its approximate age-associated categorization does present some guidelines to assist in broadly estimating a patient's level of spiritual development.

▶ Nursing Assessment of Spiritual Needs

The Spiritual Assessment Scale

In their fundamentals of nursing text, Taylor, Lillis, and LeMone (1993) asserted that assessment of a patient's spirituality should be considered part of any "comprehensive nursing history" because, they reasoned, "a person's spirituality and religious beliefs have the potential to influence every aspect of being" (p. 1173). Although an initial spiritual assessment or history can provide baseline information regarding a patient's spirituality, it is important to remember that spiritual needs may change, or new spiritual concerns may arise during an illness experience. And, because a patient may find it difficult to discuss spiritual problems, the nurse is advised to look for signs of possible spiritual distress such as "sudden changes in spiritual practices [rejection, neglect, fanatical devotion]; mood changes [frequent crying, depression, apathy, anger]; sudden interest in spiritual matters [reading religious books or watching religious programs on television, visits to clergy]; and disturbed sleep" (p. 1174).

Nurse researchers Sessanna, Finnell, Undershill, Chang, and Peng (2011) assert that "Assessing spiritual needs and preferences is an essential and critical aspect of holistic and multidisciplinary patient care practice" (p. 1692). The authors admit, however, that "conceptual and operational definitions of spirituality vary greatly among nursing and health related literature" (p. 1692). They found that the concept of "religiosity" was often included in the ostensible measuring of "spirituality."

One set of questions describing a patient's spirituality that may be included as part of a nursing history are those contained in the spiritual history guide developed by Ruth Stoll (1979). The guide is divided into four subsections or "areas of concern": "The person's concept of God or deity; the person's source of strength and hope; the significance of religious practices and rituals to the person; and the person's perceived relationship between his spiritual beliefs and his state of health" (p. 1574). Some standardized spiritual assessment tools created by nurses include the Spiritual Perspective Scale, which measures adult spiritual views (Reed, 1991); Kerrigan and Harkulich's (1993) Spiritual Assessment Tool, developed to identify the spiritual needs of nursing home residents; the JAREL Spiritual Well-Being Scale, a tool to assess the spiritual attitudes of older adults (Hungelmann, Kenkel-Rossi, Klassen, & Stollenwerk, 1996); Puchalski's (2000) "Spiritual History," which includes four domains: "Faith, Importance, Community, and Address" (p. 129); the multidimensional "Spiritual Needs Survey," which includes seven major constructs: "belonging, meaning, hope, the sacred, morality, beauty, and acceptance of dying" (Galek, Flannelly, Vane, & Galek, 2005, p. 62); the spiritual assessment model, including focus on one's "spiritual belief system, personal spirituality, integration/involvement in a spiritual community, ritualized practices and restrictions, implications for care and terminal events planned (advanced directives)" (Dameron, 2005, p. 16); the "Serenity Scale," which measures spirituality and well-being and has three subscales that explore "acceptance, inner haven and trust" (Kreitzer, Gross, Waleekhachonloet, Reilly-Spong, & Byrd, 2009); and the "Spiritual Care Inventory," which measures nurses' attitudes toward and behaviors in providing patients' spiritual care (Burkhart, Schmidt, & Hogan, 2011).

The author's standardized instrument to assess adult, cognitively aware individuals' spiritual beliefs and practices, entitled the "Spiritual Assessment Guide," was initially developed and published in 1982 (O'Brien, 1982a, pp. 99–102). The 53-item tool contained six subscales: General Spiritual Beliefs, Personal Spiritual Beliefs, Identification with Institutionalized Religion, Spiritual/Religious Support Systems, Spiritual/Religious Rituals, and Spiritual Deficit/Distress. Items contained in the instrument were derived from content analysis of qualitative data generated in interviews with 126 chronically ill hemodialysis patients. The patients had been asked to discuss their spiritual beliefs, practices, concerns, and needs in relation to living with a long-term life-threatening illness. It was admitted at the time of construction that this early version of the tool, which contains a mix of both closed- and open-ended questions, was more detailed than appropriate for nursing use in short-term care but could prove valuable in nursing research on the spiritual beliefs and behaviors of the chronically ill patient.

During the past two decades, the Spiritual Assessment Guide has been revised several times and selected items were used in research with such populations as nursing home residents (O'Brien, 1989), persons living with human immunodeficiency virus (HIV) and acquired immunodeficiency syndrome (AIDS) (O'Brien, 1992, 1995; O'Brien & Pheifer, 1993), and the homebound elderly (Brennan, 1994).

The Spiritual Assessment Guide has recently been significantly revised again and retitled the Spiritual Assessment Scale (SAS). The standardized instrument, which measures the construct of SWB, now contains 21 items organized into three subscales: Personal Faith (PF), 7 items; Religious Practice (RP), 7 items; and Spiritual Contentment (SC), 7 items. In its newly abbreviated form, the SAS, which takes approximately 3 to 4 minutes to complete, can be used by practicing nurses in the health-care setting, as well as being employed as a research instrument. The tool, as revised, will provide nursing staff and nurse researchers with a broad overview of a patient's personal faith beliefs, the type of spiritual support he or she receives from religious practices, and the type and degree of spiritual contentment/distress the patient is currently experiencing. The 21-item scale is organized with Likert-type scale response categories (SA—Strongly Agree, A—Agree, U—Uncertain, D—Disagree, SD—Strongly Disagree) following each item to facilitate administration; the appropriate categories may be checked by the patient or read aloud and marked by the nurse if a patient is unable to write.[*]

Validity and Reliability of the SAS

The construct measured by the SAS, SWB, includes the dimensions of both spirituality and religiousness, or "religiosity," operationally defined in terms of three discrete concepts: Personal Faith, Religious Practice, and Spiritual Contentment.

Spiritual Well-Being

The term *spiritual well-being* is described historically as having emerged following a 1971 White House Conference on Aging. Sociologist of religion David Moberg (1979) identified SWB as relating to the "wellness or health of the totality of the inner resources of people, the ultimate concerns around which all other values are focused, the central philosophy of life that guides conduct, and the meaning-giving center of human life which influences all individual and social behavior" (p. 2). The concept of hope is central to a number of definitions of SWB. In a discussion of holistic nursing care, SWB is described as "an integrating aspect of human wholeness, characterized by meaning and hope" (Clark, Cross, Deane, & Lowry, 1991, p. 68). Lindberg, Hunter, and Kruszewski (1994) included "the need to feel hopeful about one's destiny" (p. 110) in a litany of patient needs related to SWB; and Droege (1991), in discussing the "faith factor" in healing, suggested that when an individual does not experience SWB, serious "spiritual maladies" may occur, such as "depression, loneliness, existential anxiety and meaninglessness" (p. 13).

---

*The Spiritual Assessment Scale does assume belief in a Supreme Being, or God.

Most notions of SWB also contain some reference to philosophy of life and transcendence. Blaikie and Kelson (1979) described SWB as "that type of existential well being which incorporates some reference to the supernatural, the sacred or the transcendental" (p. 137); and Barker (1979) observed that SWB is "to be in communication, in communion with that which goes beyond oneself in order to be whole in oneself" (p. 154). For the Christian, SWB is identified as "a right relationship of the person to God, and, following that, a right relationship to neighbor and self" (Christy & Lyon, 1979, p. 98).

Spirituality is generally identified as being related to issues of transcendence and ultimate life goals. Nurse theorist Barbara Dossey (1989) explained spirituality as encompassing "values, meanings, and purpose" in life; it includes belief in the existence of a "higher authority"; and it may or may not involve "organized religion" (p. 24). O'Brien (1989), in reporting on research with the chronically ill, suggested that spirituality is a broad concept relating to transcendence [God]; to the "non-material forces or elements within man [or woman]; spirituality is that which inspires in one the desire to transcend the realm of the material" (p. 88).

Religiousness, or "religiosity," as it is sometimes identified in the sociological literature, refers to religious affiliation and/or practice. Kaufman (1979) described religiousness as "the degree to which religious beliefs, attitudes and behaviors permeate the life of an individual" (p. 237). In their classic work, Stark and Glock (1968) identified five primary elements of religiousness: belief, religious practice (ritual, devotional), religious experience, religious knowledge, and consequence of religious practice on day-to-day living.

The "spirituality" dimension of SWB is measured in terms of the concepts of Personal Faith and Spiritual Contentment; the "religiousness" element of the construct is reflected in the concept of Religious Practice.

▶ Personal Faith

Personal faith, as a component concept of the SWB construct, has been described as "a personal relationship with God on whose strength and sureness one can literally stake one's life" (Fatula, 1993, p. 379). Personal faith is a reflection of an individual's transcendent values and philosophy of life.

Religious Practice

Religious practice is primarily operationalized in terms of religious rituals such as attendance at formal group worship services, private prayer and meditation, reading of spiritual books and articles, and/or the carrying out of such activities as volunteer work or almsgiving.

Spiritual Contentment

Spiritual contentment, the opposite of spiritual distress, is likened to spiritual peace (Johnson, 1992), a concept whose correlates include "living in the now of God's love," "accepting the ultimate strength of God," knowledge that all are "children of God," knowing that "God is in control," and "finding peace in God's love and forgiveness" (pp. 12–13). When an individual reports minimal to no notable spiritual distress, he or she may be considered to be in a state of "spiritual contentment."

Construct Validity of the SAS

In research with young adults, Moberg (1979) identified eight correlates or characteristics of SWB: Peace with God (PG), Inner Peace (IP), Faith in Christ (God) (FG), Good Morals (GM), Faith in People (FP), Helping Others (HO), Good Health (GH), and Being Successful (BS) (p. 8). Moberg reported that study participants placed greatest importance on the concepts Peace with God, Inner Peace, and Faith in Christ. The majority of respondents believed that Good Health and Being Successful were not critical elements to SWB. Those persons, however, who did not seem to possess SWB were reported as being "more likely to interpret these [health and success] as essential or most likely to be present" with overall SWB (p. 9).

The SAS, developed to assess SWB, was constructed to broadly reflect Moberg's eight correlates. In some cases a liberal interpretation of the characteristic was accepted; for example, Faith in Christ is understood also as Faith in God, to include the tradition of the non-Christian believer; Good Health, which Moberg described as physical, may also include good mental health, for the person whose body is suffering the ravages of illness; and Being Successful may relate to an individual's positive feeling about self related to the strength of his or her spiritual beliefs.

The SAS items relate to Moberg's conceptualization of SWB as follows: Peace with God—item 2; Inner Peace—items 13, 14; Faith in God/Christ—items 1, 3, 5, 6; Good Morals—items 8, 9; Faith in People—items 7 (also GH), 11, 12; Helping Others—item 10; Good Health—item 7 (also FP); Being Successful—item 4.*

Construct validity of the SAS is also derived, in part, from the association of individual items with James Fowler's (1981) conceptualization of the stages of faith development (p. 113), proceeding from the prestage, infancy (Undifferentiated Faith), to the late adult stage (Universalizing Faith):Prestage (trust, courage, hope, and love): items 3, 6

Stage 1 (child learns examples of faith from related adults): items 11, 12

Stage 2 (internalization of stories of one's own faith community): items 1, 4

Stages 3 and 4 (religious faith as a basis for identity and world outlook): items 2, 5

Stage 5 (conjunctive faith): items 7, 13, 14

Stage 6 (universalizing faith; one recognizes imperatives of love and justice toward all humankind): items 8, 9, 10*

---

*SAS items 15–21 assessing spiritual contentment/spiritual distress explore negative or lack of negative experiences associated with Moberg's correlates of Inner Peace and Faith in God.

*SAS items 15–21 assessing spiritual contentment/spiritual distress explore negative or lack of negative experiences associated with Fowler's stages of faith development; focus is placed especially on internalization of trust and hope (stage 1) and the development of one's personal reflective faith (stage 5).

Content Validity of the SAS

Content validity of the SAS was established through submission of the revised items to a panel of experts in the area of spirituality and health/illness. Following the expert judges' review, certain tool items were modified and/or reworded.

Reliability of the SAS

Reliability of the newly revised 21-item SAS was determined through administration to a sample population of 179 chronically ill persons who agreed to respond to the tool items for the purpose of statistical analysis.

The sample group, employed for the purpose of establishing instrument reliability, consisted of 36 men and 143 women. One hundred thirty-eight members of the group (76 percent) were Roman Catholic; 34 were Protestant; 3 were Jewish; and 4 identified no specific religious belief system. Sixty-three persons attended church services weekly; 26 individuals attended daily church services; and 6 persons reported never going to church or synagogue. The mean age of the sample group was 49 years, with ages ranging from 19 to 89. Seventy-seven persons were single; 79 individuals were married. The participants were well educated, with 70.3 percent reporting some level of college education; the range was from 16.2 percent with 2 years of college or AA degrees to 5 percent who had achieved an MD or PhD.

Selected occupations of the sample group members included physician, nurse, teacher, social worker, secretary, pastoral minister, nursing aide, counselor, engineer, chaplain, and speech pathologist. Some examples of the chronic illnesses reported by the study population, as categorized by body system, included gastrointestinal—ulcer, gastroesophageal reflux disease (GERD), colitis, esophageal cancer, colorectal cancer; genitourinary—end-stage renal disease (ESRD), nephritis, polycystic kidneys; cardiovascular—hypertension, rheumatic heart disease, prolapsed mitral valve, pernicious anemia; respiratory—chronic obstructive pulmonary disease (COPD), asthma, lung cancer, emphysema; neurologic—brain cancer, epilepsy; musculoskeletal—osteoarthritis, osteoporosis, arthritis, multiple sclerosis; gynecological—uterine cancer, breast cancer, ovarian tumors, herpes; psychiatric—chronic depression, bipolar disease, transient amnesia, bulimia/anorexia.

Statistical reliability was calculated for a sample of 171 cases (11 cases were deleted because of missing data). Items 15–21, comprising a subscale measuring the degree of spiritual distress, were recorded in the opposite direction to reflect the concept of Spiritual Contentment.

Cronbach's alpha coefficients for the overall SAS and the subscales Personal Faith (PF), Religious Practice (RP), and Spiritual Contentment (SC) demonstrated statistically significant reliability for the instrument, both in regard to the overall tool and its subscales as examined individually:

> **SPIRITUAL ASSESSMENT SCALE (SAS)—21 ITEMS**
>   Alpha coefficient = 0.92
> Personal Faith (PF)—7 items
>   Alpha coefficient = 0.89
> Religious Practice (RP)—7 items
>   Alpha coefficient = 0.89
> Spiritual Contentment (SC)—7 items
>   Alpha coefficient = 0.76

Mean total scale and subscale scores reflected a sample population with a strongly positive sense of SWB. The overall mean SAS score was 91.7, out of a possible total scale score of 105. The subscales reflected a similar pattern with a PF subscale mean of 32.2 (possible total subscale score of 35); and RP and SC subscale means of 29.7 and 29.6, respectively (possible total scores of 35 for each subscale).

Spiritual Assessment Scale

Instructions: Please check the response category that best identifies your personal belief about the item (response categories: SA—Strongly Agree; A—Agree; U—Uncertain; D—Disagree; SD—Strongly Disagree).

A. Personal Faith
1. There is a Supreme Being, or God, who created humankind and who cares for all creatures.
   SA ✓ A ____ U ____ D ____ SD ____
2. I am at peace with God.
   SA ✓ A ____ U ____ D ____ SD ____
3. I feel confident that God is watching over me.
   SA ✓ A ____ U ____ D ____ SD ____
4. I receive strength and comfort from my spiritual beliefs.
   SA ✓ A ____ U ____ D ____ SD ____
5. I believe that God is interested in all the activities of my life.
   SA ✓ A ____ U ____ D ____ SD ____
6. I trust that God will take care of the future.
   SA ✓ A ____ U ____ D ____ SD ____
7. My spiritual beliefs support a positive image of myself and of others, as members of God's family.
   SA ✓ A ____ U ____ D ____ SD ____

B. Religious Practice
8. Belonging to a church or faith group is an important part of my life.
   SA ✓ A ____ U ____ D ____ SD ____
9. I am strengthened by participation in religious worship services.
   SA ✓ A ____ U ____ D ____ SD ____
10. I find satisfaction in religiously motivated activities other than attending worship services, for example, volunteer work or being kind to others.
    SA ✓ A ____ U ____ D ____ SD ____
11. I am supported by relationships with friends or family members who share my religious beliefs.
    SA ✓ A ____ U ____ D ____ SD ____
12. I receive comfort and support from a spiritual companion, for example, a pastoral caregiver or friend.
    SA ✓ A ____ U ____ D ____ SD ____
13. My relationship with God is strengthened by personal prayer.
    SA ✓ A ____ U ____ D ____ SD ____
14. I am helped to communicate with God by reading or thinking about religious or spiritual things.
    SA ✓ A ____ U ____ D ____ SD ____

C. Spiritual Contentment

15. I experience pain associated with my spiritual beliefs.
    SA _____ A _____ U _____ D _____ SD __✓__
16. I feel "far away" from God.
    SA _____ A _____ U _____ D _____ SD __✓__
17. I am afraid that God might not take care of my needs.
    SA _____ A _____ U _____ D _____ SD __✓__
18. I have done some things for which I fear God may not forgive me.
    SA _____ A _____ U _____ D _____ SD __✓__
19. I get angry at God for allowing "bad things" to happen to me, or to people I care about.
    SA _____ A _____ U _____ D _____ SD __✓__
20. I feel that I have lost God's love.
    SA _____ A _____ U _____ D _____ SD __✓__
21. I believe that there is no hope of obtaining God's love.
    SA _____ A _____ U _____ D _____ SD __✓__

▶ Nursing Diagnoses: Alterations in Spiritual Integrity

Nursing diagnoses are currently used in selected health-care facilities to label those patient conditions whose treatment falls within the purview of the nurse. From early in the nursing diagnosis movement, spiritual issues have been addressed with such diagnoses as "alterations in faith" (Gebbie, 1976; Gebbie & Lavin, 1975) and "nursing diagnoses related to spiritual distress" (Campbell, 1978). This concern for the identification of patients' spiritual needs and deficits has continued among contemporary theorists of nursing diagnosis. The nursing diagnosis "high risk for spiritual distress related to confrontation with the unknown" was described by Holloway (1993). Two other diagnoses related to faith beliefs, "potential for spiritual well-being" and "spiritual distress," were identified in 1994 by the North American Nursing Diagnosis Association (Brennan, 1994, p. 852). The potential for SWB is associated with "the process of an individual's developing an unfolding of mystery through harmonious interconnections that spring from inner strength"; "spiritual distress is a disruption of the life principle that pervades a person's entire being and that integrates and transcends one's biological and physiological nature" (Brennan, 1994, p. 852). A recently advanced nursing diagnosis for human response in the domain of spirituality is that of "enhanced spirituality" (Cavendish et al., 2000).

As contemporary nurses become more involved with diagnosis and intervention in the spiritual arena, some basic knowledge of the beliefs and behaviors associated with the major religious cultures is essential (Engebretson, 1996). This information will allow nurses to accurately identify and address significant spiritual needs and problems exhibited or reported by their patients.

Seven nursing diagnoses related to "alterations in spiritual integrity," which were identified from the author's research (O'Brien, 1982a) on spirituality and life-threatening illness, include:

"Spiritual Pain, as evidenced by expressions of discomfort or suffering relative to one's relationship with God; verbalization of feelings of having a void or lack of spiritual fulfillment, and/or a lack of peace in terms of one's relationship to one's creator" (O'Brien, 1982a, p. 106). A terminally ill patient, experiencing such "spiritual pain," may verbalize a fear that he or she has not lived "according to God's will"; this concern is exacerbated as the possibility of imminent death approaches.

"Spiritual Alienation, as evidenced by expressions of loneliness, or the feeling that God seems very far away and remote from one's everyday life; verbalization that one has to depend upon oneself in times of trial or need; and/or a negative attitude toward receiving any comfort or help from God" (O'Brien, 1982a, p. 106). Often, a chronically ill person expresses frustration in terms of closeness to God during sickness; the comment may be heard: "Where is God when I need Him most?"

"Spiritual Anxiety, as evidenced by an expression of fear of God's wrath and punishment; fear that God might not take care of one, either immediately or in the future; and/or worry that God is displeased with one's behavior" (O'Brien, 1982a, p. 106). Some cultural groups entertain a concept, although not held by all members of the culture, that illness may be a "punishment" from God for real or imagined faults or failures.

"Spiritual Guilt, as evidenced by expressions suggesting that one has failed to do the things which he or she should have done in life, and/or done things which were not pleasing to God; articulation of concerns about the 'kind' of life one has lived" (O'Brien, 1982a, p. 106). Certain individuals, especially those schooled in more fundamentalist religious traditions, experience "guilt" related to their perceived failure to follow God's will, as they understand it. This "guilt" frequently is exacerbated during times of physical or psychological illness.

"Spiritual Anger, as evidenced by expressions of frustration, anguish or outrage at God for having allowed illness or other trials; comments about the 'unfairness' of God; and/or negative remarks about institutionalized religion and its ministers or spiritual caregivers" (O'Brien, 1982a, p. 107). Family members of those who are ill may express anger at God for allowing a loved one to suffer.

"Spiritual Loss, as evidenced by expression of feelings of having temporarily lost or terminated the love of God; fear that one's relationship with God has been threatened; and/or a feeling of emptiness with regard to spiritual things" (O'Brien, 1982a, p. 107). A sense of "spiritual loss" may frequently be associated with psychological depression; for an individual who feels useless and powerless, there may also be a resultant feeling of alienation from anything or any person perceived as good, such as God.

"Spiritual Despair, as evidenced by expressions suggesting that there is no hope of ever having a relationship with God, or of pleasing Him; and/or a feeling that God no longer can or does care for one" (O'Brien, 1982a, p. 107). Although spiritual despair is generally rare among believers, such a diagnosis may be associated with serious psychiatric disorders. If such thoughts or feeling are expressed by a patient, the nurse needs to be alerted, also, to the potential for suicidal ideation or possible behavior.

▶ Spirituality and Nursing Research

Although clinical nursing research efforts in the area of spirituality and nursing practice have not been extensive, some nurse investigators have addressed the spiritual needs of particular patient groups. Examples include Soeken and Carson (1987), "Responding to the Spiritual Needs of the Chronically Ill"; Clifford and Gruca (1987), "Facilitating

Spiritual Care in the Rehabilitation Setting"; Reed (1991), "Preferences for Spiritually Related Nursing Interventions Among Terminally Ill and Nonterminally Ill Hospitalized Adults and Well Adults"; Toth (1992), "Faith in Recovery: Spiritual Support After an Acute M.I."; Highfield (1992), "Spiritual Health of Oncology Patients"; Mickley, Soeken, and Belcher (1992), "Spiritual Well-Being, Religiousness, and Hope Among Women with Breast Cancer"; Harris et al. (1995), "The Role of Religion in Heart-Transplant Recipients' Long-Term Health and Well-Being"; Smith (1995), "Power and Spirituality in Polio Survivors: A Study Based on Roger's Science"; Twibell, Wieseke, Marine, and Schoger (1996), "Spiritual and Coping Needs of Critically Ill Patients: Validation of Nursing Diagnoses"; and Post-White et al. (1996), "Hope, Spirituality, Sense of Coherence, and Quality of Life in Patients with Cancer."

Nursing studies, especially those in the arena of chronic illness, have frequently included the concepts of spirituality, religion, and/or religiosity (religious practice) as key variables in a larger matrix. Some examples include the author's research with chronic renal failure (CRF) patients, migrant farmworkers, nursing home residents, and persons living with HIV infection and AIDS. Brief examples of the studies are described here; more detailed qualitative data elicited in the research can illustrate instances of spiritual need and spiritual care.

Study Title: Religious Faith and Adaptation to Maintenance Hemodialysis

The purpose of this study was to examine the relationship between religious faith and adaptation to chronic renal failure and its treatment regimen of maintenance hemodialysis. The religious faith question represented one variable in a multivariate study of adaptation to renal disease and dialysis. The study subjects consisted of 126 adult hemodialysis patients who were interviewed first to obtain baseline data and again in a three-year follow-up, when 63 of the original sample were identified (O'Brien, 1982c, p. 75).

Study Title: Spirituality and Health Beliefs and Practices of Migrant Farmworkers

The research consisted of an exploratory descriptive qualitative study of the overall health attitudes and behaviors of a sample group of Mexican American migrant farmworkers. Central to the study was an examination of the spirituality and religious beliefs of the population, as related to health/illness beliefs and practices. The methods of data collection were observation and focused interview. During the three-month data collection phase of the study, the investigator attended many of the group's religious services and rituals, including weekly Spanish Masses, evening Mass in migrant camps, Baptisms, First Communion services, a Mass of departure as the migrants moved from one work setting to another, and a "coming of age" religious service for a teenage girl. The author visited several Mexican American religious shrines and interviewed three practitioners of folk religion/medicine. Focused interviews were also conducted with 125 adult migrant workers in three Midwestern states (O'Brien, 1982b, p. 13).

Study Title: Spiritual Beliefs and Behaviors of the Institutionalized Elderly

The purpose of this exploratory case study, conducted over a two-year period, was to examine and describe the overall institutional nursing home setting, as well as the patterns of attitude and behavior exhibited by the residents, family members, medical and nursing caregivers, and ancillary staff. A key variable of interest was spirituality, or the spiritual perceptions, attitudes, behaviors, and needs of the residents. The nursing home studied was a 230-bed residential facility that provided three levels of care: skilled, semiskilled, and domiciliary. The author collected data by means of direct and participant observation, as well as through focused interviews with staff, family members, and 71 alert and cognitively aware residents (62 women and 9 men). Variables of particular interest related to the spiritual/religious attitudes, experiences, and practices of the residents. Selected data on religion and spirituality are presented as excerpted from verbatim interview transcripts (O'Brien, 1989, p. 47).

Study Title: Religious Faith and Living with HIV Infection

Personal faith beliefs, as well as the support of an individual's church group or religious denomination, were examined in a study of coping response in HIV infection. The overall aim of the longitudinal project was to establish a database of physical, psychosocial, and spiritual needs associated with HIV infection, from which appropriate caregiving strategies could be derived. The study population consisted initially of 133 men and 3 women, all of whom were categorized within the CDC IV classification: "Constitutional Disease, Secondary Infections, Secondary Cancers, or Other Conditions Related to HIV Infection." A number had diagnoses of AIDS. A subgroup of 41 men with HIV/AIDS was followed over a five-year period, as long-term survivors of the infection. Data were collected by both quantitative (interview schedule) and qualitative (tape-recorded focused interview) measures. Data on the relationship of religion and spirituality revealed the importance of personal faith beliefs and church affiliation in coping with HIV (O'Brien, 1992, 1995).

Although not all nurses may or must feel comfortable in providing spiritual care, the assessment of a patient's spiritual needs is a professional responsibility. Contemporary holistic health care mandates attention to the problems and concerns of the spirit as well as to those of the body and mind. In carrying out an assessment of the patient's SWB, a nurse may glean information important to supporting the medical and nursing therapies planned for the ill person. Following a spiritual assessment, appropriate spiritual or religious interventions may be provided either by the nurse or through referral to a designated pastoral caregiver.

▶ References

Ameling, A., & Povilonis, M. (2001). Spirituality, meaning, mental health and nursing. *Journal of Psychosocial Nursing & Mental Health Services, 39*(4), 15–20.

Barker, E. (1979). Whose service is perfect freedom. In D. O. Moberg (Ed.), *Spiritual well-being: Sociological perspectives* (pp. 153–171). Washington, DC: University Press of America.

Blaber, M., Jones, J., & Willis, D. (2015). Spiritual care: Which is the best assessment tool? *Journal of Palliative Nursing, 21*(9), 430–438.

Blaikie, N. W., & Kelson, G. P. (1979). Locating self and giving meaning to existence. In D. O. Moberg (Ed.), *Spiritual well-being: Sociological perspectives* (pp. 133–151). Washington, DC: University Press of America.

Brennan, M. R. (1994). *Spirituality in the homebound elderly* (Unpublished doctoral dissertation). The Catholic University of America. Ann Arbor, MI.

Brush, B. L., & Daly, P. R. (2000). Assessing spirituality in primary care practice: Is there time? *Clinical Excellence for Nurse Practitioners, 4*(2), 67–71.

Burkhart, L., Schmidt, L., & Hogan, N. (2011). Development and psychometric testing of the spiritual care inventory. *Journal of Advanced Nursing, 67*(11), 2463–2472.

Campbell, C. (1978). *Nursing diagnosis and intervention in nursing practice.* New York, NY: Wiley.

Cavendish, R., Luise, B. K., Horne, K., Bauer, M., Medefindt, J., Gallo, M. A., . . . Kutza, T. (2000). Opportunities for enhanced spirituality relevant to well adults. *Nursing Diagnosis, 11*(4), 151–163.

Christy, R. D., & Lyon, D. (1979). Sociological perspectives on personhood. In D. O. Moberg (Ed.), *Spiritual well-being: Sociological perspectives* (pp. 91–98). Washington, DC: University Press of America.

Clark, C. C., Cross, J. R., Deane, D. M., & Lowry, L. W. (1991). Spirituality: Integral to quality care. *Holistic Nursing Process, 3*(1), 67–76.

Clark, P., Drain, M., & Malone, M. (2003). Addressing patients' emotional and spiritual needs. *Joint Commission Journal on Quality and Safety, 29*(12), 659–670.

Clifford, M., & Gruca, J. (1987). Facilitating spiritual care in the rehabilitation setting. *Rehabilitation Nursing, 12*(6), 331–333.

Dameron, C. (2005). Spiritual assessment made easy . . . with acronyms. *Journal of Christian Nursing, 22*(1), 14–16.

Dossey, B. M. (1989). The transpersonal self and states of consciousness. In B. M. Dossey, L. Keegan, L. G. Kolkmeier, & C. E. Guzzetta (Eds.), *Holistic health promotion* (pp. 23–35). Rockville, MD: Aspen.

Driscoll, J. (2003). HIPAA: Calling the question. *Vision, 13*(5), 4–5.

Droege, T. (1991). *The faith factor in healing.* Philadelphia, PA: Trinity Press International.

Engebretson, J. (1996). Considerations in diagnosing in the spiritual domain. *Nursing Diagnosis, 7*(3), 100–107.

Fatula, M. A. (1993). Faith. In M. Downey (Ed.), *The new dictionary of Catholic spirituality* (pp. 379–390). Collegeville, MN: The Liturgical Press.

Fowler, J. W. (1981). *Stages of faith development.* New York, NY: HarperCollins.

Galek, K., Flannelly, K., Vane, A., & Galek, R. (2005). Assessing a patient's spiritual needs: A comprehensive instrument. *Holistic Nursing Practice, 19*(2), 62–69.

Gebbie, K. M. (1976). *Summary of the second national conference, classification of nursing diagnoses.* St. Louis, MO: C. V. Mosby.

Gebbie, K. M., & Lavin, M. A. (1975). *Classification of nursing diagnoses, proceeds of the first national conference.* St. Louis, MO: C. V. Mosby.

Govier, I. (2000). Spiritual care in nursing: A systematic approach. *Nursing Standard, 14*(17), 32–36.

Harris, R. C., Dew, M. A., Lee, A., Amaya, M., Bushes, L., Rettz, D., & Coleman, G. (1995). The role of religion in heart-transplant recipients' long-term health and well-being. *Journal of Religion and Health, 34*(1), 17–32.

Haugan, G. (2014). The FACIT-SP spiritual well-being scale: An investigation of the dimensionality, reliability and construct validity in a cognitively intact nursing home population. *Scandinavian Journal of Caring, 29*(1), 152–164.

Highfield, M. (1992). Spiritual health of oncology patients. *Cancer Nursing, 15*(1), 1–8.

Hodge, D. R. (2015). Administering a two-stage assessment in healthcare settings: A necessary component of ethical and effective care. *Journal of Nursing Management, 23*(1), 37–38.

Hodge, D. R. (2006). A template for spiritual assessment: A review of the JCAHO requirements and guidelines for implementation. *Social Work, 51*(4), 317–326.

Holloway, N. M. (1993). *Medical surgical care planning* (2nd ed.). Springhouse, PA: Springhouse Corporation.

Hsaio, Y., Chiang, Y., Lee, H., & Han, C. (2013). Psychometric testing of the properties of the Spiritual Health Care Scale Short Form. *Journal of Clinical Nursing, 22*(21/22), 2981–2990.

Hungelmann, J., Kenkel-Rossi, E., Klassen, L., & Stollenwerk, R. (1996). Focus on spiritual well-being: Harmonious interconnectedness of mind-body-spirit—Use of the JAREL spiritual well-being scale. *Geriatric Nursing, 17*(6), 262–266.

Johnson, R. P. (1992). *Body, mind, spirit: Trapping the healing power within you.* Liguori, MO: Liguori.

Joint Commission. (2003). *Comprehensive accreditation annual for hospitals: The official handbook.* Oakbrook Terrace, IL: The Joint Commission.

Joint Commission. (2008). *Standards FAQ details: Spiritual assessment.* Retrieved from http://www .jointcommission.org/standards_information/jcfaqdetails.aspx?StandardsFaqId=290& ProgramId=1

Kaufman, J. H. (1979). Social correlates of spiritual maturity among North American Mennonites. In D. O. Moberg (Ed.), *Spiritual well-being: Sociological perspectives* (pp. 237–254). Washington, DC: University of America Press.

Kerrigan, R., & Harkulich, J. T. (1993). A spiritual tool. *Health Progress, 74*(5), 46–49.

Kreitzer, M. J., Gross, C., Waleekhachonloet, O., Reilly-Spong, M., & Byrd, M. (2009). The brief serenity scale: A psychometric analysis of a measure of spirituality and well-being. *Journal of Holistic Nursing, 27*(1), 7–16.

LaPierre, L. (2003). JCAHO safeguards spiritual care. *Holistic Nursing Practice, 17*(4), 219.

Lindberg, J. B., Hunter, M. L., & Kruszewski, A. Z. (1994). *Introduction to nursing: Concepts, issues and opportunities.* Philadelphia, PA: J. B. Lippincott.

Lutheran Services in America. (2004, July). Intersections of HIPPA and pastoral care. *Q & A, Lutheran Services in America Newsletter, 1.*

Mickley, J., Soeken, K., & Belcher, A. (1992). Spiritual well-being, religiousness and hope among women with breast cancer. *Image, 24*(4), 267–272.

Moberg, D. O. (Ed.). (1979). The development of social indicators of spiritual well-being and quality of life. In *Spiritual well-being: Sociological perspectives* (pp. 1–13). Washington, DC: University of America Press.

North American Nursing Diagnosis Association (NANDA). (1994). *NANDA, nursing diagnoses: Definitions and classification, 1995–1996.* Philadelphia, PA: Author.

Nouwen, H. J. M. (1986). *Reaching out.* New York, NY: Doubleday.

O'Brien, M. E. (1982a). The need for spiritual integrity. In H. Yura & M. Walsh (Eds.), *Human needs and the nursing process* (Vol. 2, pp. 82–115). Norwalk, CT: Appleton-Century-Crofts.

O'Brien, M. E. (1982b, April). Pragmatic survivalism: Behavior patterns affecting low level wellness among minority group members. *Advances in Nursing Science, 4*(3), 13–26.

O'Brien, M. E. (1982c). Religious faith and adjustment to long-term hemodialysis. *Journal of Religion and Health, 21*(1), 68–80.

O'Brien, M. E. (1989). *Anatomy of a nursing home: A new view of resident life.* Owings Mills, MD: National Health Publishing.

O'Brien, M. E. (1992). *Living with HIV: Experiment in courage.* Westport, CT: Auburn House.

O'Brien, M. E. (1995). *The AIDS challenge: Breaking through the boundaries*. Westport, CT: Auburn House.

O'Brien, M. E., & Pheifer, W. G. (1993). Nursing care of persons infected with HIV. In M. Maas, K. Buckwalter, & M. Titler (Eds.), *Nursing clinics of North America, 23*(2), 303–315.

Pesut, B., Fowler, M., Reimer-Kirkham, S., Taylor, E., & Sawatzky, R. (2009). Particularizing spirituality in points of tension: Enriching the discourse. *Nursing Inquiry, 16*(4), 337–346.

Post-White, J., Ceronsky, C., Kreitzer, M. J., Nickelson, K., Drew, D., Mackey, K. W., . . . & Gutknecht, S. (1996). Hope, spirituality, sense of coherence, and quality of life in patients with cancer. *Oncology Nursing Forum, 23*(10), 1571–1579.

Power, J. (2006). Spiritual assessment: Developing an assessment tool. *Nursing Older People, 18*(2), 16–18.

Puchalski, C. (2000). Taking a spiritual history allows clinicians to understand patients more fully. *Journal of Palliative Medicine, 3*(1), 129–137.

Reed, P. G. (1991). Preferences for spiritually related nursing interventions among terminally ill and nonterminally ill hospitalized adults and well adults. *Applied Nursing Research, 4*(3), 122–128.

Sanders, C. (2002). Challenges for spiritual care-giving in the millennium. *Contemporary Nurse, 12*(2), 107.

Sessanna, L., Finnell, D., Underhill, M., Chang, Y., & Peng, H. (2011). Measures assessing spirituality as more than religiosity: A methodological review of nursing and health-related literature. *Journal of Advanced Nursing, 67*(8), 1677–1694.

Smith, D. W. (1995). Power and spirituality in polio survivors: A study based on Roger's science. *Nursing Science Quarterly, 8*(3), 133–139.

Smyth, T., & Allen, S. (2011). Nurses' experiences assessing the spirituality of terminally ill patients in acute clinical practice. *International Journal of Palliative Care Nursing, 17*(7), 337–343.

Soeken, K., & Carson, V. B. (1987). Responding to the spiritual needs of the chronically ill. *Nursing Clinics of North America, 22*(3), 603–611.

Stark, R., & Glock, C. (1968). *American piety: The nature of religious commitment*. Berkeley, CA: University of California Press.

Stoll, R. I. (1979). Guidelines for spiritual assessment. *American Journal of Nursing, 79*(9), 1574–1577.

Tanyi, R. A. (2006). Spirituality and family nursing: Spiritual assessment and interventions for families. *Journal of Advanced Nursing, 53*(3), 287–294.

Taylor, E. J. (2013). New Zealand hospice nurses' self-rated comfort in conducting spiritual assessment. *International Journal of Palliative Nursing, 19*(4), 178–185.

Taylor, C., Lillis, C., & LeMone, P. (1993). *Fundamentals of nursing: The art and science of nursing care* (2nd ed.). Philadelphia, PA: J. B. Lippincott.

Timmins, R., & Kelly, J. (2008). Spiritual assessment in intensive and cardiac care nursing. *Nursing in Critical Care, 13*(3), 124–131.

Toth, J. C. (1992). Faith in recovery: Spiritual support after an acute M.I. *Journal of Christian Nursing, 9*(4), 28–31.

Twibell, R. S., Wieseke, A. W., Marine, M., & Schoger, J. (1996). Spiritual and coping needs of critically ill patients: Validation of nursing diagnoses. *Dimensions of Critical Care Nursing, 15*(5), 245–253.

White, L. (2003). Pastoral care providers are members of the health care team in accordance with the regulations of the Department of Health and Human Services. *APC News, 6*(1), 1–2.

White, L., & Pierce, R. (2002a). HIPPA regulations raise questions for chaplains. *APC (Association of Professional Chaplains) News, 5*(1), 1–2.

White, L., & Pierce, R. (2002b). HIPPA regulations impact on visitation by clergy, lay ministers and faith group representatives. *APC News, 5*(3), 1–2.

Young, C., & Koopsen, C. (2011). *Spirituality, health and healing: An integrative approach*. Sudbury, MA: Jones & Bartlett Learning.

CHAPTER 3

The Nurse–Patient Relationship: A Caring Ministry

"Therefore, since it is by God's mercy that we are engaged in the ministry, we do not lose heart."

2 Corinthians 4:1

"When I do nursing, when I care for someone who is sick, I have a real feeling that I'm ministering to that person; that I am doing ministry. That goes back to the idea that the gospel tells us, as Christians, to care for the sick and that when we care for them we care for the Lord. Nursing is definitely a ministry".

Megan, Nurse Practitioner in Community Health

▶ The Nurse–Patient Relationship

For centuries, the nurse–patient relationship has been unique and individualized. Both patient and nurse bring into the partnership a multiplicity of personal life variables, including such factors as demographics (age, gender, marital status, ethnicity, religion, and socioeconomic status), family history, illness experience, and spiritual orientation. All of the characteristics associated with these variables may affect how the nurse–patient relationship is played out during the course of an interaction. Recent literature has also begun to explore, in more specificity, the topic of professional boundaries related to the nurse–patient relationship (Griffith, 2013), focusing especially on such issues as: the nurse's power and the patient's vulnerability (Benbow, 2013, p. 30); trust in nurse–patient relationships (Dinc & Gastmans, 2013); person-centered practice (Devenny & Duffy, 2014); communication (Reblin, Otis-Green, Ellington, & Clayton, 2014); and spirituality and the nurse's penchant for innate compassion (Wright &

Neuberger, 2012). Any or all of these variables, as well as sociodemographic characteristics, may impact the nurse–patient relationship.

The research data in this chapter poignantly describe the ministerial dimension of the nurse–patient relationship as identified by a cadre of practicing nurses. The nurses' own words are employed to label concepts in a paradigm of interaction that reveals the nurse as an anonymous minister. In this ministerial role, the nurse enters into a sacred covenant of caring for the sick.

▶ Spirituality and the Nurse

In discussing nurses' spiritual needs, Philip Burnard (1988) posed a number of questions that may help a nursing practitioner explore his or her own spirituality in relation to caregiving. These questions focus on such topics as understanding the term *spiritual*, religious education, the importance of spirituality to the nurse, feelings about spiritual beliefs different from one's own, the potential for changing personal spiritual beliefs, feelings regarding talking about spiritual beliefs with other nurses, and the perception of how one's own spiritual beliefs affect patient care (p. 36). For seasoned nurses, these questions may have been well explored in the course of their own faith development; for the newer clinician, exploring spiritual beliefs can be a valuable and growth-producing faith experience. Ultimately, responses to Burnard's questions may have an important impact on the nurse–patient ministerial relationship. Writing on the subject of a nurse's spirituality in 1912, distinguished nurse educator Isabel Hampton Robb (1912) asserted that indeed "the nurse's work is a ministry; it should represent a consecrated service, performed in the spirit of Christ, who made Himself of no account but went about doing good. The woman who fails to bring this spirit into her nursing misses the pearl of greatest value that is to be found in it" (p. 38). Nursing's spiritual dimension has been described as including the fact that attention to the "spirit should be regarded as an important part of spiritual care" (Myers, 2009, p. 22); that there should be "a systematic provision of spiritual care to patients" (Dunn, 2008, p. 4); that the concept of spiritual care should be included in nursing fundamentals textbooks (Pesut, 2008); and that nurses have a duty to facilitate the meeting of patients' spiritual and/or religious needs (Ledger, 2005).

In a 2010 literature review exploring the integration of spirituality into nursing practice, Tiew and Creedy identified five themes that impact spiritual care: these include "a lack of shared understanding of spirituality, lack of emphasis on spirituality in nursing education, attitudes, organizational and cultural factors, and individuality" (p. 15). Among these authors' recommendations following the review was the notion that "more research is required to develop a better understanding of how nurses perceive spirituality and the types of difficulties or barriers they face integrating spirituality into practice" (p. 19). A paper in *Nursing Ethics* addresses one of the themes identified by Tiew and Creedy, that of a lack of emphasis on spirituality education. Annette Becker (2009) asserts that "despite the evidence in college students indicating a hunger for spiritual insight and spirituality's application in health care, there continues to be a guardedness within the academy toward the inclusion of curricula that address spirituality" (p. 697). Becker offers a model for teaching spirituality and health that contains four guidelines: "approach teaching spirituality as any other 'difficult topic'";

"develop . . . a pragmatic course including learning activities that engage depth of learning"; "create and sustain a secure environment of learning"; and "be a trustworthy citizen of the college community" (p. 703).

In line with Becker's concept of creating activities that promote learning, one nurse author suggests that "creative modalities offer nurses a new perspective on how to care for patients" in an article entitled "Creativity and Spirituality in Nursing: Implementing Art in Healing" (Lane, 2005, p. 122). Dr. Mary Lane focuses on the accomplishment of healing using such arts as music, painting, and sculpture (p. 122). Other authors who link the concepts of spirituality with healing include: Glen McCabe (2008), who suggests the integration of body, mind, and spirit with traditional healing practices in psychotherapy; Dr. Jane Hart, of the Center for Spirituality and Healing at the University of Minnesota, which offers programs based on an integrative healing model (2010, p. 50); and Pipe, Hansen, Hentz, and Hartsell, who describe a program of spirituality and healing using "Watson's Theory of Human Caring (as) the framework guiding the project" (2010, p. 47).

Tyler and Raynor (2006) remind nurses that "there has been consistent use of spiritual practices to address health concerns by individuals for thousands of years" (p. 63); they note further that "incorporating spiritual care into practice is an integral dimension of holistic care that is the crux of nursing practice in the 21st century" (p. 63). Research employing focus groups, including patients, nurses, and hospital chaplains, showed that spirituality "played various roles in patients' lives during their illness" (van Leeuwen, Tiesinga, Jochemsen, & Post, 2007, p. 482), and myriad investigations have revealed that "spirituality is a fundamental quality that contributes to health and wellness" (Shores, 2010, p. 8).

Although the author's interviews with practicing nurses described in the following pages did address the nurses' own spiritual needs, only a modest amount of data was elicited on the topic. Nurses who participated in the study were clearly more interested in talking about the spiritual concerns and needs of their patients, how they had attempted to meet these, and how they might better practice spiritual care in the future. Nursing has historically been a discipline of service to others; the concern with one's personal well-being, spiritual or otherwise, was secondary to meeting the needs of the ill. The study nurses who did speak about their own spirituality, however, described the importance of such religious activities as prayer and Scripture reading in providing support for their practice.

Ellie, a pediatric oncology nurse practitioner who had worked with terminally ill children for more than 15 years, explained the significance of her personal spirituality:

> In this job, in this work I do with little ones, some of them are so, so sick. It hurts a lot to watch them get sicker and sicker; they are so brave, some of them. And the parents! It can get to you. Some days you just want to run away and say "no more!" I can't keep doing this job. You want to forget that babies are dying. . . . I truly do believe it's my faith in God, in the Lord Jesus, that holds me up. I try to pray every morning while I'm getting myself together for work. And when I can steal a few minutes I read some Scripture or something like Henri Nouwen; I love his books. And my church, they're a big, big support. I guess I could say that it is the spiritual that keeps me in oncology nursing.

▶ The Nurse: The Anonymous Minister

In addition to the nurse's personal spirituality, a number of other factors are relevant to the spiritual dimension of nurse–patient interactions, including the nurse's comfort level in discussing spiritual issues with patients, the degree of spiritual support provided in the care setting (i.e., support for both patients' and caregivers' spiritual needs), and the emphasis or lack of emphasis on providing spiritual care to patients in the course of professional nursing education. "Ministry denotes service and servanthood," asserts nurse educator Do-rhen Angking (2012). Although "the notion of nursing as a service has been de-emphasized, mainly due to the vigorous efforts to raise nursing to the realms of science as a profession," Angking points out that "for many nurses, especially Christian nurses, nursing is indeed the ministry they are called to by Christ" (p. 59). In order to explore, empirically, these questions and issues regarding spirituality and the covenantal nurse–patient relationship, the author conducted focused interviews with 66 contemporary nurses employed in two East Coast metropolitan areas, soliciting individual experiences, attitudes, and behaviors regarding the relationship between spirituality and nursing practice. The nursing cadre was purposely chosen to include a broad range of experience and education. The 6 men and 60 women comprising the population of nurses reported the following religious affiliations: 39 Roman Catholics; 25 Protestants (4 Baptists, 3 born-again Christians, 2 Methodists, 2 Episcopalians, 2 Presbyterians, 1 Lutheran, 1 "Christian," and 10 persons who described themselves broadly as "Protestant"); 1 Jewish nurse; and 1 nurse who reported having no religious affiliation.

Two members of the group were licensed practical nurses, five were diploma registered nurses, and one had an associate in arts nursing degree. Eleven individuals had baccalaureate degrees in nursing, 25 had master's in nursing degrees, 14 had doctorates in nursing science, and 8 were registered nurses with doctorates in the biologic or behavioral sciences.

The largest subgroup of 38 nurses identified a history of 16 to 25 years of nursing experience; 19 had been nurses for 26 to 40 years; and only 9 had practiced nursing for less than 15 years. Thirty-three percent of the group described their specialty area as medical–surgical nursing. Seven nurses worked in the area of psychiatric-mental health, and seven worked in pediatrics. Five critical care nurses and five cardiovascular nurses were included in the group; there was one oncology nurse, as well as three hospice and five gerontologic nurses. Three nurses worked in the area of maternal–child health, and two each represented the areas of community health, emergency room, and operating room nursing. Three of the study nurses worked with the mentally retarded/developmentally disabled, and three worked in home health-care nursing; one of the latter group of nurses was primarily involved with the health care of homeless persons.

Sixteen of the study nurses were employed at military health-care facilities; 10 were faculty members in schools of nursing. Ten nurses were employed by medical centers, 7 by research institutions, 12 by private religiously affiliated hospitals, 3 by hospice facilities, 7 by city-run health-care facilities, and 1 nurse worked for an HMO. More than half of the group were identified as working in the area of nursing practice; 10 were nurse educators, 10 were nurse administrators, and 4 were employed as nurse researchers.

Interviews with the nursing group explored experiences and attitudes associated with nursing and spirituality, focusing on such topics as nurse–patient interactions related to patients' spiritual needs and/or spiritual care, the nurse's personal spirituality and/or spiritual needs, spiritual support provided in the health-care setting, and the inclusion or lack of inclusion of spiritual concepts in the nurse's educational program. Discussions were tape-recorded to preserve the nurses' attitudes, perceptions, and experiences in their own words. Confidentiality was assured to the nurses participating in the interviews; wherever naming is warranted, pseudonyms are used.

Tape-recorded interviews were transcribed and content analyzed to identify dominant themes related to nursing and spirituality. A multiplicity of concepts emerged associated with such broad areas as nurses' attitudes toward spirituality and spiritual care, the identification of patients' spiritual needs, nursing behaviors regarding the spiritual care of patients, and nurses' perceptions of their roles in ministering to patients' spiritual needs. All dominant themes and related concepts are derived from the practicing nurses' own words.*

Study Findings

Ultimately, an overall construct describing the association between spirituality and the nurse–patient relationship emerged from analysis of the interview data and was labeled "The Nurse: The Anonymous Minister."

This construct, which identifies the nurse's frequently unrecognized role in spiritual ministry, consists of three dominant themes: A Sacred Calling, Nonverbalized Theology, and Nursing Liturgy. Each theme incorporates six key concepts reflective of the category's content and orientation (see **TABLE 5.1**).

A Sacred Calling

The first concept of the empirically derived construct, The Nurse: The Anonymous Minister, is reflected in a dominant theme derived from the nurses' interviews and labeled A Sacred Calling. This theme relates to a perceived professional nursing role in ministering to the spiritual needs of patients. A majority of the nurse practitioners, educators, administrators, and researchers interviewed described nursing as being a vocation or calling, reflecting a spiritual element incorporated within their profession.

---

*The nurses who participated in the Nursing and Spirituality interviews were identified through informal sampling. The author requested key nurses, in the various types of health-care facilities described, to approach members of their staff who might be willing to meet and discuss the topic of spirituality. No criteria regarding the nurses' religious affiliations were specified. As demonstrated in the demographic profile, 64 of the overall group of 66 nurses who agreed to participate in the project identified themselves as Christian. Thus, many of the themes and concepts relating to spirituality and the nurse–patient relationship presented in this chapter are undergirded by Christian theology and spirituality. It is expected, however, that the reader affiliated with another religious tradition will be able to appreciate the universal themes of love, caring, compassion, and ministry to those in need.

TABLE 3.1 The Nurse: The Anonymous Minister		
A Sacred Calling	Nonverbalized Theology	Nursing Liturgy
A Send of Mission	United in Suffering	Healing Rituals
Messenger of Good Faith	Proddings of the Holy Spirit	Experiencing the Divine
The Almost Sacred	The Day the Lord has Made	Touching the Core
Touching the Hand of God	Crying for More	Being Present
Sensing the Vibrations	Needing Ventilation	Midwifing the Dying
A Healing Ministry	Praying a Lot	Privileged Moments

Peg, a master's-prepared psychiatric–mental health nurse with eight years of experience in the field, observed:

> When I was 16 I felt a "calling" to be a nurse; it's like a Sacred Calling. Over time you develop a devotion. I can't imagine doing anything else.

And Catherine, a doctorally prepared medical–surgical practitioner with 25 years of experience, perceived nursing as a calling from early on in her education:

> I went to school because I felt called to be a nurse. I see nursing as a spiritual vocation. It's much more than work; I find it a way of serving.

The term *vocation*, which is derived from the Latin word *vocare*, "to call," has been identified as a key theme "in both Hebrew and Christian scriptures" (O'Connell, 1993). "[V]ocation is central to understanding the relationship between Divine initiative and human response" (O'Connell, 1993, p. 1009). The concept of vocation is broadly understood as defining an individual's felt call to a particular ministry or work. In theological terminology the word *vocation* generally refers to "a Divine call to undertake a particular activity or embrace a particular 'stage of life' on behalf of God or the community" (Holland, 1990, p. 1087).

One of the younger study discussants, Amy, a 24-year-old baccalaureate-prepared nurse with one year of experience in the pediatric intensive care unit, asserted that although it had been a real "challenge" to master the health-care technology used in the care of critically ill children, it was the spiritual dimension of nursing that appealed to her: "When the day comes that I don't minister spiritually to that child or the family, then I need to get out. This is why I felt called to go into nursing; I don't just want to be a technician."

Supportive of envisioning nursing as a vocation, also, is the recent resurgence of interest among nurse researchers and educators in the relationship of moral belief to the practice of nursing. Ray (1994) observed that nurse theorist Jean Watson "illuminated caring as the moral ideal in nursing where protection, preservation, and enhancement of human dignity are the mandates for the nurse" (p. 106).

The theme of vocation, or a Sacred Calling, may be further explained in terms of six key concepts derived from the data elicited in the Nursing and Spirituality discussions. These include A Sense of Mission, Messengers of Good Faith, The Almost Sacred, Touching the Hand of God, Sensing the Vibrations, and A Healing Ministry.

A Sense of Mission

A number of nurses described their perceptions of and experiences with spiritual care in terms of a call to mission or ministry. For Christians, all are called to ministry as pointed out in the New Testament:

> Then the king will say to those at his right hand, "Come you that are blessed by my Father, inherit the kingdom prepared for you from the foundation of the world; for I was hungry and you gave me food, I was thirsty and you gave me something to drink, I was a stranger and you welcomed me, I was naked and you gave me clothing, I was sick and you took care of me, I was in prison and you visited me . . . I tell you, just as you did it to one of the least of these . . . you did it to me. (Matthew 25:34–36; 40)

Although several terms are used to indicate the concept of ministry in the New Testament, interestingly, one used at least 20 times is the word *therapeu*, which means "to care for," "attend," "serve," "treat," especially by a physician, hence, "to heal" (Rademacher, 1991, pp. 39–40). Rademacher pointed out as well that "since the Jews, unlike some of the Greeks, did not divide the person into body and soul, we must assume the word describes a holistic healing of the total person" (p. 40). Most practicing nurses used the terms *ministry* and *mission* interchangeably; they also linked the concept of holistic nursing assessment and nursing care with a sense of ministering to the "whole" person, which they perceived as including the patient's spiritual needs.

Sarah, a baccalaureate-prepared nurse with 12 years of experience in hospice care and pediatric oncology, explained that, although she did need to work for financial reasons, she would not have chosen nursing if it were not for the ministry aspect, "I feel a real 'sense of mission' in nursing. It's a spiritual ministry. If I didn't feel that, I wouldn't be here." She added:

> I really depend on God to direct me. Every morning I try to spend some time in prayer and reading Bible verses to give myself strength. I try, when I have time off, to be alone and have a sense of God's presence. I know that I can't heal the children, but to just be there, that helps, and I pray that Jesus will work through me, to use my hands to in some way comfort or do the right thing for the patients.

A doctorally prepared pediatric nurse educator with 14 years of experience in practice described a strong sense of congruence between nursing and ministry:

> My nursing is my service to God. I believe that this is what I am supposed to be doing; this is my ministry. For me nursing and spirituality are intertwined.

I deal with people in their hour of greatest need; whether it's rocking a dying child or helping to support a family. People need more than physical care; they need love and acceptance. And this is when your mission, your ministry, can be a healing presence.

Paula, a master's-prepared medical–surgical nurse, perceived ministry as a key role in nursing practice:

> We are ministering when we sit and counsel with patients; you are ministering to them when you are talking spiritual beliefs. This is part of our mission; we nurses wear so many different hats. We go from teacher, to being ministers, to doing the technical things of our trade like catheters and IVs. But the ministry part is a special gift; it is central to caring and to nursing.

And Martha, a critical care nurse, described how she learned the importance of spiritual ministry to those living with HIV/AIDS:

> I've found that ministering to [people with HIV], to be open, to listen to them, has led to some very humbling experiences for me, and [they] have also been some of my most rewarding experiences. Once I learned that it was OK to cry with the patients; to scream with them. It was OK to just sit there and say nothing because I just didn't know what to say. I learned to just sit there and hold their hand; they will let you know if they want to talk. They don't want anything a lot of times. All they want is a touch or just to know that you are there; they don't want anything else.

Finally, Shannon, in describing her ministry to intensive care unit (ICU) patients, spoke about her approach to critical care, which included a reluctance to impose her personal faith beliefs on patients:

> I try to figure out where a patient or their family is in terms of spirituality, and if there are needs there and they don't know how to bring it up. So, when something good comes up in a conversation, I'll say something like, "Well, you really have been blessed, haven't you?" And about 98 percent of the time that gives them the permission to let me know about their spirituality. I discovered that this way I can get to their spiritual side without being real threatening; it's just a word choice. . . . I've always been real sensitive to the fact that I have no right to impose my faith on anybody else, but to give folks a chance to articulate their own. If they're not clear on what they believe, sometimes just talking it out with a caring listener puts those issues in perspective. . . . There have been a number of times when folks have asked for a prayer after a conversation like that.

In sum, the spiritual mission of nursing might well be encapsulated in the challenge of Brother Roger of Taizé (1991) who asked, "Who will give the best of their creative gifts so that suffering throughout the world may be alleviated, in places where there is sickness, or hunger, or appalling housing conditions?" (p. 13). Brother Roger advised, "Perhaps you could place these Gospel words on the wall of your home; they come straight from the heart of Christ: 'Whatever you do to the least of my brothers and sisters, you are doing to me,' Matthew 25:40" (p. 13).

Messengers of Good Faith

A baccalaureate-prepared pediatric oncology nurse, Maria, described her perceived nursing vocation as related to the comments of a priest–chaplain at her hospital orientation. Maria explained:

> In our orientation Fr. O'Connor told us that we were "messengers of good faith." I really feel that is right but don't always see it happening on the units. The advanced technology has taken us somewhat away from the patients. But this is the kind of nurse I want to be, a nurse with a sense of vocation, of "good faith." . . . The spirituality, the strength of these children and their families amazes me; going through chemo and all that really affects their lives. I, being Catholic, attribute that strength to God. I need to support them with my faith.

Anna, a long-term hospice nurse, also spoke about the importance of spiritually supporting patients and families without imposing one's own beliefs:

> The idea of spiritual care is particularly important in the hospice setting. The spiritual component is just as important to hospice personnel as the physical component is. At every team meeting the spirituality of the patients is discussed; it is very holistic. . . . But we can't just go in and force our spirituality or our belief system on any patient. We need to meet patients wherever they are.

In their roles as messengers of good faith, nurses walk "among the hurting" attempting to "heal" and to "comfort"; they need to proclaim the love of God for His people. In her deeply moving book, *May I Have This Dance?*, Joyce Rupp (1992) reminded us that "[t]he Spirit of God dances among us, calls us to appreciate and enjoy life, and invites us to participate in the Divine Song that makes melody in the heart of all of creation" (p. 95).

No one is ignored; no one is excluded from the call to loving participation in the "Divine Song."

The Almost Sacred

The term *sacred* is defined variously as relating to "the service or worship of a deity"; "a thing worthy of religious veneration, or Holy"; or "something associated with religion or the religious" (*Merriam-Webster's Seventh New Collegiate Dictionary*, 1976, p. 757). A number of practicing nurses who shared spiritual thoughts or experiences used the word *sacred* in relating to some dimension of their interaction with patients. This is exemplified in the comments of Anne Marie and Karen.

A master's-prepared psychiatric–mental health nurse presently working at a research institution, Anne Marie noted that her choice of nursing had been strongly motivated by an "idealistic desire to help people." She reported:

> I considered other careers along the way but nursing gives you an opportunity to make a difference in people's lives. In nursing you deal with the "almost sacred." I know that sounds like strong words but nursing almost touches on the religious. Our work with patients is a real gift. The deep experiences and talks I have had with patients are the closest thing to a spiritual experience.

These are the times when you make these deeper connections with people that are spiritual; that is Christ within. Although you don't always recognize it or define it as God's presence within. I have been personally touched by those times.

And Karen, a doctorally prepared medical–surgical nurse, spoke about her approach to patient spiritual care as being a sacred trust:

> I try to look and see if there is a way that patients are signaling me that they need spiritual support. I look to see if maybe they have a Bible laying out and if they're in pain or not sleeping, and I say, "I see you have your Bible here; is there a favorite passage you'd like me to read?" I might also ask, "What kinds of things are important to you?" to see if they might want to go to church or to talk to a chaplain.
>
> I know that my calling as a Christian is to share the Gospel, the good news of Christ; this is a sacred trust. But also, the patient is a captive there and I struggle with getting the balance of "OK, how much am I injecting my values?" So that's why I look for clues to see what's important in their lives; so if it's meditation or listening to music, or whatever, I can pick up on that but if they do mention something to do with the Lord then I can either talk about Scripture or call a chaplain without hitting the person over the head with denominational religion. . . . We have to separate religion and spirituality. Religion is a lot different from spirituality and may be tied up with a lot of rules and prejudices and judgments, but spirituality is about how God reaches out to us and how we respond to that.

Frequently, practicing nurses noted that, although they might not be affiliated with the same religious denomination as a patient, there was, nevertheless, a common sense of spirituality to which they could relate. This provided a starting point from which the nurse could then assess the patient's spiritual needs or concerns.

Touching the Hand of God

The sacredness of a nurse's spiritual ministry was recognized clearly in instances of care for those facing life-threatening illness. In discussing ministry to the terminally ill, Niklas and Stefanics (1975) admitted that this may represent a time when the patient, faced with the reality of his or her own mortality, is open to the presence and the love of God. They suggested that the one ministering actually "walks with the dying person through the valley of the shadow of death" (p. 115). Thus, ministers need to be secure in their own relationship with God and in the understanding of their role in spiritual care.

Christian, a doctorally prepared nurse with 18 years of experience in hospice care, which had recently included a significant amount of care for those with HIV or AIDS, related his nursing vocation to work in the area of death and dying:

> In nursing we have many opportunities to minister but we sometimes miss the opportunity to do this. But when facing death you really face the concept of spirituality, your own and your patients'. AIDS patients really articulate their spirituality in their coping. When you work with people who are dying, you touch the hand of God. . . . Spirituality is an area of nursing that would provide a really wonderful expanded role; for me, [spirituality] is primary.

Peg, a master's-prepared medical–surgical nurse with more than 20 years of experience, also described such a perception of closeness to God in caring for seriously ill patients:

> I remember working with some really critically ill patients, and really sensing the presence of God and their spiritual closeness. And especially at night when the hospital is quieter and more lonely, I felt that they [the patients] just wanted me to be there and to understand what they were going through. They may have only a few days to live but I could hold their hand and give them that presence of God's love and caring.

Sensing the Vibrations

Joyce, a master's-prepared nursing administrator with approximately 24 years of experience in medical–surgical and intensive care nursing, understood the concept of nursing as a Sacred Calling. She commented, "Spirituality, for me, is to allow both nurses and patients to self-actualize; to love, that is what brings about healing. That is what makes nursing, caring." Joyce observed that when she entered a nursing unit, she considered that part of her role as a clinical nursing administrator was in sensing the vibrations:

> When I walk on a ward, I can sense the vibrations, whether there's a lot of sickness, whether there's a lot of anxiety, a "darkness," and I think that those vibrations are part of spirituality. And I think that the more we love the more we send out our own vibrations of peace and we can lower the anxiety. As we love people we can bring them light; we can make them feel "lighter" and happier. I think that nurses need to do this to their stressful environments, to promote a wholesome, healthy, healing environment. . . . We are all connected in God.

A Healing Ministry

Jesus taught about the concept of ministry through His example of preaching, teaching, and especially of healing the ill and infirm. McGonigle (1993) pointed out that "Jesus sealed the truth of His ministry by the total gift of Himself for the Salvation of all those whom He came to serve" (p. 658). Many Christian health caregivers feel most appropriate in envisioning their work as a spiritual ministry when they relate their activities to Jesus' healing ministry.

This is well exemplified in the comments of Emily, a master's-prepared critical care nurse with 15 years of experience:

> Nurses, I believe, minister to patients, just as I believe that certified clergy do, as Christ did in his healing ministry. I look at the person in totality, the holistic approach. Sometimes it's just by being there, by listening. We talk about God and the love of God, and that He looks at the whole person, not just the last things you did. I have had many patients ask me to pray with them. . . . Nursing is a calling, a healing ministry. You can read and study but it has to be something that is within you, something you are called to do spiritually. . . . Especially in working with dying or critically ill patients you call on your spirituality. Sometimes if someone is suffering a lot you even pray that they will die but it's OK because of faith in God. We say,

"I see an angel on the foot of the bed." ... "Growing up" in critical care you can become focused on the technology but you need to go beyond that. You can cry with the family; I have cried with so many patients and families.

Finally, Emily observed that there was a "definite need for staff nurses to 'marry-up' with chaplains and begin to talk about their spiritual experiences."

The comments from the Spirituality and Nursing study group represent only a few selected examples of the nurses' perceptions of their chosen profession as representing a Sacred Calling. As observed earlier, virtually all of the group members viewed some dimension of vocation or spiritual ministry as integral to their profession. Although this perception might be articulated through different concepts or anecdotes, the essential theme of nursing as a Sacred Calling pervaded the discussions.

Nonverbalized Theology

The second concept supporting the construct of the nurse as anonymous minister is described as Nonverbalized Theology. Repeatedly, discussions revealed individual nurses' "God-relationships" and "God-understanding" as being supported by such practices as the reading of Scripture, attendance at formal religious worship services, and personal prayer and meditation. None of the group, however, reported having formally studied theology, although several nurses suggested that it was something they had thought about and might consider doing in the future.

For Christians, theology is the study of "Divinely revealed religious truths. Its theme is the being and nature of God and His creatures and the whole complex of the Divine dispensation from the fall of Adam to the Redemption through Christ" (Livingstone, 1990, p. 509). Gerald O'Collins (1981), in his classic text *Fundamental Theology,* noted that the common understanding of the theological discipline is "faith seeking understanding" (p. 5). Although O'Collins accepted that we must come to the study of theology from a position of personal faith, he posited that the discipline "can help believers to describe, explain, interpret, and account for their faith" (p. 10). O'Collins added, "[Christians] know that they believe in the God revealed in Jesus Christ. Theology makes it easier or even possible to say just what it is they believe. With this help they can state their faith to both themselves and others" (p. 11).

Most of the nurses interviewed were articulate in describing their own faith beliefs, especially in terms of the Christian admonition to care for brothers and sisters in need. Many, however, admitted that they generally did not spend a lot of time speaking or consciously thinking about the dimension of spiritual ministry incorporated into their nursing practice; it was simply considered part of the caring activity central to the profession.

The concept of Nonverbalized Theology was suggested by Paula, a doctorally prepared medical–surgical nurse administrator with 22 years of experience. Paula asserted that nurses "minister" spiritually throughout their professional careers, although the underlying theology may never be verbalized:

Ministry is not a discreet function; a separate task. It is embedded in the careful giving of the meds, the wiping of the brow, the asking of the right questions, the acknowledgment of the patients' humanness, and what they are experiencing in their sickness. I can be there, to be a person of the love of God. You want to alleviate suffering, convey hope, bring love. It is in giving your care in a caring way; but there is no theology being verbalized; it's a nonverbalized theology. It's in our nursing that we recognize the spiritual side of ourselves and others.

Judith, a doctorally prepared cardiovascular nurse, supported the position:

> I believe that nurses have been doing, and still do, spiritual care a whole lot but we just haven't called it that. . . . Before we didn't verbalize our theology or spirituality but now at least we have an official "nursing diagnosis" for "spiritual distress." I think that gives us a big opening for spiritual assessment of our patients. . . .
>
> Nursing is a ministry but you don't have to speak Scriptures every time you see a patient. When you do spiritual care it can be like Jesus; He just didn't go in and do teaching; He went in and took care of the needs of people first. He fed them and healed them. So when you go in to a patient, take care of their physical needs before you do spiritual care; I believe that nursing is a combination between the art of caring and science. . . . We need to be sensitive. You can turn somebody off by coming on too strong; but you never turn them off by loving them. You always draw them to the Lord; by letting His love flow through you to them. That is the "Cup of Cold Water"; "you did it unto me."

Peter, a master's-prepared psychiatric–mental health nurse with 25 years of experience, also envisioned the concept of Nonverbalized Theology as supporting his clinical nursing practice:

> We are oriented to look at patients holistically, as having a biological, psychological, and spiritual dimension. So, if you're dealing holistically with a patient, and if your underlying theology is that man is made in the image and likeness of God, and you have the perspective of an Incarnational theology, then this is how you approach the patient, even if not on a conscious or verbal level. I am an instrument through which God is present to this person, and in this person is the suffering, or the joyful, Christ. Christ is always present to the other person through you and you encounter Christ in that patient. So even if this theology is not always spoken, or conscious in your mind, but is your underlying theology, then, in holistic nursing, you are relating to the patient's spiritual needs as well as his physiological and psychological; you can't compartmentalize man.

In content analyzing the discussion data, six key concepts articulated by the nurses were identified as being reflective of the overall theme of Nonverbalized Theology: United in Suffering, Proddings of the Holy Spirit, The Day the Lord Has Made, Crying for More, Needing Ventilation, and Praying a Lot.

United in Suffering

Frequently during the discussions, nurse practitioners movingly demonstrated a non-verbalized theological concept of community by revealing a deep sense of empathy with and understanding of their patients' pain. Without sharing specific details, some of the nurses reported that personal experiences of pain and suffering had helped them become more sensitive caregivers; their interpretation was that having "been there" helped them better identify, at least broadly, with the concerns and anxieties of their patients. This is supported by Henri Nouwen's (1979) concept of the wounded healer, which he explained this way: "Making one's own wounds a source of healing . . . does not call for a sharing of superficial personal pains but a constant willingness to see one's own pain and suffering as rising from the depth of the human condition which all men share" (p. 88).

Sharon, a doctorally prepared gerontologic nurse with 19 years of experience, observed:

The older I get, the more confident I feel in sharing spiritual issues with my patients; we are all united in suffering, all children of God. I may not talk about my own pain, my own theology, a lot but I feel comfortable praying with my patients or assisting with a person's rituals. I understand where they're coming from if they're hurting. At this point in my career I am secure in my spirituality. . . . Some nurses are afraid of saying the wrong thing. I think it is a fear of confronting their own spirituality in dealing with patients. . . . Spirituality is that sense of community where God is most, through the presence of other people; Grace in our lives comes through other people.

The concept that we are all united in suffering is well reflected in 1 Corinthians 12:12–26:

As a body is one though it has many parts, and all the parts of the body though many, are one body, so also Christ. For in one Spirit we were all baptized into one body, whether Jews or Greeks, slaves or free persons, and we were all given to drink of one Spirit; . . . The eye cannot say to the hand, "I do not need you," nor again the head to the feet, "I do not need you." Indeed the parts of the body that seem to be weaker are all the more necessary, and those parts of the body that we consider less honorable, we surround with greater honor and our less presentable parts are treated with great propriety. . . . But God has so constructed the body . . . that the parts may have the same concern for one another. If one part suffers, all the parts suffer with it.

Proddings of the Holy Spirit

In Christian theology the Holy Spirit is understood as "the Third Person of the Trinity, distinct from, but consubstantial, co-equal and co-eternal with the Father and the Son, and in the fullest sense God" (Livingstone, 1990, p. 245). Farrelly (1993) suggested that in the early Church the "dynamism of Christian life" was ascribed to the Holy Spirit as the vehicle of God's love given to His people (p. 496). In John's Gospel, the "personal character" of the Holy Spirit is demonstrated. "'I will ask the Father and He will give you another advocate to be with you always, the Spirit of Truth'; John 14:16–17" (Farrelly, 1993, p. 499). A number of the nurse respondents spoke of the importance of the Holy Spirit's guidance in their work with patients, staff, or students. Maggie, a nursing administrator for over 11 years, who described herself as a Southern Baptist and born-again Christian, noted that, although she would never impose her spirituality on a patient, she was "comfortable discussing her own beliefs," if this seemed warranted. Maggie believed that there was definitely a "spiritual care" role for nurses "if you take the time to go a little deeper." She advised that the nurse has to observe and listen carefully to what a patient may be seeking, prior to any spiritual intervention, however. Her suggestion was, "Be attuned to the proddings of the Holy

Spirit." Maggie reported, "I have prayed with patients. The times I have felt good about a spiritual interaction [with a patient], I knew I was ministering."

Maggie described a specific instance in which she recognized the guidance of the Holy Spirit in her nursing ministry:

> I was working with a mom whose little girl was having some diagnostic tests and they didn't know what was going on and she was really worried. And when they were getting ready to transfer her, the mom came to me and said, "Are you a Christian?" And I said, "Yes, I am," and she said, "I thought you were. And I wanted you to know that you were an answer to prayer; because I prayed for a guardian angel during this hospital experience, because we didn't know what was going on and you were there for me, from the first day to the last.

Maggie concluded, "In those types of experiences I give credit to God; to the Holy Spirit. It was not me; I was just His instrument."

In commenting on the characterization of the Holy Spirit in St. John's Gospel, the ecumenical community of the Brothers of Taizé (Taizé Community, 1992) explained that we are not expected to actually see or experience the Spirit who dwells in us. "What is asked . . . is that we believe in the Holy Spirit, that we trust in Him, that we abandon ourselves to Him. Far from being another demand made on us, this call to faith sets us free" (p. 75).

The Day the Lord Has Made

Several nurses spoke of their gratitude for the spiritual ministry involved in their nursing practice. They saw it as a gift from God to whom they now gave thanks, as directed in Psalm 118:

> Give thanks to the Lord for He is good; His mercy endures forever. . . . The Lord is with me; He is my helper. . . . The Lord is my strength and my song. . . . This is the day the Lord has made; let us rejoice and be glad in it.

Margaret, a practical nurse with 16 years of experience who worked more recently with HIV and AIDS patients, asserted strongly:

> I may not discuss religion a lot but I couldn't do this work without my faith. I ask God to help me and then I can be calm. Prayer is important to me and seeing God in the smallest of things; in the miracles of flowers and birds. To deal with AIDS I have to do this. . . . I am so grateful to God for all that He has given me. I look at the trees in the morning and say, "this is the day the Lord has made." That's what will get you through.

Evelyn, an LPN with extensive experience working with mentally and physically challenged adults, also described her perception that each day was a day to give thanks for serving the Lord. "There is no separation of my day-to-day nursing and my spirituality. I live with it 24 hours a day; prayer in the morning, prayer at night. Each day is a gift of God. I'm not always conscious of it. I think it's like living prayer. It's all the time." Evelyn related her conscious awareness of the spiritual dimension of nursing to when she did hands-on care:

> I don't get to do as much "hands on" as I would like but when I do it's such a gift. I'm so grateful. There is something so holy. You say, "This person is

completely dependent upon my hands and my compassion to be cared for."
It's seeing Christ there.

Crying for More

Repeatedly, nurses' comments reflected their perceptions of patients' spiritual hunger for God, their need for spiritual care and healing, even if not articulated in theological terminology. In his classic book *Reaching Out* (1975), Henri Nouwen observed that increased sophistication of the healing professions has resulted in depersonalizing the "interpersonal aspects" of the work (p. 92). Caregivers often are forced, by the demands of their jobs, to "keep some emotional distance to prevent over-involvement with . . . patients" (p. 73). Thus, Nouwen advised that "the healer has to keep striving for a spirituality . . . by which the space can be created in which healer and patient can reach out to each other as fellow travelers sharing the same broken human condition" (p. 93).

Anna, a doctorally prepared nurse educator who has worked with students in the clinical medical–surgical area for more than 28 years, expressed concern about patients' spiritual needs not being met:

> People have psychological and emotional needs, but deep down they have real spiritual needs; they are crying for more. . . . I think it's a real gap in our nursing practice; we get so caught up with the technology, there's no time for theology. There are times in life, especially when you're ill, when you really need spiritual support. . . . I try to get the students to see the whole person. They often don't get to that; especially the values, beliefs, religion. If we're going to look at the whole person, you have to include spirituality.

In the preface to her classic spiritual allegory *Hinds' Feet on High Places*, Hannah Hurnard (1975) reminded us that, as the Song of Songs expresses, there is in each human heart a cry for more, a desire for a deeper union with God. "He has made us for Himself, and our hearts can never know rest and perfect satisfaction until they find it in Him" (p. 11).

Needing Ventilation

Related to the concept of patients' spiritual "cry for more," is that of a need to verbalize spiritual and theological concerns and anxieties in the presence of a caring and supportive listener. Allowing a patient to tell his or her story was a concept that emerged frequently in discussions. Emotional pain, often long held at arm's length, may emerge vividly when the physiologic component of one's persona has been wounded. Defenses may be at an all-time low; this is a time when important healing can begin. Nouwen (1992) asserted that old wounds can only be healed by allowing them out of the dark corners of "forgetfulness." Caregivers must "offer the space in which the wounding memories of the past can be reached and brought back into the light without fear" (p. 23).

Karen, an ICU nurse with 30 years of experience, spoke at length about her intensive care unit patients' need to talk about their old anxieties and fears, especially related to the topics of illness and death. She recounted that when physicians suggest the administration of tranquilizing medication to calm patient anxieties, she reminds the staff that the patients "need ventilation, not sedation!" Karen, as ICU head nurse, directs her staff nurses to "sit down and hold their patients' hands: Be open to listen; it's a humbling and rewarding experience." Karen advises, "It's OK to say nothing!" And she encourages the staff to do continual assessments of their patients' spiritual needs. She also teaches that "It's OK to cry with patients; crying is not a weakness. This may validate the patient's legitimacy in ventilating anxiety through tears."

During periods of illness or physical debilitation, a patient's latent emotional stresses may surface, generating responses such as anxiety and feelings of loneliness and alienation. It is important, as demonstrated by the nurses' anecdotes, that these stress responses be ventilated.

Praying a Lot

Prayer is as unique as the individual who prays. Whether one's prayer is of petition, adoration, reparation, or thanksgiving, both the form and the content may vary greatly. A few generalizations about prayer, however, can be offered.

The term *prayer* means "a petition or request": "Although the word may be used to mean a petition made to anyone at all, its customary use is . . . more particular, made to God or some holy person reigning with God" (Wright, 1993, p. 764). Some methods of prayer identified by Jesuit John Wright (1993) include "vocal prayer," which employs a specific word formula; "mental prayer," which is more of a conversation with God; "discursive prayer," which is led by one's reason; "affective prayer," in which love, joy, or other emotions may predominate; "meditation," in which one considers different aspects of God's activity; "contemplation," which involves a "simple gazing" lovingly upon God; "centering prayer," in which one contemplates God at the center of one's being; "mystical prayer," which is led by God's grace; and finally, "private" and "communal prayer," the latter consisting of a group of worshippers praying together (pp. 773–775).

In relation to the theme of Nonverbalized Theology, the majority of practicing nurses admitted that prayer, in some form, was an important part of their lives. Mark, a baccalaureate-prepared eight-year nursing veteran working with HIV/AIDS patients, reported that his personal faith was critical to his nursing practice:

> I have strong faith. I truly believe that God puts you where He wants you. God tests us as Christians and as nurses. You become friends with your patients; it hurts to lose them. I pray a lot; I can't do what I do without a lot of prayer. . . . Some AIDS patients feel guilty and not worthy of healing; they are afraid that God won't hear their prayers. I tell them that God does not punish illness. I tell them to pray.

And a long-term critical care nurse spoke about prayer in the midst of technology:

> Critical care nurses have to deal with a lot of technology; but the beauty of technology is that after a while it becomes so rote that you can do it without thinking. Once you've got the moves down, I think it is quite possible for you, in the midst of a "Code," while you are pulling up drugs, to pray for that patient, to pray for whoever is making the decisions, to pray for the families who have to cope with whatever happens.

Although most of the nurses interviewed admitted that they did not often speak about theology or spirituality with nursing colleagues, it was definitely an underlying theme related to their practice. Frequently, at the end of the discussions, nurses offered such comments as, "At first, I didn't think I had much to say, but I really enjoyed talking about these spiritual things"; or "I do give spiritual care but I don't often take the time to think about it, or talk about it." The latter seems an excellent reflection of the overall theme of Nonverbalized Theology.

Nursing Liturgy

The third and final concept supporting the research-derived construct of the nurse as an anonymous minister is labeled Nursing Liturgy. Anecdotes describing creative nursing behaviors involving worship related to spiritual care of patients and families abound in the transcripts of the Spirituality and Nursing discussions. The term *liturgy* is broadly understood as relating to rites or rituals associated with public worship; the word *liturgy* is derived from the Greek, *leitourgia*, meaning "the work of the people" (*The Liturgy Documents*, 1991, p. xiv). In its early pre-Christian use, the term was understood to mean any public activities undertaken to promote communal well-being (Collins, 1990, p. 592). Christian usage focused the word's meaning on "the public worship of the Church" (p. 592).

Nursing Liturgy is conceptualized here as consisting of communal, worship-related, spiritual care activities carried out by nurses in the context of their professional practice. In its broadest meaning, the term *communal* may include worshipful interactions of the nurse–patient dyad only; that is, a nurse and patient praying together. The latter activity constitutes liturgy, for, as noted in Scripture, "Wherever two or three come together in My Name, I am there among them" (Matthew 18:20). Key concepts reflective of the Nursing Liturgy theme include Healing Rituals, Experiencing the Divine, Touching the Core, Being Present, Midwifing the Dying, and Privileged Moments.

Healing Rituals

The term *ritual* is derived from the Latin word *ritus*, meaning "structure." "Ritual is understood as a social, symbolic process which has the potential for communicating, creating, criticizing, and even transforming meaning" (Kelleher, 1990, p. 906). Madigan (1993) noted that "Religious rituals, like social rituals, are intended to be formative and expressive of personal and communal identity" (p. 832). Madigan asserted that, essentially, "Religious rituals are symbolic actions that unify the doer with the sacred" (p. 832).

In relating instances of what they perceived to be "spiritual care," many nurses described poignant worship-associated "rituals" that provided healing to both patients and caregivers; several discussants labeled these "graced moments."

Cathy, a pediatric nurse clinician with 15 years of experience, much of it in the area of pediatric critical care, told a touching story of the "liturgy" that she and two other staff members created to mark the passing of an anencephalic newborn.

> The baby, a "preemie," had lived for a couple of weeks, but there were so many congenital anomalies that there was no hope; so the family signed the papers to terminate life support. The parents just couldn't be there, though, so we decided to plan something. It was a very young neonatologist, it was really hard on him, and myself, and the peds ICU head nurse. We came into the NICU [neonatal intensive care unit] at about 5 am on a Saturday, when there weren't a lot of staff around. We took the baby into a separate little

isolation room and discontinued the vent and the IVs, all the life support systems. And then we prayed and we sang hymns and we just held her and loved her until she died. It was her special ritual to go to God, and we shared it with her; that baby gave a lot to us, too.

Julia, a master's-prepared nurse educator with 22 years of experience in medical–surgical and ICU nursing, described a nursing ritual she had created for her students on completion of their clinical experience:

At the end of the semester I wanted to do something special for the students, to acknowledge their gifts and their talents in caring for patients. It was to provide some type of rite of passage that they were finished with their clinical. I called it an "anointing of the hands"; it was a "blessing with oil." I would explain that oil is healing and say something specific to each student about her gifts as I rubbed the oil on her hands. As I was massaging the oil into the palms of their hands, I would describe their giftedness and their talents in terms of who they were. I would bless them in the name of the Lord. After I had been with them for 15 weeks, I could make the prayer specific to each one. It was acknowledging the sacredness within them. Some students would cry.

Megan, a doctorally prepared nursing administrator with 27 years of experience in hospital care, described what she labeled a "para-liturgical" service, during which she also conducted an "anointing of the hands." In this liturgy, she anointed and blessed with oil the hands of her hospital's medical interns at their closing assembly of the year. Megan prayed over each young physician as she did the anointing. She reported that many were close to tears during the experience.

The symbol of anointing has always had a special place in the care of the sick. Oil is used sacramentally as a sign of healing and provides comfort for those who are ill and their loved ones. The concept of anointing the sick is found repeatedly in Scripture, for example, Mark 6:13. "And they cast out many demons, and anointed with oil many that were sick and healed them." Cunningham (1990) suggested that any "anointing" of a person may result in "a change in the person physically [health, strength, fertility] or in the relationship one has with the community" (p. 21).

Several of the nurse educators teaching in schools of nursing reported that they began their classes with a ritual of prayer or spiritual meditation. Frequently these rituals were nondenominational in order to include all of the students present. One nursing faculty member explained, "At the beginning of each class I give about a 2-minute spiritual reflection. One day, when we started into some questions about an exam without doing it, the students stopped me and said, 'Aren't we going to pray today?'"

Experiencing the Divine

The majority of practicing nurses indicated having at some time experienced God through interactions with their patients. For some the experience was conscious and ongoing; for others "critical incidents" highlighted a sense of experiencing the divine in a patient. This varied to some degree according to age and nursing experience, with more than a few nurses explaining that the longer they practiced their profession, the more "tuned in" they became to the presence of God within; this occurred in regard to both themselves and their patients. One nurse observed, "I feel like this kind of caring, this kind of experiencing and caring for God in your patients, is like going to church; it's a worship experience."

Julia, with her 22 years of experience in nursing practice, commented, "Nurses are always involved in spiritual care but they don't talk about it; they don't put a label on it" (as reflected in the theme Nonverbalized Theology). She went on to identify some nursing encounters that she perceived as reflecting spiritual experiences in nurse–patient interactions:

> I remember the first time that I ever experienced the divine in another person, in the woundedness of an individual. It just happened. It was an unattractive little old man who was drooling and unable to feed himself. His name was Tom. He seemed repulsive to me. He wasn't pleasant to look at and couldn't even respond to you. But I was caring for him and all of a sudden I thought, "Oh, this is what is meant by Christ within. Christ is present within this man who I initially saw as repulsive." . . . This was a graced moment for me. It was like a quiet kind of awakening; it was parallel to a faith experience!

Touching the Core

As a dimension of the dominant theme of Nursing Liturgy, several nurses spoke about the unique nature of the relationships developed in providing spiritual care for those who are ill. This was true whether the interactions consisted of formal spiritually oriented rites or rituals or more informal types of behaviors, such as praying with patients or discussing spiritual needs or concerns. Repeatedly the concept of depth in nurse–patient interactions related to spirituality emerged from discussion data; nurses spoke of the special opportunity to relate to patients intimately at a time when they are particularly open and vulnerable. This was perceived as a rewarding experience for the caregiver as well as for the patient.

Kinast (1990) asserted that in spiritual ministry to the sick "the deepest and richest human experiences are those which are shared between persons" (p. 9); that is, those in which the minister is able to touch the heart of another person.

Barbara, a doctorally prepared nurse educator with 23 years of experience in the area of pediatrics, commented that "Nursing is much more important than what you are doing [technically] to people; healing takes place just by being with people, by touching their spirituality. A gift to us as nurses is to be able to touch the core of someone."

Barbara's concept of touching the (spiritual) core, or holy place, of another is supported by a description of ministry to those living with HIV infection, in which a caregiver labeled his patient interactions "holy places we share when we have time together" (O'Brien, 1992, p. 99). The caregiver continued, "There is an incredible sweetness in being with these persons [with HIV], even when they are very ill and death is imminent; it gives one the incredible sense of 'holding a sacredness'".

Being Present

Barbara also spoke about the concept of being present, which she perceived as "integral to the spirituality of the nurse–patient relationship." Barbara described being present as the idea of "listening with a loving heart." She affirmed, "I don't know how you can relate to somebody, to be with them in their loneliness, without that dimension."

Holst (1992) highlighted the loneliness of being ill in his discussion of the hospital as "paradox." Although, he noted, privacy is rare, "there can be an eerie loneliness in the midst of all those human contacts" (p. 6). This is, in part, related to the fact that, although advanced technology is devoted to carefully monitoring disease, the person experiencing the disease may be neglected. Technology, Holst (1992) observed, makes us "more preoccupied with the heart as a pump, than with the heart as the seat of emotions" (p. 7).

This paradox is also addressed by James Nelson (1976) who asserted that fundamental to a patient's healing process is the presence of caring persons in the health-care facility. "Caring," Nelson added, "is an active attitude which genuinely conveys to the other person that he or she really does matter. It is different from wanting to care for another in the sense of making that person dependent on us. Rather it involves a profound respect for the otherness of the other" (p. 63). To take the concepts of presence and caring a step further, Henri Nouwen (1991) observed that the basis of caring ministry, the point at which ministry and spirituality touch each other, is compassion (p. 33). "Compassion," Nouwen continued, "is hard because it requires the inner disposition to go with others to the place where they are weak, vulnerable, lonely and broken" (p. 34). This, he added, is not our natural response to suffering; we generally either desire to flee from it or to find a "quick cure" (p. 34). In so doing, however, Nouwen argued "we ignore our greatest gift, which is our ability to enter into solidarity with those who suffer" (p. 34).

Many other project participants highlighted the importance of being present to patients in their suffering.

Pat, a baccalaureate-prepared critical care nurse with three years of experience, observed that in providing spiritual care "You have to have intuition beyond the psychological. We're the ones right there at the bedside. You can be the facilitator, find out what the patient and family need spiritually, just by being present."

Kathryn, a master's-prepared psychiatric–mental health nursing administrator with more than 30 years of experience in nursing, noted that "Taking care of the sick is a ministry in and of itself. The idea of ministering and really being present to people helps me to see them as whole individuals, and my own spirituality leads me to see the individual through the eyes of Christ."

And, Diane, a master's-prepared operating room nurse with 19 years of experience, described her conceptualization of being present to her OR patients by praying for them during surgery. "Especially when open-heart surgery patients are in the OR, on the 'Pump,' and we are literally touching their hearts; that's the time when I especially pray for that patient." Diane added, "I serve God through being present for my patients."

Midwifing the Dying

In his article "Religious Approaches to Dying," Anglican Father David Head (1994) reminded us that "Death is integrated as a concept into religious belief systems, and also the religious belief systems integrate death and life" (p. 306). For many "religious" people the beliefs surrounding death "may be comforting" (p. 305). Their tenets often include such concepts as "the transitory nature of the state of death" and "entry into an unknown mystery that is congruent to human experience" (p. 305).

In ministering to a dying person, the caregiver must understand not only the patients' beliefs and feelings about death, but his or her own as well. Niklas and Stefanics (1975) pointed out that if a caregiver is "not in tune with his feelings [about death], they become a weapon or a barrier preventing the dying person and his family from expressing their feelings, or cause him to lack appreciation of the feelings that are being expressed" (p. 114).

Although a number of nurses spoke about the importance of being present to their patients and their families during the death and dying experience, two actually described themselves as being like midwives helping their patients to be "born into a new life." One was Jan, a master's-prepared medical–surgical clinician with 21 years of nursing experience, a significant portion of which involved working with terminally ill patients. She observed, "I help patients to 'cross-over' in the last few days. Part of our job is being like midwives in assisting people in getting to that next state, to their new life in God. We are not only nurses and spiritual caregivers, we are family."

And Sarah, a peds oncology nurse with extensive experience in dealing with death and dying among children, related a special midwifing experience:

> I just got a letter at Christmastime from a family of a little boy who died about 5 years ago. And it was such a precious experience for me; how I bonded with him and with the family. When he was dying we picked him up and we held him and prayed with him and sang to him, and I felt like a midwife; that was really a gift. Being a midwife; it was like helping him to be born into eternal life. You feel so humbled and so privileged just being a part of it.

Sherrie, a master's-prepared critical care nurse with 15 years of experience, described her privileged experience in working with a family whose baby died shortly after birth:

> This was a gift for me and I hope I helped the family. We spent a lot of time with [the baby] in the 3 days before she died. We dressed her and held her and sang to her. I told the family, "We are all God's angels and some of us He wants back with Him sooner." . . . God had a special role for that baby. In the 3 days' time this baby gave and received more love than you will ever know. . . . It's a gift to us to be with anyone who is so close to being with God, to be with them in this special time of transition from this life to a new life.

Privileged Moments

As noted earlier, gratitude for the opportunity for spiritual encounters with patients emerged frequently as a theme in the Nursing and Spirituality discussions. Our nurse project participants reported a multiplicity of privileged moments related to spiritual care interactions with patients. A number of these are evident in the comments and anecdotes already presented. Especially touching are those related by Mary, Daniel, and Sarah.

Mary, a master's-prepared community health nurse with approximately 16 years of experience, most of it in hospice care, described her perception of spiritual care:

> Nurses should never force their spiritual beliefs on patients. . . . Just sitting with a patient, especially one who is dying, I think that is very much spiritual care. . . . Being a hospice nurse is so humbling; it's such a privilege. As hospice nurses, people really take us into their hearts. We have the opportunity to be with people during that time of life transition. We are connecting with

the very depth of a person who is facing death. And when they actually pass on, that is a very privileged moment to share with them.

Daniel, a 25-year nursing veteran, also spoke about the privilege of working with patients close to death:

I have always felt so privileged to work with patients in the final chapter of their lives on earth because it is such a rewarding experience. It is the tremendous privilege of being there. You try to do things that the patient is comfortable with. I remember especially the time I was caring for Mark; he was terminal with AIDS and he wanted me to take him upstairs to the bathroom. So I got him up there and then I thought, "Now, how can I get him back down?"; getting him up had been challenging enough! And I just said, "Well, Mark, I think the best thing is if you just get on my back." And I carried him that way, and it was really a privileged moment, like a mystical experience, I guess. It was like carrying Christ, a really powerful experience. . . . In situations like this you see yourself as merely an instrument through which God's love is present in the life of the suffering person. It's a mystery to us but it's through grace that I am here and can do what needs to be done in order to make God's love and compassion present to this person in his time of need. . . . We don't usually think of this consciously but there are times when it raises our consciousness, to be used by God, like when I carried Mark down the stairs.

Finally, Sarah related a poignant story that she described as a special and privileged moment with one of her small oncology patients:

Timmy was very disfigured with basal cell sarcoma and he hated to have his blood drawn. He usually screamed and his mom cried, so I'd started praying when I drew it; we prayed together. And so one day we prayed, and I got right in and got the blood, and Timmy was very happy. And it was the first time he had really made a connection with me. So he came into the utility room with me to help label the tubes, and he picked one up to put on the label and dropped it; and it shattered all over the floor. And I thought, "Oh God, how could you have let this happen after we all prayed?" But when I talked to the doctor he said that we could do without the blood that day. But Timmy felt really bad, and as a result, I spent a lot of time with him, and when they went to leave, I went over and hugged and kissed him; that was the first time that we really had connected like that. Since that time Timmy, when he comes in, always runs up and we hug and kiss. And, I realized that God was really working in our lives that day, except maybe not in the way I expected; that hug was much more important than the blood getting drawn. When God reveals something like that to you it is a very privileged moment.

▸ The Mysticism of Everyday Nursing

The comments of Mary, Daniel, and Sarah, like those of other nursing practitioners reported in the previous pages, exemplify a concept identified by theologian Karl

Rahner as the "mysticism of everyday life." Rahner contended that "the human person is 'homo mysticus'—one who experiences God because of an orientation to God rooted in the way God has made human nature" (Egan, 1989, p. 8). In Rahner's mind "everyone is at least an anonymous mystic" (p. 8). Egan observed that for Karl Rahner nothing about day-to-day life was "profane": "Wherever there is radical self-forgetting for the sake of the other . . . surrender to the mystery that embraces all life, there is . . . the mysticism of everyday life" (p. 8). Rahner's concept might appropriately be translated to read: the mysticism of everyday nursing.

Throughout this chapter members of the professional nursing community have, through their anecdotes and reflections, demonstrated themselves to be not only "anonymous ministers" but also "anonymous mystics." This is evidenced by the many reports of tender care and compassion provided for patients. Although contemporary nurses, whether practitioners, educators, administrators, or researchers, generally do not consciously think of themselves as either mystics or ministers, the data, as exemplified in their attitudes and behaviors, warrant the use of both labels. These findings indeed explain why at least one author has called nursing "the finest art" (Donahue, 1985), why nurse authors Joanne Widerquist and Ruth Davidhizar have described nursing as "ministry" (1994), and why mysticism and ministry may truly be considered integral dimensions of everyday nursing.

▶ References

Angking, D. (2012). Preparing for nursing ministry. *Journal of Christian Nursing, 29*(1), 59.

Becker, A. L. (2009). Ethical considerations of teaching spirituality in the academy. *Nursing Ethics, 16*(6), 697–706.

Benbow, D. (2013). Professional boundaries: When does the nurse-patient relationship end? *Journal of Nursing Regulation, 4*(2), 30–33.

Burnard, P. (1988). Search for meaning. *Nursing Times, 84*(37), 34–36.

Collins, M. (1990). Liturgy. In J. Komonchak, M. Collins, & D. Lane (Eds.), *The new dictionary of theology (NDT)* (pp. 591–601). Collegeville, MN: The Liturgical Press.

Cunningham, J. L. (1990). Anointing. In J. Komonchak, M. Collins, & D. Lane (Eds.), *The new dictionary of theology (NDT)* (pp. 21–23). Collegeville, MN: The Liturgical Press.

Devenny, B., & Duffy, K. (2014). Person-centered reflective practice. *Nursing Standard, 28*(28), 37–43.

Dinc, L., & Gastmans, C. (2013). Trust in nurse-patient relationships: A literature review. *Nursing Ethics, 20*(5), 501–516.

Donahue, M. P. (1985). *Nursing: The finest art, an illustrated history.* St. Louis, MO: C. V. Mosby.

Dunn, L. (2008). Spirituality and nursing: Personal responsibility. *Journal of Rural Nursing and Health Care, 8*(1), 3–4.

Egan, H. D. (1989, February). The mysticism of everyday life. *Studies in Formative Spirituality, 10*(1), 7–25.

Farrelly, M. J. (1993). Holy Spirit. In M. Downey (Ed.), *The new dictionary of Catholic spirituality (NDCS)* (pp. 492–503). Collegeville, MN: The Liturgical Press.

Griffith, R. (2013). Professional boundaries in the nurse-patient relationship. *British Journal of Nursing, 22*(18), 1087–1088.

Hart, J. (2010). The Center for Spirituality & Healing at the University of Minnesota. *Alternative and Complementary Therapies, 16*(1), 50–54.

Head, D. (1994). Religious approaches to dying. In I. Corless, B. Germino, & M. Pittman (Eds.), *Dying, death, and bereavement* (pp. 229–314). Sudbury, MA: Jones & Bartlett Learning.

Holland, P. D. (1990). Vocation. In J. Komonchak, M. Collins, & D. Lane (Eds.), *The new dictionary of theology (NDT)* (pp. 1087–1092). Collegeville, MN: The Liturgical Press.

Holst, L. E. (1992). *Hospital ministry*. New York, NY: Crossroad.

Hurnard, H. (1975). *Hinds' feet on high places*. Wheaton, IL: Tyndale House.

Kelleher, M. M. (1990). Ritual. In J. Komonchak, M. Collins, & D. Lane (Eds.), *The new dictionary of theology (NDT)* (pp. 906–907). Collegeville, MN: The Liturgical Press.

Kinast, R. L. (1990). Caring for God's covenant of freedom: A theology of pastoral care. In H. Hayes & C. Van der Poel (Eds.), *Health care ministry* (pp. 7–21). New York, NY: Paulist Press.

Lane, M. R. (2005). Creativity and spirituality in nursing: Implementing art in healing. *Holistic Nursing Practice, 19*(3), 122–125.

Ledger, S. D. (2005). The duty of nurses to meet patients' spiritual and/or religious needs. *British Journal of Nursing, 14*(4), 220–225.

The liturgy documents: A parish resource. (1991). Chicago, IL: Liturgy Training Publications.

Livingstone, E. A. (1990). *The concise Oxford dictionary of the Christian church*. New York, NY: Oxford University Press.

Madigan, S. (1993). Ritual. In M. Downey (Ed.), *The new dictionary of Catholic spirituality (NDCS)* (pp. 832–833). Collegeville, MN: The Liturgical Press.

McCabe, G. (2008). Mind, body, emotions and spirit: Reaching to the ancestors for healing. *Counseling Psychology Quarterly, 21*(2), 143–152.

McGonigle, T. (1993). Ministry. In M. Downey (Ed.), *The new dictionary of Catholic spirituality (NDCS)* (pp. 658–659). Collegeville, MN: The Liturgical Press.

Merriam-Webster's seventh new collegiate dictionary. (1976). Springfield, MA: Merriam-Webster.

Myers, J. (2009). Spiritual calling. *Nursing Standard, 23*(40), 22.

Nelson, J. (1976). *Rediscovering the person in medical care*. Minneapolis, MN: Augsburg.

Niklas, G., & Stefanics, C. (1975). *Ministry to the hospitalized*. New York, NY: Paulist Press.

Nouwen, H. J. M. (1975). *Reaching out*. New York, NY: Doubleday.

Nouwen, H. J. M. (1979). *The wounded healer*. Garden City, NY: Image Books.

Nouwen, H. J. M. (1991). *Creative ministry*. New York, NY: Image Books.

Nouwen, H. J. M. (1992). *The living reminder: Service and prayer in memory of Jesus Christ*. New York, NY: HarperCollins.

O'Brien, M. E. (1992). *Living with HIV: Experiment in courage*. Westport, CT: Auburn House.

O'Collins, G. (1981). *Fundamental theology*. New York, NY: Paulist Press.

O'Connell, L. J. (1993). Vocation. In M. Downey (Ed.), *The new dictionary of Catholic spirituality (NDCS)* (pp. 1009–1010). Collegeville, MN: The Liturgical Press.

Pesut, B. (2008). Spirituality and spiritual care in nursing fundamentals textbooks. *Journal of Nursing Education, 47*(4), 167–173.

Pipe, T., Hansen, P., Hentz, J., & Hartsell, Z. (2010). Rediscovering the art of healing by creating the tree of life poster. *Journal of Gerontological Nursing, 36*(6), 47–54.

Rademacher, W. (1991). *Lay ministry: A theological, spiritual and pastoral handbook*. New York, NY: Crossroad.

Ray, M. A. (1994, May–June). Communal moral experience as the starting point for research in health care ethics. *Nursing Outlook, 43*(3), 104–109.

Reblin, M., Otis-Green, S., Ellington, L., & Clayton, M. F. (2014). Strategies to support spirituality in healthcare communication. *Journal of Holistic Nursing, 32*(4), 269–277.

Robb, I. H. (1912). *Nursing ethics: For hospital and private use*. Cleveland: E.D. Koeckert Publishing.

Roger of Taizé. (1991). *No greater love*. Collegeville, MN: The Liturgical Press.

Rupp, J. (1992). *May I have this dance?* Notre Dame, IN: Ave Maria Press.

Shores, C. (2010). Spiritual perspectives of nursing students. *Nursing Education Perspectives, 31*(1), 8–11.

Taizé Community. (1992). *Listening with the heart.* Collegeville, MN: The Liturgical Press.

Tiew, L., & Creedy, D. (2010). Integration of spirituality in nursing practice: A literature review. *Singapore Nursing Journal, 37*(1), 15–22.

Tyler, I., & Raynor, J. (2006). Spirituality in the natural sciences and nursing: An interdisciplinary perspective. *ABNF (Association of Black Nursing Faculty) Journal, 17*(2), 63–66.

van Leeuwen, R., Tiesinga, L., Jochemsen, H., & Post, D. (2007). Aspects of spirituality concerning illness. *Scandinavian Journal of Caring Science, 21*, 482–489.

Widerquist, J., & Davidhizar, R. (1994). The ministry of nursing. *Journal of Advanced Nursing, 19*, 647–652.

Wright, J. H. (1993). Prayer. In M. Downey (Ed.), *The new dictionary of Catholic spirituality (NDCS)* (pp. 764–775). Collegeville, MN: The Liturgical Press.

Wright, S., & Neuberger, J. (2012). Why spirituality is essential for nurses. *Nursing Standard, 26*(40), 19–21.

CHAPTER 4

Spiritual Care: The Nurse's Role

And remember every nurse should be one who is to be depended upon . . . she must have a respect for her own calling, because God's precious gift of life is often literally placed in her hands.

Florence Nightingale, 1859

I look at nursing's role definitely as a calling to serve the sick. Because I think any nurse has to give 100% of herself or himself into the profession and to truly be a professional, they have to look at it beyond being an ordinary type of job; to include spiritual as well as physical and psychosocial care. I think it is truly a caring profession; nurses need to give of themselves sometimes when they are not feeling up to giving of themselves.

Annemarie, School Health Nurse

In years past, spiritual care was generally not considered a dimension of nursing therapeutics. With the advent of the holistic health movement, however, together with the notion of holistic nursing, assessment of an ill person's spiritual needs, and in some cases the practice of spiritual care, became recognized as legitimate activities within the domain of nursing. In light of the current interest in the nurse's role in patients' spiritual care, the present chapter explores the practice of spiritual care as nursing intervention; the attention given to patients' spiritual needs and concerns within the grand theories of nursing; some basic tenets of key Eastern and Western religious traditions; and the nurse's use of spiritual and religious resources such as prayer, Scripture, and sacred music. Referral to a formally designated pastoral caregiver is an acceptable option for the nurse not personally comfortable with the practice of spiritual care.

▶ The Nurse's Role in Spiritual Care

Clinical and research professionals sometimes question whether indeed the nurse has a relevant role in providing spiritual care to patients in his or her charge. The topic was addressed briefly in terms of nursing assessment of spiritual needs. The point bears repeating, however, that identification of the nurse's role in providing spiritual care is in no way meant to devalue the role of the hospital chaplain or the pastor ministering to the ill in the community. Rather, the nurse and pastoral care provider can work together to assess the spiritual needs of the ill person and support a comprehensive plan of spiritual care. Although not all nurses may feel comfortable providing spiritual care in all situations, the nurse should always be sensitive to the spiritual needs of his or her patients. With the advent of the holistic health-care concept, it is suggested that the "nursing profession must expand its awareness and competence in the spiritual dimension" (Nelson, 1984, p. 26).

Nursing textbooks, particularly those addressing fundamentals of nursing and medical–surgical nursing, reveal that the nurse's role in both assessment of patients' spiritual needs and the provision of spiritual care is a significant component of overall nursing. Several fundamental texts contain chapters with titles such as "Spirituality," "Spiritual Health," and "Spirituality and Religion" (Kozier, Erb, Blais, & Wilkinson, 1995; Potter & Perry, 1997; Taylor, Lillis, & LeMone, 1997). These chapters include such topics as spiritual health, spiritual problems, assessment of patients' spiritual needs, religious practices, spirituality and family needs, spirituality and the nursing process, and nursing diagnosis of spiritual distress. Many medical–surgical nursing texts also contain discussions of the nurse's role in spiritual care of the patient. Topics included are spirituality and nursing practice, spiritual care, assessment of patients' spiritual needs, nursing diagnoses, religious beliefs and practices, death-related spiritual beliefs, and spiritual beliefs in coping with acute and chronic illness (Black & Matassarin-Jacobs, 1997; Ignatavicius, Workman, & Mishler, 1995; Phipps, Cassmeyer, Sands, & Lehman, 1995; Smeltzer & Bare, 1996). In discussing the psychosocial dimensions of medical–surgical nursing, Edmision (1997) stated unequivocally that "meeting the spiritual needs of clients has become a recognized part of nursing care" (p. 68).

In the periodical nursing literature also, spiritual care is identified as a recognized element of holistic practice (Bruner, 1985; Labun, 1988; Sims, 1987) and is viewed as central to quality care (Clark, Cross, Dean, & Lowry, 1991; Simsen, 1988). A number of spiritual care models (Ceronsky, 1993; Karns, 1991) and creative approaches to spiritual care (Praill, 1995) have been advanced. Julia Lane (1987) suggested that the spiritual care of patients be addressed in three parts: first, by identifying the characteristics of spiritual care in relation to the essential nature of the human person; second, by identifying spiritual care interventions; and finally, by viewing nursing as a vocation (p. 332). Emblen and Halstead (1993) identified five spiritual care interventions appropriate to nursing: "listening to the patient express key concerns; praying with the patient; reading favorite portions of religious readings; spending time with the patient; and making a referral to a chaplain" (pp. 181–182). Dennis (1991), in a study of 10 nurses who reported providing spiritual support from a nonreligious perspective, also found the concepts of listening and spending time with patients to be important components of spiritual care. Recent research has demonstrated that there is a need for educational strategies to prepare nurses for spiritual caregiving (Greenstreet, 1999);

spiritual care infiltrates all aspects of nursing care (Carroll, 2001); there are cultural aspects involved in spiritual care (Sellers, 2001); and nurses themselves derive much satisfaction from providing spiritual care to their patients (Kumar, 2004; Narayanasamy & Owens, 2001; Nolan, 2000; Stephenson & Wilson, 2004; Treloar, 2001). From a review of the literature, three key competencies of spiritual care were identified, including "awareness of the use of self; spiritual dimensions of the nursing process; and assurance and quality of expertise" (van Leeuwen & Cusveller, 2004, p. 234).

Explorations into the nature and role of spiritual care in nursing were conducted by Ellis and Narayanasamy (2009) and Pearce (2009). Tanyi, McKenzie, and Chapek (2009) investigated the incorporation of spiritual care into practice by nurse practitioners and other health-care professionals. Spiritual care was defined by Hummell, Galek, Murphy, Tannenbaum, and Flannelly (2008). Nurses' understanding of spiritual care was explored by P. Kemp (2009); Chung, Wong, and Chan (2007); Swift, Calcutawalla, and Elliott (2007); and R. Moore (2007).

How can the nurse not grounded in a religious tradition or spiritual philosophy practice spiritual care? Should such a nurse attempt to intervene relative to the spiritual needs of an ill person? Ultimately the response must lie with the individual nurse.

As noted earlier, all nurses are responsible for being aware of and sensitive to their patients' spiritual needs as a dimension of holistic health care. It is suggested that nurses may even "be called upon to pray with or for patients as a part of holistic care" (Narayanasamy & Narayanasamy, 2008, p. 394), and in a discussion of "ethical principles of spirituality," Cheryl Lantz (2007) observed that nurses are "ethically obligated to provide spiritual care to clients" (p. 36). It has also been noted, however, that the lack of a clear definition of spirituality may hinder nurses from providing adequate spiritual care (Denholm, 2008, pp. 451–452).

The minimizing or neglect of this aspect of patient care may have serious implications for the overall illness adaptation. The nurse must consider spiritual needs as part of a comprehensive nursing assessment. What may vary, however, is the degree to which individual nurses carry out therapeutic intervention in response to spiritual needs. Many nurses do feel both comfortable and confident in engaging in such spiritual care activities as praying with patients, sharing the reading of Scripture passages, and listening to and counseling a patient about spiritual concerns. These activities may be appropriately carried out by a nurse if acceptable to the patient and family. For the nurse who does not feel adequately prepared to be involved in the practice of spiritual care, the appropriate course of action is referral to another nurse comfortable with providing spiritual intervention or to a formally trained pastoral caregiver.

Related to the nurse's role as anonymous minister, the majority of spiritual care provided as a component of nursing activity is unrecognized and unacknowledged. Spiritual care is rarely documented on patients' charts (Broten, 1997, p. 29). Nevertheless, current nursing research and clinical evaluations continue to identify the value placed on the nurse's role in providing spiritual care, by both patients and families.

A number of 21st-century professional articles confirm the importance of the role of spirituality in nursing practice. Nursing leader Phillip Kemp (2009) points out that spiritual care is so central to nursing practice that it is incorporated in "the way in which [a nurse] behave[s], talk[s], care[s], guide[s] or treat[s] people" (p. 334). Spiritual care, it is asserted, "is widely recognized in nursing theory," and "involves a complexity of social processes, of which developing caring relationships is core" (Carr, 2008, p. 686). Nevertheless, it is also recognized that spiritual care is not always understood and sometimes "dwells on the periphery of the profession" (Carr, 2010, p. 1379). Nursing leader Anna-Marie Stevens (2011) suggests that there can be "a role for spirituality in palliative care leadership" (p. 315), and nurse educator Donia Baldacchino reported the introduction of an experience in spiritual care for nursing students in order to expose them to the practice (2010).

The contemporary nurse's role in providing spiritual care to patients also seems to be cemented by a proliferation of journal articles discussing related issues such as: "Who can give spiritual care?" (Kevern, 2012); nurses' perceptions of spiritual care (McSherry & Jamieson, 2013; McSherry & Jamieson, 2011); a health services framework of spiritual care (Daaleman, 2012); perspectives of spiritual care among nurse managers (Battey, 2012); "creating conditions for good nursing by attending to the spiritual" (Biro, 2012, p. 1002); research on spiritual care in nursing (Cockell & McSherry, 2012); and studying "the lived experience of giving spiritual care" (Deal & Grassley, 2012). A spiritual care values model to guide what is described as one having a "careful nursing perspective" was published by nurse educator Therese Connell Meehan (2012, p. 990).

The importance of the nurse's role in spiritual care is also reflected in journal articles discussing the importance of education on patients' spiritual needs and spiritual care interventions in undergraduate nursing programs. Some examples include: "the efficacy of integrating spirituality into undergraduate nursing curricula" (Yilmaz & Gurler, 2014, p. 929); introducing spirituality into a baccalaureate nursing program (Yuan & Porr, 2014, p. 240); use of simulation techniques to teach students spiritual care (Costello, Atinaja-Faller, & Hedberg, 2012); undergraduate nursing educators teaching spiritual care (Cone & Giske, 2012); nursing students learning spiritual care (Giske & Cone, 2012); undergraduate nursing students learn to care spiritually (Giske, 2012); and nurse educators promote inclusive spiritual care (Barss, 2012).

Pediatric nurse practitioner Mary Sweat (2012) observes that part of spiritual care may be simply providing a "quiet place" for the patient and suggests four premises to support the idea; these ask the nurse to "respect privacy," "create an environment that promotes respect," "respect individual preferences," and "respect yourself" (p. 180). Wright and Neuberger (2012) offer "a seven point manifesto" for integrating spirituality into nursing care. The positions include:

1.   Spiritual care is not a luxury . . . but goes to the heart of care.
2.   Educational programs that nurses undertake must provide an in-depth understanding of what people mean by spirituality.
3.   Imaginative educational programs for nurses relating to spiritual care [should be offered].
4.   The workplaces of nurses should ideally provide all patients with access to spiritual support.
5.   Spirituality has a direct effect on health and well-being.
6.   Spiritual care . . . is essential for the ongoing training of all nurses.
7.   Spiritual care is also a part of enhancing the healing environment (p. 21).

▶ Spiritual Care and Religious Tradition

In order to engage in the assessment of spiritual needs and the provision of spiritual care for patients whose personal spirituality is intimately interwoven with religious beliefs and practices, the nurse should have some basic knowledge about the traditions of the major world religions. Obviously, the nurse may not herself subscribe to the religious tenets and practices of a particular patient; however, a broad understanding of the patient's religious culture will assist in identifying spiritual problems and in making referrals to an appropriate pastoral caregiver. The spiritual care of the atheist, who denies the existence of God, and the agnostic, who questions the existence of God, may consist of listening to and providing emotional support for the patient.

It is neither the intent nor within the scope of this text to present a comprehensive review of world religions. The following discussion is intended only as an overview of key tenets of the religious groups described. This delineation of selected spiritual and religious beliefs and practices may, however, provide the nurse with a starting point in interaction with patients of different faiths. The best strategy in conducting a spiritual assessment is to attempt to learn from the patient or a family member which religious beliefs and practices are most important, especially those pertinent to health and illness issues.

Two major categories of religious tradition are generally considered to be Western spiritual philosophy and Eastern spirituality. The three key Western religions are Judaism, Christianity, and Islam; all are founded on a monotheistic theology. Major Eastern traditions include Buddhism, Hinduism, and Confucianism, the tenets of which differ, especially in regard to the worship of God or of a multiplicity of gods.

Native American religions, of which there are many, generally look to the earth and the spirits of nature for comfort, sustenance, and support. Most Native American religions share a common view of the cycle of life and death and use ritual ceremonies to mark life transitions (Taylor, Lillis, & LeMone, 1997).

Western Religious Traditions

Within the Western religions of Judaism, Christianity, and Islam, the one supreme being is named Yahweh, God, or Allah.

Judaism is described as one of the oldest religions "still practiced in western civilization" and "the foundation on which both Christianity and Islam were built" (Taylor, Lillis, & LeMone, 1997, p. 885). The major religious Jewish groups are Orthodox, Conservative, and Reform; a more recently identified fourth Jewish tradition, which emerged out of a conservative mind-set, is Reconstructionist Judaism (Pawlikowski, 1990, p. 543). The groups differ significantly in regard to religious beliefs and practices. Orthodox Jews follow the traditional religious practices, including careful observance of the Talmudic laws; the Conservative and Reform movements interpret the laws more broadly (Charnes & Moore, 1992). All Jewish traditions emphasize the practice of good deeds or mitzvahs each day (Nutkiewicz, 1993, p. 561). Although daily religious rituals are central to the faith of most Jewish persons, health is so valued that "almost all religious injunctions may be lifted to save a life or to relieve suffering" (Charnes & Moore, 1992, p. 66). Jewish people tend to believe that the occurrence of illness is not an accident but rather a time given one to reflect on life and the future (Beck & Goldberg, 1996, p. 16). The keeping of a kosher dietary regimen, if not injurious to health, is very important to many Jewish patients' coping with an illness experience (Fine, 1995), as is the keeping of Shabbat or Sabbath, which is observed from sunset on Friday evening to sunset on Saturday. "It is suggested that home visits should not be scheduled on the Sabbath [*Shabbos,* from sundown Friday to sundown Saturday] for this is a day set apart for God, to honor him and use for prayer, studying scripture and special family time" (Salladay & Bitting, 2012, p. 15). Death, for the Jewish believer, is viewed as part of life; it is important to document the precise hour when death occurs in order to establish the time of mourning, shiva, and the annual "honoring of the dead, Yahrzeit" (Beck & Goldberg, 1996, p. 18).

Christianity, the largest of the world religions, consists of three main divisions: Roman Catholicism, Eastern Orthodox religions, and the Protestant faiths.

Roman Catholicism identifies that group of Christians who remain in communion with Rome, and who profess allegiance to the doctrines, traditions, philosophies, and practices supported by the pope, as religious leader of the Church. Roman Catholics are trinitarian in theology and place great importance on the seven sacraments: Baptism, Reconciliation (Confession), Holy Eucharist, Confirmation, Matrimony, Holy Orders, and Anointing of the Sick (formerly called "Extreme Unction"); participation in the holy sacrifice of the Mass is the central element of worship.

The Eastern Orthodox tradition, which represents a group of churches whose international leaders are located in Eastern Europe, differs from the Roman Church on both theological issues and aspects of ritual and worship. These churches respect the primacy of the patriarch of Constantinople and include reverence for the Holy Trinity as a central spiritual tenet of the faith. Veneration of holy icons is an important devotion leading ultimately to worship of God the Father, God the Son, and God the Holy Spirit. Currently the term *Eastern Orthodox Church* refers to four ancient patriarchates (Constantinople, Alexandria, Antioch, and Jerusalem), as well as a number of other churches such as those of Russia and Romania, Cyprus, Greece, Egypt, and Syria (Farrugia, 1990, p. 306).

The term *Protestant* generally refers to the churches that originated during the 16th-century Reformation (Gros, 1990). Some characteristics of original Protestantism are "the acceptance of the Bible as the only source of revealed truth, the doctrine of justification by faith alone, and the universal priesthood of all believers" (Livingstone, 1990). Protestant Christians generally regard Baptism and Holy Communion as important sacraments, although denominations may differ on associated rituals. Some of the major Protestant denominations are Adventist, Baptist, Church of the Brethren, Church of the Nazarene, Episcopal (Anglican), Friends (Quakers), Lutheran, Mennonite, Methodist, and Presbyterian.

Christianity is based on the worship of God and promotion of the Kingdom of God through the living out of the Gospel message of Jesus of Nazareth. For the Christian patient, the nurse will need to be sensitive to a multiplicity of religious beliefs and rituals associated with such health-related events as birth, childbearing, organ donation, and death. For example, infant Baptism is required by Roman Catholics and Episcopalians, and Last Rites or the Sacrament of the Sick is optional for some Protestant groups, but traditional for Eastern Orthodox Christians (Krekeler & Yancey, 1993). In a study of Christian patients' attitudes toward spiritual care, Conco (1995) found that three key themes emerged from interview data. Christian patients described the spiritual care they received as "enabling transcendence for higher meaning and purpose," which helped the patients find meaning in their illness and suffering; "enabling hope," which included the belief that the patients could find a better future; and "establishing connectedness," a theme that spoke to the support provided by the caregiver in terms of such activities as touching, listening, and being present to the patient (pp. 271–272).

Other Western churches of which the practicing nurse should be aware include Christian Science, Church of Jesus Christ of Latter Day Saints (Mormons), Jehovah's Witnesses, and Unitarian Universalist Association of Churches (Taylor, Lillis, & LeMone, 1997, p. 886).

Islam is frequently viewed as having been founded by the prophet Muhammed in the seventh century, with the revelation of the Holy Qur'an. Muslims themselves, however, do not regard Islam as a new religion; "they believe that Allah is the same God who revealed His will to Abraham, Moses, Jesus and Muhammed" (Esposito, 1990). A key tenet of Islam is Tauhid, which means faith in the total Lordship of Allah as ruler of heaven and earth; allied with this concept is the understanding that one's life must be centered on this belief (Abdil-Haqq Muhammad, 1995). Important religious practices for Muslims include the ritual prayer, prayed five times each day (preceded by ritual washing) while facing Mecca (the east); honoring Ramadan, the month of fasting from sunup to sundown, which occurs in the ninth lunar month of the Islamic calendar; and the experience of a hajj, a pilgrimage to Mecca, once in one's lifetime, if possible. Spiritual care for a hospitalized Muslim patient should be focused on providing the time (about 15 minutes) and the setting (a quiet, private place) for the five-times-daily ritual prayer (C. Kemp, 1996, p. 88). Most hospitals have access to the services of a Muslim spiritual leader, an imam, if requested by the patient (Rassool, 2000).

A Muslim registered nurse, Selia, spoke about some of the needs of Muslim patients who have entered into the health-care system:

> A Muslim patient, what they need during their sickness is similar to what a Christian patient needs: they need a faith in God; they need someone to listen to them; someone to talk about God with them; to know the support coming from God. We have some people in Islam, Muslim women, like who you might say is a "nun," and they are very prayerful and we might ask them to visit and to pray for someone who is sick. We also have in Islam, an imam, who is the spiritual leader of the mosque; he can be called to visit and pray with patients.

Selia also spoke of the importance of faith in helping her own sister accept a diagnosis of cancer. "The staff nurse helped her see that the cancer was not a punishment from God. The nurse sat with her and prayed with her in Arabic and after this she was able to accept her chemotherapy. The 'spiritual' was the most important thing in helping my sister accept her cancer and her treatment." Selia noted that if a patient was not physically able to pray facing Mecca during an illness or treatment, "They can pray while they are lying in bed; they can pray in their minds, even if they are not able to talk. Nurses should encourage Muslim patients to pray to accept their disease because it will help them to cope." She added, "One does not mourn if a family member dies from an illness; they accept this as the will of Allah and one does not contradict this."

Selia continued, "Although a Muslim patient who is very ill is not required to pray five times each day, Muslim hospitals usually prepare prayer rooms; one for women and one for men, who are able to move about. During Ramadan, a patient is not required to fast. The Qur'an says that the sick person, after he gets well, can fast then. She explained, however, that some patients "insist on fasting because they think it is like a prayer; it is something from God."

Finally, Selia spoke of the importance in Islam of visiting the ill:

The Prophet Mohammed, in the Holy Qur'an, it is written in his own words, that each Muslim should visit patients who are sick and support them and pray with them. It is a must for each Muslim to pray; to ask Allah to help that patient and to help all patients all over the world, whatever their religion.

Eastern Religious Traditions

The major Eastern traditions—Buddhism, Hinduism, and Confucianism—incorporate beliefs about God that differ significantly from those of religions of the Western tradition.

Buddhism derives its beliefs and practices from the life and teachings of the Buddha, the "enlightened one," who lived in India some 2500 years ago (Borelli, 1990). Myriad Buddhist traditions are associated with the cultures of particular geographical communities, such as Tibetan Buddhism or Chinese Buddhism. Wherever Buddhists are found, there are usually monasteries of monks, and sometimes nuns, who preserve the Buddhist teachings and liturgies. Buddhists believe that suffering can be ended by following the eightfold path: "right understanding, right intention, right speech, right action, right livelihood, right effort, right mindfulness and right contemplation" (Borelli, 1990, p. 146). Buddhists do not revere any particular sacraments.

Hinduism does not embrace one particular body of beliefs and practices; the name Hindu is derived from the geographical region of the Indus river valley and the subcontinent, Hindustan, where many of those who practice Hinduism reside (Cenkner, 1990). Key concepts in Hinduism relate to reincarnation or rebirth and the idea of karma, or "the law by which one's personal deeds determine one's present and future status in this life and in future lives" (Cenkner, 1990, p. 467). Hindus who have lived well do not fear death; it is seen as the preparation for reincarnation into another life.

Confucianism is an Eastern tradition derived primarily from the personal philosophy of the ancient Chinese scholar Confucius. Inherent in Confucian thought is belief in the importance of maintaining harmony and balance in the body. Two potentially conflicting forces are thought to occur in the world, the "yin" and the "yang"; it is critical that these dimensions of function be kept in balance in order to achieve and maintain a good and productive life.

▶ Nursing Theory and Spiritual Care

In the ideal world of nursing, clinical practice would be based on and directed by well-validated nursing theory; this includes the practice of spiritual care. Nursing theory, however, is still relatively new, having been developed primarily over the past three decades. And in a number of the grand theories of nursing, the spiritual needs of the ill person are given only minimal attention. As more grand nursing theory, as well as theory of the middle range, is generated, scholars anticipate that spirituality will be an important concept of interest. One example is the work of Judith Allen Shelly and Arline Miller, *Called to Care: A Christian Theology of Nursing* (1999).

Speaking from the practitioner's perspective, hospital charge nurse Andrew Oldnall (1995) decried the fact that many nurse theorists have either omitted discussion of the concept of spirituality from their models or have "referred to it only implicitly" (p. 417). There has, however, been a recent reawakening to the importance of the spiritual nature of the human person among contemporary nurse theorists. Barbara Barnum (1995) posited three reasons for what she describes as a "spiritual resurgence" in nursing; these include "a major shift in the normative world view," "a spiritual focus in the growing self-help movement," and "a renewed drive on the part of traditional religious groups and individuals within nursing" (p. 24). Barnum's suggestion that the "self-help movement" has been a catalyst for nursing's current interest in spirituality may be related to the holistic health-care concept, a central premise of the holistic approach being patient autonomy and participation in therapeutic planning.

In examining the writings of some of the key nurse theorists of past and present, one finds significant variability in terms of interest in spirituality or the spiritual needs of the ill person. One of the earliest theorists, Virginia Henderson, writing with Harmer in 1955, observed that "sickness may threaten the patient's faith in the ultimate 'goodness' of life. He cannot believe in a God that lets terrible things happen; or he may fear he has lost favor in the sight of God, considering illness a punishment for real or imagined sins" (p. 74). In her later work, Henderson (1966) identified as 1 of 14 "Components of Basic Nursing Care" provision for "Worship according to one's faith" (p. 17); she did not, however, explore this precept in any detail. Faye Abdellah (Abdellah & Levine, 1979), in "Criterion Measures of Patient Care," also included a patient care component related to personal faith "to facilitate progress toward achievement of personal spiritual goals"; Abdellah, like Henderson, viewed attention to the patient's spiritual needs as a key component of nursing care.

Joyce Travelbee (1971), in her theory of illness as a "self-actualizing experience," was more explicit in her concern with both the patient's and the nurse's spirituality, observing, "It is believed the spiritual values a person holds will determine, to a great extent, his perception of illness. The spiritual values of the nurse or her philosophical beliefs about illness and suffering will determine the degree to which he or she will be able to help ill persons find meaning, or no meaning, in these situations" (p. 16). Travelbee further asserted that a patient's religious beliefs will greatly influence the experience of, and the ability to cope with, suffering (p. 64). She admitted, however, that the degree to which a person actually practices his or her religion is a mediating factor in relation to coping with distress and suffering (p. 71).

Nurse theorist Betty Neuman's systems model is a conceptual framework that addresses the spiritual dimension and needs of the ill person. In Neuman's model, the patient system is assessed holistically from five perspectives: physiologic, psychological, developmental, sociocultural, and spiritual (Sohier, 1997, p. 112). For Neuman, the spiritual dimension of a person supports and permeates all other systems (Fawcett, 1989, p. 172). In her earlier work, Betty Neuman placed less emphasis on the spiritual; the spiritual aspects of her theory were first significantly displayed in her 1989 understanding of the patient system (Meleis, 1991, p. 294). In the third edition of the theorist's book *The Neuman Systems Model*, Neuman's "spiritual variable" is described as the pivot on which the framework centers and as having important implications for patients from a variety of world cultures (Curran, 1995, p. 581).

Callista Roy's adaptation model, which focuses on the adaptive needs of the ill person and family, includes a self-concept adaptive mode that emphasizes the psychological and spiritual characteristics of an individual. This model addresses the "self-consistency, self-ideal and moral-ethical-spiritual self" of a patient (Phillips, 1997, p. 177). Religion or religious practice is considered one of the significant cultural influences on a patient's adaptation. Although Roy identified the concept of religion as primarily associated with the major organized traditions of Eastern and Western society, she noted that this cultural category may also include "spiritual beliefs, practices and philosophies that are not necessarily attached to institutional forms of religion" (Sato, 1984, p. 69). Callista Roy views religion as an important variable in the adaptive process, as she perceives religiosity or religious practice as potentially influencing all dimensions of a person's life view and functional capacity, especially in terms of attitudes and behaviors related to health and illness.

Two other nursing theories that indirectly address the concept of the patient's spiritual nature in terms of phenomenological and humanistic approaches are the models of Parse (1981) and Paterson and Zderad (1976). Parse accepted the transcendent nature of humanity. "Nursing is unfolding in simultaneous mutual interchange with the world transcending with greater diversity and complexity" (p. 172). Paterson and Zderad viewed the human person as "an incarnate being, always becoming, in relation with men and things in a world of time and space" (p. 19).

And finally, nurse theorist Jean Watson (1985) explained the nature of personhood by placing significant emphasis on the existence of the "human soul [spirit or higher sense of self] that is greater than the physical, mental and emotional existence of a person at any given point in time" (p. 45). Sarter (1992) asserted that Jean Watson is the only nurse theorist who explicitly describes the concept of the soul (p. 152).

In examining the writings of the select group of nursing theorists mentioned, one finds key words related to patients' spiritual needs, including faith, worship, spiritual goals, spiritual values, transcendence, human soul, higher authority, and organized religion. Identifying the patient's understanding of these concepts is important for a nurse undertaking the practice of spiritual care.

▶ Nursing Intervention: The Practice of Spiritual Care

Admittedly, a nurse may not know precisely which nursing therapeutics to employ when faced with a patient experiencing spiritual need. Simple guidelines presented in an earlier publication may provide some basic ground rules for spiritual care:

> The nurse must attempt to respect and understand a patient's religious beliefs and practices, even if very different from his or her own. The nurse must take time to allow the patient to express religious, ethical, or philosophical views, as well as any fears and anxieties related to the patient's spiritual belief system. The nurse must be spiritually supportive, assisting the patient whenever it is within the realm of his or her understanding or expertise, and recognize the need to seek outside spiritual or ministerial counseling, either personally or for the patient, when the situation warrants. (O'Brien, 1982, p. 108)

Nurses should keep two important principles of spiritual intervention in mind when ministering to those who are ill. First, because each person has a unique spirituality, the provision of spiritual care cannot be derived from a procedure book of orders; and second, to intervene in the spiritual needs of others, the nurse must first understand his or her own spirituality or relationship to God (Fish & Shelly, 1979, p. 68).

In his best-selling book, *Care of the Soul*, Thomas Moore (1992) observed that spiritual caring forces one to transcend the self and to "recover a sense of the sacredness of each individual life" (p. 19). Moore asserted that spiritual care of the soul incorporates the mystery of suffering and does not deny life's problems (pp. 19–20). Ultimately, Moore contended that spiritual care "requires craft (techne), skill, attention and art" (p. 285).

A number of factors, both positive and negative, have been identified that can affect the practice of spiritual care by nursing staff. In a study of 110 nurses, nursing professor Moon Fai Chan (2009) learned that "the greater the nurse's [positive] spiritual care perceptions, the more frequently spiritual care is included in that nurse's practice" (p. 2128). Chan's tool measuring "perceptions" of spiritual care included such topics as the importance of spiritual care to the sick, the strength that can be drawn from spiritual care, and the relevance of spiritual care as an "important dimension of nursing" (p. 2132). Family practice physicians and nurse practitioners were studied to determine how spiritual care was carried out "in spite of documented barriers" (Tanyi, McKenzie, & Chapek, 2009, p. 690). Five key themes emerged from this phenomenological research: "(1) discerning instances for overt spiritual assessment; (2) displaying a genuine and caring attitude; (3) encouraging the use of existing spiritual practices; (4) documenting spiritual care for continuity of care; (5) managing perceived barriers to spiritual care" (p. 690).

▶ Nursing Intervention in Spiritual Distress

A patient's experience of spiritual suffering, or spiritual distress, may pose unique challenges for nursing intervention (Kahn & Steeves, 1994). Spiritual distress may be experienced by any ill person questioning the reason for his or her suffering (Harrison, 1993). Defining characteristics of spiritual distress include questioning one's relationship with God, attempting to identify religious idols, guilt feelings, and a variety of somatic symptoms (Heliker, 1992, p. 16); questioning the meaning and purpose of life; expressing anger toward God; refusing to participate in usual religious practices; regarding illness as God's punishment; and seeking spiritual assistance, other than usual spiritual or religious support (Tucker, Canobbio, Paquette, & Wells, 1996, p. 52).

The nurse does not need religious training to meet the needs of a patient in spiritual distress (DiMeo, 1991, p. 22); nurses continually engage in the process of assessing, planning, intervening, and evaluating (the nursing process) related to physical and emotional nursing diagnoses. In assessing spiritual need, the nurse must determine whether he or she may provide the spiritual care, such as listening and counseling, or whether referral should be made to a chaplain or formally trained minister of the patient's denomination (Duff, 1994).

Counseling a person in spiritual distress can constitute a growth experience for the nurse while also providing support for the patient (Burnard, 1988). This was validated in the observations of Gail, a 16-year veteran of nursing interviewed by the author:

> Spiritual care, listening, advising is so important, because people are hurting so much. They suffer a lot and the main thing is to listen and let them tell you their pain. I can't tell them there's a cure and they know that; they lean on God, because there is no other answer. Sometimes chaplains come up

and do a "quickie": "I'll keep you in my prayers." But sometimes the patient just needs somebody to sit and listen to her, and be with her. . . . I have seen and listened to much more spiritual distress in patients than I would ever have imagined, and I think it has made me grow spiritually. It's helped me to think about Christ's forsakenness. Suffering in itself can be a prayer.

Spiritual care interventions were identified in response to a nursing diagnosis of spiritual distress in a 41-year-old AIDS patient who demonstrated symptoms of fear of death and questioning belief in God. These nursing therapeutics included assisting the client to explore the spiritual meaning of coping with the HIV experience, providing support for the expression of feelings, and allowing the patient to proceed through the grief process related to physical and psychosocial losses (O'Brien & Pheifer, 1993, p. 314).

The success of spiritual interventions such as prayer in patients with spiritual distress, related to a number of disease/illness conditions, has been documented in the literature. Some examples are: "seeking comfort through prayer" among coronary artery bypass graft patients (Hawley & Irurita, 1998); prayer as a health strategy in managing HIV-related symptoms (Coleman, Nokes, Corless, Kirksey, Nicholas, & Tsai, 2006); and the benefits of prayer for cancer survivors (Levine, Aviv, Yoon, Ewing, & Au, 2009; Ross, Hall, Fairley, Taylor, & Howard, 2008). The importance of spirituality in coping with the distress of early Alzheimer's disease was documented by Beuscher and Grando (2009).

Findings from an online survey of 4,054 nurses in the United Kingdom revealed that "nurses recognize that attending to the spiritual needs of patients enhances the overall quality of nursing care" (McSherry & Jamieson, 2011, p. 1757). In addition, two nursing authors contend that spiritual care includes considering the "soul" of the patient being served: Stephen Wright (2011) asserts that spiritual care is "an essential feature of high-quality patient care" (p. 18) in "The Heart and Soul of Nursing," as does Fenske (2011), an advanced practice nurse who used "multiple theoretical frameworks to make meaning of her severely developmentally disabled son's untimely death" (p. 229) in "Soul Mate: Exploring the Concept of Soul."

The Problem of Suffering

Perhaps the most difficult challenge a practicing nurse may face in attempting to carry out the theological mandate of caring is addressing a patient's suffering. Washholtz, Pearce, and Koenig (2007) explored the relationship between spirituality and the suffering of chronic pain in order to understand why "some people rely on their faith to cope with pain" (p. 311). These authors concluded that "spiritual and religious coping may affect a number of physiological, psychological, neurological and emotional domains that influence pain perception and tolerance" (p. 316). Nurse theorist Katie Eriksson (2007) has asserted that "the mission of caring is the alleviation of human suffering and the serving of life and health" (p. 8). And a team of palliative care providers report that addressing the "spiritual issues in suffering . . . is recognized as a very important component of palliative care" (Hinshaw, Carnahan, Breck, Mosoiu, & Mosoiu, 2011, p. 7).

In some cases, the nurse's therapeutic toolbox will contain instruments to alleviate the suffering, at least for a time. In other situations, the pain, whether physical, emotional, or spiritual, seems to take on a life of its own; no techniques or supplies in the nurse's armamentarium prove effective. At such an impasse the nurse, like the chaplain, must wrestle with the imponderable "why." And for the caregiver with a strong religious foundation, be it of the Judeo-Christian tradition or some other belief system, the "why" of suffering may take on a powerful spiritual élan. Why does an all-powerful God allow an infant to be born with multiple congenital anomalies? Why does a loving and compassionate God not intervene to alleviate a teenage cancer patient's intractable pain? Why does a merciful God not use his strength to heal a terminally ill mother whose death will leave orphaned children?

The nurse may also be called on to respond to patients' and family members' inability to understand or accept the reason for an injury or illness. Joyce Travelbee (1971) focused specifically on this point when she defined the purpose of nursing as being "to assist an individual, family or community to prevent or cope with the experiences of illness and suffering, and, if necessary, to find meaning in their experiences" (p. 16). Often, however, it is difficult to articulate a profound existential meaning in an illness experience; thus, the nurse must indeed draw on Moore's thesis of accepting suffering as mystery and of not attempting to offer a patient or family false hope or an unreal prognosis.

Several years ago, the author spent a summer as a chaplain intern at a research medical center whose treatment was directed primarily to those with life-threatening illness. Most of the patients were coping with the potential for a relatively imminent death or at least a shortened life; many were burdened with pain and suffering, both physical and spiritual. For the patients, the families, the staff, and the chaplains, the "why" question always seemed to be lurking in the background. Sometimes it was spoken aloud; at other times it could be read in the eyes of the patients and those who loved and cared for them. The following excerpt from the author's chaplaincy journal describes a mother's distress over the suffering of her son:

> This morning Catherine, the mother of a teenage son, Michael, who was facing mutilating surgery in hope of slowing the progress of advanced rhabdomyosarcoma, came to me in great spiritual pain; she said: "I need you to answer a question: Why? Why my beautiful, generous, loving son? Why not me; I've lived a full life? Why is the God I pray to letting this happen to him? I don't understand." I tried to respond to Catherine's question with some thoughts about the mystery of God's ways; mostly I just listened. Catherine spoke for over an hour, pouring out all of the pain in her heart, all of the love for her son, stopping only once to remind me gently, "You still haven't answered my question: Why?"

At the end of our meeting Catherine said, "Thank you for spending this time with me; it's helped more than I can ever tell you." She did not raise the "why" question again; I breathed a sigh of relief.

When this experience was shared with other medical center chaplains, one observed, "I'm sure that mother knew in her heart there was no answer to the question, 'why?'; she just needed someone to be with her while she asked it."

Most patients and families who suffer, especially those with spiritual foundations, understand that in the realm of the Holy Mystery, the why question has no answers that we, as humans, can comprehend. Rather, what they ask of us as caregivers is, like Catherine, that we be there with them while they ask the questions, that we accept with them the mystery of human suffering, and that we offer no false illusions. This is the essence, the heart of spiritual caregiving.

Suffering as a concept has been defined as "any experience that impinges on an individual's or a community's sense of well-being" (Sparks, 1993, p. 950). Sparks added that suffering may be "physical, psychological, interpersonal or spiritual," though he commented that generally it is a combination of all four (p. 950). Suffering is usually understood as a state rather than an incident. It is described not "by sharp pains and moments of terror but by an almost unbearable duration and inescapability" (Maes, 1990, p. 29). Suffering defines an ongoing and consistent state of distress, not merely a brief encounter with painful stimuli. Many of those who are chronically ill well understand the notion of an ongoing state of distress; they may experience, at any one time, a combination of physical, emotional, and spiritual suffering related to an illness condition.

A dimension of suffering frequently encountered in the health-care setting and explored in the theological literature relates to the question of "why"; what or who is responsible for the suffering? Suffering, religious faith, and illness have long been associated concepts (Hufford, 1987). The "why" query is highlighted in the classic biblical story of Job. "They [Job's friends] sat down upon the ground with him seven days and seven nights, but none of them spoke a word to him, for they saw how great was his suffering" (Job, 2:13). Job was, seemingly, a good man, and yet he suffered great physical trials, which both he and his friends questioned. In his anger and frustration Job cried out to God, "Why?" According to the Scripture, God never answered Job's question but simply asked him to have faith, which ultimately Job accepted. Theologians agree that the story of Job, often quoted in relation to suffering, leaves the "why" question unanswered and supports the need for absolute faith in God (Baird, 1994; Bergant, 1990; Kidner, 1983).

Robert, a young man who had been living with cancer for more than five years, described a kind of "Job-like" anger at God. Like Job, Robert ultimately was able to trust in his long-standing faith relationship with his creator:

> When I found out I had cancer I was depressed and really mad at God. But then, because I was so scared, I started to pray. And, you know, I learned about praying and about how you really can talk to God. God has always been with me and he'll be with this too. I just have to trust his love.

Robert's conclusion is supported by theologian Kathleen O'Conner's commentary on the "Job Story." O'Conner (1990) observed that the book of Job is not really about suffering but about one's relationship to God while experiencing suffering (p. 104). She asserted, like Robert, that the lesson to be learned is to pray, to ask God for answers, and then to accept and trust.

In discussing religious interpretations of sickness-related suffering, Emeth and Greenhut (1991) decried explanations claiming that illness is a form of God's punishment or that God gives illness and suffering to those He loves (p. 63). While obviously God allows suffering and may use a suffering experience to draw an ill person to Him, most contemporary theologians would argue that a loving God could not purposely choose to hurt or cause pain. This thinking was reflected by Eriksson (1994) who warned against attempting to find "premature" or "quick-fix" explanations for suffering, asserting that to do so might block an individual from discovering his or her own phenomenological understanding of the meaning of a suffering experience (p. 7). As Eriksson observed, "Suffering in itself has no meaning, but people could, having lived through it, realize that it was in fact meaningful to do so" (p. 7).

In a pastor's response to the suffering experience, especially as related to illness, Rabbi Harold Kushner, author of the best-selling book *When Bad Things Happen to Good People* (1981), asserted, "The God I believe in does not send us the problem; He gives us the strength to cope with the problem" (p. 127). Rabbi Kushner's position is reflected in the comments of Paul, a middle-aged cancer patient:

> God doesn't design diseases; He is a God of love. Why does God allow His people to suffer from sickness? I don't know! But I do know He holds us up. We are His. We belong to Him and He will sustain us. We may walk the way of suffering but we will not be alone.

For the individual who denies or is uncertain about the existence of God, the condition of human suffering is more difficult to manage. Nurses need to be aware of the secular humanist philosophy of such a person. In the case of a patient who professes to be either an atheist or an agnostic, the listening, loving presence of a caring nurse may provide spiritual support and comfort in an experience of suffering.

The most difficult suffering for a nurse to work with is that which is unrelieved. Hospice physician Ira Byock (1994), in discussing persistent suffering, admitted that he sometimes asks himself the question, "how complete is my commitment?" (p. 8). Sister Rosemary Donley (1991) believes that part of the nurse's mission is to "be with people who suffer, to give meaning to the reality of suffering"; it is in these activities, Donley asserted, that the "spiritual dimension" of nursing lies (p. 180).

▶ Spiritual and Religious Resources

In order to provide spiritual care to patients from a variety of religious traditions, the nurse must have some familiarity with the available resources, particularly pastoral care, prayer, Scripture, religious rituals, devotional articles, and sacred music. The importance of nurses' understanding the meaning of spiritual and religious resources for patients from a variety of ethnic and religious groups was identified through hospital-based interviews and panel discussions (Davidson, Boyer, Casey, Matzel, & Walden, 2008).

Pastoral Care

Pastoral care describes the interventions carried out by religious ministers in response to the spiritual or religious needs of others. The activities of the pastoral caregiver, "including sacramental and social ministries, can be as informal as conversational encounters and as formal as highly structured ritual events" (Studzinski, 1993, p. 722). Howard Clinebell (1991), identified five specific pastoral care functions: "healing, sustaining, guiding, reconciling, and nurturing" (p. 43). Such spiritual care interventions may promote significant healing on the part of ill persons.

Shelly and Fish (1988) noted the importance of the clergy as a resource in spiritual care of the ill; they asserted that spiritual care given by clergy and nurses should be complementary (p. 138). For such complementarity to exist, three conditions are suggested: mutuality of goals in the caregiving, a delineation of role responsibilities, and communication (p. 138). The activities of the minister or pastoral caregiver offer an important religious comfort dimension by providing the patient with familiar symbols and experiences (Atkinson & Fortunato, 1996, p. 99). A pastoral advisor understands the patient's religious belief system and can plan care to be congruent with the individual's religious heritage (Krekeler & Yancey, 1993, p. 1010).

In making a pastoral care referral, the nurse may contact a priest, minister, rabbi, imam, or other spiritual advisor of the patient's acquaintance and tradition, or refer the patient to a health-care facility's department of pastoral care. To facilitate a pastoral care visit, the nurse may prepare a place close to the patient for the spiritual minister to sit, provide privacy to the degree possible in the setting, and cover the bedside table with a white cover if a sacrament such as Anointing of the Sick is to be administered (Taylor, Lillis, & LeMone, 1997, p. 896).

A renal failure patient, Catherine, spoke about the importance of pastoral ministry in helping her cope with the acute onset of her disease:

> When I first went on dialysis and was in the hospital, I was sick as a dog. I had pneumonia plus the kidney failure and I thought I might die. But the response that I got from my minister and the church was just fantastic. The minister prayed for me, and I had everybody wanting to know how's my dialysis going, and I got a list of 35 people from the church, especially the deacons, who were willing to drive me anyplace I need to go.

Prayer

The word *prayer* is generally understood as a request or a petition to obtain some good outcome. There are a number of other kinds of prayer, such as prayers of thanksgiving, as well as specific methods of prayer, including vocal prayer, contemplation, and centering prayer.

Spiritual writer Carlo Carretto (1978) observed that "we can never define what prayer is . . . prayer is communicating with the mystery" (p. 75). Prayer is envisioned as the spiritual action one takes to bring an individual "into connection with God" (Johnson, 1992, p. 148). Prayer, whether formal or informal, may be central to healing the sick (Normille, 1992, p. 74). Healing prayer has been described as bringing oneself and a situation of disease before God, "with at least one other person to listen, discern, speak and respond, so that healing in relation to or with God can take place" (Bacon, 1995, p. 15).

Although prayer may be engaged in individually by a patient, and often is, it is important to remember that illness, especially acute illness, may create a "barrier to personal prayer" (Shelly & Fish, 1995, pp. 9–10). In such instances a nurse's prayer for and with the patient can be an important spiritual care intervention. Shelly and Fish remind the nurse that his or her prayer should reflect what the patient would pray for if capable of doing so; they advised, "The most helpful prayer is usually a short, simple statement to God of the patient's hopes, fears and needs, and a recognition of God's ability to meet the patient in his [or her] situation" (p. 11). Prayer as a nursing intervention was described by a practicing nurse as "possible in any setting, as long as we ask people's permission" (Mason, 1995, p. 7). Mason believes that prayer can be an important source of peace and comfort for an ill person (p. 7).

In a 1995 editorial in the *Journal of Christian Nursing*, editor Judith Shelly posed the rhetorical question, "Is prayer unprofessional?" In answering, decidedly in the negative, Shelly cited an address by Florence Nightingale to students at the Nightingale School of Nursing. Nightingale commented, in part, "Did you ever think how Christ was a nurse; and stood by the bedside, and with His own hands, nursed and did for the suffering?" (p. 3). In supporting prayer as an appropriate dimension of holistic nursing, Lewis (1996) also drew on the wisdom of Florence Nightingale as mentor and guide. "Nightingale recognized that the use of prayer attuned the inward man to the universal laws of God . . . and . . . contended that prayer could be applied to daily life for health, wholeness and healing" (p. 309). The importance of the healing power of prayer in holistic nursing was supported by Narayanasamy and Narayanasamy (2008), DiJospeh and Cavendish (2005), and Ameling (2000).

Two chronically ill persons experiencing bouts of acute exacerbation of their conditions described the comfort personal prayer afforded them. Agnes, a maintenance hemodialysis patient who was hospitalized at the time, reported, "I believe in a hereafter, and in a God someplace, and that makes you feel like, OK, I can go on. If I feel bad, I can lay in bed and talk to Him, when I don't want to talk to anybody else about my feelings. That's it. That's what religion is all about." Nicholas, an AIDS patient suffering from acute symptoms of cytomegalovirus, admitted, "Sometimes when I'm having a bad day, you know, Why is this happening to me? I say to God, 'could you give me a little hand here?' And usually what happens is I get overwhelmed with gratitude, and I get a sense that God's saying, 'You can handle it, Nicholas; I'm right here.' Sometimes His words actually come to me. I mean, I don't hear a booming voice, but I hear real words in my heart."

A family member of an AIDS patient who had recently died in the ICU after a bout with *Pneumocystis carinii* pneumonia, described the importance of a nurse's prayer in the unit:

> I was particularly touched when [she] prayed for Jonathan in the hospital. I didn't say it at the time but when she prayed aloud it was like I was burning inside. And I prayed too. She really had a way with words and I hoped to emulate that.

As advised by Shelly and Fish, the nurse praying aloud for a patient should try to pray as the patient would. An example is a prayer said by the author while in chaplaincy training. Michael, a 36-year-old hospitalized patient suffering from an anaplastic astrocytoma, had described himself as a born-again Christian. Michael loved to talk to and about Jesus in a very direct and simple manner; however, it was difficult for him to articulate a prayer, so he asked that it be done for him. The prayer, recorded in a clinical pastoral education report, is as follows:

> Lord Jesus, put your arms around Michael as he prepares for his chemo treatment. Let him know that he is not walking on this path alone, that you are right there by his side; you are holding him up and supporting him with your strength. Let him know that you are holding his hand. Remind Michael that his name is written on the palm of your hand. [Michael frequently responded, "Amen" or "Thank you, Jesus."] Michael knows you, Jesus, and knows that you are His Lord. Help him to feel your love and care during this illness. Bless the doctors and the nurses who are giving Michael his treatments, that their hands may be Your Hands as they care for him on this journey. God, our Father, you know what Michael needs in these days, and you know the prayers that are in his heart. Bless his prayer, protect him, guide him and comfort him, we ask this in the name of your son, our Lord Jesus. Amen.

Michael responded to the prayer by saying, "Thank you, your coming here and ministering means a lot to me."

Scripture

Scripture, or the "word of God," is written material that represents venerated and guiding principles for many religious traditions. For the Jewish community, the Hebrew Scripture as contained in the Torah represents God's word and laws for his people. For a Christian, both Old (or "First") and New Testaments contained in the Bible are revered. The Old Testament, shared with the Jewish religion, contains "the story of God's work in the world from creation to the period of the second temple (built in 515 bce)"; the second, or "New Testament . . . begins with the story of Jesus, and contains documents and letters and visions of the early Christian community in the 1st century ce" (Nowell, 1993, p. 857). *Merriam-Webster's New Collegiate Dictionary* (1976) defines the term *scripture*, not only as "the books of the Old and New Testaments," but also, broadly, as "the sacred writings of a religion" (p. 775). Thus, other scriptural materials, comforting for patients of the appropriate denominations, might include the Holy Qur'an (for Muslims) or the Book of Mormon (for members of the Church of Jesus Christ of Latter Day Saints).

Shelly and Fish (1988) cautioned that a "principle of appropriate timing" should govern the nurse's use of Scripture (p. 121). If a patient is angry or depressed, or experiencing severe discomfort, such as that accompanying acute pain, the seemingly glib quoting, even of an apparently comforting Scripture passage, may seem like "rubbing salt into the wounds" of the sufferer. If, however, it seems that a patient might benefit from a Scripture passage, the nurse can always ask permission in a noncontrolling manner, leaving the patient free to refuse without discomfort. Related to nurses' sensitivity to timing in the use of Scripture, a study of the spiritual caring behaviors of 303 nurses (Hall & Lanig, 1993) revealed that of three types of interventions (conversing, praying, and reading Scripture), nurses were least likely to read Scripture to their patients (p. 736). Ultimately, Piles (1990) suggested that prior to a nurse initiating the sharing of Scripture with patients, he or she should have acquired some sense of when the use of Scripture is an "appropriate intervention" (p. 39).

When a nurse feels comfortable sharing a passage of Scripture with a patient or family member, the reading can represent an important and valid dimension of spiritual care. Following are some suggested Scripture passages and their underlying messages:

> For comfort in times of fear and anxiety—Psalm 23; Philippians 4:4–7; 1 Peter 5:7; Romans 8:38–39
> For fear of approaching death—Psalm 23; John 14:17
> For one in need of healing—Isaiah 53:4–6
> For one seeking God's care and protection—Isaiah 43:2; Isaiah 40:28–31; Psalm 25; Psalm 121; Psalm 139:11–19; Deuteronomy 8:2–3; Jeremiah 29:11; Matthew 10:26–33; Luke 12:22–31
> For one seeking God's mercy and forgiveness—Isaiah 1:18; Isaiah 53:5–6; Hebrews 4:14–16; 1 John 1:9
> For one who is fatigued by illness or life stress—Isaiah 40:31

Religious Rituals

"One must observe the proper rites"....."What is a rite?" asked the little prince. "These are actions too often neglected," said the fox.

—**Antoine de Saint-Exupéry**, *The Little Prince*

The concept of rite or ritual may be understood theologically as "a social, symbolic process which has the potential for communicating, creating, criticizing and even transforming meaning" (Kelleher, 1990, p. 906). Religious rituals are sets of behaviors that reflect and honor spiritual or religious beliefs on the part of the participant. There can be a profoundly healing value in participation in religious ritual, especially for the acutely ill person (Texter & Mariscotti, 1994). Thus, the use of or support for religious rituals meaningful to a patient should be an integral part of spiritual care intervention provided by a nurse. Some important religious rituals in relation to health and healing have been identified by Young and Koopsen (2011) as including such activities as prayer, meditation, visualization, guided imagery, dance, and storytelling.

A number of religious rituals may be appropriate for an ill person, whether at home or in the hospital setting. For the Muslim patient whose theology is anchored in the five pillars of Islam, formal prayer (salat) is prayed five times daily, facing the east (Mecca). To support the Muslim's daily prayer requirement, a nurse may provide a prayer rug facing the east, situated in a place of privacy, as well as facilities for the ritual washing of hands and face. Advice from an imam may have to be sought regarding fasting if a Muslim falls ill during the holy period of Ramadan. Some other important Muslim rituals are those associated with birth and death. At the birth of an infant the husband stands near his wife's head; when the infant is born, the new father whispers a prayer from the Qur'an in the child's ear. Usually a dying Muslim chooses to lie facing Mecca (the east); he or she may also wish to confess prior sins and to recite the words, "There is no God but Allah, and Muhammed is His prophet."

The Orthodox Jewish patient is required to pray three times each day. A male patient, if able, may wish to wear a yarmulke (skull cap) and prayer shawl, as well as phylacteries (symbols of the Ten Commandments) when praying (Charnes & Moore, 1992, p. 66). On the eighth day after birth, a Jewish male child must be circumcised. Circumcision may be done in the hospital, if necessary, or in the home by a mohel or Jewish rabbi trained in the procedure. When a Jewish patient is dying, family and friends consider it a religious duty to visit and pray with the dying person and his or her family. In the case of an Orthodox Jew, the nursing personnel may not need to perform postmortem care, as a group from the patient's synagogue, the "burial society," will come to care for the body.

For the Christian person who is ill, the sacraments, as mentioned earlier, as well as prayers particular to each denomination, may be an important part of the healing process. Some years ago, a Roman Catholic could only receive Anointing, then called Extreme Unction, when death was perceived to be imminent. Current Church teaching allows the Catholic patient to request the Anointing in the revised ritual of the Sacrament of the Sick at any point during an illness experience. Receiving Holy Communion at that time, or at any time during one's illness, is an important religious ritual for the Catholic and also for many Protestant patients.

Infant Baptism is also an important Roman Catholic ritual. Ordinarily it is carried out in the parish church several weeks after mother and baby have left the hospital. If, however, an infant is in danger of death, any nurse may perform an emergency Baptism by pouring a small amount of water on the child's head and reciting simultaneously, "I baptize you in the name of the Father and of the Son and of the Holy Spirit." Many other Christians practice infant Baptism; some of these church groups include the Episcopal, Lutheran, Methodist, and Presbyterian denominations. Baptismal rites may vary slightly. For example, in the Methodist tradition, "the one baptizing should put his or her hands in the water and then place the wet hand on the baby's head and repeat the baptismal words. In the Lutheran rite, the water is poured on the head three times, while saying the baptismal words" (Reeb & McFarland, 1995, p. 27).

Rosemarie, an operating room nurse for more than 20 years, described a situation in which she felt that she was providing spiritual care by supporting a patient's religious ritual belief, even though she was of a different faith.

> In this situation I was a fairly new nurse, and the patient came in [to the OR suite], and I just had a sense that this patient was going to die. The patient was very ill; he was elderly and had a bowel obstruction. He had come in the middle of the night for emergency surgery. The man was Catholic, and I thought, "well if this man is this bad, then he needs to see a priest." I felt strongly about supporting that and the surgeon got angry with me for not taking the patient in. I literally stepped in front of the gurney, and didn't let the patient get rolled into the OR until the priest came and he was able to give his last confession. That patient died on the table!? . . . It was scary for me. I don't know why I felt so strongly; normally I wouldn't go up against an authoritative role like the surgeon. I don't know what drove me to do it but it was based on my own religious beliefs. . . . The wife of the patient was so grateful that I insisted on waiting for the priest; the family never got to see him alive again.

Devotional Articles

Frequently the first clue to an ill patient's religious beliefs and practices is the presence or use of religious or devotional articles. A Jewish person, especially one of the Orthodox tradition, may use a prayer shawl and phylacteries during times of prayer. A Muslim may choose to read passages from the Holy Qur'an, or to pray with prayer beads, which identify the 99 names of Allah. A Christian patient, as well as reading sacred books such as the Bible or the Book of Mormon, will often display devotional items such as relics, medals, crosses, statues, and holy pictures with symbolic meaning for the person. For example, an ill Mexican American of the Christian tradition will frequently carry a medal or picture of Santo Niño de Atocha, a religious personage believed to be instrumental in healing the sick. Other religious symbols an ill person might display include sacred threads tied around the neck of a Hindu, Native American medicine bags, or mustard seeds used by Mediterranean groups to ward off the "evil eye" (Morris & Primomo, 1995, p. 111).

A medical–surgical nurse caring for acutely ill patients validated the notion that the visible presence of patients' devotional articles signaled religious belief and practice. "Usually we get a cue; if you see a Bible or a prayer book, or if they have a cross or a rosary, you think the patient probably has an interest in spiritual matters."

Sacred Music

Music, especially music reflecting an interest in the transcendent, expresses the depth of feeling of one's spirit. Music is a part of all cultures and religious traditions, especially as a central dimension of religious worship (Hurd, 1993, p. 675). Music is frequently used by individuals to relieve stress, and music therapy may be used as an adjunct to healing (Keegan, 1994, p. 169). In a nursing study exploring the use of music in the postoperative recovery period, researchers learned that experimental group patients reported that the music served to relax them, as well as serving as a distracter from pain and discomfort (Heiser, Chiles, Fudge, & Gray, 1997).

Karen Sutherland (2005) observed that "the first recorded use of music as an instrument of healing is in the Bible" and cited the story of the young shepherd David who was "summoned to play his music to heal King Saul's emotional and spiritual distress" (p. 29). "The therapy was so successful," Sutherland adds, "Saul requested that David remain in his service (1 Samuel 16:14–23)" (p. 29). The story of a contemporary David is reported in *The Nurse with an Alabaster Jar: A Biblical Approach to Nursing*. The author was told an anecdote about a hospitalized elderly end-stage emphysema patient who was experiencing severely compromised breathing. While she received prescribed nebulizer treatments periodically throughout the day, her breathing and her anxiety became more and more pronounced toward the end of each afternoon. Thus, "a young respiratory therapist, who had been working with the patient, asked the head nurse if he could try an intervention with music; he was a folk guitarist. The head nurse, desperate for any kind of relief for her patient, agreed. The respiratory therapist brought his guitar to the unit and began to play gently for the patient during the periods when her breathing became extremely labored. Everyone, including the head nurse, was amazed at how this gentle 'folk guitar therapy' eased the rapid, labored breathing of the anxious patient" (O'Brien, 2006, p. 104).

Religious music ranges from religious rock, folk, or country-western music, which may appeal to younger patients, to the traditional religious hymns and classical religious pieces such as Handel's *Messiah*, often preferred by the older generation. Playing a recording of religious music, or even softly singing a hymn with a patient, may be incorporated into spiritual care (Folta, 1993, p. 29), if nurse and patient find it meaningful. Music has been identified as a "therapeutic intervention for healing" by Young and Koopsen (2011, p. 175).

Anna, a 13-year-old Ewing's sarcoma patient from a Christian missionary family, loved the traditional hymns of her church. Anna was very ill and experiencing severe pain from her disease; she also required periodic painful bone marrow exams to determine the side effects of her chemotherapy. Anna's mother and the nursing staff decided that singing hymns would be a good way to distract her during the procedure. It was deeply moving to hear the gentle singing of "Abide with me, fast falls the eventide," coming from the pediatric clinic treatment room during Anna's "bone marrows."

If a nurse believes that a patient of any religious tradition might find comfort and support in sacred music, yet the ill person has little experience with religious music, one suggestion might be the beautiful ecumenical chants of Taizé, known throughout the world. The community of Taizé, founded by Lutheran Brother Roger Shutz, has become a center of ecumenical prayer and reconciliation for people from all countries and of all religious traditions. The simple and beautiful chants were created so that Taizé visitors of all cultures and religious persuasions might be able to sing together as one choir. Recordings of the Taizé chants, which include a short scripture verse or brief prayer, with refrains such as "Alleluia," "Bless the Lord," and "Stay with us O Lord," are available at most religious bookstores.

This chapter describes the importance of the nurse's role in spiritual care. Many contemporary nurses find assessment, and in some cases intervention, relative to patients' spiritual needs to be a treasured part of their clinical practice. It is nevertheless important to reiterate that not all nurses will feel competent or comfortable undertaking nursing therapeutics in the area of spiritual care. These nurses should, however, be sensitive to the importance of nursing assessment of patients' spiritual needs; referral to a pastoral caregiver for support or intervention is always an acceptable option.

▶ References

Abdellah, F. G., & Levine, E. (1979). *Better patient care through nursing research*. New York, NY: Macmillan.

Abdil-Haqq Muhammad, K. (1995, June). What Muslims believe and why. *Muslim Community News*, 1–2.

Ameling, A. (2000). Prayer: An ancient healing practice becomes new again. *Holistic Nursing Practice*, *14*(3), 40–48.

Atkinson, L. J., & Fortunato, N. M. (1996). *Berry & Kohn's operating room technique*. St. Louis, MO: C. V. Mosby-Yearbook.

Bacon, J. (1995). Healing prayer: The risks and the rewards. *Journal of Christian Nursing*, *12*(1), 14–17.

Baird, R. H. (1994). On bad luck: Job and Jesus. *Journal of Religion and Health*, *33*(4), 305–312.

Baldacchino, D. (2010). Caring in Lourdes: An innovation in students' clinical placement. *British Journal of Nursing*, *19*(6), 358–366.

Barnum, B. S. (1995, Spring). Spirituality in nursing. *Nursing Leadership Forum*, *1*(1), 24–30.

Barss, K. S. (2012). Building bridges: An interpretive phenomenological analysis of nurse educators clinical experience with the T.R.U.S.T. model for inclusive spiritual care. *International Journal of Nursing Education Scholarship*, *9*(1), 1–17.

Battey, B. W. (2010). Perspectives on spiritual care for nurse managers. *Journal of Nursing Management*, *20*(8), 1012–1020.

Beck, S. E., & Goldberg, E. K. (1996). Jewish beliefs, values and practices: Implications for culturally sensitive nursing care. *Advanced Practice Nursing Quarterly*, *2*(2), 15–22.

Bergant, D. (1990). The book of Job (introduction). In D. Senior, M. Getty, C. Stuhlmueller, & J. Collins (Eds.), *The Catholic study Bible* (pp. 611–612). New York, NY: Oxford University Press.

Beuscher, L., & Grando, V. (2009). Using spirituality to cope with early-stage Alzheimer's disease. *Western Journal of Nursing Research*, *31*(1), 583–598.

Biro, A.L. (2012). Creating conditions for good nursing by attending to the spiritual. *Journal of Nursing Management*, *20*(8), 1002–1011.

Black, J. M., & Matassarin-Jacobs, E. (1997). *Medical–surgical nursing: Clinical management for continuity of care* (5th ed.). Philadelphia, PA: W. B. Saunders.

Borelli, J. (1990). Buddhism. In J. A. Komonchak, M. Collins, & D. A. Lane (Eds.), *The new dictionary of theology* (pp. 144–147). Collegeville, MN: The Liturgical Press.

Broten, P. (1997). Spiritual care documentation: Where is it? *Journal of Christian Nursing*, *14*(2), 29–31.

Bruner, L. (1985). The spiritual dimension of holistic care. *Imprint*, *31*(4), 44–45.

Burnard, P. (1988). Spiritual distress and the nursing response: Theoretical considerations and counseling skills. *Journal of Advanced Nursing*, *12*(3), 377–382.

Byock, I. R. (1994). When suffering persists. *Journal of Palliative Care, 10*(2), 8–13.

Carr, T. (2008). Mapping the processes and qualities of spiritual nursing care. *Qualitative Health Research, 18*(5), 686–700.

Carr, T. (2010). Facing existential realities: Exploring barriers and challenges to spiritual nursing care. *Qualitative Health Research, 20*(10), 1379–1392.

Carretto, C. (1978). *Summoned by love*. Maryknoll, NY: Orbis Books.

Carroll, B. (2001). A phenomenological exploration of the nature of spirituality and spiritual care. *Mortality, 6*(1), 81–98.

Cenkner, W. (1990). Hinduism. In J. A. Komonchak, M. Collins, & D. A. Lane (Eds.), *The new dictionary of theology* (pp. 466–469). Collegeville, MN: The Liturgical Press.

Ceronsky, C. (1993). Creative models of spiritual care. *Health Progress, 74*(4), 58–61.

Chan, M. F. (2009). Factors affecting staff in practicing spiritual care. *Journal of Clinical Nursing, 19*, 2128–2136.

Charnes, L., & Moore, P. (1992). Meeting patients' spiritual needs: The Jewish perspective. *Holistic Nurse Practitioner, 6*(3), 64–72.

Chung, L. Y., Wong, F. K., & Chan, M. F. (2007). Relationship of nurses' spirituality to their understanding and practice of spiritual care. *Journal of Advanced Nursing, 58*(2), 158–170.

Clark, C. F., Cross, J. R., Dean, D. M., & Lowry, L. W. (1991). Spirituality: Integral to quality care. *Holistic Nursing Practice, 5*(3), 67–76.

Clinebell, H. (1991). *Basic types of pastoral care and counseling*. Nashville, TN: Abington Press.

Cockell, N., & McSherry, W. (2010). Spiritual care in nursing: An overview of published international research. *Journal of Nursing Management, 20*(8), 958–969.

Coleman, C., Nokes, K., Corless, I., Kirksey, K., Nicholas, P., & Tsai, Y. (2006). Prayer as a complementary health strategy for managing HIV-related symptoms among ethnically diverse patients. *Holistic Nursing Practice, 20*(2), 65–72.

Conco, D. (1995). Christian patients' views of spiritual care. *Western Journal of Nursing Research, 17*(3), 266–276.

Cone, P. H., & Giske, T. (2012). Teaching spiritual care: A grounded theory study among undergraduate nurse educators. *Journal of Clinical Nursing, 22*(13/14), 1951–1960.

Costello, M., Atinaja-Faller, J., & Hedberg, M. (2012). The use of simulation to instruct students on the provision of spiritual care. *Journal of Holistic Nursing, 30*(4), 277–281.

Curran, G. (1995). The spiritual variable, a world view. In B. Newman (Ed.), *The Neuman systems model* (3rd ed., pp. 581–589). Stamford, CT: Appleton & Lange.

Daaleman, T. P. (2012). A health services framework for spiritual care. *Journal of Nursing Management, 20*(8), 1021–1028.

Davidson, J., Boyer, M., Casey, D., Matzel, S., & Walden, D. (2008). Gap analysis of cultural and religious needs of hospitalized patients. *Critical Care Nursing Quarterly, 31*(2), 119–126.

Deal, B., & Grassley, J. S. (2012). The lived experience of giving spiritual care: A phenomenological study of nephrology nurses. *Nephrology Nursing Journal, 39*(6), 471–496.

Denholm, B. (2008). Staff nurses and prayer. *AORN Journal, 88*(3), 451–455.

Dennis, P. (1991). Components of spiritual nursing care from the nurse's perspective. *Journal of Holistic Nursing, 9*(1), 27–42.

DiJoseph, J., & Cavendish, R. (2005). Expanding the dialogue on prayer relevant to holistic care. *Holistic Nursing Practice, 19*(4), 147–154.

DiMeo, E. (1991). Patient's advocate: Rx for spiritual distress. *RN, 54*(3), 22–24.

Donley, R. (1991). Spiritual dimensions of health care. *Nursing and Health Care, 12*(4), 178–183.

Duff, V. (1994). Spiritual distress: Deciding to care. *Journal of Christian Nursing, 11*(1), 29–31.

Edmision, K. W. (1997). Psychosocial dimensions of medical–surgical nursing. In J. M. Black & E. Matassarin-Jacobs (Eds.), *Medical–surgical nursing: Clinical management for continuity of care* (5th ed., pp. 50–74). Philadelphia, PA: W. B. Saunders.

Ellis, H. K., & Narayanasamy, A. (2009). An investigation into the role of spirituality in nursing. *British Journal of Nursing, 18*(14), 886–890.

Emblen, J., & Halstead, L. (1993). Spiritual needs and interventions: Comparing the views of patients, nurses and chaplains. *Clinical Nurse Specialist, 7*(4), 175–182.

Emeth, E. V., & Greenhut, J. H. (1991). *The wholeness handbook.* New York, NY: Continuum.

Eriksson, K. (1994). Theories of caring as health. In D. A. Gaut & A. Boykin (Eds.), *Caring as healing: Renewal through hope* (pp. 3–20). New York, NY: National League for Nursing Process.

Eriksson, K. (2007). Becoming through suffering on the path to health and holiness. *International Journal of Human Caring, 11*(2), 8–16.

Esposito, J. L. (1990). Islam. In J. A. Komonchak, M. Collins, & D. A. Lane (Eds.), *The new dictionary of theology* (pp. 527–529). Collegeville, MN: The Liturgical Press.

Farrugia, E. G. (1990). Oriental orthodoxy. In J. A. Komonchak, M. Collins, & D. A. Lane (Eds.), *The new dictionary of theology* (pp. 306–310). Collegeville, MN: The Liturgical Press.

Fawcett, J. (1989). *Analysis and evaluation of conceptual models of nursing* (2nd ed.). Philadelphia, PA: F. A. Davis.

Fenske, J. M. (2011). Soul mate: Exploring the concept of soul. *Journal of Holistic Nursing, 29*(3), 229–232.

Fine, J. (1995). Long-term care in the Jewish tradition. *The Nursing Spectrum, 5*(22), 2.

Fish, S., & Shelly, J. A. (1979). *Spiritual care: The nurse's role.* Downer's Grove, IL: InterVarsity Press.

Folta, R. H. (1993). Music: Arousing the human spirit. *Journal of Christian Nursing, 10*(2), 27–29.

Giske, T. (2012), How undergraduate nursing students learn to care for patients spiritually. *Journal of Nursing Management, 20*(8), 1049–1057.

Giske, T., & Cone, P. H. (2012). Opening up to learning spiritual care of patients: A grounded theory study of nursing students. *Journal of Clinical Nursing, 21*(13/14), 2006–2015.

Greenstreet, W. M. (1999). Teaching spirituality in nursing: A literature review. *Nurse Education Today, 19*(8), 649–658.

Gros, J. (1990). Protestantism. In J. A. Komonchak, M. Collins, & D. A. Lane (Eds.), *The new dictionary of theology* (pp. 811–815). Collegeville, MN: The Liturgical Press.

Hall, C., & Lanig, H. (1993). Spiritual caring behaviors as reported by Christian nurses. *Western Journal of Nursing Research, 15*(6), 730–741.

Harmer, B., & Henderson, V. (1955). *Textbook of the principles and practice of nursing* (5th ed.). New York, NY: Macmillan.

Harrison, J. (1993). Spirituality and nursing practice. *Journal of Clinical Nursing, 2*(3), 211–217.

Hawley, G., & Irurita, V. (1998). Seeking comfort through prayer. *International Journal of Nursing Practice, 4*(1), 9–18.

Heiser, R., Chiles, K., Fudge, M., & Gray, S. (1997). The use of music during the immediate postoperative recovery period. *Association of Operating Room Nurses Journal, 65*(4), 777–785.

Heliker, D. (1992). Re-evaluation of a nursing diagnosis: Spiritual distress. *Nursing Forum, 27*(4), 15–20.

Henderson, V. (1966). *The nature of nursing: A definition and its implications for practice, research and education.* New York, NY: Macmillan.

Hinshaw, D., Carnahan, J., Breck, J., Mosoiu, N., & Mosoiu, D. (2011). Spiritual issues in suffering: Creating a dialogue between clergy and palliative care providers. *Progress in Palliative Care, 19*(1), 7–14.

Hufford, D. J. (1987). The love of God's mysterious will: Suffering and the popular theology of healing. *Listening, 22*(2), 115–126.

Hummel, L., Galek, K., Murphy, K. M., Tannenbaum, H. P., & Flannelly, L. T. (2008). Defining spiritual care: An exploratory study. *Journal of Health Care Chaplaincy, 15*, 40–51.

Hurd, B. (1993). Music. In M. Downey (Ed.), *The new dictionary of Catholic spirituality* (pp. 674–677). Collegeville, MN: The Liturgical Press.

Ignatavicius, D. D., Workman, M. L., & Mishler, M. A. (1995). *Medical-surgical nursing: A nursing process approach.* Philadelphia, PA: W. B. Saunders.

Johnson, R. P. (1992). *Body, mind, spirit: Tapping the healing power within you.* Liguori, MO: Liguori Publications.

Kahn, D. L., & Steeves, R. H. (1994). Witnesses to suffering: Nursing knowledge, voice and vision. *Nursing Outlook, 42*(6), 260–264.

Karns, P. S. (1991). Building a foundation for spiritual care. *Journal of Christian Nursing, 8*(3), 11–13.

Keegan, L. (1994). *The nurse as healer.* Albany, NY: Delmar.

Kelleher, M. M. (1990). Ritual. In J. A. Komonchak, M. Collins, & D. A. Lane (Eds.), *The new dictionary of theology* (pp. 906–907). Collegeville, MN: The Liturgical Press.

Kemp, C. (1996). Islamic cultures: Health care beliefs and practices. *American Journal of Health Behavior, 20*(3), 83–89.

Kemp, P. (2009). Spirituality in health care: What can you do? *British Journal of Healthcare Assistants, 3*(7), 333–335.

Kevern, P. (2012). Who can give spiritual care? The management of spiritually sensitive interactions between nurses and patients. *Journal of Nursing Management, 20*(8), 981–989.

Kidner, D. (1983). Poetry and wisdom literature. In D. Alexander & P. Alexander (Eds.), *Eerdmans' handbook to the Bible* (pp. 316–369). Grand Rapids, MI: W. B. Eerdmans.

Kozier, B., Erb, G., Blais, K., & Wilkinson, J. (1995). *Fundamentals of nursing: Concepts, process and practice* (5th ed.). Menlo Park, CA: Addison-Wesley.

Krekeler, K., & Yancey, V. (1993). Spiritual health. In P. A. Potter & A. G. Perry (Eds.), *Fundamentals of nursing: Concepts, process and practice* (3rd ed., pp. 1000–1013). St. Louis, MO: C. V. Mosby.

Kumar, K. (2004). Spiritual care: What's worldview got to do with it? *Journal of Christian Nursing, 21*(1), 24–27.

Kushner, H. (1981). *When bad things happen to good people.* New York, NY: Avon.

Labun, E. (1988). Spiritual care: An element in nurse care planning. *Journal of Advanced Nursing, 13*(3), 314–320.

Lane, J. A. (1987). The care of the human spirit. *Journal of Professional Nursing, 3*(6), 332–337.

Lantz, C. (2007). Teaching spiritual care in a public institution: Legal implications, standards of practice and ethical obligations. *Journal of Nursing Education, 46*(1), 33–38.

Levine, E., Aviv, C., Yoon, G., Ewing, C., & Au, A. (2009). The benefits of prayer on mood and well-being of breast cancer survivors. *Support Care Cancer, 17*, 295–306.

Lewis, P. J. (1996). A review of prayer within the role of the holistic nurse. *Journal of Holistic Nursing, 14*(4), 308–315.

Livingstone, E. A. (1990). *The concise Oxford dictionary of the Christian church.* New York, NY: Oxford University Press.

Maes, J. (1990). *Suffering: A caregiver's guide.* Nashville, TN: Abington.

Mason, C. H. (1995). Prayer as a nursing intervention. *Journal of Christian Nursing, 12*(1), 4–8.

McSherry, W., & Jamieson, S. (2011). An online survey of nurses' perceptions of spirituality and spiritual care. *Journal of Clinical Nursing, 20*, 1757–1767.

McSherry, W., & Jamieson, S. (2013). The qualitative findings from an online survey investigating nurses' perceptions of spirituality and spiritual care. *Journal of Clinical Nursing, 22*(21/22), 3170–3182.

Meleis, A. I. (1991). *Theoretical nursing, development and progress* (2nd ed.). Philadelphia, PA: J. B. Lippincott.

Meehan, T. C. (2012). Spirituality and spiritual care from a careful nursing perspective. *Journal of Nursing Management, 20*(8), 990–1001.

Merriam-Webster's new collegiate dictionary (7th ed.). (1976). Springfield, MA: Merriam-Webster.

Moore, R. (2007). Higher connection. *Nursing Standard, 22*(12), 20–21.

Moore, T. (1992). *Care of the soul.* New York, NY: HarperCollins.

Morris, D. L., & Primomo, J. (1995). Nursing practice with young and middle-aged adults. In W. J. Phipps, V. L. Cassmeyer, J. K. Sands, & M. K. Lehman (Eds.), *Medical–surgical nursing: Concepts and clinical practice* (5th ed., pp. 45–64). St. Louis, MO: C. V. Mosby.

Narayanasamy, A., & Narayanasamy, M. (2008). The healing power of prayer and its implications for nursing. *British Journal of Nursing, 17*(6), 394–398.

Narayanasamy, A., & Owens, J. (2001). A critical incident study of nurses' responses to the spiritual needs of their patients. *Journal of Advanced Nursing, 33*(4), 446–455.

Nelson, B. (1984). Who should give spiritual care? *Journal of Christian Nursing, 1*(2), 20–26.

Nightingale, F. (1859). *Notes on nursing: What it is and what it is not.* London, UK: Hamson, Bookseller to the Queen.

Nolan, P. (2000). Learning from the past, not living in it. *Nursing Review, 17*(4), 92–95.

Normille, P. (1992). *Visiting the sick: A guide for parish ministers.* Cincinnati, OH: St. Anthony Messenger Press.

Nowell, I. (1993). Scripture. In M. Downey (Ed.), *The new dictionary of Catholic spirituality* (pp. 854–863). Collegeville, MN: The Liturgical Press.

Nutkiewicz, M. (1993). Jewish spirituality. In M. Downey (Ed.), *The new dictionary of Catholic spirituality* (pp. 561–565). Collegeville, MN: The Liturgical Press.

O'Brien, M. E. (1982). The need for spiritual integrity. In H. Yura & M. Walsh (Eds.), *Human needs and the nursing process* (Vol. 2, pp. 85–115). Norwalk, CT: Appleton-Century-Crofts.

O'Brien, M. E. (2006). *The nurse with an alabaster jar: A biblical approach to nursing.* Madison, WI: NCF Press.

O'Brien, M. E., & Pheifer, W. G. (1993). Physical and psychosocial nursing care for patients with HIV infection. *Nursing Clinics of North America, 28*(2), 303–315.

O'Conner, K. M. (1990). *The wisdom literature.* Collegeville, MN: The Liturgical Press.

Oldnall, A. S. (1995). On the absence of spirituality in nursing theories and models. *Journal of Advanced Nursing, 21*(3), 417–418.

Parse, R. R. (1981). *Man, living, health: A theory for nursing.* New York, NY: Wiley.

Paterson, J. G., & Zderad, L. T. (1976). *Humanistic nursing.* New York, NY: Wiley.

Pawlikowski, J. (1990). Judaism. In J. Komonchak, M. Collins, & D. A. Lane (Eds.), *The new dictionary of theology* (pp. 543–548). Collegeville, MN: The Liturgical Press.

Pearce, L. (2009). Delivering spiritual care. *Nursing Standard, 23*(28), 22–23.

Phillips, K. D. (1997). Roy's adaptation model in nursing practice. In M. R. Alligood & A. Marriner-Tomey (Eds.), *Nursing theory: Utilization and application* (pp. 175–198). St. Louis, MO: Mosby-Yearbook.

Phipps, W. J., Cassmeyer, V. L., Sands, J. K., & Lehman, M. K. (1995). *Medical–surgical nursing: Concepts and clinical practice* (5th ed.). St. Louis, MO: C. V. Mosby.

Piles, C. L. (1990). Providing spiritual care. *Nurse Educator, 15*(1), 36–41.

Potter, P. A., & Perry, A. G. (1997). *Fundamentals of nursing: Concepts, process and practice* (4th ed.). St. Louis, MO: C. V. Mosby.

Praill, D. (1995). Approaches to spiritual care. *Nursing Times, 91*(34), 55–57.

Rassool, G. H. (2000). The crescent and Islam: Healing, nursing and the spiritual dimension. *Journal of Advanced Nursing, 32*(6), 1476–1484.

Reeb, R. H., & McFarland, S. T. (1995). Emergency baptism. *Journal of Christian Nursing, 12*(2), 26–27.

Ross, L., Hall, I., Fairley, T., Taylor, Y., & Howard, D. (2008). Prayer and self-reported health among cancer survivors in the United States, National Health Interview Survey, 2002. *The Journal of Alternative and Complimentary Medicine, 14*(8), 931–938.

Salladay, S., & Bitting, M. (2012). Caring for familiar strangers. *Journal of Christian Nursing, 29*(1), 15.

Sarter, B. (1992). Philosophical sources of nursing theory. In L. H. Nicoll (Ed.), *Perspectives on nursing theory* (2nd ed., pp. 147–156). Philadelphia, PA: J. B. Lippincott.

Sato, M. K. (1984). Major factors influencing adaptation. In C. Roy (Ed.), *Introduction to nursing: An adaptation model* (2nd ed., pp. 64–87). Englewood Cliffs, NJ: Prentice-Hall.

Sellers, S. C. (2001). The spiritual care meanings of adults residing in the Midwest. *Nursing Science Quarterly, 14*(3), 239–248.

Shelly, J. A. (1995). Is prayer unprofessional? (Editorial). *Journal of Christian Nursing, 12*(1), 3.

Shelly, J. A., & Fish, S. (1988). *Spiritual care: The nurse's role* (3rd ed.). Downer's Grove, IL: InterVarsity Press.

Shelly, J. A., & Fish, S. (1995). Praying with patients. *Journal of Christian Nursing, 12*(1), 9–13.

Shelly, J. A., & Miller, A. (1999). *Called to care: A Christian theology of nursing.* Downer's Grove, IL: InterVarsity Press.

Sims, C. (1987). Spiritual care as a part of holistic nursing. *Imprint, 34*(4), 63–65.

Simsen, B. (1988). Nursing the spirit. *Nursing Times, 84*(37), 32–33.

Smeltzer, S. C., & Bare, B. G. (1996). *Brunner and Suddarth's textbook of medical–surgical nursing* (8th ed.). Philadelphia, PA: J. B. Lippincott.

Sohier, R. (1997). Neuman's systems model in nursing. In M. R. Alligood & A. Marriner-Tomey (Eds.), *Nursing theory: Utilization and application* (pp. 109–127). St. Louis, MO: Mosby-Yearbook.

Sparks, R. (1993). Suffering. In M. Downey (Ed.), *The new dictionary of Catholic spirituality* (pp. 950–953). Collegeville, MN: The Liturgical Press.

Stephenson, C., & Wilson, K. (2004). Does spiritual care really help? A study of patient perceptions. *Journal of Christian Nursing, 21*(2), 26–29.

Stevens, A. (2011). A role for spirituality in palliative care leadership. *International Journal of Palliative Care Nursing, 17*(7), 315.

Studzinski, R. (1993). Pastoral care and counseling. In M. Downey (Ed.), *The new dictionary of Catholic spirituality* (pp. 722–723). Collegeville, MN: The Liturgical Press.

Sutherland, K. (2005). Can music help heal us? The first recorded use of music as an instrument of healing is in the Bible. *Journal of Christian Nursing, 22*(3), 29–31.

Sweat, M. (2012). Is respecting the "quiet place" giving spiritual care? *Journal of Christian Nursing, 29*(3), 180.

Swift, C., Calcutawalla, S., & Elliott, R. (2007). Nursing attitudes toward recording of religious and spiritual data. *British Journal of Nursing, 16*(20), 1279–1282.

Tanyi, R. A., McKenzie, M., & Chapek, C. (2009). How family practice physicians, nurse practitioners, and physician's assistants incorporate spiritual care in practice. *Journal of the American Academy of Nurse Practitioners, 21*, 690–697.

Taylor, C., Lillis, C., & LeMone, P. (1997). *Fundamentals of nursing: The art and science of nursing care* (3rd ed.). Philadelphia, PA: J. B. Lippincott.

Texter, L. A., & Mariscotti, J. M. (1994). From chaos to new life: Ritual enactment in the passage from illness to health. *Journal of Religion and Health, 33*(4), 325–332.

Travelbee, J. (1971). *Interpersonal aspects of nursing* (2nd ed.). Philadelphia, PA: F. A. Davis.

Treloar, L. L. (2001). Spiritual care: Safe, appropriate, ethical. *Journal of Christian Nursing, 18*(2), 16–20.

Tucker, S., Canobbio, M., Paquette, E., & Wells, M. (1996). *Patient care standards: Collaborative planning guides.* St. Louis, MO: C. V. Mosby.

van Leeuwen, R., & Cusveller, B. (2004). Nursing competencies for spiritual care. *Journal of Advanced Nursing, 48*(3), 234–246.

Washholtz, A., Pearce, M., & Koenig, H. (2007). Exploring the relationship between spirituality, coping and pain. *Journal of Behavioral Medicine, 30*, 311–318.

Watson, J. (1985). *Nursing: Human science and human care.* Norwalk, CT: Appleton-Century-Crofts.

Wright, S. (2011). The heart and soul of nursing. *Nursing Standard, 25*(30), 18–19.

Wright, S., & Neuberger, J. (2012). Why spirituality is essential for nurses. *Nursing Standard, 26*(40), 19–21.

Yilmaz, M., & Gurler, H. (2014). The efficacy of integrating spirituality into undergraduate nursing curricula. *Nursing Ethics, 21*(8), 929–945.

Young, C., & Koopsen, C. (2011). *Spirituality, health, and healing: An integrative approach* (2nd ed.). Sudbury, MA: Jones & Bartlett Learning.

Yuan, H., & Porr, C. (2014). Integrating spiritual care into a baccalaureate nursing program in China. *Journal of Holistic Nursing, 32*(3), 240–243.

CHAPTER 5

Spiritual Needs of the Patient with an Acute Illness

Waiting for tomorrow ... asks for ... a deep faith in the value and meaning of life, and a strong hope which breaks through the boundaries of death.

Henri Nouwen, *The Wounded Healer*, 1979

> For your patients who are suffering physically, you have to give compassion; trying to empathize [with] how they are feeling ... and always wanting to do the right thing for the patient, relieve their pain or discomfort, or try to, if you can't do anything else, just listen to them. I think that aspect of empathy and compassion sets nurses apart from other healthcare providers, the caring aspect.

Katie, Team Leader on a Medical–Surgical Unit

The spiritual needs of the adult patient suffering from an acute illness vary greatly depending on such factors as age, religious tradition, and the seriousness of the condition. These and other variables are explored in this chapter, which describes the spiritual needs of patients experiencing conditions including congestive heart failure, septicemia, pneumonia, myasthenia gravis (myasthenic crisis), toxoplasmosis, acute renal failure, and acute pain. Data documenting the importance of personal spirituality and religious support were obtained through the author's interviews of and interaction with patients, family members, and nurse caregivers of patients with acute illness.

Currently the spiritual care practices of nurses caring for acutely ill patients are being explored in relation to ease or difficulty of providing such care. The most significant barriers reported in a study of 271 acute care nurses included: "belief that patients' spirituality is private, insufficient time, difficulty distinguishing proselytizing from spiritual care and difficulty meeting spiritual needs when spiritual beliefs are

93

different from their own" (Gallison, Xu, Jurgens, & Boyle, 2013, p. 95). Specific barriers to spiritual care carried out in a hospital setting were identified as: "the difficulty in defining spirituality; the lack of clear guidelines for the nurse's role in providing spiritual care; nurses' lack of time to provide spiritual care; and a lack of training and education on spirituality" (Rushton, 2014, p. 370).

Some of the acutely ill patient populations among whom spiritual care needs have recently been examined are: coronary care patients (Abu-El-Noor & Abu-El-Noor, 2014); coronary syndrome patients (Jahani, Rajeh, Heravi-Karimooj, Vaismoradi, & Jasper, 2014); intensive care unit patients (Turan & Karamanoglu, 2012); palliative care patients (Ronaldson, Hayes, Aggar, Green, & Carey, 2012); and medical-surgical hospital patients (Barber, 2013).

▶ The Case of Acute Illness

Nursing texts distinguish between acute and chronic illnesses, differentiating the two phenomena as distinct entities. Taylor, Lillis, and LeMone (1997) described acute illness as "a rapidly occurring illness that runs its course, allowing the person to return to his or her previous level of functioning" (p. 1451), whereas Potter and Perry (1997) defined it as "characterized by symptoms that are of relatively short duration, are usually severe, and affect the functioning of the client in all dimensions" (p. 1475). These conceptualizations are appropriate to describe a multiplicity of illness conditions such as pneumonia, influenza, bronchitis, gastritis, herpes zoster ("shingles"), and a host of other self-limiting disease processes. With an uncomplicated acute illness, an individual may pass rapidly through the stages of initial symptom development, treatment and "sick role" behavior, and recovery.

However, a number of "chronic" disease conditions may begin or end with an acute illness phase or manifest acute symptoms during periods of exacerbation over the course of the illness trajectory. One example is that of chronic renal failure (CRF), which may, if undiagnosed, initially manifest in a state of acute renal failure, necessitating emergency dialytic therapy and, in some cases, critical care nursing. Human immunodeficiency virus (HIV) infection, another condition currently being categorized as chronic, may be initially diagnosed by the acute onset of an opportunistic infection such as *Pneumocystis carinii* pneumonia (PCP) or cytomegalovirus. Patients suffering from various types of carcinoma may experience acute illness symptoms related to a therapeutic regimen incorporating radical surgery and/or chemotherapy.

During periods of acute illness, whether self-limiting or associated with a chronic disease, the patient may experience significant physical discomfort and anxiety, especially if symptoms are severe or life threatening. Patients with self-limiting illness may need comfort and support in coping with the sequelae of an infectious process, such as the acute pain accompanying a bout with herpes zoster ("shingles"). Individuals experiencing acute exacerbations of a potentially life-threatening chronic illness may need help in coping with the prognosis as well as the diagnosis of their condition. For the acute renal failure patient faced with the possibility of a future of dependency on medical technology, quality of life may become questionable; in a few cases, patients have elected to die rather than continue living supported by continuous dialytic therapy (O'Brien, 1982b). Thus the need for spiritual care and assessment of spiritual concerns are important aspects of holistic nursing care during periods of acute illness.

▶ Spiritual Needs in Acute Illness

Spiritual beliefs and, for some, religious practices, may become more important during illness than at any other time in a person's life (Kozier, Erb, Blais, & Wilkinson, 1995, p. 314). While an individual is enjoying good mental and physical health, spiritual or religious practices may be relegated, in terms of both time and energy, to a small portion of one's life activities. With the onset of acute illness, however, especially if associated with the exacerbation of a chronic condition, some significant life changes may occur both physically and emotionally. First, the ill person is usually forced to dramatically curtail physical activities, especially those associated with formal work or professional involvement. This may leave the individual with a great deal of uncommitted time to ponder the meaning of life and the illness experience. Such a time of forced physical "retreat" may effect considerable emotional change in one's assessment of past and future attitudes and behaviors.

Meeting patients' spiritual needs in institutional settings such as the hospital or long-term care facility often poses unique challenges for nursing staff (Minnix, 2008). Developing a positive relationship between the nursing department and staff chaplains is an important facilitator for the provision of spiritual care (Weaver, Koenig, & Flannelly, 2008); the caring presence of nurses can be critical to the spiritual well-being of many hospitalized patients (Pipe et al., 2008). It is suggested that hospitals can, in fact, become "healing spaces" if appropriate attention to the spiritual needs of patients and families is considered and attended to (Sternberg, 2009). In discussing the spiritual needs of hospitalized patients, March and Caple (2012) pointed out that hospital-based clergy often reported "assisting patients to cope with not only their religious/spiritual concerns but also with feelings of loneliness, despair, anger, frustration, guilt and shame, physical pain and suffering, and with issues surrounding family discord" (p. 1). In essence, the clergy were coping with an expanded definition of spiritual needs for the acutely ill hospitalized patient.

It is also important for nurses to be attuned to the spiritual needs of acutely ill patients who may be at or near the end of their lives. In relation to a nurse's responsibility to either provide or facilitate the provision of spiritual care to these patients, one nursing study evaluated the relationship between nurses' personal religiosity and attitudes toward end-of-life care. Findings revealed that there was a significant positive association between the nurse's own religious beliefs and practices and his or her view of the importance of end-of-life care (Bjarnason, 2010, p. 78).

The remarks of a 32-year-old male patient reflected such an experience during an episode of acute renal failure. "It enlightened me as to just how fast I was really going. It made me reevaluate my life. Now I can place my needs before my wants. It hasn't been so difficult in looking at the good advantages. This thing has made me think a lot about the way I used to live, and put different values on things" (O'Brien, 1983, p. 146). A 47-year-old male renal failure patient who had also suffered a serious bout of acute illness at the time of disease onset, commented in a similar vein. "This illness definitely made me think; get my mind together. I know all things happen for the good. It turned me around spiritually and mentally. Now I listen better. I try to be more patient, and I have more to learn from others" (O'Brien, 1983, p. 146).

Of the 126 renal failure patients studied, 93 individuals (approximately 74 percent of the total group) reported that religious or spiritual beliefs were, to some degree, responsible for their ability to accept their disease and its prognosis.

Despite a possible positive effect, however, the onset of a sudden and unanticipated acute illness may pose serious emotional and spiritual problems related to fear of possible death or disability. Psychological depression may occur as a result of severe physical symptoms such as acute pain and fatigue. Some patients question God's will and even express anger toward God for allowing the illness to occur. At this point, especially, the nurse must be alert and astute in assessing the spiritual concerns and needs of an acutely ill patient. Although a diagnosis of spiritual distress may be masked by the physical and emotional symptoms of an illness, the patient's remarks can provide a hint as to the presence of spiritual symptoms in need of attention. For example, comments such as "God help me," or "I wonder where God is in all of this?" can give the nurse an opening for informal spiritual assessment.

In essence, meeting the spiritual needs of the acutely ill may encompass basic concepts of spiritual care such as listening, being present, praying or reading Scripture (if acceptable to the patient and comfortable for the nurse), and/or making a referral to a chaplain or other pastoral caregiver. These activities, however, must be handled sensitively, related to the severity of patient symptoms such as pain, nausea, or fatigue. Appropriate spiritual care behaviors for the acutely ill person might include sitting quietly at the patient's bedside for a brief period, saying a short prayer aloud or offering a silent prayer, or sharing a comforting Scripture passage that may help to focus the patient away from the present suffering.

Interestingly the contemporary nursing literature seems to use the terminology "serious illness" rather than "acute illness" when describing patients' spiritual needs. One example of this is an article that identifies the types of spiritual care provided for persons during serious illness. Some of the caregiving activities reported were: "help relationship with God," "help you feel at peace with God," "help you attend religious/ spiritual services," "help you with prayer," "help to better understand (one's) faith," and "help by asking others to pray for you" (Hanson et al., 2008, p. 911). Another paper focused on the spiritual needs of patients with serious illness at an urban public hospital. The authors contend that providers of spiritual care need to consider "difficult life events such as estrangement, homelessness, substance abuse, and imprisonment (which may have) shaped patients' approaches to serious illness" (Dzul-Church, Cimino, Adler, Wong, & Anderson, 2010, p. 695).

Nurses must assess the spiritual needs of seriously/terminally ill patients in clinical practice in order to "incorporate spiritual care into their clinical practice" (Smyth & Allen, 2011, p. 337; Hayden, 2011). Clinical conditions such as heart failure or the final stage of cardiac disease warrant assessment of spiritual needs to "improve life satisfaction" (Westlake, Dyo, Vollman, & Heywood, 2008, p. 257). A similar case is made for victims of serious illness related to hematological malignancies or "those individuals surviving the confrontation with death caused by a life threatening illness" (McGrath, 2004, p. 227).

Spiritual care is considered an intrinsic feature of palliative care for those with critical or terminal illnesses (Amoah, 2011). Amoah asserts that "spirituality should be considered on an equal footing with other key themes in palliative care, like relieving pain and advance care planning" (p. 353). Finally, spiritual care is identified as important for acutely ill or terminally ill persons as they may be "at special risk of spiritual crisis" (Agrimson & Taft, 2008, p. 454). "Spiritual crisis," explain Agrimson and Taft, may be described as "a unique form of grieving or loss, marked by a profound questioning of or lack of meaning in life" (p. 454).

▶ Spiritual Health in Acute Illness

Even though an acutely ill person may be facing a potentially life-threatening situation, the concept of spiritual health is not only possible, but may be the key factor in his or her coping successfully with the physiologic deficit. In discussing the spiritual health of the acutely ill patient, Peterson and Potter (1997) suggested that "the strength of a client's spirituality influences how he or she copes with sudden illness, and how quickly he or she can move to recovery" (p. 443).

Spiritual health can be defined as "a state of well-being and equilibrium in that part of a person's essence and existence which transcends the realm of the natural and relates to the ultimate good. Spiritual health is recognized by the presence of an interior state of peace and joy; freedom from abnormal anxiety, guilt, or a feeling of sinfulness; and a sense of security and direction in the pursuit of one's life goals and activities" (O'Brien, 1982a, p. 98). Spiritual health is also understood as relating to the ability to identify and describe one's purpose in life (Chapman, 1986; Levin & Schiller, 1987). Health-care researchers found a significant correlation between spiritual health and an individual's subjective evaluation of overall physical health (Michello, 1988), and that spiritual health can be predictive of how a person confronts his or her personal mortality (Hart, 1994). In emphasizing the value of the concept, Seidl (1993) argued that, as spiritual health organizes the values, meaning, and purpose in one's life, it also motivates an individual to "optimize" personal health so that he or she can serve God and community (p. 48). This places the notion of spiritual health in a religious context, which indeed is appropriate for many persons. An individual who professes no particular religious beliefs, however, may also be in a state of spiritual health. The terms *spiritual* and *religious* are not synonymous. Spirituality may, however, undergird religious practice, and thus, both concepts become relevant to a discussion of spiritual health (Fahlberg & Fahlberg, 1991).

An acutely ill person who is spiritually healthy can find comfort and strength in his or her spiritual or religious philosophy of life. This is reflected in the comments of Evan, HIV-positive for three years, who had recently experienced an acute episode of an opportunistic infection, *Pneumocystis carinii* pneumonia. "It's the spiritual dimension of religion that I want to practice. I meditate a lot. I sing the refrain from 'Day by Day.' Remember that? That's what I want to do; love Him more dearly. That's the most important thing in my life right now, with this disease" (O'Brien, 1992, pp. 47–48).

For the atheist or the agnostic who may be struggling to find a state of spiritual health, coping with the acute symptoms of an illness may be expressed very differently and, for some, may be much more difficult. Atheism, denial of the existence of God, or agnosticism, uncertainty about the existence of God, may leave a person diagnosed with serious illness struggling to find meaning and purpose in the experience. Burnard (1988) pointed out that patients with such beliefs also have spiritual needs, however, and nurses must be creative and compassionate in carrying out assessment and interventions.

Kent, an HIV-positive patient with cytomegalovirus, described his belief system as basically universal. "I believe in a superior force or being. It's an energy that I tap into. It's everywhere and it speaks to everything. I call on it when I need some reinforcement and encouragement in dealing with the stress of this illness" (O'Brien, 1992, p. 48).

Gerry, still in the process of recovering from a bout with toxoplasmosis, poignantly expressed the distress of his personal struggle to find spiritual health. "I don't think I believe in God. But it is hard not to believe in God because I am so afraid of death.

If there is no God, then death is really going to be the 'death' that I am afraid of, which is nothingness" (O'Brien, 1992, p. 48).

For an acutely ill patient such as Evan, the nurse might anticipate spiritual needs related to traditional religious belief and practice as reflected in his comment about wanting to love God more dearly. For patients such as Kent and Gerry, however, whose belief systems are either humanistic or currently in a state of crisis, spiritual care must be creative and tailored to assist the patient in relation to his or her faith or lack of faith.

The comments of those living with acute sequelae of HIV and acquired immunodeficiency syndrome (AIDS) demonstrate that spiritual health correlates importantly with one's ability to cope with an illness experience. The patients themselves recognized that their spiritual or religious beliefs or lack thereof were significantly related to their adaptation to living with their illness conditions.

As well as being associated with the acute illness conditions and the acute phases of chronic illness, serious physiologic and psychological challenges requiring spiritual support are also present in such experiences as the perioperative journey, the critical care experience, the emergency room experience, and the experience of pain; these are reflected in the following sections.

▶ Spiritual Needs of the Perioperative Patient

The term *perioperative* refers to the period encompassing the preoperative, intraoperative, and postoperative experiences for a surgical patient. Specifically, the preoperative phase begins with the plan to carry out surgery and ends with the actual transfer of the patient to the operating room (OR); the intraoperative phase covers the period of the actual surgical procedure; and the postoperative phase begins with the transfer of the patient out of the OR to recovery, and continues through the healing process to the time of discharge from the physician's care. The perioperative client may be found in a hospital, a community-based surgery center, or, for minor procedures, a physician's office.

The perioperative patient and family may pose significant challenges to the nursing staff related to the anxiety experienced prior to, during, and immediately after the surgery; yet, the perioperative nurse often has little time to develop a relationship with the patient due to the fast-paced nature of the nursing (Dearing, 1997). Some of the most frequently identified causes for fear in the preoperative period are "fear of the unknown," "fear of pain or death," and "fear of changes in body image and self-concept" (Taylor et al., 1997, pp. 676–677); fear of the unknown may encompass the other fears. Fear of the unknown may also include fear of the postoperative diagnosis, especially if the surgical procedure is focused on an exploration to determine the possible presence of a malignancy. Fear of surgical death or of a painful postoperative death lurks in the minds of most patients and families during the intraoperative period. Even if the surgery has been described as a "simple procedure," preoperative patients often express fear of "going under the knife" or going under anesthesia, especially if general anesthesia is used.

A dimension of the perioperative nurse's role is to provide comfort and support to patients and families, especially during the pre- and post-operative periods (Fairchild, 1996). Meeker and Rothrock (1995) described the perioperative nurse's role as including a "continuous awareness of the dignity of persons and their physical, emotional, cultural, ethnic, and spiritual needs." In a 1994 statement, the Association of Operating Room Nurses asserted that "the perioperative nurse designs, coordinates, and delivers care to meet the identified physiologic, psychologic, sociocultural and spiritual needs of patients whose protective reflexes or self-care abilities are potentially compromised because they are having invasive procedures. The nursing activities address the needs and responses of patients and their families or significant others" (cited in Atkinson & Fortunato, 1996, p. 22).

The perioperative nurse can identify a patient's spiritual beliefs through use of the nursing history and thus can provide spiritual care through "acceptance, participation in prayer, or referral to clergy or chaplain" (Taylor et al., 1997, p. 678). Although some nurses may feel that raising spiritual issues may be threatening to the patient, Burns (1996) asserted that regardless of religious tradition, discussing spiritual concerns is therapeutic during the perioperative period (p. 361). Burns believes that simply asking if a perioperative patient's pastor is aware of impending surgery is a supportive approach (p. 361).

The model of perioperative nursing developed by Phippen, Wells, and Martinelli (1994) contains the earlier identified assumption of the appropriateness of holistic health care, including attention to the patient's spiritual nature (p. 3). The individual's spiritual component is viewed as the "animating" principle of life, and this spiritual dimension of the patient is influenced by underlying "religious and philosophical beliefs" (p. 4). If the nurse diagnoses "spiritual distress" manifested by symptoms of fear of death, anger at God, or disruption of spiritual practices on the part of a perioperative patient, appropriate spiritual care interventions may be carried out. The strategy suggested by Phippen et al. involves an exploration of the type of spiritual or religious practices to which the patient relates (e.g., spiritual reading or a visit with a chaplain); the nurse may then intervene by providing materials or making an appropriate referral (p. 66).

In a study of perioperative nurses' perceptions of caring practices, McNamara (1995) found that spiritual care was viewed as primarily including those activities and behaviors that "comforted patients or increased their feelings of security" (p. 385). The perioperative nurses interviewed in McNamara's study asserted the importance of avoiding judgmental attitudes about patients' religious beliefs and practices. Listening and being aware of the patient's religious tradition was considered essential to spiritual care. Several nurses reported praying with patients; others made referral to a pastor of the patient's choice (p. 385). In a discussion of the meaning of spirituality to perioperative nurses and their patients, Rothrock (1994) advocated supporting hope as a "healing force." Heiser, Chiles, Fudge, and Gray (1997) advocated that perioperative nurses use music therapy in the immediate postoperative recovery period as a contemporary spiritual intervention strategy.

Carol, a nurse anesthetist with 18 years of experience in perioperative nursing, explained the importance of spiritual care in the immediate preoperative period:

> I try to talk to patients when they arrive in the OR suite. They are just scared to death. I might be the last person to talk to them before they go to sleep. I talk to them outside the OR while the surgeons are changing clothes. We usually have a few minutes of privacy. I listen to their concerns. I listen to hear if they say anything like, "I'm in God's hands," and then I just take it

from there. I say it's OK to put all your trust in God; He'll be with you in there [the OR]. Especially if a person is in for cancer surgery, I reassure them of God's love and care during the surgery. This is when people are at their most vulnerable; they feel like they are losing all control of their lives. They don't know what the surgery will bring and their future is in the balance. This is the most logical time to think of God, to think, "Am I ready to die?" This is the time they really need some spiritual care . . . I pray silently while the patient is under anesthesia; if they're having a hard time, I ask God to give them strength.

Diane, a master's-prepared operating room nurse with 19 years of experience, spoke of spiritual care as "being with" the patient during the intraoperative phase; she also incorporates touch in her caring. "I think there isn't a patient that has gone to sleep here that I haven't held their hand while they're being put to sleep. That is spiritual care as far as I'm concerned. You stand beside them and hold their hand and talk to them. I consider all that part of spiritual care." Diane also admitted that she prayed for patients during surgery, while performing her duties as a scrub nurse or circulating nurse. "I especially pray for the 'open hearts.' When they go on and off that pump, believe me, I'm praying like crazy. When open heart surgery patients are in the OR and on the pump, and we are literally touching their hearts; that's the time when I especially pray for that patient." Diane added, "I serve God through being present for my patients."

Opportunities for spiritual care of the perioperative patient in the postoperative period may vary significantly depending on the nature of the surgical procedure. Many patients currently experiencing less complex surgeries, classified as "same day surgery," are in and out of the hospital very quickly. Nevertheless, a gentle touch or a word of comfort or support may still be possible during the recovery room stay. This is also a time when anxious family members or friends greatly welcome a kind word of encouragement from the nursing staff. For the patient immediately postoperative from a complex surgical procedure, such as a coronary artery bypass graft (CABG) who may emerge from the OR on mechanical ventilation, the intensive care unit (ICU) will be the setting where spiritual intervention is needed and much appreciated by both patients and families.

▶ Spiritual Needs of the ICU Patient

In the contemporary critical care unit, with its ever more complex therapeutic technology, the persona of the patient may seem lost in the myriad tubes, wires, and sophisticated monitoring devices. Obviously, a central responsibility of the critical care nurse is to skillfully employ the technology at hand in the service of intensive patient care. If the nurse is to provide truly holistic care to the critically ill patient, however, attention to the needs of the mind and the spirit must accompany the delivery of high-quality physical care. Dossey, Guzzetta, and Kenner (1992) in the introduction to their text *Critical Care Nursing: Body, Mind, Spirit*, admitted that their subtitle may seem inappropriate to some readers who might regard the emphasis on mind and spirit as irrelevant to contemporary science. The authors argued, however, that sensitivity to the patient's emotional and spiritual needs is an essential dimension of the subfield of critical care nursing. They suggested that during a period of critical illness "patients frequently search for how to create new perceptions for their life as well as to find wholeness and spirituality" and that they "need guidance in their transformation" (p. 11). Dossey et al. explained that the critical care nurse, therefore, needs to be sensitive to a variety of factors in order to help patients deal with spiritual issues, including the pluralism of spiritual beliefs and religious practices that patients may adhere to, the difference between spiritual and religious concepts, and the nurse's own possible personal confusion in regard to spiritual or religious values (p. 12). Meeting the spiritual and/or religious needs of acutely ill patients such as those suffering from heart failure (Westlake et al., 2008) can greatly alleviate anxiety over the illness condition.

Critical care units (CCUs) or ICUs, first created in the early 1960s, were developed to sustain individuals who might not otherwise survive a serious physiologic deficit or complex surgical procedure, such as acute myocardial infarction or a coronary artery bypass graft. The critical care patient in the ICU is considered physiologically unstable and at great risk for developing life-threatening complications (Kidd, 1997). Like acutely ill patients in general, ICU patients may include persons experiencing bouts of severe symptomatology related to a chronic illness, such as myasthenic crisis in a myasthenia gravis patient, or a sudden onset acute illness or trauma, as in the case of patients diagnosed with meningococcal meningitis or multiple fractures sustained in an accident.

Among the current variety of specialized critical care units are neonatal ICUs (NICUs), pediatric ICUs (PICUs), surgical ICUs (SICUs), medical ICUs (MICUs), neurologic and neurosurgical ICUs, and coronary care units (CCUs). These contemporary critical care units, as centers for advanced health-care technology, are host to many medical "machines" such as cardiac, hemodynamic, and intracranial pressure monitors, ventilators, and defibrillators, the sight of which may be anxiety provoking to patients and their families. Another particularly frightening aspect of the ICU environment is the potential for observing crisis intervention in another patient (Hopkins, 1993, p. 1564); a patient or family member might unexpectedly be witness to an emergency intubation or a "code blue" occurring close to their own assigned space in the unit.

Virtually all cognitively aware adult patients report significant stress associated with the ICU experience. As well as those discussed already, other identified stressors include "social isolation, enforced immobility, pain from procedures, poor communication with staff, excessive noise and lack of sleep" (Dracup, 1995, pp. 12–13). Lack of personal autonomy (Walleck, 1989) and a feeling of utter helplessness (Niklas & Stefanics, 1975, p. 75) are perhaps the most devastating emotions that the ICU patient experiences. This may result in an overwhelming sense of depersonalization as a result of such factors as "powerlessness, emotional/touch deprivation, loss of privacy, invasion of personal space, and transfer anxiety" (Clochesy, 1988, p. 193). Thus, concepts such as prayer and spirituality are becoming more and more sought after as dimensions of care by critically ill patients and their families (Holt-Ashley, 2000).

Related to the stress of critical illness, with its painful sequelae, as well as the sometimes persistent fear of death and the added stressor of hospitalization in a critical care unit, Busch (1994) recognized that the experience may either enhance or challenge a patient's spiritual or religious beliefs (p. 16). A first step in providing spiritual care for the critically ill patient, then, is to carry out an assessment of the person's spiritual and/or religious beliefs, practices, and current needs. Some pertinent information about spiritual or religious history may be obtained from the patient's chart and from the family; hopefully, information about current spiritual needs will emerge through personal interaction between patient and nurse.

Because of the patient's possible isolation from usual religious practices, such as attending worship services or reading Scripture or other spiritual books, and because of the fear and anxiety about his or her illness condition, the nurse may diagnose spiritual distress in the ICU patient. Twibell, Wieseke, Marine, and Schoger (1996) identified some defining characteristics of a spiritual distress diagnosis for a critically ill patient, including a request of spiritual guidance or support, the verbalization of distress over not being able to carry out usual religious practices, expression of "spiritual emptiness," questioning the credibility of one's belief system, and expressing anger or frustration over the meaning of the present illness experience (p. 249). Following such a diagnosis, the nurse may intervene or may elect to contact a chaplain or other pastoral care provider. Bell (1993) advised that if the nurse chooses to pray with the critically ill patient, using "the patient's own words" in relation to illness-related needs may be comforting (p. 27).

Gillman, Gable-Rodriguez, Sutherland, and Whitacre (1996) identified some basic postures in providing spiritual care in a critical care setting: "inclusion," meaning that the nurse should try to imagine what the ICU experience must actually be like for the patient; "confirmation," that the nurse should support the patient's personal spiritual goals; and "mutuality," a spirit of cooperation between nurse and patient in seeking healing (p. 13). Stromberg (1992) described the role of the spiritual care provider in a coronary care unit as encompassing three tasks: listening empathetically, confronting reality, and being a "fellow pilgrim" on the patient's current spiritual journey (p. 127). Listening and "being there" are central to spiritual care in the ICU. The concept of presence, "enhanced by empathetic listening," reflects the nurse's sense of "genuineness, trust and positive regard," which will allow the patient freedom to express his or her spiritual needs or concerns (Shaffer, 1991, p. 45). Beverly Hall (1997), in discussing the nurse's role as spiritual caregiver in life-threatening illness, observed that "what patients need from us is not psychology or theology but caring and presence while they seek answers" (p. 93). As well as providing a listening presence for the critically ill patient in the ICU, and praying with him or her if acceptable to the patient, nurses should refer patients to clergy when appropriate (Bardanouve, 1994; Bucher, Wimbush, Hardie, & Hayes, 1997; Reed, 1991; Shelly & Fish, 1995).

A sometimes neglected yet no less important dimension of spiritual care for the ICU patient that should be included in the nurse's role is that of providing care and support to the patient's family (Chesla & Stannard, 1997). The ICU hospitalization of one of its members may create great anxiety on the part of the rest of the family (Rukholm, Bailey, & Coutu-Wakulczyk, 1991); thus, spending even a brief period of time with family visitors is an important dimension of spiritual care (DiSarcina, 1991, p. 23).

ICU nurse Joyce Hahn related a poignant anecdote about taking the times allocated for her mealtime and break in order to sit with a dying patient's husband. After his beloved wife's death, the husband returned with a lovely poem he had written for their nurse. The meditation included the thought that he had experienced an "angel clothed in white" and ended with the words, "It was one of God's children, a nurse from the ICU" (Hahn, 2001, p. 32).

In discussing spirituality in the CCU, Gloria Nussbaum (2003), MSN, points out that nurses must be available to provide spiritual care when it is needed, noting that "The critical care unit is most vulnerable because the intensity of the illness is so great. Conscious or unconscious, the patient needs human touch and consolation which transcends technology. Indifference to this is all but negligence on the part of the nurse" (p. 214). Spiritual care is provided in the ICU by "giving mental support, facilitating religious rituals, communicating with patients and patients' families, assessing the spiritual needs of patients and showing respect" (Lundberg & Kerdonfag, 2010, p. 1121). A program titled "Embrace Hope," which included spiritual care, was created to support neurological critical care patients and their families in another unit (Yeager et al., 2010).

The concept of spiritual assessment in intensive and cardiac care nursing is advocated in order to "formulate a care plan of spiritual care that provides a powerful inner resource to critically ill patients in acute clinical environments" (Timmins & Kelly, 2008, p. 124). As a result, spiritual care such as that provided for a critically ill elderly woman with "rapidly advancing small cell lung cancer" can be given; the result was described by the coordinator of a cardiac critical medical care unit as "spirituality shining through in a magnet moment" (Monroe, 2011, p. 98).

For the majority of critical care patients, regardless of professional credentials or life history, the ICU experience is new and exceedingly traumatic. This concept was clearly exemplified in the case of an ordained minister who was hospitalized in the same ICU where he himself ministered to others. Pastor Norton, who was a longtime myasthenia gravis patient, was brought to the unit late one evening in myasthenic crisis; he was immediately intubated and placed on mechanical ventilation. He remained on ventilatory support for approximately two weeks. Shortly after his critical care experience, Pastor Norton admitted that although the physical and technical care had been excellent, he had in fact felt isolated during the intubation period and longed for more caring "touch." There were times, the minister admitted, when he would have liked a nurse simply to come and sit by the bed, take his hand, and be with him. As he reflected on the experience, Pastor Norton's conclusion about the lack of "spiritual care" related to his personal identity as a minister; he speculated that the staff probably felt shy about attempting to comfort or support him spiritually, thinking that he already possessed a vast store of resources to draw on. With honesty and humility, Pastor Norton confessed that despite his own strong faith, he had experienced significant feelings of anxiety, loneliness, and helplessness during his stay in the intensive care unit.

An older female patient, Mrs. McCarthy, who was experiencing an exacerbation of a chronic endocrine disorder, and who had also been intubated for several weeks, admitted to feelings of devastating helplessness while on mechanical ventilation, as had Pastor Norton. Mrs. McCarthy, who reported after extubation that her nursing care had been fine, confessed that while on the ventilator she had fantasized that because of the physical deterioration of her body, an ICU staff member, questioning the quality of her life, might "pull the plug" while she was sleeping. This was very threatening to her as she was looking forward to the high school graduations of two of her grandchildren. Obviously, the ICU nursing staff expressed shock when told of this fear. Mrs. McCarthy's frightening fantasy, however, was a reminder of the fragility of the ICU patient's emotional state, and of the constant need for reassurance and support.

In the case of a confused or comatose patient, caregivers should provide spiritual care and support directly toward the family of the person receiving intensive care. One such case was that of a 67-year-old patient, Mr. Lundquist, who was critically ill as the result of a rampant septicemia following bowel surgery; he was mechanically ventilated and his physiologic functioning was being maintained by the continual use of pharmacologic agents (the use of multiple "pressors"). As his illness progressed,

Mr. Lundquist was only minimally responsive to verbal or tactile stimuli. Mr. Lundquist's family, including his wife and several adult children, spent many hours in the critical care waiting room, as well as at the bedside. Their pastor visited frequently and helped them begin the process, on the physician's advice, of facing the patient's imminent death. The adult children's concern, which was verbalized on several occasions to the nursing staff, especially as new therapeutic procedures were initiated, was, "how long would Dad want to live like this?" They were very concerned about their father's suffering. Mr. Lundquist's wife and children reported that he had never discussed his wishes in regard to the use of "extraordinary measures" to prolong life. A nurse researcher working with patients and families in the ICU was able to spend time at Mr. Lundquist's bedside and also be with the family in order to provide a caring presence when such issues as the "DNR" (Do Not Resuscitate) option were discussed. The family expressed gratitude for this supportive nursing presence in a note sent after Mr. Lundquist's death.

Critical care nurses often comment on the need for the practice of spiritual care in the ICU. Margaret, a relatively new ICU staff nurse, observed:

> My patients are all very sick, and communication is a key issue. When I talk to them about religious things, they often exhibit strengths related to how they are handling their illness. For some of these patients it's really tough, like with young bone marrow transplants in the MICU flunking the second transplant, and they're not going to live and they know it and the family knows it. They really need spiritual support. The physicians get to leave the room but it's the nurses who have to stay and be with the patients while they suffer . . . I'm trying to work on the nonpharmacologic approach to decreasing anxiety. Patients may be anxious because of unmet spiritual needs, so we're trying to use music, listening, visitors, communication . . . just being open to whatever the patients' spiritual needs are, whether they're religious like associated with a church or just their own spirituality.

Coleen, a 22-year veteran of ICU nursing, spoke about critically ill patients' fear of death:

> I've worked in critical care for many, many years and I can't even count the number of patients who have said to me, "Am I going to die?" This is the biggest opening for spiritual care that anybody could present. Usually what I say back is, "Do you mean if or when?" Then we can get down to what's really bothering them. The only answer you can give is "I don't know"; it also depends on where the nurse is spiritually herself. If you're Christian and the patient is, you can give them a parable like the man who built his house on rock and it will not be blown away, or if the patient is Jewish, something "Old Testament." You can pray out loud with the patient or silently, and just help them be at peace . . . Most people will let you know if they have a religious background and want you to pray or read the Scripture with them. Sometimes you just have to go with the Holy Spirit, and hope you say what the Holy Spirit wants you to say.

Coleen related a personal prayer experience in the ICU:

> I've been reading about some scientific research where nurses were praying for cardiac surgical patients; an experimental group who got prayers and a control group that didn't, and the experimental group didn't have any

complications and did a lot better than the control group. I had a hint of that last year when one of the unit nurses I was working with said, "Watch my patient; I'll be right back." There wasn't anything to do so I just started to pray for the patient. When his nurse came back she said, "Coleen, what did you do? His O_2 sat [oxygen saturation] has never been this good!"

Coleen concluded with advice about spiritual intervention in the ICU:

You want to be careful to respect the religious practice of the patient. You don't want to shock anybody by a religious practice that might seem strange or different, or inappropriate in their eyes. When we are going to do spiritual care for patients I think that it is better to be on the conservative side until they give us clues as to what they want or need, if it's prayer or whatever. If you have the love of God in you, they are going to respond to that regardless of what their religious affiliation is.

Judith, a master's-prepared nurse with 24 years of experience in critical care nursing, shared her perception of the change in attitude toward the provision of spiritual care by the ICU nurse:

When I first went into critical care I did it because of the focus on the technical aspect, but shortly into my career I really kept looking for the person; that you are not just taking care of the equipment, but that there is a person there in the bed. I believe there's been a change, especially in the last five to eight years. Patients are not afraid to share how they feel spiritually. It used to be, years ago, I remember, that the nurse never talked about God or church or praying with a patient. The minister came and prayed with the patient and everybody else left the room. What I've seen over these last few years is nurses being less anxious and more comfortable in their own spirituality; then they can comfort others . . . Sometimes you are really busy in ICU and you don't have much time to talk to the patient about spirituality but you can find out where they are with it and maybe call the chaplain. You can get the ball rolling for the chaplain to come in. We are the ones right there at the bedside, especially in critical care. You can sense what the patient needs and pick up on it . . .

I'm not Catholic, but this past week I had a Catholic patient who was really anxious, and one of the other nurses was Catholic so she went and they had a talk. She gave the patient a little "Lady of Perpetual Help" charm [medal], pinned it on her, blessed her with some holy oil, and shared prayer with her . . . I think that is a prime example of a nurse attending to a patient's spiritual needs. We shouldn't ever foster one religion over another, and sometimes we don't know what a person believes really, but just to be there with them. Death is really hard in the ICU so just sitting with a family, I am sometimes at a loss for words but just to be there, I think is part of caring.

An excerpt from the author's research journal, maintained during the course of a five-year study of the nursing needs of persons living with HIV and AIDS, presents a final example of spiritual care that a practicing nurse might carry out in the ICU setting.

It was a clear, crisp Friday morning in autumn, my favorite season, as I headed off to a local medical center, but my heart was heavy. I had just received a phone call from Luke, the friend of Jonathan, an AIDS patient with whom

I had been working. Luke apologized for calling early but, he said, "Jonathan asked that I get in touch with you. He was admitted to ICU during the night and they're putting him on the ventilator; it doesn't look good."

As I drove to the hospital I tried to imagine, or perhaps to not imagine, what condition I would find Jonathan in. I couldn't help but reminisce about when we had first met some 2 years previously; it was shortly after he had been diagnosed with HIV infection. I was searching for persons living with HIV to participate in a five-year NIH-supported study of coping strategies, and Jonathan had agreed to speak with me. His enthusiasm for the study matched his enthusiasm for life: it was infectious. During the past months we had laughed and worried and cried over the strange twists and turns which the human immunodeficiency virus had introduced into his life, but always, underneath it all, Jonathan maintained a serenity and a joy that were exquisite to behold.

When I arrived in the intensive care unit, Jonathan had already been placed on the ventilator and was barely conscious; Luke was standing at his bedside. After filling me in on the events of the past few hours, Luke looked across the bed and said, "Mary Elizabeth, would you do something for Jonathan?" I immediately responded, "Of course," wondering, considering the setting, what it could be. I assumed Luke's request was for some nursing task, a comfort measure perhaps, yet Jonathan appeared to be resting peacefully, at least as peacefully as one can when attached to a ventilator, IVs, and the multiple system monitoring devices usual to the ICU environment. Luke, who was an aeronautical engineer, explained, "Religion is not something that is very big with me; as a scientist I have difficulty with the mystery, but for Jonathan it's important. He didn't go to church a lot but faith in God was a real part of his life. Would you say a prayer for him?"

My first reaction was something akin to panic [this occurred prior to my chaplaincy training]; where is a chaplain? I thought. As a nurse I'm not "credentialed" in prayer. But I quickly realized that since it was I, the nurse, whom Luke had asked, surely God would compensate for my perceived weakness in the prayer department.

I cannot recall the exact prayer that I prayed that morning in the medical center intensive care unit. I remember that I reached out and took one of Jonathan's hands; I also grasped Luke's hand, so that we three could be connected, as a small worship community in our makeshift chapel. The words were simple, I think. I asked God to put His arms around Jonathan and hold him close, to give him strength and comfort, to let him know how deeply he was loved and cherished as one of God's own. The musical accompaniment was provided by the rhythmic hum of the ventilator as it coaxed and supported Jonathan's labored breathing; the choir, the hushed whispers of the nurses and technicians as they quietly worked in the background. Together, hand in hand, amidst the tubes and lines and wires apropos of contemporary intensive care, our small community celebrated a liturgy. When we had finished Luke's eyes filled with tears and he whispered, "Thank you"; my eyes also filled with tears and I silently prayed "Thank you" to the God of love who carries us in His arms when we feel most fragile.

The experience with Jonathan and Luke taught me that we, as nurses, are indeed called to a lived reality of God's love which may be manifested in terms of spiritual care, as well as physical and emotional support. I recognized the importance of allowing myself to be "used" as God's instrument in the midst of feelings of personal inadequacy. Although I did not feel competent to minister spiritually, through prayer, at the time, the Spirit provided the courage and the words. Luke told me several days later, after Jonathan's death, that he felt peace after we prayed together; that this was a turning point, and that he had now begun to think about his own spiritual life and how he might understand God. I believe that not only the praying together, but also our joining hands, as a worshipping community, was an important dimension of our ICU liturgy. Through the intimate touch of palm against palm, we became aware of our connectedness both as a human family and as the spiritual family of God. We were thus able to support and strengthen each other, even as we sought the support and strength of our Creator.

▶ Spiritual Needs of the Emergency Room Patient

An emergency is defined as "any sudden illness or injury that is perceived to be a crisis threatening the physical or psychological well-being of a person or a group" (Lazure & DeMartinis, 1997, p. 2501). Although most large hospitals house emergency departments to care for those persons and groups, it is well known that a number of individuals seek care at an emergency room for nonlife-threatening, and even routine, problems. This occurs most frequently in large urban inner-city areas, where indigent and homeless individuals have no other available and accessible source of medical care.

The goal of emergency departments is to provide care for "the acutely sick and injured" (Santacaterina & Stein-Spencer, 1990, p. 3). Most hospital emergency rooms (ERs) are also involved in prehospital care, provided prior to arrival at the health-care facility; for example, care provided at an emergency scene by emergency medical technicians (EMTs) and carried on during ambulance transport. Sophisticated telemetry systems may connect the EMTs with the hospital emergency room staff physicians and nurses (Robinson, 1992).

The Emergency Nurses Association defines *emergency nursing care* as "assessment, diagnosis and treatment of perceived, actual or potential, sudden, or urgent physiologic or psychosocial problems that are primarily episodic or acute. These may require medical care or life support measures, client and significant other education, appropriate referral, and knowledge of legal limitations" (Lazure & DeMartinis, 1997, p. 2503). A key role of the emergency department nurse is that of triage, or initial nursing assessment of the patient's condition in order to determine priority care needs (Blair & Hall, 1994, pp. 21–23). Following triage, the patient may be assigned to one of several types of ER space such as "major trauma or arrest room, minor suture room, gynecologic examination room, psychiatric room, family room, or general examination room" (MacPhail, 1992, p. 7).

The Emergency Nurses Association has articulated comparative standards for working with individual patients. Standard 1, Assessment, states, "The emergency nurse initiates accurate and ongoing assessment of physical, psychological and social problems of patients within the emergency care system" (Emergency Nurses

Association, 1995, p. 16). The consideration of the ER patient's psychological and social problems, as well as physical assessment and triage, as part of the emergency nurse's role, is underscored in a list of ER nurse activities. This is identified in a contemporary fundamentals of nursing text, which includes caring for the patient with severe anxiety (Long, 1993, p. 1540). The current philosophy of emergency care has become so broad as to consider an emergency "whatever the patient or family considers it to be" (Miller, 1996, p. 2000).

Spiritual care and support may be an important need for both patient and family in an emergency situation, especially if the admitting diagnosis contains a life-threatening dimension. In 1993, Eileen Corcoran (1993), president of the Emergency Nurses Association, posed the question, "Is it reasonable to believe that the emergency room nurse's role includes addressing spiritual needs of patients and their families?" (p. 183). In posing her rhetorical question in the *Journal of Emergency Nursing*, Corcoran admitted that a significant amount of the ER nurse's time must be spent on meeting the patient's physical needs, but she argued that this does not relieve the ER nurse from attention to spiritual needs. Some suggestions Corcoran offered for spiritual care intervention by emergency nurses include establishing a trusting relationship with the patient; maintaining a supportive environment, including providing privacy for patient and family if necessary and identifying religious resources such as the availability of on-call clergy; and finally, recognizing the role of the nurse in "healing the whole person" (p. 184).

Anecdotal reports in the nursing literature document ER patients questioning God's will. See "Has God forsaken the emergency department?" (Schlintz, 1987) and "Would God listen to me now?" (Schlintz, 1988). Guthrie (1985), an ER nurse, also recorded the distress of ER patients. Three contemporary ER nurses spoke of the need for and experiences in spiritual care in their setting.

Pat, a 19-year ER nursing veteran, worried:

In the ER you really see the need for spiritual care but sometimes you are moving and working; you feel you are not able to provide much. With death, you always ask, "Would you like us to call a chaplain?" But there are a lot of other needs to minister to, like thinking from a staff nurse's point, dealing with abuse cases, especially the kids.

Ann, with 8 years of ER experience, expressed gratitude for her own spirituality:

Having my own spiritual base really helped me because I've done so much work in the ER and trauma. You see so much death and dying. You only have a few minutes with the patient before you see them die, and you have to support them in that little bit of time. You also deal with supporting the families; they need a lot of spiritual care. It makes you look at life differently; it makes you a different person . . . Sometimes the chaplains don't get there at the time of a crisis and you are the only one giving support. I can think of many times when I have been the only one there to talk with a family who had just lost a patient . . .

Nurses need to know how to do ministry especially in the crisis times. I see nursing as a ministry, no question about it. Taking care of these patients in the ER is a ministry in and of itself. There are individuals who incorporate that into their nursing. There are some nurses who may not consciously think about it all the time, but they allow themselves to be used by God . . . I think that nurses have to work at being truly spiritual people. I think that my own spirituality leads me to being a more feeling individual, to see a client through their own eyes instead of mine.

Helen, head nurse of an emergency department for five years, spoke of spiritual care interventions she had carried out in the ER:

My coping comes out of a belief that there is a God and that He is loving and generous and forgiving. I always believe that He allows things for a reason and that we can learn from it, the trials and tribulations. For my patients it's the idea that I am given the gift of taking care of them in the ER, to get them through this crisis. I spend a lot of time talking and listening to them. I touch their hand. I believe there are energies from God that we are not necessarily aware of. I think nursing supports the person in giving this kind of spiritual care.

Finally, Helen spoke about her ER nursing staff:

I am very proud of the spiritual care they give; that is one of our strong points. Sometimes we need to get someone in on the patient, and we call pastoral care to come and sit with the family. It works well in our ER. You need a sense of your own spirituality to function well and take care of patients. I think ideally you address the patients' needs by knowing what you believe in yourself.

▶ Spiritual Needs of the Patient in Pain

Although no common definition of pain exists, many nurse clinicians still rely on the pragmatic description first articulated in 1968 by McCaffery. "Pain is whatever the experiencing person says it is, existing whenever the experiencing person says it does" (p. 95). A more contemporary, yet also practical, definition identifies pain as "the state in which an individual experiences and reports the presence of severe discomfort or an uncomfortable sensation" (Gunta, 1993, p. 1538). Pain is broadly understood as a word used to reflect a "subjective perception of distress"; the concept may be divided into three major categories: acute pain, chronic pain, and the pain of malignancy (Gildenberg & DeVaul, 1985, pp. 4–5). Acute pain is described as that which "follows acute injury, disease or surgical intervention, and has a rapid onset, varying in intensity [mild to severe], and lasting for a brief time" (Potter, 1997, p. 1160). Chronic pain has been characterized as pain that "persists longer than three months," "cannot be eliminated," "often becomes diffuse," "may originally have been acute," and has an "insidious onset" (Watt-Watson & Long, 1993, p. 167). The chronic pain of malignancy is identified as pain that lasts for more than 6 months, "after tissue damage has healed or in the absence of evident tissue damage" (Gunta, 1993, p. 1541).

Pain, whether acute, chronic, or related to a malignancy, is influenced by a multiplicity of physiologic, psychological, sociocultural, and spiritual factors. Therapeutic interventions for the relief of pain include pharmacologic (e.g., analgesic drugs) and physiologic (e.g., acupuncture, acupressure, cutaneous stimulation, surgery) measures, as well as nonpharmacologic measures such as biofeedback, meditation, relaxation, and guided imagery.

Potter (1997) advised that in attempting to provide relief for those in pain, the nurse must remember that the patient interprets and experiences both pain and comfort in light of his or her own "physiological, social, spiritual, psychological, and cultural characteristics" (p. 1154). The National Institute of Nursing Research report, submitted by the priority expert panel on symptom management of acute pain, while including spiritual factors as influential in pain perception and response, also identified the religious ethic as a mediating variable (National Institute of Nursing Research, 1994, p. 30).

Any pain diagnosis may, as noted, be influenced by or contain within its boundaries a spiritual dimension; thus, a nursing diagnosis of spiritual distress may be identified in a patient experiencing chronic pain such as that of malignancy. In a study to explore the management of "spiritual distress in patients with advanced cancer pain," Georgensen and Dungan (1996) identified a list of questions to be used in the assessment of spiritual distress, including, "Has your illness affected your faith/belief system?" "Do you pray? What do you think the power of prayer means?" "Is God or other power important to you?" "How can I assist you in maintaining spiritual strength?" and "Are there religious rituals that are important to you now?" (p. 379). Some defining characteristics for the diagnosis of spiritual distress in patients with advanced cancer pain were anger at God, expressions of helplessness, questioning the meaning and purpose in life, grief, and concerns regarding religious beliefs (p. 381).

Religious beliefs can be particularly important to the pain experience as they may provide support and strength through such activities as prayer (Springhouse Corporation, 1985, p. 21). Religious or spiritual beliefs may also provide the person in pain with a vehicle for finding meaning in suffering, or for "offering" the pain experience to God, in expiation for one's failings or the failings of others. Some individuals, however, may also view pain or suffering as a punishment from God, for example, the concept of *castigo* (punishment) in the Mexican-American culture. A nurse or pastor familiar with contemporary theology may be helpful in counseling a patient with this negative perception of God and of the pain experience (Kumasaka, 1996).

As well as recommending or participating in prayer (if acceptable to the patient in pain) and seeking counsel of a chaplain, another therapeutic spiritual care activity that the nurse may recommend and teach is the use of spiritual imagery (Ferszt & Taylor, 1988). A suggestion that the patient imagine God as a loving parent holding him or her in His arms and gently loving and caring may do much to comfort the person in pain. Some other spiritual care strategies for alleviating patients' pain include listening with a caring manner to the individual's fears and anxieties related to the pain experience, and facilitating the participation of family members or other significant persons who may be a primary source of support (Turk & Feldman, 1992; Warner, 1992). As it is appropriately observed, "spiritual views can have a substantial impact on patients' understanding of pain and decisions about pain management" (Unruh, 2007, p. 67).

Ultimately, as described in spiritual care of acutely ill patients in general, sometimes simply the nurse's presence is an important spiritual intervention. Molly, an advanced cancer patient, although medicated with self-administered analgesics, was experiencing acute pain during her final hospitalization at a clinical research facility. Molly had consistently refused the ministrations of a pastoral caregiver with the excuse that she was too tired and in too much pain to be bothered. One day a chaplain desperate to provide some support for Molly asked gently if she might just sit by her bed and pray silently; the chaplain promised not to talk. Molly acquiesced. She seemed to drowse during most of the chaplain's visit, but opened her eyes periodically to see if the pastoral caregiver was still there. A few days later, as Molly was dying, she asked the staff to call the chaplain to be with her. Molly told the staff, "She's the only one who knows what to say!"

Spiritual care is an important dimension of holistic care for the person with an acute illness or an acute exacerbation of a chronic condition. Spiritual care is also essential for persons experiencing a serious physical or psychosocial challenge related to a perioperative experience, a critical care experience, an emergency room experience, or a pain experience. Often the nurse must employ creative strategies to intervene spiritually for persons who may be experiencing a crisis of faith as well as a serious illness. Ultimately, however, spiritual care is appropriate and acceptable for the nurse working with acutely ill patients.

▶ References

Abu-El-Noor, M., & Abu-El-Noor, A. (2014). Importance of spiritual care for cardiac patients admitted to coronary care units in the Gaza strip. *Journal of Holistic Nursing, 32*(2), 104–105.

Agrimson, L., & Taft, L. (2008). Spiritual crisis: A concept analysis. *Journal of Advanced Nursing, 65*(2), 454–461.

Amoah, C. (2011). The central importance of spirituality in palliative care. *International Journal of Palliative Care Nursing, 117*(7), 353–358.

Atkinson, L. J., & Fortunato, N. M. (1996). *Berry & Kohn's operating room technique.* St. Louis, MO: Mosby-Yearbook.

Barber, C. (2013). Spirituality 7: Spiritual support in a ward or in a care home. *British Journal of Healthcare Assistants, 7*(6), 278–281.

Bardanouve, V. E. (1994). Spiritual ministry in the ICU. *Journal of Christian Nursing, 11*(4), 38–39.

Bell, N. (1993). Caring: The essence of critical care nursing. In N. M. Holloway (Ed.), *Nursing the critically ill adult* (4th ed., pp. 14–29). New York, NY: Addison-Wesley.

Bjarnason, D. (2010). Nurse religiosity and end-of-life care. *Journal of Research in Nursing, 17*(1), 78–91.

Blair, F., & Hall, M. (1994). The Klein nursing process: Assessment and priority setting. In A. Klein, G. Lee, A. Manton, & P. Parker (Eds.), *Emergency nursing core curriculum* (4th ed., pp. 3–23). Philadelphia, PA: W. B. Saunders.

Bucher, L., Wimbush, F., Hardie, J., & Hayes, E. (1997). Near death experiences: Critical care nurses' attitudes and interventions. *Dimensions of Critical Care Nursing, 16*(4), 194–201.

Burnard, P. (1988). The spiritual needs of atheists and agnostics. *The Professional Nurse, 4*(3), 130–132.

Burns, L. (1996). Preoperative nursing management. In S. C. Smeltzer & B. G. Bare (Eds.), *Brunner and Sudarth's textbook of medical–surgical nursing* (8th ed., pp. 357–367). Philadelphia, PA: J. B. Lippincott.

Busch, K. D. (1994). Psychosocial concepts and the patient's experience with critical illness. In C. M. Hudak, B. M. Gallo, & J. J. Benz (Eds.), *Critical care nursing: A holistic approach* (pp. 8–22). Philadelphia, PA: J. B. Lippincott.

Chapman, L. S. (1986, Summer). Spiritual health: A component missing from health promotion. *American Journal of Health Promotion, 1*(1), 38–41.

Chesla, C., & Stannard, D. (1997). Breakdown in the nursing care of families in the ICU. *American Journal of Critical Care, 6*(1), 64–71.

Clochesy, J. M. (1988). *Essentials of critical care nursing.* Rockville, MD: Aspen Systems.

Corcoran, E. (1993). Spirituality: An important aspect of emergency nursing. *Journal of Emergency Nursing, 19*(3), 183–184.

Dearing, L. (1997). Caring for the perioperative client. In P. A. Potter & A. G. Perry (Eds.), *Fundamentals of nursing: Concepts, process and practice* (pp. 1379–1427). St. Louis, MO: C. V. Mosby.

DiSarcina, A. (1991). Spiritual care at a code. *Journal of Christian Nursing, 8*(3), 20–23.

Dossey, B. M., Guzzetta, C. E., & Kenner, C. V. (Eds.). (1992). Body, mind, spirit. In *Critical care nursing: Body, mind, spirit* (pp. 10–16). Philadelphia, PA: J. B. Lippincott.

Dracup, K. (1995). Key aspects of caring for the acutely ill. In S. G. Funk, E. M. Tornquist, M. T. Champagne, & R. A. Wise (Eds.), *Key aspects of caring for the acutely ill* (pp. 8–22). New York, NY: Springer.

Duzl-Church, V., Cimino, J., Adler, S., Wong, P., & Anderson, W. (2010). I'm sitting here by myself . . . experiences of patients with serious illness at an urban public hospital. *Journal of Palliative Care Medicine, 13*(6), 695–701.

Emergency Nurses Association. (1995). *Standards of emergency nursing practice* (3rd ed.). St. Louis, MO: Mosby-Yearbook.

Fahlberg, L. L., & Fahlberg, L. A. (1991). Exploring spirituality and consciousness with an expanded science. *American Journal of Health Promotion, 5*(4), 273–281.

Fairchild, S. S. (1996). *Perioperative nursing: Principles and practice* (2nd ed.). Boston, MA: Little, Brown and Company.

Ferszt, G. G., & Taylor, P. B. (1988). When your patient needs spiritual comfort. *Nursing '88, 18*(4), 48–49.

Gallison, B. S., Xu, Y., Jurgens, C. Y. & Boyle, S. M. (2013). Acute care nurses' spiritual practices. *Journal of Holistic Nursing, 31*(2), 95–103.

Georgensen, J., & Dungan, J. M. (1996). Managing spiritual distress in patients with advanced cancer pain. *Cancer Nursing, 19*(5), 376–383.

Gildenberg, P. L., & DeVaul, R. A. (1985). *The chronic pain patient: Evaluation and management.* New York, NY: Karger.

Gillman, J., Gable-Rodriguez, J., Sutherland, M., & Whitacre, J. (1996). Pastoral care in a critical care setting. *Critical Care and Nursing Quarterly, 19*(1), 10–20.

Gunta, K. E. (1993). Chronic pain. In J. M. Thompson, G. K. McFarland, J. E. Hirsch, & S. N. Tucker (Eds.), *Mosby's clinical nursing* (3rd ed., pp. 1538–1543). St. Louis, MO: C. V. Mosby.

Guthrie, J. (1985). E.R.: One nurse's struggle with problem patients and self-righteousness. *Journal of Christian Nursing, 2*(4), 20–21.

Hahn, J. (2001). Ministry in ICU. *Journal of Christian Nursing, 18*(2), 31–32.

Hall, B. A. (1997). Spirituality in terminal illness. *Journal of Holistic Nursing, 15*(1), 82–96.

Hanson, L., Dobbs, D., Usher, B., Williams, S., Rawlings, J., & Daaleman, T. (2008).

Providers and types of spiritual care during serious illness. *Journal of Palliative Medicine, 11*(6), 907–914.

Hart, C. W. (1994). Spiritual health, illness, and death. *Journal of Religion and Health, 33*(1), 17–22.

Hayden, D. (2011). Spirituality in end-of-life care: Attending the person on their journey. *British Journal of Community Nursing, 16*(11), 546–551.

Heiser, R., Chiles, K., Fudge, M., & Gray, S. (1997). The use of music during the immediate postoperative recovery period. *Association of Operating Room Nurses Journal, 65*(4), 777–785.

Holt-Ashley, M. (2000). Nurses pray: Use of prayer and spirituality as a complimentary therapy in the intensive care setting. *AACN Clinical Issues: Advanced Practice in Acute and Critical Care, 11*(1), 60–67.

Hopkins, M. (1993). Care of the patient in a critical care unit. In B. Long, W. J. Phipps, & V. L. Cassmeyer (Eds.), *Medical–surgical nursing: A nursing process approach* (3rd ed., pp. 1564–1585). St. Louis, MO: C. V. Mosby.

Jahani, R., Rejeh, N., Heravi-Karimooj, M., Vaismoradi, M., & Jasper, M. (2014). Spiritual well-being of Iranian patients with acute coronary syndromes: A cross-sectional descriptive study. *Journal of Research in Nursing, 19*(6), 518–527.

Kidd, P. S. (1997). Caring for the critically ill patient: Patient, family and nursing considerations. In P. S. Kidd & K. D. Wagner (Eds.), *High acuity nursing* (2nd ed., pp. 3–24). Stamford, CT: Appleton & Lange.

Kozier, B., Erb, G., Blais, K., & Wilkinson, J. (1995). *Fundamentals of nursing: Concepts, process and practice* (5th ed.). Menlo Park, CA: Addison-Wesley.

Kumasaka, L. (1996). My pain is God's will. *American Journal of Nursing, 96*(6), 45–47.

Lazure, L. A., & DeMartinis, J. E. (1997). Basic concepts of emergency care. In J. H. Black & E. Mahassarin-Jacobs (Eds.), *Medical–surgical nursing: Clinical management for continuity of care* (5th ed., pp. 2501–2516). Philadelphia, PA: W. B. Saunders.

Levin, J. S., & Schiller, P. L. (1987). Is there a religious factor in health? *Journal of Religion and Health, 26*(1), 9–36.

Long, B. C. (1993). Problems encountered in emergencies and disasters. In B. Long, W. J. Phipps, & V. L. Cassmeyer (Eds.), *Medical–surgical nursing: A nursing process approach* (3rd ed., pp. 1537–1560). St. Louis, MO: C. V. Mosby.

Lundberg, P., & Kerdonfag, P. (2010). Spiritual care provided by Thai nurses in intensive care units. *Journal of Clinical Nursing, 19*, 1121–1128.

MacPhail, E. (1992). Overview of emergency nursing and emergency care. In S. Sheehy (Ed.), *Emergency nursing principles and practice* (pp. 1–8). St. Louis, MO: Mosby-Yearbook.

March, P., & Caple, C. (2012, June). Spiritual needs of hospitalized patients. *Cinahl Information Systems, 14*(2), 1–2.

McCaffery, M. (1968). *Nursing practice theories related to cognition, bodily pain, and man-environment interaction.* Los Angeles, CA: University of California at Los Angeles.

McGrath, P. (2004). Reflections on serious illness as spiritual journey by survivors of haematological malignancies. *European Journal of Cancer Care, 13*, 227–237.

McNamara, S. (1995). Perioperative nurses' perceptions of caring practices. *Association of Operating Room Nurses Journal, 61*(2), 377–388.

Meeker, M. H., & Rothrock, J. C. (1995). *Alexander's care of the patient in surgery* (10th ed.). St. Louis, MO: C. V. Mosby.

Michello, J. A. (1988). Spiritual and emotional determinants of health. *Journal of Religion and Health, 27*(1), 62–70.

Miller, K. (1996). Emergency nursing. In S. C. Smeltzer & B. B. Bare (Eds.), *Brunner and Suddarth's textbook of medical-surgical nursing* (8th ed., pp. 2000–2018). Philadelphia, PA: J. B. Lippincott.

Minnix, L. (2008). Maintaining spirituality in institutional settings. *Generations, 32*(2), 65–67.

Monroe, C. (2011). Spirituality shines through in a magnet moment. *Critical Care Nurse, 31*(4), 98–99.

National Institute of Nursing Research. (1994). *Symptom management: Acute pain, a report of the NINR priority expert panel.* Bethesda, MD: Author.

Niklas, G. R., & Stefanics, C. (1975). *Ministry to the hospitalized.* New York, NY: Paulist Press.

Nouwen, H. J. M. (1979). *The wounded healer.* Garden City, NY: Image Books.

Nussbaum, G. (2003). Spirituality in critical care: Patient comfort and satisfaction. *Critical Care Nursing Quarterly, 26*(3), 214–220.

O'Brien, M. E. (1982a). The need for spiritual integrity. In H. Yura & M. B. Walsh (Eds.), *Human needs and the nursing process* (Vol. 2, pp. 85–115). Norwalk, CT: Appleton-Century-Crofts.

O'Brien, M. E. (1982b). Religious faith and adjustment to long-term hemodialysis. *Journal of Religion and Health, 21*(1), 68–80.

O'Brien, M. E. (1983). *The courage to survive: The life career of the chronic dialysis patient.* New York, NY: Grune & Stratton.

O'Brien, M. E. (1992). *Living with HIV: Experiment in courage.* Westport, CT: Auburn House.

Peterson, V., & Potter, P. A. (1997). Spiritual health. In P. A. Potter & A. G. Perry (Eds.), *Fundamentals of nursing: Concepts, process and practice* (4th ed., pp. 441–456). St. Louis, MO: C. V. Mosby.

Phippen, M. L., Wells, M. P., & Martinelli, A. M. (1994). A conceptual model for peri-operative nursing practice. In M. L. Phippen & M. D. Wells (Eds.), *Perioperative nursing practice* (pp. 3–67). Philadelphia, PA: W. B. Saunders.

Pipe, T. B., Kelly, A., LeBrun, G., Schmidt, D., Atherton, P., & Robinson, C. (2008). A prospective descriptive study exploring hope, spiritual well-being, and quality of life in hospitalized patients. *Medsurg Nursing, 17*(4), 247–257.

Potter, P. A. (1997). Comfort. In P. A. Potter & A. G. Perry (Eds.), *Fundamentals of nursing: Concepts, process and practice* (4th ed., pp. 1153–1190). St. Louis, MO: C. V. Mosby.

Potter, P. A., & Perry, A. G. (1997). *Fundamentals of nursing: Concepts, process and practice* (4th ed.). St. Louis, MO: C. V. Mosby.

Reed, P. (1991). Preferences for spiritually related nursing interventions among terminally ill and non-terminally ill hospitalized adults and well adults. *Applied Nursing Research, 4*(3), 122–128.

Robinson, K. (1992). Pre-hospital care. In S. Sheehy (Ed.), *Emergency nursing: Principles and practice* (3rd ed., pp. 9–18). St. Louis, MO: Mosby-Yearbook.

Ronaldson, S., Hayes, L., Aggar, C., Green, J., & Carey, M. (2012). Spirituality and spiritual caring: Nurses' perspectives and practice in palliative and acute care environments. *Journal of Clinical Nursing, 21*(15/16), 2126–2135.

Rothrock, J. C. (1994). The meaning of spirituality to perioperative nurses and their patients. *Association of Operating Room Nurses Journal, 60*(6), 894–895.

Rukholm, E. E., Bailey, P. H., & Coutu-Wakulczyk, G. (1991). Family needs and anxiety in ICU: Cultural differences in Northeastern Ontario. *The Canadian Journal of Nursing Research, 23*(3), 67–81.

Rushton, L. (2014). What are the barriers to spiritual care in a hospital setting? *British Journal of Nursing, 23*(7), 370–374.

Santacaterina, S., & Stein-Spencer, L. (1990). Emergency medicine services. In S. Kidd & J. Kaiser (Eds.), *Emergency nursing: A physiologic and clinical perspective* (pp. 3–12). Philadelphia, PA: W. B. Saunders.

Schlintz, V. (1987). Has God forsaken the emergency department? *Journal of Christian Nursing, 4*(1), 18–19.

Schlintz, V. (1988). Would God listen to me now? *Journal of Christian Nursing, 5*(2), 14–16.

Seidl, L. G. (1993, September). The value of spiritual health. *Health Progress, 10*(1), 48–50.

Shaffer, J. (1991). Spiritual distress and critical illness. *Critical Care Nurse, 11*(10), 42–45.

Shelly, J. A., & Fish, S. (1995). Praying with patients. *Journal of Christian Nursing, 12*(1), 9–13.

Smeltzer, S. C., & Bare, B. G. (1996). *Brunner and Suddarth's textbook of medical-surgical nursing* (8th ed.). Philadelphia, PA: J. B. Lippincott.

Smyth, T., & Allen, S. (2011). Nurses' experiences assessing spirituality of terminally ill patients in acute clinical practice. *International Journal of Palliative Nursing, 17*(7), 337–343.

Springhouse Corporation. (1985). *Nursing now series: Pain*. Springhouse, PA: Author.

Sternberg, E. M. (2009). *Healing spaces: The science of place and well-being*. Cambridge, MA: Harvard University Press.

Stromberg, R. (1992). The voices on coronary care: A confrontation with vulnerability. In L. E. Holst (Ed.), *Hospital ministry: The role of the chaplain today* (pp. 127–138). New York, NY: Crossroad.

Taylor, C., Lillis, C., & LeMone, P. (1997). *Fundamentals of nursing: The art and science of nursing care* (3rd ed.). Philadelphia, PA: J. B. Lippincott.

Timmons, F., & Kelly, J. (2008). Spiritual assessment in intensive and cardiac care nursing. *Nursing in Critical Care, 13*(3), 124–131.

Turk, D. C., & Feldman, C. S. (1992). Facilitating the use of noninvasive pain management strategies with the terminally ill. *The Hospice Journal, 8*(1), 193–214.

Turan, T., & Karamanoglu, A. Y. (2012). Determining intensive care unit nurses' perceptions and practice levels of spiritual care. *Nursing in Critical Care, 18*(2), 70–78.

Twibell, R., Wieseke, A., Marine, M., & Schoger, J. (1996). Spiritual and coping needs of critically ill patients: Validation of nursing diagnosis. *Dimensions of Critical Care Nursing, 15*(5), 245–253.

Unruh, A. (2007). Spirituality, religion and pain. *Canadian Journal of Nursing Research, 39*(2), 66–86.

Walleck, C. A. (1989). Spinal cord injury. In K. T. Von Rueden & C. Walleck (Eds.), *Advanced critical care nursing* (pp. 181–203). Rockville, MD: Aspen Systems.

Warner, J. E. (1992). Involvement of families in pain control of terminally ill patients. *The Hospice Journal, 8*(1), 155–170.

Watt-Watson, J. H., & Long, B. C. (1993). Pain. In B. Long, W. J. Phipps, & V. L. Cassmeyer (Eds.), *Medical–surgical nursing: A nursing process approach* (3rd ed., pp. 163–179). St. Louis, MO: C. V. Mosby.

Weaver, A. J., Koenig, H. G., & Flannelly, L. T. (2008). Nurses and healthcare chaplains: Natural allies. *Journal of Health Care Chaplaincy, 14*(2), 91–98.

Westlake, C., Dyo, M., Vollman, M., & Heywood, J. T. (2008). Spirituality and suffering of patients with heart failure. *Progress in Palliative Care, 16*(5–6), 257–265.

Yeager, S., Doust, C., Epting, S., Iannantuono, B., Indian, C., Lenhart, B. . . . Thomas, K. (2010). Embrace hope: An end-of-life intervention to support neurological critical care patients and their families. *Critical Care Nurse, 30*(1), 47–58.

CHAPTER 6

Spiritual Needs of the Chronically Ill Person

Those who wait for the Lord shall renew their strength, they shall mount up with wings as eagles, they shall run and not be weary, walk and not faint.

Isaiah 40:31

Virtually all of our cancer patients are in some way or another in a psychological, emotional, or spiritual crisis at some point, and they all address it in different ways . . . and of course, one of the things you run into is, like, "Why should I get treatment? I trust God." Then I like to explain to them that God does help those who help themselves, not in those words specifically. On occasion you seek outside help [for someone] who is really just beyond what you can do. But most times people just need to talk, get it off their chest. If I were in their place I would want a nurse there.

Sarah, Oncology Research Nurse

For the chronically ill individual, personal spirituality and/or religious beliefs and practices often constitute an important, even critical, dimension of coping with the life changes necessitated by the illness experience. This was clearly recognized in the author's longitudinal research with persons facing long-term adaptation to such illnesses as chronic renal failure (CRF) and human immunodeficiency virus (HIV) infection. The corporate élan of both groups was reflected in the titles of books reporting their coping strategies: *The Courage to Survive: The Life Career of the Chronic Dialysis Patient* (O'Brien, 1983) and *Living with HIV: Experiment in Courage* (O'Brien, 1992). For the CRF and HIV-positive study participants, as for many persons living with serious, life-threatening chronic illnesses, it is exquisitely courageous to go on about the business of living, knowing that each new day may possess myriad physical or emotional threats to one's quality of life. For many persons living with chronic illness, transcendent belief and experience provide the impetus to live and to love in the midst of significant pain and suffering. As one 8-year survivor of an HIV-positive diagnosis put it:

> God is the one reliable constant in my life. When I'm feeling unsure about everything else, I know that God is with me. I feel it. It's not a "head thing." It's in my heart. I almost think I'm being arrogant but it really is indescribable, the feeling of the presence of God; it's like the hymn puts it: "Standing on Solid Rock."
>
> (O'Brien, 1995, p. 129)

A topic currently under study is that of "spirituality self-care," especially as it relates to quality of life among persons diagnosed with chronic illness (White, 2013, p. 23). In research with 142 outpatients it was found that "spiritual self-care practices helped manage the chronic illness, specifically heart failure and quality of life" (p. 23). Other chronic illness conditions in which spiritual support was found to be particularly important included cancer (Egan, McKechnie, Jobson, Herbison, & Richards, 2013; Nixon, Narayanasamy, & Penny, 2013; and Blanchard, Dunlap, & Fitchett, 2012); mental health conditions such as dementia (Odbehr, Kvigne, Hauge, & Danbolt, 2014); and acute psychiatric inpatient conditions (Raffay, 2014). It has been reported that "people with mental health needs are increasingly identifying spirituality as a vital part of their recovery" (Elliott, 2011, p. 4). This chapter documents spiritual needs in chronic illness as identified in interviews with persons living with such conditions as cancer (including Burkitt's lymphoma), chronic renal failure, depression, and multiple chronic sequelae of HIV infection and acquired immunodeficiency syndrome (AIDS). The patients' spiritual needs are further explained through analysis of interview data elicited from families and professional nurse caregivers. In addition, practicing nurses report and describe specific instances of spiritual care in a variety of settings.

▶ The Case of Chronic Illness

Any experience of illness may bring about a degree of disruption in a person's life. Usual patterns of life activity are temporarily, or in some cases permanently, changed or modified to cope with the situation. The need for a major life change occurs more frequently in patients facing chronic illness. Corbin (1996) defined chronic illness as "a medical condition or health problem with associated symptoms or disabilities that require long-term management" (p. 318). Taylor, Lillis, and LeMone (1997) described chronic illness as having the following characteristics: results in "permanent change," "causes or is caused by irreversible alterations in normal anatomy and physiology," "requires special client education for rehabilitation," and "requires a long period of care or support" (p. 61). Currently, chronic illness is considered the "primary health problem in the United States," with some 50 percent of the population experiencing one or more conditions (Ignatavicius, Workman, & Mishler, 1995, p. 213).

Chronic illness symptoms may range from mild to severe, and often fluctuate between periods of exacerbation and remission (LeMone & Burke, 1996, p. 44). Medical sociologists point out that in cases of chronic illness, frequently the fulfillment of previous roles and responsibilities becomes impossible, and significant reorganization of an individual's patterns of behavior is required. Major changes may occur in social relationships and future life plans, as well as in personal self-concept and self-esteem (Turk & Rudy, 1986, p. 309). The family, especially, may be significantly disrupted by the chronic illness of one of its members, especially when well family members are intimately involved with the care and support of the ill person. Both current and prior nursing research suggest that spiritual well-being is, for many chronically ill persons, a key factor in successful long-term adaptation to the illness condition (Landis, 1996).

▶ Spiritual Care of the Chronically Ill Patient

If, as the literature suggests, an individual's spiritual well-being is central to coping with the physical and psychosocial sequelae of chronic illness, what interventions may a nurse initiate in the provision of spiritual care for a chronically ill patient? And, in what setting(s) will spiritual care for the chronically ill person need to be provided?

The chronically ill person, although most frequently living at home, may also be found in a hospital or clinic setting; the latter in times of illness exacerbation or during the carrying out of diagnostic or therapeutic procedures. The kind of spiritual care provided by the nurse will be influenced by the setting and also by the type and degree of the patient's disability. Physical disability, such as being unable to ambulate freely, may necessitate a creative strategy to facilitate participation in religious rituals, if desired by the client. Spiritual care may also be directed toward the emotional sequelae of chronic illness, which may affect overall spiritual well-being, such as "low self-esteem, feelings of isolation, powerlessness, hopelessness, and anger" (Soeken & Carson, 1987, p. 606). Spiritual interventions that a nurse can initiate in response are an affirmation of God's love and care for each person, encouragement to participate in rituals shared with others, and support for an individual's hope in God's protection (pp. 608–609).

In discussing a "spirituality for the long haul," Muldoon and King (1991) observed that the challenge for the chronically ill person is to integrate the illness experience into his or her self-concept (p. 102). Central to accomplishing this is the support of one's spiritual philosophy undergirding the ultimate meaning and purpose in life. For 181 chronic obstructive pulmonary disease (COPD) patients, a "high sense" of spirituality was associated with "low stress" and "high quality of life" as reported by nonhospitalized patients (Delgado, 2007, p. 229). This finding is supported by the idea that individuals may "make sense of chronic illness" by finding spiritual meaning in their suffering (Greenstreet, 2006, p. 938). Greenstreet presents a conceptual model that incorporates a spiritual perspective on "making sense of chronic illness in relation to coping skills" (p. 938).

Spiritual care interventions for the chronically ill are similar to those proposed for the acutely ill patient. They include listening to and being with the patient, which may facilitate the integration of spirituality into coping behaviors; praying with a patient, if the patient so desires; reading Scripture, if appropriate; providing spiritual books or other devotional materials; and referring the patient to a clergy member. These spiritual interventions need to be adapted, however, to particular illness conditions and their sequelae, such as mental illness and physical disability, and to specific settings, such as those involving home health care and homelessness, which are discussed later in this chapter. Obviously, careful attention to the patient's religious tradition should precede any spiritual interventions as well as the assessment of spiritual needs.

▶ Spiritual Needs in Chronic Illness

All individuals have spiritual needs, regardless of religious belief or personal philosophy of life. The experience of illness, especially of a long-term chronic illness, may be a time when spiritual needs previously unnoticed or neglected become apparent (Baldacchino & Draper, 2001). It has been reported that individuals with chronic illness "have identified spirituality as a resource that promotes quality of life" (Adegbola, 2007, p. 42). Spiritual needs may manifest in a multiplicity of symptoms, depending on the person's particular theology, religious tradition, or philosophical understanding of the meaning and purpose of life. For the adherent of one of the monotheistic Western religious groups, Judaism, Christianity, or Islam, spiritual needs are generally associated with one's relationship to God. Shelly and Fish (1988) identified God in the believer's life to be the source of "meaning and purpose, love and relatedness and forgiveness" (p. 38); they asserted that an absence of belief in any one of these factors will result in spiritual need (p. 39). Spiritual needs may also include hope and creativity (Highfield & Cason, 1983, p. 188), as well as reassurance and self-esteem (Cassidy, 1992).

Although assessment of a patient's spiritual needs may be more readily carried out by a practicing nurse, it is often at the stage of intervention that difficulties arise. Although most nurses profess to practice holistic patient care, Forbis (1988) asserted that "they often avoid dealing pragmatically with the spiritual realm" (p. 158). In interviewing nurses prior to designing a course on spiritual care, Ellis (1986) found that many nurses were uncomfortable discussing spiritual issues with patients and were decidedly uneasy about praying with their patients (p. 76). Nurses need to develop an understanding of and comfort with their own spiritual beliefs in order to be at ease discussing spiritual matters with others (Burnard, 1988; McSherry, 1996).

In a study of nurses' perceptions of patients' spiritual needs, Boutell and Bozeht (1988) identified the concepts of faith (in religious beliefs), peace (inner strength), hope, and trust (in the importance of religious practices) (p. 174). Additional needs, those of courage and love, were reflected in nursing research data elicited from CRF and AIDS patients (O'Brien, 1983, 1992, 1995). The spiritual needs of hope, trust, courage, faith, peace, and love on the part of chronically ill persons are explored in the following pages; examples of these characteristics are drawn from the comments of individuals experiencing such illness conditions as cancer, HIV infection and AIDS, and CRF.

Hope

And now, O Lord, what do I wait for? My hope is in you.

—**Psalm** 39:7

Hope, as a general term, relates to an anticipation that something desired will occur. Hope, or the act of hoping, defined theologically for a member of a monotheistic religious tradition, is the "focusing of attention, affectivity and commitment to action toward the future goal of fulfillment in God, the realization of the reign of God" (Hellwig, 1993, p. 506). Shelly and Fish (1988) pointed out that placing one's hope in God does not mean an immediate end to suffering or anxiety; rather, hoping relates to trust in God's support during a crisis (p. 44). Both clinical anecdotes and research have documented the fact that when a patient loses hope and the will to live, death may result (Ross, 1994, p. 440). Thus, supporting and nurturing hope is described as a "vital ingredient" in a nurse's plan of spiritual care (Gewe, 1994; Le Peau, 1996; Thompson, 1994).

Phillip, a young adult cancer patient who described himself as a born-again Christian, manifested a beautifully direct sense of hope as he faced his illness:

> I put all my hope in Jesus, in the Cross. I have my daily minute with Him. I mean, it's about an hour, but I call it my "minute." I try to always have the special "minutes." I pray to Jesus; He is with me. Jesus is my hope.

Because of his disease, an anaplastic astrocytoma, Phillip's speech patterns were sometimes difficult to follow; by listening carefully, however, one could understand his meaning; his eyes were very expressive as he spoke about his relationship with Jesus. On a page in his Bible, Phillip had written "Born again in Jesus"; he explained, "That's when I accepted Him, and now He's always with me."

Trust

I trust in you, O Lord, I say, "You are my God."

—**Psalm** 31:14

The concept of trust indicates having confidence in something or someone. Theologically, the term is considered to be a relational one, "describing the quality of a relationship among two or more persons" (Schreiter, 1993, p. 982). The Hebrew word for trust, which occurs frequently in the Old Testament, "refers most often to trust in God" (p. 982). Possessing the ability to trust in others is considered "essential to spiritual health" (Simsen, 1988, p. 33).

In discussing adaptation to chronic illness, nursing scholar Ruth Stoll (1989) noted that "a dynamic spiritual belief system enables us to trust that somehow tomorrow will not be beyond our capacities" (p. 195). Trusting, for the ill person who is a believer, will give a sense of security that God's healing power will be operative in his or her life (Johnson, 1992, p. 92). It is important to recognize, however, that the "healing" that occurs may be of a spiritual or emotional nature, rather than a physical healing.

A recently married and newly diagnosed Burkitt's lymphoma patient, David, spoke eloquently to the concept of trust:

> Well, this is not what I had expected at this time in my life but this is the Cross, the folly of the Cross they say, so I put it in the hands of the "man upstairs." I mean I'm really with Him and He's with me, you know . . . I have to tell you, though, even with my faith, we're all human, and I was really scared in the beginning. When they first brought me in to the hospital, they rolled me into that ICU, through the doors, and I saw all that equipment and those monitors, I thought: "Whoa! Is this the Cross?" But you know that God is going to be walking beside you.

David's life had, he admitted, been "turned upside down" by his diagnosis and hospitalization, and yet he described a sense of comfort in knowing that this, for him, was God's will. He laughingly commented that this kind of attitude would, he knew, be considered "folly" by some; for David it was, quite simply, a matter of trust.

Courage

I took courage for the hand of the Lord, my God, was upon me.

—**Ezra** 7:28

Courage, or emotional strength, is described not as the absence of fear, but rather as "the ability to transcend one's fears, to choose to actively face what needs to be" (Stoll, 1989, p. 196).

Martha, an adult woman in midlife diagnosed with CRF and experiencing maintenance hemodialysis, spoke openly about the need for courage to face a life dependent on technology:

You have to get yourself together and face the thing; be courageous about it because nobody is going to do it for you. I think adjusting to kidney failure and dialysis is very difficult because I can't answer why. Why did this happen to me? But my faith says that all things have a reason, and God won't put anything on us that we can't bear . . . But it's still difficult because chronic illnesses may be with you a long time before they lead to dying; you have to have some courage about it.

We, as nurses, long to do something for those with whom we work: to heal, to cure, to alleviate the suffering of our courageous patients and their families. Yet frequently we must accept that such accomplishments are beyond our power; we must learn to accept that our desire to comfort and our empathy are, of themselves, an important dimension of nursing care.

Faith

Daughter, your faith has made you well.

—**Luke** 8:48

Faith means belief or trust in someone or something. From a theological perspective, faith is the basis of our personal relationship with God "on whose strength and absolute sureness we can literally stake our lives" (Fatula, 1993, p. 379). Faith is identified as "a prerequisite for spiritual growth" (Carson, 1989, p. 28), and faith in God is often a critical element in surviving a loss (Sandin, 1996) or coping with an illness experience (Ross, 1994). A holistic nursing philosophy suggests that religious faith may give one the strength to "combat disease and facilitate healing" (Kennison, 1987, p. 29).

An example of the support provided by personal faith in coping with an advanced cancer diagnosis was reflected in Matthew's perception of his condition:

I can't question how I got this disease or what God's plan is for me. But I know my faith will get me through. At a time like this, faith is the key. My faith makes me strong. Chemo is tough but God's in that too. I don't know; I just know my faith will get me to the place I need to be.

Peace

May the Lord give strength to His people, may the Lord bless His people with peace.

—**Psalm** 29:11

Peace is a sense of being undisturbed, a feeling of freedom from anxiety and fear. Theologically, peace is described as being derived from "a right relationship with God, which entails forgiveness, reconciliation and union" (Dwyer, 1990, p. 749). In a study of spiritual well-being (SWB), researcher David Moberg (1979) found that, according to most respondents' perceptions, two significant indicators of SWB were "peace with God" and "inner peace" (p. 9).

Two chronic renal failure patients on maintenance hemodialysis described the peace their religious faith afforded them in relation to their disease and treatment regimens. Carolyn, who had been on dialysis for over 3 years, asserted:

> Well, I think if I didn't believe in God and have the religious beliefs I have, I don't think I'd be able to survive this. I don't think I'd have any peace. I think I probably would have attempted suicide at one time or another. But my faith helps me be optimistic about it; it really helps.

And Elizabeth, a two-year veteran of dialytic therapy, reported that the illness experience had a positive effect on her personal spirituality:

> My faith has really strengthened. I'm still a good old "knee-slapping" Baptist. I still love my pastor and I enjoy going to church on Sunday. I pray a lot, but I don't want to ask too much. I'm at peace. If healing is for me, then it will come to me. I just take the attitude that I don't worry about it. God will provide.

Love

How precious is your steadfast love, O God.

—**Psalm** 36:7

To love means to care for or to treasure someone or something. Love, from a religious perspective, relates to "God's benevolent love"; thus, "by association, God's love encompasses human love for God, human love for neighbor, human love for creation, and self-love" (Dreyer, 1993, p. 613). Shelly and Fish (1988) asserted that God's love will be with one, unconditionally, during a crisis such as illness (pp. 46–47), and that His supportive love is best reflected in the Old Testament Scripture, Isaiah 43:2–3:

> When you pass through raging waters, I will be with you; in the river you shall not drown. When you walk through fire, you shall not be burned; the flames shall not consume you. For I am the Lord, your God, the Holy One of Israel, your savior.

Mary Grace, a cancer patient, described the importance of God's love as manifested by her church:

> Well the one thing that helps you deal with this is that you know that your church is behind you. The pastor, he remembers to call you and the church members come to visit and the deacons bring me my Communion to the house. All those things make me feel good; they make me feel loved.

Tom, a 37-year-old lymphoma patient and a practicing attorney who described his personal spirituality as "secular humanism," also admitted the need for love in coping with his diagnosis:

> I'm not sure about the "God thing"—I mean whether God exists or not. But I believe in human goodness and the responsibility we have to each other and to the universe. I don't lean on any religion to help me live with this disease, but I do rely on my family and friends who love me. That's what gets me through the day, knowing I'm loved.

Cancer, HIV/AIDS, and CRF are three chronic illness syndromes from which many individuals currently suffer. Examples of data-based spiritual needs of the oncology patient, the HIV-positive patient, and the CRF patient can serve to guide spiritual care therapeutics for persons suffering from other chronic illnesses that a nurse may encounter.

▶ Spiritual Needs of the Cancer Patient

The term *cancer* is a broad label that covers a family of diseases characterized by un-controllable growth of mutated cells that may disseminate to various parts of the body. Cancerous growths originate in various tissues or organs, differ in size and appearance, develop in a variety of ways, and respond differently to therapeutic interventions (Petty, 1997, p. 533). Roughly 20 percent of all deaths in the United States are attributable to some form of the approximately 12 major and 50 minor types of cancer (LeMone & Burke, 1996, p. 306). Because of the serious, life-threatening nature of most cancer diagnoses, the spiritual needs of the patient may be significant. A study of 45 adult cancer patients (with diagnoses such as breast cancer, lung cancer, and leukemia) revealed that religious belief was a source of strength and comfort in coping with the illness (Moschella, Pressman, Pressman, & Weissman, 1997). Moschella et al. found that patients diagnosed with cancer reported an increase in faith, more time spent in prayer, and greater frequency of church attendance, despite the fact that their religious belief systems provided no theological explanation for suffering (p. 17). Findings from research with 114 adult cancer patients indicated a positive association between high levels of spiritual well-being and lower levels of anxiety (Kaczorowski, 1989). Spiritual well-being, as evaluated in a study of 175 breast cancer patients, was demonstrated to be highest in those women who were classified as intrinsically religious, that is, those who internalized their religious belief as a core motivator in life (Mickley, Soeken, & Belcher, 1992). Highfield (1992) found the spiritual health of 23 primary lung cancer patients to be high when normed according to the current literature on spirituality and cancer. Highfield posited some reasons: the study participants' reliance on spiritual resources, and a greater degree of spiritual development, related either to age or the terminal diagnosis (p. 7).

Research on the attitudes and beliefs about spiritual care among Oncology Nursing Society members revealed that the community held the nurse's role of pro-viding spiritual care in high regard (Taylor, Highfield, & Amenta, 1994). The study of 181 members of the Oncology Nursing Society reported spiritual care behaviors such as talking with patients about spiritual or religious matters; referring patients to other spiritual caregivers such as chaplains or clergy; praying with or for a patient; supporting a patient's family; facilitating the use of religious or devotional resources;

and being with and touching the patient, with a supportive and nonjudgmental attitude (Taylor, Amenta, & Highfield, 1995, p. 36). Recent nursing research has also demonstrated the increasing role of spiritual caring among oncology nurses (Thomas & Retsas, 1999); the importance of the nurse's sensitivity to diverse cultural and religious traditions (Lackey, Gates, & Brown, 2001); and nurses' recognition of the uniqueness of individualized spiritual experience for oncology patients (Halstead & Hull, 2001; MacDonald, 2001). In a qualitative study exploring oncology nurses' coping processes, the concepts of caritas, religiosity, and spirituality were considered and found to "have a protective function that facilitates coping as the nurse has something to turn to" (Ekedahl & Wengstrom, 2010, p. 530). The study data also suggested that "religious coping dominated by basic trust where prayer is used as a coping strategy may support the nurse" (p. 530).

Some additional research on the spiritual needs of cancer patients includes the work of McClain, Rosenfeld, and Breitbart (2003) in "Effect of Spiritual Well-Being on End-of-Life Despair in Terminally Ill Cancer Patients" and in "Spiritual Care Nursing: What Cancer Patients and Family Caregivers Want" (Taylor & Mamier, 2005). In attempting to map the "processes and qualities of spiritual care" with oncology patients, Carr (2009) conducted open-ended interviews with patients, nurses, and families that revealed that "developing caring relationships" was core in the nurse–patient interactions, and that the nurse should possess four qualities: "receptivity, humanity, competency, and positivity" (p. 686). Other studies highlighting the importance of spiritual well-being in cancer patients were conducted by Lopez, McCaffrey, Griffin, and Fitzpatrick (2009); and Schneider (2007).

Spiritual care for Mrs. Anna Smithfield, an advanced ovarian cancer patient participating in an experimental chemotherapy protocol, consisted primarily of listening and supporting the patient's existing spiritual and religious beliefs and traditions. Mrs. Smithfield's religious tradition was Methodist; her nurse, Beth, was Roman Catholic. At their first meeting, Beth and Mrs. Smithfield discussed their denominational differences; they agreed, however, that as Christians they really had more similarities in belief than differences. Mrs. Smithfield was receiving spiritual support from her pastor and church members. What she needed to talk to Beth about was her fear of leaving her husband of 26 years alone. She was also saddened over the fact that her young grandchildren would never get to know her as "grandmother." For Beth, the primary spiritual care intervention was to sit with Mrs. Smithfield, to listen, and to talk with her about her family; they also prayed together. Beth made a point to drop in when Mr. Smithfield visited, because the patient had expressed the wish that he meet her nurse; this provided Beth the opportunity to be available for Mr. Smithfield who also needed spiritual support in his anxiety over his wife's prognosis.

▶ Spiritual Needs of the HIV-Infected Person

HIV infection, identified in 1983 under the acronym LAV (lymphadenopathy associated virus), and in 1984 as HTLV III (human T-cell lymphotropic virus) has progressed through many phases and mutations over the last 33–34 years; numerous therapeutic protocols have been tested on both the virus and related opportunistic infections with varying degrees of efficacy. Although HIV infection in the United States was originally a disease of white gay men, the condition later became more prevalent in the black and Hispanic communities (Ungvarski & Matassarin-Jacobs, 1997). The clinical course of HIV infection is directed by the immune system response, with the development of opportunistic infection symptoms such as fever, malaise, sweating, headache, weight loss, sore throat, and rashes, among others (Lisanti & Zwolski, 1997). HIV infection may progress to a stage officially categorized as AIDS related to a variety of immune system parameters and symptomatology. More recent pharmacologic therapies have significantly slowed the progression of the human immunodeficiency virus and its related disease conditions. Many of those infected with HIV are living longer and with better quality of life than in the past.

Nevertheless, the anxiety and stigma often associated with HIV infection remain as concerning for some 21st-century patients as in the early days of the condition.

In the past countless psychosocial concerns related to both the seriousness and stigma of HIV infection were identified in the nursing research literature; spiritual and religious needs were central among these (Belcher, Dettmore, & Holzemer, 1989; Carson, Soeken, Shanty, & Terry, 1990; Mellors, Riley, & Erlen, 1997; O'Brien, 1992, 1995; O'Brien & Pheifer, 1993; Warner-Robbins & Christiana, 1989). There was also a plethora of early books published on the topics of spirituality, religion, and pastoral care for people living with HIV and AIDS. Some examples that may continue to prove useful as resources for the nurse in providing spiritual care are *The Gospel Imperative in the Midst of AIDS* (Iles, 1989); *The Church with AIDS* (Russell, 1990); *Ministry to Persons with AIDS* (Perelli, 1991); *Embracing the Mystery: A Prayerful Response to AIDS* (Sandys, 1993); *AIDS, Ethics and Religion: Embracing a World of Suffering* (Overberg, 1994). Nevertheless, nursing literature of the time suggested that spirituality remained a neglected area of concern in the assessment of HIV patients' needs (Newshan, 1998; Sherman, 2001). Presently, that neglect continues to be a concern. Today, as in the past, spiritual care of the person living with HIV or AIDS may take many forms depending on the stage and current symptomatology of the illness. It is important to keep in mind that some HIV-positive persons who have become alienated from their churches may not be receiving formal religious ministry because of the stigma of the disease (Perelli, 1991). That, however, is a situation that can be remedied, if the patient and church desire. Some suggestions for spiritual care for the HIV-positive person that may be carried out by a nurse include listening to the patient's "stories" surrounding the illness (Crowther, 1991); offering small gestures of friendship, which may be missing in the alienated patient's life (AIDS Ministry Program, 1991); providing empathy and emotional support (Sunderland & Shelp, 1987); allowing the patient to take the lead in the offering of prayer (Christensen, 1991); and presenting the patient with a nonjudgmental attitude (W. J. Smith, 1988). For the HIV-positive individual who is physically and cognitively well enough to participate, activities such as creating and appreciating religious art or poetry may provide healing for the heart (Roche, 1992).

John Michael, who had lost many friends to AIDS and who had been living with an HIV diagnosis for over six years, began to write poetry as a way of coping with his illness. A nurse researcher provided spiritual support by listening to and appreciating John Michael's poetry. Reading the poetry often provided an opening to discuss spiritual issues related to both living and dying with HIV. One poem, entitled "The Touch of the Maestro," reveals the impact of the HIV experience on John Michael's personal spirituality. In the piece, the poet muses on how HIV disease has alerted him to the fragility of the human condition and has brought into focus the importance of transcendent issues; this is reflected in the final stanza:

> Never again, will I find satisfaction from a mundane ordinary success.
>> There is only one reward that needs to be filled,
>> That is the plucking of the instrument that is my heart, which now only
> sings at the touch of the Maestro.
>> (O'Brien, 1995, p. 126, reprintzed with permission of the poem's author)

▶ Spiritual Needs of the Chronic Renal Failure Patient

Matassarin-Jacobs (1997) defined CRF as irreversible and "progressive reduction of functioning renal tissue such that the remaining kidney mass can no longer maintain the body's internal environment" (p. 1641). CRF may result from any one of a variety of diseases such as polycystic kidney disease, glomerulonephritis, and pyelonephritis; CRF may also accompany other illness conditions such as diabetes mellitus or hypertension. CRF, if undetected and untreated, generally progresses unilaterally through three stages: diminished renal function, renal insufficiency, and uremia. As a patient progresses toward the critical uremic stage, with symptoms of greatly decreased urine output, fatigue, nausea, and general malaise, dialytic therapy is usually considered. The four major modes of dialysis currently in use are hemodialysis, peritoneal dialysis, continuous ambulatory peritoneal dialysis (CAPD), and continuous cyclic peritoneal dialysis (CCPD). Hemodialysis employs a machine with a "semipermeable filtering membrane [artificial kidney] that removes accumulated waste products from the blood" (Kilpatrick, 1997, p. 1298). The peritoneal dialysis methods cleanse the blood by filling the abdominal cavity with dialysate (electrolyte solution) and using the peritoneum as a filter for waste not excreted by the kidneys. Any method of dialytic therapy, combined with the diagnosis of renal failure, may prove extremely stressful for the CRF patient and family (Flaherty & O'Brien, 1992; Korniewicz & O'Brien, 1994; O'Brien, 1990; O'Brien, Donley, Flaherty, & Johnstone, 1986).

Among the psychosocial sequelae of CRF and its treatment modality, perhaps the least studied yet possibly most important factor relates to the patient's spiritual or religious needs. In a nursing study of hemodialysis patients' needs, according to family perception, one of those most frequently identified was the patients' desire to feel "cared for" by their nurses (C. D. Wagner, 1996). A paper exploring successful aging among chronic renal disease patients included the concept of spirituality within the study framework as a "foundational coping process": "the process describes a person's view and feelings regarding a higher power and the extent of spiritual awareness" (Blevins & Troutman, 2011, p. 257). These authors advised that the identified theory of successful aging, which included spirituality, could be "utilized to assist nurses with enhancing and promoting successful aging" among CRF patients (p. 260). For CRF patients "who live totally dependent upon [technology] for their continued existence, the need for truly caring nursing staff is key. For these patients, also, the quality of life may become questionable"; thus, a multiplicity of spiritual or ethical concerns can result for patients and families (O'Brien, 1983, p. 35).

One early study of religious faith and long-term adaptation to CRF revealed that 78 percent of the 126 maintenance hemodialysis patients studied believed that religious beliefs were to some degree associated with their ability to cope with CRF and the related treatment regimen (O'Brien, 1983). Open-ended questioning of the same group of study respondents produced comments such as, "I knew everything would be alright [after cardiac arrest] because I asked God to carry me through. I know that He's got His arms around me." Another patient, after reporting that faith had been very important in coping with the illness, asserted, "A lot of people couldn't have gone through what I went through without faith in God" (O'Brien, 1982, p. 76).

For the CRF patient, often it is the therapeutic regimen, especially if consisting of maintenance hemodialysis carried out in a dialysis center, that is the most trying. One new hemodialysis patient admitted that the treatment regimen was the most difficult part of the CRF experience. "I pray to God all the time to help me stay on my treatment and to do what I have to do." The remarks of several other hemodialysis patients reflected a similar theme. "Without my religious faith, I couldn't make it"; "Religious faith really helps you go on"; "Without faith I don't know what I'd do"; and "If it hadn't been for my religion, I wouldn't even be here now" (O'Brien, 1983, p. 37).

Spiritual nursing care for the CRF maintenance dialysis patient should incorporate some element of spiritual or religious support that facilitates coping with the altered quality of life imposed by the disease and its treatment regimen. Virtually all dialysis patients report moderate to severe symptoms of fatigue and general malaise that periodically interfere with social and professional or work activities. As Joseph, a young businessman, described:

> You have to pull yourself up and do for yourself. You can't keep waiting for everybody else. Sometimes when I get up in the morning I feel bad, but I just get up and go to my business and make myself keep busy. You have to accept the fact that your kidneys are gone but you can still do things. A lot of it's in your own head, how you feel about it, how you accept it. (O'Brien, 1983, p. 40)

For a CRF patient who adheres to the theology of Reform Judaism, such as Joseph, a dimension of spiritual care might consist in exploring how his religious tradition views God's role in trials such as chronic illness. Joseph stated that "how you feel about" the illness influences "how you accept it." A comforting Scripture for Joseph might be Isaiah 43:2 ("When you pass through raging waters") or Jeremiah 29:11–12 ("For I know well the plans I have in mind for you, says the Lord, plans for your welfare, not for woe. Plans to give you a future full of hope."). Such a reading might provide the opportunity to discuss the need for hope in light of the CRF diagnosis and therapeutic regimen.

▶ Spiritual Needs of the Mentally Challenged

The Person with Mental Illness

Mental health and mental illness are relative terms, existing along a continuum of attitude and behavior; the label mental illness covers a vast array of diagnostic categories, ranging from mild conditions, such as situational anxiety and depression, to the frank psychosis of schizophrenic disorders. The concepts are culturally determined also. What may be considered pathologic in one society, such as the trancelike states entered into during some West Indian religious rituals, is normal according to the perception of that particular community. In order to determine functional mental status, some factors to be evaluated include "level of consciousness, orientation, memory, mood and affect, intellectual performance, judgement and insight and language and communication" (Bruegge, 1997, p. 715). Problems in any of these areas may reflect a deficit in one's mental health, whether of a temporary or a more lasting nature.

Mental health viewed from a Christian perspective is defined as "a state of dynamic equilibrium characterized by hope, joy and peace, in which positive self-regard is developed through love, relationship, forgiveness and meaning and purpose resulting from a vital relationship with God, and a responsible interdependence with others" (Shelly & John, 1983, p. 27). In exploring mental health for the person who does not embrace a monotheistic spirituality, this definition may be modified in terms of relationship with a deity.

The standards of psychiatric mental health nursing identify spiritual variables as important to the nurse, who is advised to be attentive to the "interpersonal, systemic, sociocultural, spiritual or environmental circumstances or events which affect the mental and emotional well-being of an individual, family or community" (American Nurses Association, 1994, as cited in Carson, 1997, p. 144). Nurses who work with those categorized as mentally ill admit that assessing spiritual needs for the psychiatric patient is a difficult task. Frequently, the patient's manifestation of spiritual concerns is considered to be "part of the client's pathology" (Mickley, Carson, & Soeken, 1995; Peterson & Nelson, 1987, p. 34). Assessing the psychiatric patient's spiritual needs may be confounded by the individual's altered thought processes (Varcarolis, 1994; Walgrove, 1996), including religious delusions and hallucinations (Fontaine, 1995b, p. 305). Judith Shelly (1983) pointed out, however, that it is precisely the fact that so many psychiatric clients do manifest religiously oriented delusions or distortions in thinking that highlights the presence of spiritual need (p. 55). Shelly observed, "Clients tend to distort only those things that are intensely meaningful to them" (p. 56). It is important, in providing spiritual care to the mentally disturbed, that a nurse understand how a patient's religious or spiritual beliefs may interact with illness symptoms. For example, in the case of an individual who perceives suffering as a penance for past sins, prayer may be "as much a part" of the healing as therapy (Shoemaker, 1996, p. 298). Another facet of mental illness, which may be supported by prayer, is that of loss of faith in God or a distancing from God, which is "a common occurrence during depressive episodes" (Fontaine, 1995a, p. 243). Suggesting the use of prayer to a client needs to be done judiciously, related to the individual's personal spiritual and religious tradition; for the client with a theistic worldview, however, prayer is identified as "one of the main spiritual tools for seeking God's help" (Walsh & Carson, 1996, p. 498). The lack of attention to spiritual care in some instances of mental health nursing has been associated with reliance on a medical model of care (Greasley, Chiu, & Gartland, 2001). It is suggested, nevertheless, that spiritual needs must be included in effective mental health nursing practice (Fry, 1998; Weaver, Flannelly, Koenig, & Larson, 1998).

To assist the nurse in distinguishing a psychiatric client's spiritual needs from those directly related to his or her mental health condition, John (1983) suggested a series of questions relating to such issues as whether a person's religious belief or behavior seems to contribute to the illness, whether religious concerns reflect a pathologic inner conflict, whether religious beliefs and behavior bring comfort or distress, and whether religion is used merely as a context for psychotic delusions (pp. 81–83). In the case of a religiously oriented delusion, the role of the person providing spiritual care is to "support the person but not the delusion" (W. Wagner, 1992, p. 156). A case example offered by Wagner is that of a psychiatric patient who asserted that because he has not done God's will, God has "taken away his brain"; the patient questioned whether God will give it back. In this situation, Wagner contended, the spiritual caregiver should focus not on the delusion or any interpretations, but rather "support the reality of God's continued love and care" for the patient (p. 156). As noted throughout this discussion, a different strategy of spiritual support will need to be provided for the psychiatric client who is not from a monotheistic religious tradition.

An example of a nursing diagnosis associated with a moderately serious condition such as mood disorder is "spiritual distress related to no purpose or joy in life; lack of connectedness to others; misperceived guilt" (Fontaine, 1995a, p. 253). Assessment of decreased spiritual well-being, associated with depression in older women, is also a diagnosis amenable to nursing intervention (Morris, 1996).

Angela McBride (1996) emphasized caring as a key dimension of the psychiatric-mental health nurse's role (p. 7); caring includes sensitivity to the values, beliefs, and practices of an individual, which is identified as the "first step" toward nursing competence in the provision of spiritual care for the patient with a mental health deficit (Campinha-Bacote, 1995, p. 24). In a study of 50 psychiatric–mental health nurses, the nurses' personal spiritual perspectives were found to be notably high (Pullen, Tuck, & Mix, 1996, p. 85). Spiritual interventions reported by the mental health nurses included "being with," or spending time with, the client; "doing for," or employing personal and environmental resources to care for the client; "encouraging the client to look inward for strength"; and "encouraging the client to look outward for people and objects that could be resources" (Tuck, Pullen, & Lynn, 1997, p. 351). The research of Awara and Fasey (2008) supports the value of providing spiritual care to the psychiatric outpatient population; and Wilding, Muir-Cochrane, and May's (2006) study of spirituality and mental health nursing concluded that mentally ill patients "wanted to discuss their experiences of spirituality" (p. 144). Spiritual care approaches for the dementia patient were identified by Bephage (2008).

An article published by the American Psychiatric Association entitled "Psychiatrists Urge More Direct Focus on Patients' Spirituality" noted, "Many patients have spiritual needs that when addressed in psychiatric treatment help unearth important existential issues and strengthen the therapeutic relationship" (Bender, 2004). A 2012 edition of a text on contemporary psychiatric nursing practice contains an entire chapter devoted to "Cultural and Spiritual Issues Related to Mental Health Care." The author, nursing professor Mary Ann Boyd, points out that "both spirituality and religion are factors that influence beliefs about mental illness" as well as having an "impact on treatment and recovery" (p. 24). Boyd asserts that "religion and spirituality can provide support and strength in dealing with mental illnesses and emotional problems" (p. 26). Some examples of spiritual interventions appropriate for nurses include "guided imagery" and "when appropriate, prayer" (p. 26).

Spirituality is considered the "heart of caring" (Aaron, 2008) and the strength of "whole person care" (Diggins, 2012) for patients dealing with mental health challenges. While it can admittedly be challenging for health-care professionals to sort out the meaning of spiritual concerns and beliefs articulated by some mentally challenged patients, it can also be challenging for the patients. This is reflected in the following comment by a patient: "Well if we talk about our belief systems to a mental health professional, we find that our medication dose is substantially increased" (Gilbert, Kaur, & Parkes, 2010, p. 29). Spirituality can be incorporated into mental health practice, however, in a number of creative ways. One example is described in the paper "Integrating Spirituality into Mental Health Rehabilitation" (Lloyd & O'Connor, 2007). Another model is presented by Janice Clarke (2010), who urges a holistic approach to mental health, employing a threefold conceptualization that consists of "soul (which contains the mind), spirit and body" (p. 649). "All three aspects," Clarke notes, "are connected in a constant dynamic cycle" (p. 649).

The challenge of incorporating a patient's spiritual beliefs into a mental health nursing assessment is addressed by Ruth Elliott (2011), who proposes some potential strategies to overcome a nurse's personal bias or prejudice. Elliott suggests the use of "recognized assessment methods to assess someone's spiritual beliefs" (p. 10) but admits that these have limitations and recommends further research on the topic. Perhaps one of the most difficult clinical conditions for which to assess spiritual beliefs is that of the patient with dementia. While the dementia patient may have the same spiritual needs as any ill person, complicating factors need to be considered, such as "expanding experience of discontinuation, which means not knowing places, names and faces, as well as declining memories" (Jolly, 2011, p. 388). However, in a study of dementia patients who scored "12 or more on the Mini Mental State Examination," 29 study participants "rated their beliefs as strong and considered practices associated with their beliefs to be very important" (Jolly et al., 2010, p. 311). The research team recommended that "service providers should integrate questions about spirituality and faith into their routine assessments and structure care plans to accommodate identified spiritual needs" (p. 311).

Specific spiritual care interventions for the psychiatric client will vary greatly, depending not only on the patient's identified needs, but also on personal spiritual and religious history. For this patient population, especially, the nurse will need to employ the art, as well as the science, of nursing.

Mathias Johnson was a 66-year-old patient suffering from moderate depression associated with a multiplicity of physical ailments, as well as financial and situational stressors. Mr. Johnson's chart identified him as Baptist, although he admitted that he was not a frequent church attender. After spending about 15 minutes visiting with Mr. Johnson, during which time he spoke briefly about faith, his nurse Beth asked if he would like her to say a prayer before leaving. Mr. Johnson nodded in the affirmative. Beth took Mr. Johnson's hand and offered a brief prayer, asking God to give Mr. Johnson strength and comfort during his illness; she also prayed that God would let the patient feel his love and care. As Beth was concluding the prayer, she noticed that tears were streaming down Mr. Johnson's face; she handed him a tissue without comment. After taking a few deep breaths, Mr. Johnson looked up and said with a smile, "Thank you, I really needed that!"

Attempting to analyze and understand the spiritual needs of a mentally ill patient, especially a depressed individual, is extremely challenging to the nurse. Much time may be spent in simply encouraging the patient to verbalize his or her concerns. During the interaction, however, the nurse can communicate a sense of care and empathy, sometimes opening the door to the possibility of therapeutic intervention in the area of spiritual need.

The Cognitively Impaired Client

Cognitive functioning affects both physical and psychosocial dimensions of an individual's life. Although cognition is "primarily an intellectual and perceptual process, [it is] closely integrated with . . . emotional and spiritual values" (Arnold, 1996, p. 977). The cognitively disabled person may have been diagnosed from infancy with some degree or type of mental retardation; cognitive processes may have been injured during childhood or early to middle adulthood as a result of illness or traumatic injury; or a cognitive disability may have its onset only in the elder years, in cases such as senile dementia.

In the past, the religious community has raised some concern about the role of the cognitively disabled individual in the church or worship setting. Some have questioned whether a person who is not cognitively functional can have a relationship with God, much less understand the meaning of religious practices. Reverend John Swinton (1997), a minister and former psychiatric–mental health nurse, admitted that theological confusion still exists about the spiritual and religious capabilities of persons with profound cognitive disabilities, and that some believe that to allow "sacramental participation without intellectual comprehension is dishonoring to God" (p. 21). Swinton argued, however, that "faith is not an intellectual exercise but relational reality," and that relationship to God is for any of us a mystery beyond intellectual understanding (pp. 21–22). True affective understanding of God, Swinton concluded, occurs at a much more interior level than that of intellectual comprehension (p. 23). Swinton's position is supported by ethicist Stanley Hauerwas (1995), who pointed out that, although including cognitively handicapped persons in worship services may not be easy, the extent to which they may bring about the unexpected is a reminder that "the God we worship is not easily domesticated" (p. 60). Hauerwas contended that "in worship the church is made vulnerable to a God who would rule this world not by coercion but by the unpredictability of love" (p. 60).

In a video entitled *We Are One Flock*, produced by the National Catholic Office for Persons with Disabilities (1990), a young woman with Down syndrome is shown assisting with the distribution of the Holy Eucharist during Mass. Her comments after the service reflect the validity of her active participation in the Eucharistic liturgy. "My idea about God is you feel it in your heart. When you really love God and you know He's around you, you feel it in your heart. And I feel it when I'm singing and when I'm ministering, and that brings me close to God, really close when I'm ministering."

A magnificent example of spiritual care for the profoundly cognitively impaired is that carried out in L'Arche (the Ark) communities founded by French Canadian philosopher Jean Vanier. Vanier (1975) began his work during a visit to the small town of Trosly, France, when he moved into a house with two mentally handicapped men. Gradually, other mentally challenged persons began to come, together with volunteers to live with and care for them. New L'Arche communities started to flourish under Vanier's spiritual philosophy of responsibility to care for one's brothers and sisters; this caring was to be done as in a family, where all are accepted and equal as God's children. Henri Nouwen (1988), who spent his later years living in a L'Arche community in Canada, wrote, "Today, L'Arche is a word that inspires thousands of people all over the world . . . its vision is a source of hope" (p. 13).

Evelyn, a veteran of 30 years in nursing, reported that she had worked for the past 13 years in an intermediate care facility (ICF), for the profoundly mentally retarded. Evelyn described her first encounter with the ICF patients:

The youngest was about 12 and that's around the age my children were. They looked strange, and they acted strange. I didn't have any experience in this field of nursing. And I said, "I will never be able to do this!" I questioned God. I said, "Why? I just can't see the value of their lives. This is just too sad." . . . Every day I would walk home from work and every day I would cry, because I felt like I wouldn't ever be able to help them. I wouldn't ever have any impact on their lives. But then one day something just started to happen, and I started to realize how they were God's children and they began to have an impact on my life. And then, I began to see that each one has their own personality. They became special to me. And I started to think that even if they live on earth for only 20 or 30 years, they are going to live in heaven forever . . .

Now they serve such purpose in my life, I couldn't imagine living my life without them. They have become so unique. Now I try to give them spiritual care. I try to anticipate their needs; I try to communicate with them and they do communicate, even if it is nonverbal . . .

I don't get to do as much "hands on" as I would like to but when I do it's such a gift. I'm so grateful. There is something so holy. You say, "this person is completely dependent upon my hands and my compassion to be cared for." They depend solely upon you. If you let yourself be used by God, this is what spiritual care means to me.

Another ICF nurse, Sarah, commented that her Jewish faith supported her spiritual care of cognitively impaired patients. "I don't believe that God is sitting up somewhere looking down on us, but I believe He is all around us. I believe that the Spirit of goodness and giving all around us is God; that's how I live spirituality." Sarah spoke about her interaction with the ICF patients. "I talk to them as people, even the very lowest cognitively functioning person is still a person, so I try to explain things to them. I also try to see that they get the best possible care that we can give. I think there is a 'spirituality of touch' in the holding and the caring. I know we can't change their abilities, but we can make sure the quality of their lives is as good as possible." Sarah concluded, "I think that the patients understand a lot more than we think sometimes. I think we can bring our spirituality and our God to them, even though we think it is beyond their intellectual functioning ability. I think my caring brings them spirituality."

Marti, another nurse who had worked with cognitively impaired young adults for many years, added, "I feel very humble in working with the MRDD [mentally retarded, developmentally disabled] population. I know their intelligence and cognitive functioning isn't where ours is, but they have a perception of reality that is childlike and Godlike all at the same time. I think touching them and loving them is spiritual care."

▶ Spiritual Needs in Physical Disability and Rehabilitation

Who are those persons on whom our society imposes the label "disabled"? Theologian Michael Downey (1993) believes that, excluding those who may temporarily require special attention such as infants and young children, the very elderly, and persons incapacitated for a time due to illness or accident, the term *disabled* generally describes individuals who are to some degree permanently impaired (p. 273). Downey (1993) defined the disabled as those persons "whose capacities of mind or body are diminished in any way during the pre, peri or post-natal period or at some later period in the course of psychosomatic development, so as to necessitate particular attention or special assistance in meeting basic human needs" (p. 273).

It should be pointed out that among 21st-century persons living with physical challenges there is some disagreement about the use of the term *disabled*. Some individuals feel that the disability label is pejorative and do not wish it used to describe their conditions; these persons prefer to call themselves *differently abled* or *other-abled*. However, there is another school of thought among some persons with physical deficits who feel that the concept of "disability" is not negative but rather an important descriptor in defining and clarifying their functional abilities. In attempting to determine the spiritual needs of one who is physically challenged it is important for a nurse to discern how that individual wishes to be viewed and labeled. For the following discussion of physical deficits and rehabilitation the classic term *disability* is being used.

Disability may affect all dimensions of an individual's life: physical, social, emotional, and spiritual. The goal of rehabilitation is to return to the disabled person as much pre-illness functioning in each of those life arenas as possible. Ultimately the goal of the rehabilitation process is to help an individual regain as much independence as possible. In analyzing the "anatomy of illness," Schreiter (1988) posited that experiencing illness for a disabled person is like taking a long journey to an unknown country: "disabled persons leave behind their accustomed ways of relating to their bodies, their friends, their workplaces, their families" (p. 7). J. L. McBride and Armstrong (1995) suggested, additionally, that while no standardized tests currently exist to measure "spiritual damage," "something does happen to the spiritual development of a person who is traumatized" (p. 7). Theologian Donald Senior (1995) pointed out that although an authentic response would be to bear the illness in a "spirit of Faith," persons with disabilities need spiritual support in the process of achieving fullness of life (p. 17). Even though Congress passed the Americans with Disabilities Act (ADA) in 1990, making it illegal to discriminate against the handicapped, individuals who make up our churches have not always internalized a supportive attitude for the disabled (Krafft, 1988).

In a book discussing the "psychospiritual aspects of rehabilitation," Carolyn Vash (1994) observed that "disability is a symbol we all fear"; this, she asserted, is why religion has not well supported the disabled (p. 49). Vash demonstrated through numerous examples from history that disabled individuals such as Helen Keller can use adversity to achieve significant life goals. The rehabilitation nurse may refer to such role models in providing spiritual care.

The concept of spiritual care is an appropriate dimension of rehabilitation nursing, which is concerned with the promotion of client wholeness (Solimine & Hoeman, 1996, p. 628). Some suggested spiritual interventions for a disabled patient experiencing rehabilitation are recommending a spiritual counselor; providing prayer materials, as denominationally appropriate; and introducing imagery, music, or meditative prayer to the client (Solimine & Hoeman, 1996, p. 636). In regard to the latter activity, Solimine and Hoeman suggested that through prayer, disabled individuals are able to give over their situation to God and "trade their weakness for God's strength" (p. 631). Accardi (1990) suggested three other pastoral care interventions for the disabled: listening to the patient's "spiritually significant stories," that is, walking with the patient on his or her spiritual journey; "indwelling the stories," or expressing the empathy and compassion that results from entering into another's pain; and "linking the stories" with biblical references that may help the person find meaning in, or the ability to transcend, the disability (p. 91).

For the rehabilitation patient not associated with a religious tradition that employs devotional practices, Boucher (1989) suggested that spiritual care may draw on such basic needs as "the need to belong, to feel attachment to a person or group, to reach out beyond oneself, to have a meaningful life, and to be creative" (p. 46). In general, spiritual care of the disabled person must focus on the acceptance of present life circumstances as a basis for future growth and accomplishment (Saylor, 1991). Some related activities include maximizing the client's wellness and assisting him or her to move out of the sick role, supporting the client's present talents and abilities, teaching the client to conserve energy and to avoid focusing on deficits, and promoting activities that enhance self-esteem (Davidhizar & Shearer, 1997, pp. 132–133).

An article entitled "Dance of Disability and Spirituality" presents the findings of in-depth interviews with 13 adults with physical disabilities. In general, the study participants "described disability and spirituality as essential, interactive dimensions of their lives . . . all but one participant expressed strong beliefs related to a higher being and all participants stressed the influence of these beliefs on their lives as a person with disability" (Boswell, Hamer, Knight, Glacoff, & McChesney, 2007, p. 35). The researchers concluded that "the interaction of spirituality and disability unfolded in the lives of these participants as a dance in which both partners influence the direction and rhythm of the steps. This interaction was characterized by five major themes: purpose, awareness, connections, creativity and acceptance" (p. 39). And, in a 2011 study exploring the needs of people with learning disabilities, clinical psychologist Claire Wilson found that spirituality was a "neglected topic across the lifespan for people with a learning disability" (p. 31). Through a series of questions, Wilson found that parents, service managers, and faith-based professionals believed that concern for a patient's spiritual needs was "a legitimate topic for health care professionals to inquire about during clinical contacts" (p. 31).

The rehabilitation nurse may employ usual spiritual assessment skills to determine the religious beliefs and practices and spiritual support system of the patient prior to the occurrence of the disability (Davis, 1994, p. 298). The point, of course, is to help the disabled patient return to former spiritual and religious practices to the degree possible. Because the rehabilitation nurse may have more time to provide spiritual care than a nurse in an acute illness setting, Clifford and Gruca (1987) suggested setting aside time to discuss spiritual needs and concerns with the client, reading meditations or poetry to the client, or playing spiritual music (p. 332).

Two nurses who worked in a rehabilitation setting with partially disabled persons described their perceptions of spiritual care. One reported:

> For me, rehabilitation nursing of patients has to do with spiritual care, with establishing the quality of their lives. One patient considers himself rehabilitated because he can walk from his house to his car; now he can get out. To him that establishes his need to be connected to people.

A second nurse added:

> Spiritual care is about quality of life, and quality of life is whatever the patient wants to make it. I have a patient who is very disabled. He can't

walk, so they got him a wheelchair with a motor on it, so he can get around and do his church work . . . that's what makes his quality of life. (O'Brien, 1983, p. 41)

▶ Spiritual Needs of the Client in the Community

Nursing care of the client in the community is carried out in the overall context of community health nursing, which is identified as "a synthesis of nursing practice and public health practice applied to promoting and preserving the health of populations" (American Nurses Association, 1980, cited in Nies & Swanson, 1997, p. 10). The American Nurses Association (ANA) definition goes on to explain that the primary responsibility of community health nursing is to the community as a whole or aggregate nursing (Nies & Swanson, 1997). In discussing the role of the community health nurse in providing spiritual care to clients, Burkhardt and Nagai-Jacobson (1985) advised that three questions may guide the initial assessment of need: Does the client's formal religious tradition or denomination provide a good structure for spiritual care? Does the way in which the client speaks or does not speak of God reveal spiritual concerns or needs? and Do the client's religious contacts seem to provide strength and comfort? (p. 194). The answers to such questions can then lead the nurse to a more detailed spiritual assessment and plans for intervention, if needed.

This section focuses on one specific dimension of community health nursing: spiritual needs of the home health-care client.

The Home Health-Care Client

McNamara (1982) defined *home health care* as "that component of comprehensive health care where services are provided to individuals and families in their places of residence for the purpose of promoting, maintaining or restoring health or minimizing the effects of illness and disability" (p. 61). Some examples of clients receiving home health care include acutely ill patients, especially those suffering from AIDS; terminally ill clients; the frail elderly; and at-risk women and children (Lyon, Bolla, & Nies, 1997, pp. 798–799). A primary component of home health care is nursing care, which is one of the largest contemporary nursing practice areas. Home health-care nurses help clients manage their prescribed plans of care and also help them cope with the social and environmental factors that may influence the course of illness and treatment (T. Smith, 1997).

Dealing with illness in the home, the client or family has to coordinate the meeting of a multiplicity of needs that may require such items as medications, medical supplies, special diet, or physical therapy equipment; the nurse can serve as advisor in obtaining necessary therapeutic materials (Humphrey, 1994, p. 1). Some home health-care clients are acutely ill, some have chronic debilitating health problems, and many are elderly. An individual must be seriously ill, homebound, and "in need of skilled nursing services" to receive home health care (Smeltzer & Bare, 1996, p. 18). A significant role identified for the home health nurse is that of client advocate (LeMone & Burke, 1996, p. 54); this title lends itself well to the inclusion of spiritual care as an appropriate activity in home health nursing.

Spiritual assessment and, if appropriate, the provision of spiritual care, are important activities for the home health nurse, as "hope and faith" have been identified as playing a major role in the home care client's adaptation to illness or disability (Rice, 1996, p. 47). Jaffe and Skidmore-Roth (1993) suggested several issues to be addressed in a spiritual assessment of the home health-care patient: religious beliefs and practice, how one's belief (or lack of belief) in a supreme being relates to illness, specific people who provide spiritual support, religious symbols of importance (e.g., a Bible or Sabbath candles), religious restrictions (dietary, medical treatment), requirements for church attendance, and religious leaders (pp. 42–43). Bauer and Barron (1995) noted that spiritual nursing interventions are particularly important for the elderly client who lives alone in the community with no religiously based support system available; the community health nurse may be the only visitor who is able and willing to discuss spiritual issues with such a client. In their research with elderly community-based clients, Bauer and Barron found that older individuals especially wanted nurses to be respectful, caring, and sensitive to their religious beliefs and traditions.

Dorothy, a community health nurse for more than 17 years, described the caring relationship she developed in providing spiritual care to clients:

> In my clinical practice in community health, it's like the "I–thou" relationship, where you give of your own spiritual energy to the people you're working with. You have to respect their beliefs and where they are spiritually, and then go from there. Some people will ask you to pray with them, if they're having a hard time, or they'll say, "think of me," and I think they just want you to send them some energy. Sometimes a patient has something very deep, like being away from their church, and you need to call in a priest or a minister. But that's part of the nurse's job, especially the community health nurse.

Megan, another nurse, with an MSN in community health nursing and 23 years of experience, added:

> You have to be attuned to what the client is saying. Sometimes they don't say it in spiritual words or religious words, but really the thing they need is some spiritual care. You have to listen with your heart to what is behind the words they say.

Personal spirituality and/or religious beliefs and practices may constitute an important mediating variable for the individual coping with a chronic illness. For the chronically ill patient, such concepts as hope, trust, courage, and love may take on new and deeper meaning following the illness onset. Nurses may support and facilitate the presence of positive attitudes and attributes in a patient's life through a variety of spiritual care interventions. As well as providing spiritual care for the hospitalized patient, contemporary nurses need to be sensitive to the spiritual needs and concerns of persons with a variety of other chronic conditions and in a variety of settings.

▶ References

Aaron, M. (2008). Spirituality, the heart of caring. *A Life in the Day, Pavilion Journals, 12*(4), 23–26.

Accardi, R. F. (1990). Rehabilitation: Dreams lost, dreams found. In H. Hayes & C. J. van der Poel (Eds.), *Health care ministry: A handbook for chaplains* (pp. 88–92). New York, NY: Paulist Press.

Adegbola, M. (2007). Spirituality and quality of life in chronic illness. *The Journal of Theory Construction & Testing, 10*(2), 42–46.

AIDS Ministry Program, the Archdiocese of St. Paul and Minneapolis. (1991). *For those we love: A spiritual perspective on AIDS.* Cleveland, OH: The Pilgrim Press.

American Nurses Association. (1980). *A conceptual model of community health nursing* (ANA publication #CHI0). Kansas City, MO: Author.

American Nurses Association. (1994). *A statement on psychiatric–mental health clinical nursing practice and standards of psychiatric–mental health clinical nursing practice.* Washington, DC: Author.

Arnold, E. N. (1996). The journey clouded by cognitive disorders. In V. B. Carson & E. N. Arnold (Eds.), *Mental health nursing: The nurse–patient journey* (pp. 977–1019). Philadelphia, PA: W. B. Saunders.

Awara, M., & Fasey, C. (2008). Is spirituality worth exploring in psychiatric outpatient clinics? *Journal of Mental Health, 17*(2), 183–191.

Baldacchino, D., & Draper, P. (2001). Spiritual coping strategies: A review of the nursing research literature. *Journal of Advanced Nursing, 34*(6), 833–841.

Bauer, T., & Barron, C. R. (1995). Nursing interventions for spiritual care. *Journal of Holistic Nursing, 13*(3), 268–279.

Belcher, A. E., Dettmore, D., & Holzemer, S. P. (1989). Spirituality and sense of well-being in persons with AIDS. *Holistic Nurse Practice, 3*(4), 16–25.

Bender, E. (2004). Psychiatrists urge more direct focus on patients' spirituality. *Psychiatric News, 39*(12), 30.

Bephage, G. (2008). Care approaches to spirituality and dementia. *Nursing & Residential Care, 10*(3), 134–137.

Blanchard, J., Dunlap, D., & Fitchett, G. (2012). Screening for spiritual distress in the oncology inpatient: A quality improvement pilot project between nurses and chaplains. *Journal of Nursing Management, 20*(8), 1076–1084.

Blevins, C., & Troutman, M. (2011). Successful aging theory and the patient with chronic renal disease: Application in the clinical setting. *Nephrology Nursing Journal, 38*(3), 255–270.

Boswell, B., Hamer, M., Knight, S., Glacoff, M., & McChesney, J. (2007). Dance of disability and spirituality. *Journal of Rehabilitation, 73*(4), 33–40.

Boucher, R. J. (1989). Nursing process. In S. S. Dittmar (Ed.), *Rehabilitation nursing: Process and application* (pp. 45–62). St. Louis, MO: C. V. Mosby.

Boutell, K. A., & Bozeht, F. W. (1988). Nurses' assessment of patients' spirituality: Continuing education implications. *Journal of Continuing Education in Nursing, 21*(4), 172–176.

Boyd, M. A. (2012). Cultural and spiritual issues related to mental health care. In M. A. Boyd (Ed.), *Psychiatric nursing, contemporary practice* (5th ed., pp. 21–28). Philadelphia, PA: Lippincott, Williams & Wilkins.

Bruegge, M. V. (1997). Assessment of clients with neurologic disorders. In J. M. Black & E. Matassmarin-Jacobs (Eds.), *Medical–surgical nursing: Clinical management for continuity of care* (5th ed., pp. 709–742). Philadelphia, PA: W. B. Saunders.

Burkhardt, M. A., & Nagai-Jacobson, M. G. (1985). Dealing with spiritual concerns of clients in the community. *Journal of Community Health Nursing, 2*(4), 191–198.

Burnard, P. (1988, December). Discussing spiritual issues with clients. *Health Visitor, 61*, 371–372.

Campinha-Bacote, J. (1995). Spiritual competence: A model of psychiatric care. *Journal of Christian Nursing, 12*(3), 22–44.

Carr, T. (2009). Mapping the processes and qualities of spiritual nursing care. *Qualitative Health Research, 18*(5), 686–700.

Carson, V. B. (1989). Spiritual development across the lifespan. In V. B. Carson (Ed.), *Spiritual dimensions of nursing practice* (pp. 24–51). Philadelphia, PA: W. B. Saunders.

Carson, V. B. (1997). Spirituality and patient care. In A. W. Burgess (Ed.), *Psychiatric nursing: Promoting mental health* (pp. 143–149). Stamford, CT: Appleton & Lange.

Carson, V. B., Soeken, K. L., Shanty, J., & Terry, L. (1990). Hope and spiritual well-being: Essentials for living with AIDS. *Perspective in Psychiatric Care, 26*(2), 28–34.

Cassidy, J. (1992, April). What keeps people well? A new paradigm for pastoral care. *Health Progress, 73*(3), 34–36.

Christensen, M. J. (1991). *The Samaritans imperative: Compassionate ministry to people living with AIDS.* Nashville, TN: Abington Press.

Clarke, J. (2010). Body and soul in mental health care. *Mental Health, Religion and Culture, 13*(6), 649–657.

Clifford, M., & Gruca, J. (1987). Facilitating spiritual care in the rehabilitation setting. *Rehabilitation Nursing, 12*(6), 331–333.

Corbin, J. (1996). Chronic illness. In S. C. Smeltzer & B. G. Bare (Eds.), *Brunner and Suddarth's textbook of medical–surgical nursing* (8th ed., pp. 317–324). Philadelphia, PA: J. B. Lippincott.

Crowther, C. E. (1991). *AIDS: A Christian handbook.* London, UK: Epworth Press.

Davidhizar, R., & Shearer, R. (1997). Helping the client with chronic disability achieve high level wellness. *Rehabilitation Nursing, 22*(3), 131–134.

Davis, M. C. (1994). The rehabilitation nurse's role in spiritual care. *Rehabilitation Nursing, 19*(5), 298–301.

Delgado, C. (2007). Sense of coherence, spirituality, stress and quality of life in chronic illness. *Journal of Nursing Scholarship, 39*(3), 229–234.

Diggins, K. (2012). Hope yields health: Offering whole person care. *Journal of Christian Nursing, 29*(1), 11–12.

Downey, M. (Ed.). (1993). Disability: The disabled. In M. Downey (Ed.), *The new dictionary of Catholic spirituality* (pp. 273–274). Collegeville, MN: The Liturgical Press.

Dreyer, E. (1993). Love. In M. Downey (Ed.), *The new dictionary of Catholic spirituality* (pp. 612–622). Collegeville, MN: The Liturgical Press.

Dwyer, J. A. (1990). Peace. In J. A. Komonchak, M. Collins, & D. A. Lane (Eds.), *The new dictionary of theology* (pp. 748–753). Collegeville, MN: The Liturgical Press.

Egan, R., McKechnie, R., Jobson, J., Herbison, P., & Richards, R. (2013). Perspectives on psychosocial and spiritual cancer support services in New Zealand. *Journal of Psychosocial Oncology, 31*(1), 659–674.

Ekedahl, M., & Wengstrom, Y. (2010). Caritas, spirituality and religiosity in nurses' coping. *European Journal of Cancer Care, 19*, 530–537.

Elliott, R. (2011). Spirituality, mental health nursing and assessment. *Journal of Community Nursing, 25*(3), 4–10.

Ellis, C. (1986, April). Course prepares nurses to meet patients' spiritual needs. *Health Progress, 9*(1), 76–77.

Fatula, M. A. (1993). Faith. In M. Downey (Ed.), *The new dictionary of Catholic spirituality* (pp. 379–390). Collegeville, MN: The Liturgical Press.

Flaherty, M. J., & O'Brien, M. E. (1992). Family styles of coping in end-stage renal disease. *ANNA Journal, 19*(4), 345–350.

Fontaine, K. L. (1995a). Mood disorders. In K. L. Fontaine & J. S. Fletcher (Eds.), *Essentials of mental health nursing* (3rd ed., pp. 236–258). New York, NY: Addison-Wesley.

Fontaine, K. L. (1995b). Schizophrenic disorders. In K. L. Fontaine & J. S. Fletcher (Eds.), *Essentials of mental health nursing* (3rd ed., pp. 300–321). New York, NY: Addison-Wesley.

Forbis, P. A. (1988). Meeting patients' spiritual needs. *Geriatric Nursing, 9*(3), 158–159.

Fry, A. (1998). Spirituality communication and mental health nursing: The tacit interdiction. *Australian New Zealand Journal of Mental Health Nursing, 7*(1), 25–32.

Gewe, A. (1994). Hope: Moving from theory to practice. *Journal of Christian Nursing, 11*(4), 18–21.

Gilbert, P., Kaur, N., & Parkes, M. (2010, October). Let's get spiritual. *Mental Health Today, 20*(6), 28–33.

Greasley, P., Chiu, L. F., & Gartland, M. (2001). The concept of spiritual care in mental health nursing. *Journal of Advanced Nursing, 33*(5), 629–637.

Greenstreet, W. (2006). From spirituality to coping strategy: Making sense of chronic illness. *British Journal of Nursing, 15*(17), 938–942.

Halstead, M. T., & Hull, M. (2001). Struggling with paradoxes: The process of spiritual development in women with cancer. *Oncology Nursing Forum, 28*(10), 1534–1544.

Hauerwas, S. (1995). The church and mentally handicapped persons: A continuing challenge to the imagination. In M. Bishop (Ed.), *Religion as a disability: Essays in scripture, theology and ethics* (pp. 46–64). Kansas City, MO: Shead & Ward.

Hellwig, M. K. (1993). Hope. In M. Downey (Ed.), *The new dictionary of Catholic spirituality* (pp. 506–515). Collegeville, MN: The Liturgical Press.

Highfield, M. F. (1992). Spiritual health of oncology patients. *Cancer Nursing, 15*(1), 1–8.

Highfield, M. F., & Cason, C. (1983). Spiritual needs of patients: Are they recognized? *Cancer Nursing, 6*(6), 187–192.

Humphrey, C. J. (1994). *Home care nursing handbook*. Gaithersburg, MD: Aspen.

Ignatavicius, D. D., Workman, M. L., & Mishler, M. A. (1995). *Medical–surgical nursing: A nursing process approach*. Philadelphia, PA: W. B. Saunders.

Iles, R. (Ed.). (1989). *The gospel imperative in the midst of AIDS*. Wilton, CT: Morehouse.

Jaffe, M. S., & Skidmore-Roth, L. (1993). *Home health nursing care plans*. St. Louis, MO: C. V. Mosby.

John, S. D. (1983). Assessing spiritual needs. In J. A. Shelly & S. D. John (Eds.), *Spiritual dimensions of mental health* (pp. 73–84). Downers Grove, IL: InterVarsity Press.

Johnson, R. P. (1992). *Body, mind, spirit: Tapping the healing power within you*. Liguori, MO: Liguori Publications.

Jolly, D. (2011). Dementia care: Spiritual and faith perspectives. *Nursing & Residential Care, 13*(8), 388–391.

Jolly, D., Bnebow, S., Grizzell, M., Willmott, S., Bawn, S., & Kingston, P. (2010). Spirituality and faith in dementia. *Dementia, 9*, 311–325.

Kaczorowski, J. M. (1989). Spiritual well-being and anxiety in adults diagnosed with cancer. *The Hospice Journal, 5*(3), 105–116.

Kennison, M. M. (1987). Faith: An untapped health resource. *Journal of Psychosocial Nursing, 25*(10), 28–30.

Kilpatrick, J. A. (1997). Urinary elimination. In P. A. Potter & A. G. Perry (Eds.), *Fundamentals of nursing: Concepts, process and practice* (4th ed., pp. 1293–1334). St. Louis, MO: C. V. Mosby.

Korniewicz, D., & O'Brien, M. E. (1994). Evaluation of a hemodialysis patient education and support program. *ANNA Journal, 21*(1), 33–38.

Krafft, J. (1988). *The ministry to persons with disabilities*. Collegeville, MN: The Liturgical Press.

Lackey, N. R., Gates, M. F., & Brown, G. (2001). African American women's experiences with the initial discovery, diagnosis and treatment of breast cancer. *Oncology Nursing Forum, 28*(3), 519–527.

Landis, B. J. (1996). Uncertainty, spiritual well-being and psychosocial adjustment to chronic illness. *Issues in Mental Health Nursing, 17*(1), 217–231.

LeMone, P., & Burke, K. M. (1996). *Medical–surgical nursing: Critical thinking in client care.* New York, NY: Addison-Wesley.

Le Peau, P. J. (1996). Finding hope when everything's up for grabs. *Journal of Christian Nursing, 13*(1), 16–19.

Lisanti, P., & Zwolski, K. (1997). Understanding the devastation of AIDS. *American Journal of Nursing, 97*(7), 26–34.

Lloyd, C., & O'Connor, C. (2007). Integrating spirituality into mental health rehabilitation. *International Journal of Therapy and Rehabilitation, 14*(4), 168–172.

Lopez, A. J., McCaffrey, R., Griffin, M. T., & Fitzpatrick, J. J. (2009). Spiritual well-being and practices among women with gynecologic cancer. *Oncology Nursing Forum, 36*(3), 300–305.

Lyon, J. C., Bolla, C. D., & Nies, M. A. (1997). The home visit and home health care. In J. M. Swanson & M. A. Nies (Eds.), *Community health nursing: Promoting the health of aggregates* (pp. 798–821). Philadelphia, PA: W. B. Saunders.

MacDonald, B. H. (2001). Quality of life in cancer care: Patients' experiences and nurses' contributions. *European Journal of Oncology Nursing, 5*(1), 32–41.

Matassarin-Jacobs, E. (1997). Nursing care of clients with renal disorders. In J. M. Black & E. Matassarin-Jacobs (Eds.), *Medical–surgical nursing: Clinical management for continuity of care* (5th ed., pp. 1625–1681). Philadelphia, PA: W. B. Saunders.

McBride, A. B. (1996). Psychiatric–mental health nursing in the twenty-first century. In A. B. McBride & J. K. Austin (Eds.), *Psychiatric–mental health nursing* (pp. 1–10). Philadelphia, PA: W. B. Saunders.

McBride, J. L., & Armstrong, G. (1995). The spiritual dynamics of chronic post traumatic stress disorder. *Journal of Religion and Health, 34*(1), 5–16.

McClain, C., Rosenfeld, B., & Breitbart, W. (2003). Effect of spiritual well-being on end-of-life despair in terminally ill cancer patients. *The Lancet, 361*(9369), 1603.

McNamara, E. (1982). Hospitals discover comprehensive home care. *Hospital, 56*(1), 60–66.

McSherry, W. (1996). Raising the spirits. *Nursing Times, 92*(3), 49–50.

Mellors, M. P., Riley, T. A., & Erlen, J. A. (1997). HIV, self-transcendence, and quality of life. *Journal of the Association of Nurses in AIDS Care, 8*(2), 59–69.

Mickley, J. R., Carson, V. B., & Soeken, K. L. (1995). Religion and adult mental health: State of the science in nursing. *Issues in Mental Health Nursing, 16*(1), 345–360.

Mickley, J. R., Soeken, K., & Belcher, A. (1992). Spiritual well-being, religiousness and hope among women with breast cancer. *Image Journal of Nursing Scholarship, 24*(4), 267–272.

Moberg, D. O. (Ed.). (1979). The development of social indicators of spiritual well-being for quality of life research. In *Spiritual well-being: Sociological perspectives* (pp. 1–13). Washington, DC: University Press of America.

Morris, L. E. (1996). A spiritual well-being model: Use with older women who experience depression. *Issues in Mental Health Nursing, 17*(1), 439–455.

Moschella, V. D., Pressman, K. R., Pressman, P., & Weissman, D. E. (1997). The problem of theodicy and religious response to cancer. *Journal of Religion and Health, 36*(1), 17–20.

Muldoon, M. H., & King, J. N. (1991). A spirituality for the long haul: Response to chronic illness. *Journal of Religion and Health, 30*(2), 99–108.

National Catholic Office for Persons with Disabilities. (1990). *We are one flock.* Washington, DC: Author.

Newshan, G. (1998). Transcending the physical: Spiritual aspects of pain in patients with HIV and/or cancer. *Journal of Advanced Nursing, 28*(6), 1236–1241.

Nies, M. A., & Swanson, J. M. (1997). Health: A community view. In J. M. Swanson & M. A. Nies (Eds.), *Community health nursing: Promoting the health of aggregates* (pp. 4–15). Philadelphia, PA: W. B. Saunders.

Nixon, A., Narayanasamy, A., & Penny, V. (2013). An investigation into the spiritual needs of neuro-oncology patients from a nurse perspective. *BMC Nursing, 12*(2), 1–11.

Nouwen, H. (1988). *The road to daybreak: A spiritual journey.* New York, NY: Doubleday.

O'Brien, M. E. (1982). Religious faith and adjustment to long-term hemodialysis. *Journal of Religion and Health, 21*(1), 68–80.

O'Brien, M. E. (1983). *The courage to survive: The life career of the chronic dialysis patient.* New York, NY: Grune & Stratton.

O'Brien, M. E. (1990). Compliance behavior and long-term maintenance dialysis. *American Journal of Kidney Disease, 15*(3), 209–214.

O'Brien, M. E. (1992). *Living with HIV: Experiment in courage.* Westport, CT: Auburn House.

O'Brien, M. E. (1995). *The AIDS challenge: Breaking through the boundaries.* Westport, CT: Auburn House.

O'Brien, M. E., Donley, R., Flaherty, M., & Johnstone, B. (1986). Therapeutic options in end-stage renal disease: A preliminary report. *ANNA Journal, 13*(6), 313–318.

O'Brien, M. E., & Pheifer, W. G. (1993). Physical and psychosocial nursing care for patients with HIV infection. *Nursing Clinics of North America, 28*(2), 303–315.

Odbehr, L., Kvigne, K., Hauge, S., & Danbolt, L. (2014). A qualitative study of nurses' attitudes toward and accommodations of patients' expressions of religiosity and faith in dementia care. *Journal of Advanced Nursing, 71*(2), 359–369.

Overberg, K. R. (Ed.). (1994). *AIDS, ethics and religion: Embracing a world of suffering.* Maryknoll, NY: Orbis Books.

Perelli, R. J. (1991). *Ministry to persons with AIDS.* Minneapolis, MN: Augsburg.

Peterson, E. A., & Nelson, K. (1987). How to meet your client's spiritual needs. *Journal of Psychosocial Nursing, 25*(5), 34–39.

Petty, J. (1997). Basic concepts of neoplastic disorders. In J. M. Black & E. Matassarin-Jacobs (Eds.), *Medical–surgical nursing: Clinical management for continuity of care* (5th ed., pp. 533–590). Philadelphia, PA: W. B. Saunders.

Pullen, L., Tuck, I., & Mix, K. (1996). Mental health nurses' spiritual perspectives. *Journal of Holistic Nursing, 14*(2), 85–97.

Raffay, J. (2014). How staff and patient experience shapes our perception of spiritual care in a psychiatric setting. *Journal of Nursing Management, 22*(7), 940–950.

Rice, R. (Ed.). (1996). Developing the plan of care and documentation. In *Home health nursing practice, concepts and application* (pp. 41–60). St. Louis, MO: C. V. Mosby.

Roche, J. (1992, March). Spiritual care of the person with AIDS. *Health Progress, 73*(2), 78–81.

Ross, L. A. (1994). Spiritual aspects of nursing. *Journal of Advanced Nursing, 9*(1), 437–440.

Russell, L. M. (Ed.). (1990). *The church with AIDS.* Louisville, KY: Westminister/John Knox Press.

Sandin, F. C. (1996). Walking through fire: Fostering faith in times of loss. *Journal of Christian Nursing, 13*(1), 23–26.

Sandys, S. (Ed.). (1993). *Embracing the mystery: A prayerful response to AIDS.* Collegeville, MN: The Liturgical Press.

Saylor, D. E. (1991). Pastoral care of the rehabilitation patient. *Rehabilitation Nursing, 16*(3), 138–140.

Schneider, M. A. (2007). Broadening our perspective on spirituality and coping among women with breast cancer and their families: Implications for practice. *Indian Journal of Palliative Care, 13*(2), 25–31.

Schreiter, R. J. (1988). The faces of suffering. *New Theology Review, 1*(4), 3–14.

Schreiter, R. (1993). Trust. In M. Downey (Ed.), *The new dictionary of Catholic spirituality* (pp. 982–983). Collegeville, MN: The Liturgical Press.

Senior, D. (1995). Beware of the Canaanite woman: Disability and the Bible. In M. Bishop (Ed.), *Religion and disability: Essays in scripture, theology and ethics* (pp. 1–26). Kansas City, MO: Sheed & Ward.

Shelly, J. A. (1983). What are spiritual needs? In J. A. Shelly & S. D. John (Eds.), *Spiritual dimensions of mental health* (pp. 55–60). Downers Grove, IL: InterVarsity Press.

Shelly, J. A., & Fish, S. (1988). *Spiritual care: The nurse's role* (3rd ed.). Downers Grove, IL: InterVarsity Press.

Shelly, J. A., & John, S. D. (1983). *Spiritual dimensions of mental health.* Downers Grove, IL: InterVarsity Press.

Sherman, D. W. (2001). The perceptions and experiences of patients with AIDS: Implications regarding quality of life and palliative care. *Journal of Hospice and Palliative Nursing, 3*(1), 7–16.

Shoemaker, N. (1996). Getting to know the traveler: Mental health assessment. In V. B. Carson & E. N. Arnold (Eds.), *Mental health nursing: The nurse-patient journey* (pp. 273–302). Philadelphia, PA: W. B. Saunders.

Simsen, B. (1988). Nursing the spirit. *Nursing Times, 84*(37), 32–33.

Smeltzer, S. C., & Bare, B. G. (1996). *Brunner and Suddarth's textbook of medical-surgical nursing* (8th ed., pp. 17–24). Philadelphia, PA: J. B. Lippincott.

Smith, T. (1997). Restorative and home health care. In P. A. Potter & A. G. Perry (Eds.), *Fundamentals of nursing: Concepts, process and practice* (4th ed., pp. 79–95). St. Louis, MO: C. V. Mosby.

Smith, W. J. (1988). *AIDS: Issues in pastoral care.* New York, NY: Paulist Press.

Soeken, K. L., & Carson, V. B. (1987). Responding to the spiritual needs of the chronically ill. *Nursing Clinics of North America, 22*(3), 603–611.

Solimine, M. A., & Hoeman, S. P. (1996). Spirituality: A rehabilitation perspective. In S. P. Hoeman (Ed.), *Rehabilitation nursing: Process and application* (2nd ed., pp. 628–643). St. Louis, MO: C. V. Mosby.

Stoll, R. I. (1989). Spirituality and chronic illness. In V. B. Carson (Ed.), *Spiritual dimensions of nursing practice* (pp. 180–216). Philadelphia, PA: W. B. Saunders.

Sunderland, R. H., & Shelp, E. E. (1987). *AIDS: A manual for pastoral care.* Philadelphia, PA: The Westminister Press.

Swinton, J. (1997). Restoring the image: Spirituality, faith and cognitive disability. *Journal of Religion and Health, 36*(1), 21–27.

Taylor, C., Lillis, C., & LeMone, P. (1997). *Fundamentals of nursing: The art and science of nursing care* (3rd ed.). Philadelphia, PA: J. B. Lippincott.

Taylor, E. J., Amenta, M., & Highfield, M. (1995). Spiritual care practices of oncology nurses. *Oncology Nursing Forum, 22*(1), 31–39.

Taylor, E. J., Highfield, M., & Amenta, M. (1994). Attitudes and beliefs regarding spiritual care. *Cancer Nursing, 17*(6), 479–487.

Taylor, E. J., & Mamier, I. (2005). Spiritual care nursing: What cancer patients and family caregivers want. *Journal of Advanced Nursing, 49*(3), 260–267.

Thomas, J., & Retsas, A. (1999). Transacting self-preservation: A grounded theory of the spiritual dimensions of people with terminal cancer. *International Journal of Nursing Studies, 36*(3), 191–201.

Thompson, M. (1994). Nurturing hope: A vital ingredient in nursing. *Journal of Christian Nursing, 11*(4), 11–17.

Tuck, I., Pullen, L., & Lynn, C. (1997). Spiritual interventions provided by mental health nurses. *Western Journal of Nursing Research, 19*(3), 351–363.

Turk, D., & Rudy, T. (1986). Living with chronic disease: The importance of cognitive appraisal. In J. S. McHugh & T. Vallis (Eds.), *Illness behavior: A multidisciplinary model* (pp. 309–320). New York, NY: Plenum Press.

Ungvarski, P. J., & Matassarin-Jacobs, E. (1997). Nursing care of clients with altered immune systems. In J. M. Black & E. Matassarin-Jacobs (Eds.), *Medical-surgical nursing: Clinical management for continuity of care* (5th ed., pp. 614–651). Philadelphia, PA: W. B. Saunders Company.

Vanier, J. (1975). *Be not afraid*. New York, NY: Paulist Press.

Varcarolis, E. M. (Ed.). (1994). Alterations in mood: Grief and depression. In *Foundation of psychiatric-mental health nursing* (2nd ed., pp. 415–464). Philadelphia, PA: W. B. Saunders.

Vash, C. L. (1994). *Personality and adversity: Psychospiritual aspects of rehabilitation*. New York, NY: Springer.

Wagner, C. D. (1996). Family needs of chronic hemodialysis patients: A comparison of perceptions of nurses and families. *ANNA Journal, 23*(1), 19–26.

Wagner, W. (1992). The voices on psychiatry: Inner tumult and the quest for meaning. In L. E. Holst (Ed.), *Hospital ministry: The role of the chaplain today* (pp. 151–162). New York, NY: Crossroad.

Walgrove, N. J. (1996). Unique attributes of successful travelers: Personal strengths for the journey. In V. B. Carson & E. N. Arnold (Eds.), *Mental health nursing: The nurse-patient journey* (pp. 175–190). Philadelphia, PA: W. B. Saunders.

Walsh, M. B., & Carson, V. B. (1996). Mind, body, spirit therapies. In V. B. Carson & E. N. Arnold (Eds.), *Mental health nursing: The nurse-patient journey* (pp. 487–502). Philadelphia, PA: W. B. Saunders.

Warner-Robbins, C. G., & Christiana, N. M. (1989). The spiritual needs of persons with AIDS. *Family Community Health, 12*(2), 43–51.

Weaver, A. J., Flannelly, L. T., Flannelly, K. J., Koenig, H. G., & Larson, D. B. (1998). An analysis of research on religious and spiritual variables in three major mental health nursing journals, 1991–1995. *Issues in Mental Health Nursing, 19*(3), 263–276.

White, M. L. (2013). Spirituality self-care effects on quality of life for patients diagnosed with chronic illness. *Self-Care, Dependent-Care and Nursing, 20*(1), 23–32.

Wilding, C., Muir-Cochrane, E., & May, E. (2006). Treading lightly: Spirituality issues in mental health nursing. *International Journal of Mental Health Nursing, 15*, 144–152.

Wilson, C. (2011). Is there a case for community learning disability teams considering the spiritual needs of people with learning disabilities? *Tizard Learning Disability Review, 16*(3), 31–40.

CHAPTER 7

Spiritual Needs of Children and Families

We are made by relationships with other people.

Carlo Carretto, *Summoned by Love*, 1978

We've sent dying children home on palliative care, and that is very challenging, knowing that you're stopping all your care. But it may be best for their future illness trajectory. I think that at times like this, viewing nursing as a vocation, we had to put our own emotions aside and help the family make the best decision. . I think your personal faith comes in a lot in that situation . . . I think that if you view nursing as a vocation, you're able to have more open conversations with the family; about what all this means spiritually and help them make the decisions they need to make.

Tara, Team Leader on a Pediatric Unit

I n this chapter, the spiritual needs of the ill child are identified and described through reports of the author's interactions with children living with such illnesses as cancer, including leukemia and lymphoma, and human immunodeficiency virus (HIV) infection. The spiritual needs of family members of both ill children and ill adults are also documented in data elicited through formal and informal interviews and observations. Patient and family data are supplemented through interviews with nurses caring for ill children and their families. The first part of the chapter is directed toward the spiritual needs of the ill child in a variety of settings; the latter part explores the spiritual needs of the family, beginning with those of the new and expanding family at the time of childbirth and concluding with a discussion of family needs in terminal illness.

▶ Spiritual Needs of the Child

Perhaps no therapeutic intervention calls on the nurse's creative skills as much as that of providing spiritual care to an ill child. Children are unique and challenging in their varied developmental stages (Kenny, 1999); as frequently noted, a child is much more than a small adult. Children, especially ill children, tend to be astoundingly straightforward in expressing their questions and concerns. They expect no less from their caregivers. Honesty and directness, to the degree possible and appropriate, is the most therapeutic approach for a nurse in the provision of spiritual care to an ill child.

It is suggested that children are "born with 'spiritual competence,' an inner quality or power for faith development, thus assessment and intervention techniques must be developed unique to the population" (Mueller, 2010, p. 197). Spiritual care must be considered from a child's earliest days in a neonatal intensive care unit (Caldeira & Hall, 2012), through school-age years (Quinlivan, 2014) up to adolescence (Spurr, Berry, & Walker, 2013). Spiritual needs of ill children, such as those critically ill with cancer, should be specifically addressed focusing on such issues as "assessing spiritual needs; assisting the child to express feelings; guiding the child in strengthening relationships; helping the child to be remembered; assisting the child to find meaning; and aiding the child to find hope" (Peterson, 2013, p. 1243).

Spirituality and the Child

Children! They are such a joy and such a mystery in our lives! Who can ever express sufficiently all that they are able to communicate, through gifts unknown to themselves . . . ? They make us understand something of the living God by the trust they show us.

—**Roger of Taizé**, 1990

The term *child* is broadly understood to refer to a young person from the developmental stage following infancy to the onset of adolescence; that is, from approximately 1 to 12 years of age. Moran (1997) identified the formal stages of growth and development as newborn (birth to 1 month), infancy (1 month to 1 year), toddlerhood (1 to 3 years), preschool age (3 to 6 years), school age (6 to 11 or 12 years), and adolescence (11 or 12 to 21 years of age) (p. 28). A child's trajectory of physical and psychological growth is accompanied by a parallel process of moral development (Kohlberg, 1984) and spiritual or faith development (Fowler, 1981).

In describing a child's moral development, Lawrence Kohlberg (1984) posited three phases of morality: the preconventional level (early childhood), the conventional level (later childhood to adolescence), and the postconventional level (adulthood). In brief, Kohlberg's schema suggests that the child progresses from an initial stage of simple acceptance of right and wrong, as identified through punishment or non-punishment for an act; to the school-age phase of more abstract understanding of morality; and later, to the adolescent/adult stage, encompassing a societal view of right and wrong.

James Fowler (1981) proposed a paradigm of spiritual development across the life span, labeled "stages of faith development." Of Fowler's seven faith stages, three may be associated with the child's parallel physical and psychological development. Stage 2, intuitive–projective faith, is the period when the preschool child is influenced by the example of adults. During this period, God is often imagined as appearing similar to adult figures with whom the child interacts, and the child may imitate the religious practices of the family without really understanding the meaning. Many preschoolers, around age 5 or 6, can create their own prayers, and a number attend church services with the family. Stage 3, mythic–literal faith, occurs during the school-age period, as the child begins to internalize religious beliefs. The child understands and accepts a more sophisticated God from a monotheistic tradition and develops a conscience. Early school-age children pray and trust that prayers will be answered. Religious stories are often appreciated during this period, especially those describing biblical or religious heroes. Stage 4, synthetic–conventional faith, is developed during the adolescent period. The teen may begin to question some or all of the religious beliefs and practices of the family. Faith experiences occur outside of the home, and the adolescent begins to claim his or her own faith identity. Some teens become very involved in their faith and religious experience during the adolescent years; they may interact with other young people of similar religious belief as a significant peer group.

Burkhardt (1991) believes that children "live in their spirits more than adults," because they are less inhibited and more intuitive about spiritual matters (p. 34); she noted that while understanding the work of the developmental theorists is important, one should adopt a broad definition of spirituality in working with children (p. 34). Spirituality related themes suggested by Burkhardt (1991) include the child's capacity for searching for meaning in life; a sense of relationship to "self, others, nature, and God or Universal Force"; and spirituality, viewed as the "deepest core" of the child's being (p. 34). The comments of Anne Marie, a doctorally prepared pediatric nurse practitioner, reflect Burkhardt's perception related to a child's intuition:

> Working with children you have to have a very clear sense of your own spirituality, because they are very sensitive to the spiritual in others. You have to have a spirituality that projects total acceptance because, if not, the kids can read right through it; anything that's a facade or put on, they know it in a heartbeat . . . In my nursing with children and families I have learned a lot about spiritual needs. I think some nurses are uncomfortable with spiritual care, to go into a 9-year-old's room and ask if he wants to talk about something religious. You just need to be open and give them the chance. They're not afraid of the hard questions, like "what's it like to die?" or "will I die?"; but you have to not be afraid to let them ask. Children will give you spiritual clues; you just have to pick up on them.

In exploring the spirituality of 40 children, ages 4 to 12, David Heller (1985) discovered differences in prayer styles among children from Jewish, Catholic, Protestant, and Hindu traditions. For example, whereas Baptist children reported being comfortable with silent devotion, both Catholic and Jewish children perceived prayer as associated with more formal religious ritual; Hindu children preferred chanting (p. 14). Psychologist Robert Coles (1990) offered poignant examples of differing religious beliefs of school-age children in his book *The Spiritual Life of Children*. Coles identified four spiritual themes from his conversations with children of different traditions: Christian salvation, Islamic surrender, Jewish righteousness, and secular soul-searching. Mary, a 9-year-old Christian with whom Coles conversed, explained that Jesus "died so we will live forever" (p. 203). Rita, a 10-year-old Muslim, asserted, "God is the one who made us, and He'll be the one to decide where we go" (p. 233). Joseph, a 12-year-old Jewish boy, explained, "We have the book, our Bible; it tells us what we should believe . . . a Jew is someone who lives the law" (p. 253). Finally, in examining the concept of secular soul-searching, Robert Coles spoke with 12-year-old Eric, who reported that although he did not belong to any church, he did sometimes "wonder" about things such as the existence of God (pp. 281–283).

The Ill Child and Religious Practice

"Children," Young and Koopsen (2011) point out "unlike adults, do not make clear distinctions between spirituality and religion" (p. 285). Children do, however "draw on previous experiences of life, including religious and spiritual beliefs . . . to cope with crises" (McSherry & Smith, 2006, p. 17). For a child of any religious tradition who is experiencing illness, the ability to participate in religious devotions or practices, such as prayer, may provide a source of comfort and stability. Religious practices and beliefs can affect a child's health; illness may be interpreted in light of a child's religious understanding (Spector & Spertac, 1990, p. 58). The presence in a sickroom of devotional articles such as holy pictures, statues, crucifixes, crosses, or Bibles may provide a sense of security and stability during the disruption of usual life activities. For the preschooler who has a concrete concept of God as protector and father, simple bedtime prayers, such as "Now I lay me down to sleep, I pray the Lord my soul to keep," may help the child to feel more at ease during the night. The reading of a religious story or looking at images from a children's picture Bible can be comforting. If mealtime grace is usual in the family, this may be carried out in the sickroom. A preschooler, ill during a religious holiday such as Christmas, Easter, or Hanukkah, should be encouraged to participate in as many of the associated rituals as possible, to help maintain some sense of normalcy in the child's life.

In the case of an ill school-age child, use of a Bible or prayer book, if part of one's tradition, can be encouraged. A Jewish child may want to experience the lighting of Sabbath candles on Friday evening and have traditional passages from Hebrew Scripture read to him or her. The early school-age child can be encouraged to pray, but will, as noted earlier, expect to have prayers answered, so some counseling may need to be done around that issue. The older school-age child will have learned that prayers are not always directly answered; thus a discussion about the meaning of prayer will be helpful. Some school-age children find it important when ill to continue to participate in certain religious practices such as reception of the sacraments (Holy Eucharist and the Sacrament of Reconciliation), also. Special religious anniversaries, such as Christmas, Easter, Rosh Hashanah, Yom Kippur, Hanukkah, and Ramadan, may be very important to the school-age child, especially if participation in the associated worship rituals is usual in the family. Some reflections of the religious meaning of the celebrations may be brought into the child's sickroom, for example, the setting up of a small Christmas crèche or a menorah. These spiritual symbols can help the child cope with the frightening nature of an illness experience.

The ill adolescent may need spiritual counseling about the relationship of his or her sickness to the religious or spiritual meaning of life. During this developmental period, when the teen may question many of the tenets of organized religion, the young person might well question "why me?" in relation to an illness. The adolescent who has a strong commitment to his or her church and has experienced consistent participation in activities such as weekly Sunday school, church youth group, youth choir, or Bible study group may experience significant anxiety over not being able to participate in these activities, which are social as well as religious. Visits from an adolescent's peers in such a church group can provide support and comfort, as well as distracting the teen from the illness experience. Adolescence is also a time when young people cherish privacy. Teens often choose to keep their deepest and most treasured feelings to themselves. Thus, adolescents may "reject formal worship services, but engage in individual worship in the privacy of their rooms" (Wong, 1997, p. 472).

It is important, even in illness, to allow for such periods of privacy, to the degree possible, for an adolescent patient.

In a study of hope and spiritual well-being in adolescent cancer patients, Hendricks-Ferguson (2008) found higher levels of spiritual well-being and religious well-being in the earlier time periods after diagnosis; it was suggested that health-care professionals assess and plan spiritual care interventions for this patient population (p. 397).

Sometimes a very ill adolescent will request a church-associated ritual. Evelyna was a hospitalized 16-year-old from a Latin American country whose lymphoma was terminal. As a Catholic, Evelyna requested the sacrament of the Eucharist each day. One afternoon, after the chaplain, Sister Elizabeth, had administered the sacrament and offered a prayer, Evelyna looked up and said, "Sister, will you lay hands on me?" Because the "laying on of hands" is not a common practice in the Roman Catholic tradition, Sister Elizabeth was not certain what Evelyna desired, but wanted to honor her request. Several members of the family were present, so the chaplain asked that all gather around the bed with her and place their hands on Evelyna while God's blessing was sought. Especially in the case of an ill child, nurses and chaplains often have the opportunity to create small religious rituals appropriate to the sickroom setting and yet helpful in meeting the spiritual needs of the patient and the family.

Assessment of the Ill Child's Spiritual and Religious Needs

As to the question of whether a child is capable of having a serious relationship with God, Judith Shelly (1982) noted that "stories abound of very young children who made serious and lasting commitments to God" (p. 12). Obviously a child's spiritual interests and concerns will vary greatly depending on age and the religious or denominational tradition of the family. Some broad measurement items reflective of religious tradition contained in a "family assessment interview" (Wong, 1997, p. 90) include identification of usual religious beliefs and practices, whether the family associates with a particular denomination or church, how religious beliefs influence the family's perception of illness, whether the family relies on religious healers or remedies for illness, and who provides religious support for the family (e.g., clergy, relatives, or healers). Pediatric head nurse Judith Van Heukelem-Still (1984) wrote that, in assessing the spiritual needs of children, it is important not only to ask questions but also to observe the child for unusual behaviors such as nightmares or withdrawal from social activities (p. 5). She pointed out that the kind of visitors and cards a child receives may give some hint of whether spiritual influences and support are present (p. 5).

Spiritual assessment questions that Van Heukelem (1982) identified for an ill child focused on such topics as how the child behaves when frightened, who provides support in times of trouble, and what the child's understanding is of God and prayer (p. 89). A nursing diagnosis of spiritual distress can be identified for the ill child. Some defining characteristics of the diagnosis might relate to the child or family's lack of spiritual support or spiritual strength (Marlow & Redding, 1988, p. 78). Nursing interventions for a child reflecting spiritual distress may begin by encouraging the child to verbalize his or her feelings to a caring adult. Elkins and Cavendish (2004) assert that "developing a plan for pediatric spiritual care" should include attention to "the child's spirituality, religion, culture, developmental stage, age-appropriate spiritual care activities, and the needs of the family" (p. 179).

Some of the needs of ill children identified by nursing professor Carolyn Mueller (2010) as important in assessment of spiritual needs include "assistance in dealing with feelings of fearfulness, anxiousness or for coping with pain or other physical symptoms . . . and help exploring such questions as 'Why me?' 'What is the meaning and purpose of suffering?' and 'When or how will death occur'" (p. 200). Peter, a six-year-old lymphoma patient, confronted his pediatric nurse practitioner one day with the question, "What will heaven be like?" His nurse, who really had no idea what kind of response Peter was hoping for, responded that "Heaven is where God lives and heaven will be beautiful, with green grass and flowers and big trees to climb with lots of leafy branches to sit on and a swing." Peter was comforted; his nurse's assessment of what information was needed at that point seemed accurate.

Spiritual Needs of the Acutely Ill Child

Pediatric nursing care, as defined by the American Nurses Association and the Society of Pediatric Nurses (1996), "focuses on helping children and their families and communities achieve their optimum health potentials" (cited in Ashwill, Droske, & Imhof, 1997, p. 11). Spiritual care of the pediatric patient is directed toward helping the child and family achieve and maintain the greatest degree of spiritual health possible, in light of the present illness experience. As noted, in terms of assessment of spiritual need, the defining characteristics of spiritual health will vary according to the child's age, religious tradition, and the severity of the illness. Pediatric chaplain George Handzo (1990) advised that, regardless of religious background, one must be direct and frank in talking about spirituality with an ill child. "Children think a lot about faith and have more ability in theological reflection than most adults give them credit for" (p. 17). Chaplain Handzo asserted that children have essentially the "same faith needs as adults"; they need to view God as one who will care for and support them, especially in times of crisis such as that of illness (p. 18).

The child experiencing an acute illness, even if being cared for at home, may suffer psychosocial sequelae such as loneliness related to isolation from a peer group and interruption of school and school-related social activities (Melamed & Bush, 1985). For the older school-age child or adolescent, missing classes may cause not only a sense of alienation from peers, but also anxiety about future goals related to college and career. The adolescent may worry about "keeping up" with classes, even in the case of a relatively temporary condition. The ill teen whose schoolwork has been interrupted may feel some anger at God or at religious beliefs and question "Why me?" Spiritual counseling at such a time will allow the adolescent to verbalize frustration and potentially achieve a degree of peace and patience, a sense that ultimately all will be well.

Sixty children with advanced cancer, ages 6 to 17, were asked to respond to a spiritual quality-of-life interview; "seventy-eight percent of the interviewees reported that they did something to 'feel close to God.' Children prayed for a 'sense of normalcy' (59%) and relational concerns (31%)" (Kamper, VanCleve, & Savedra, 2010, p. 301). Kamper, VanCleve, and Savedra point out that "Children's care will be enhanced when given the opportunity to express their spiritual and relational concerns" (p. 301).

For the young child who is acutely ill, spiritual care may be directed toward interaction with a parent or parents. Hashim was a six-year-old Muslim child with acute lymphocytic leukemia; his father Mr. Mukti stayed with him almost continuously during a hospitalization, while his mother cared for the family's other children. On a first visit, the unit's chaplain, Elizabeth, asked Mr. Mukti if it would be acceptable, even though she was a Christian, to say a prayer for Hashim, who was receiving chemotherapy. Mr. Mukti responded, "Oh, yes, yes, we all worship the same God; you call him God; we say Allah! But He is the same God." This, and subsequent interactions with Hashim and Mr. Mukti gave Elizabeth the opportunity to discuss and learn more about Islam and the spiritual needs of a Muslim patient. One of Elizabeth's colleagues taught her a Muslim greeting in Arabic: *A salaam a le kum* (Peace be unto you). She asked Mr. Mukti if it would be appropriate for her to greet him and Hashim with the blessing when she visited. Mr. Mukti replied enthusiastically, "Oh, yes, that's wonderful. It means may you be filled with God's blessing. You can say the words when you arrive and when you leave and we will answer asking a blessing for you, *A le kum a salaam.*"

The Hospitalized Child

The hospitalized child is generally experiencing an acute illness or an acute exacerbation of a chronic condition. Such factors as the severity of illness, type of care unit (e.g., pediatric intensive care unit versus general pediatric care unit), previous hospital experience, and family support will influence the child's emotional and spiritual needs. Ashwill and Volz (1997) identified some universal stressors for the hospitalized child, however, including separation from family, fear of pain or physical injury, and fear of the unknown. Although the primary goal of a pediatric hospital unit is care of the ill child, parents, an important resource, also need attention (Hardgrove & Roberts, 1989; Leavitt, 1989). The spiritual care of the child should include spiritual support of the parents. In discussing spiritual ministry in a pediatric unit, Arnold (1992) asserted that pediatric ministry must include the entire family (p. 94). Because, Arnold noted, hospitalization of a child represents a crisis situation, needs are usually identified in spiritual language: "hope, trust, love and acceptance"; such needs may be met through the use of religious resources or simply by developing caring relationships with the child and family (p. 95).

A study of the identified spiritual needs of five hospitalized children revealed key themes emerging from the interview data related to "the role of the child's relationship with family, friends, and healthcare professionals, the impact of the hospital environment on the child, coping with invasive procedures and (the child's religious) beliefs" (Bull & Gillies, 2007, p. 34). The study authors assert that all health-care professionals must recognize that children have spiritual needs that can include religious beliefs, and that it is part of their duty of care to attempt to identify and meet such needs (p. 38). This can best be done by "taking time to talk and listen with each child, [which] enables a health care professional to identify, and therefore try to meet, the needs of children" (p. 38).

Anna was a 13-year-old hospitalized for evaluation and staging of her escalating Ewing's sarcoma with metastasis; there was a question of surgery, which would include a radical amputation of her right leg, including a hemipelvectomy. Anna's disease was progressing rapidly and known sources of chemotherapy had been exhausted. Anna relied on her own and her family's religious resources and demonstrated spiritual peace in her hope and trust in God; this was reinforced by hospital nursing staff and chaplains. Anna resisted the surgery, which physicians agreed had little chance of successfully alleviating the disease process; she decided to place her trust in God, fully aware that a physical cure might not happen. That was okay, Anna assured the staff, because, in her words, she was in a "win–win situation." She explained, "If God heals my body, then it will be wonderful and I can be a missionary and tell people about Him; but if He doesn't, then I will die and be with Jesus, so there's no way I can lose" (O'Brien, 1995, p. 141).

Spiritual Needs of the Chronically Ill Child

Childhood chronic illness is a long-term condition for which there is no cure, and which may affect the child's physical and psychological functioning. Statistics suggest that 10 to 15 percent of the pediatric population is chronically ill (Martin, 1997). Management of a child's chronic illness is complicated because of the necessity of family involvement in the provision of care (Johnson, 1985). A situation of childhood chronic illness may interfere in sibling relationships because parental attention is often heavily focused on the sick child. Although some non-ill siblings cope well, jealousy and emotional distress can occur for the well child (Holiday, 1989); the situation may thus engender feelings of guilt and inadequacy in the chronically ill sibling.

Fulton and Moore (1995) believe that the spiritual well-being of the school-age child with a chronic illness significantly affects the course of illness and treatment (p. 224). They described two nursing approaches to providing spiritual care as "therapeutic play," to generate understanding of the child's perception of spirituality vis-à-vis the illness experience; "bibliotherapy," employing such techniques as storytelling or journaling to help the child explore the meaning of life; and "use of self" in establishing rapport that may comfort the child and decrease anxiety associated with the illness and treatment (Fulton & Moore, 1995, pp. 228–231). The importance of providing devotional material to an older chronically ill child is described by a mother who reported that until her physically and cognitively disabled son's "beloved and much read Children's Bible" had recently fallen apart, he had carried it daily, attached to his walker (Cichon, 1995, p. 24).

Tony, an 18-year-old with recurrent lymphoma, was hospitalized for a course of chemotherapy. Although he talked mostly about sports with the nurses, his chaplain, Elizabeth, noticed a small worn Bible on the bedside stand. Tony's religious preference was listed on his chart simply as "Christian." As she was leaving the room one day, Elizabeth asked Tony if he would like her to read a passage from Scripture. Tony smiled and said, "Yes, that would be good. You pick something." Elizabeth chose a comforting passage about God's care from Matthew 6:25–30, commonly called the "lilies of the field" passage. "Therefore I tell you, do not worry about your life . . . If God so clothes the grass of the fields . . . how much more will he not provide for you." Tony responded, "When I think like that, there really isn't anything to worry about. I get pretty scared about this cancer sometimes but when I put my thoughts to God, I know it's going to be okay. If God takes care of the birds and the flowers, He'll take care of me."

▶ Spiritual Needs of the Dying Child

It has been asserted that "caring for a child at the end of life stage is one of the greatest challenges a nurse can encounter in practice" (Pearson, 2010, p. 31). The manner in which a nurse cares for a dying child may well "help shape the experience the young patient is about to face" (p. 31). Children, especially dying children, do have a spiritual dimension and it thus becomes very important to address their spiritual, as well as physical and emotional, needs (Hufton, 2006, p. 240). In describing the spirituality of an eight-year-old with terminal leukemia, Jerome (2011) reported that "although her short life was filled with challenges . . . [her] spirituality was an innate essence . . . it supported her in shoring up her resources and bearing the burden of her illness and impending death" (p. 200).

Like other ill children, the dying child's spiritual needs are reflective of age, spiritual or religious background, and degree of physiologic and cognitive functioning. As a rule, the broad needs of dying children model those of dying adults; they desire comfort and freedom from pain, and the security that they will not be alone at the time of death (Martin, 1997, p. 414). These needs, Martin added, will be more acutely manifested in the school-age child and the adolescent (p. 414). Four of the most frequently occurring emotional reactions of dying children are "fear, depression, guilt and anger" (Winkelstein, 1989, p. 231). A school-age child, especially, may experience fear related not so much to the death itself but rather to the dying process. Children of this age may have witnessed the deaths of older family members or friends and are fearful of having to go through the pain and suffering they observed. The preschooler can feel guilty about dying, and leaving parents and siblings; he or she may feel responsible for the illness. The dying adolescent, while also experiencing some degree of fear and guilt, frequently goes through a period of depression and anger over the illness and impending death. As noted earlier, adolescence is the time of questioning spiritual and religious beliefs, as well as being the developmental stage when privacy is valued. Thus the dying adolescent may internalize and hide feelings of anger and depression for some time, resulting in an unexpected eruption of emotion as death nears.

To provide spiritual care to dying children, pediatric chaplain Dane Sommer (1989) advised that the caregiver become "theologically honest" (p. 231); that is, in order to help the child cope with suffering and death, nurses must be able to imagine their own deaths and admit that their personal faith may not provide satisfactory answers to the question, why? An exercise integral to most hospice training programs is imagining one's death and writing a personal obituary. A second requirement for those caring for dying children, identified by Chaplain Sommer, is to be able to "speak the language of children" and "enter into" the child's world (p. 231). The nurse must be sensitive to the age-related developmental stage of the child and also keep in mind that children can "see through" dishonesty and subterfuge quite easily; they find security in truth and directness, even if the information is painful. Caregivers must remember as well that a dying child who has experienced significant contact with the health-care system may be very knowledgeable about his or her disease; such children expect information at a level of sophistication that may seem far beyond that warranted by chronological age. In an article presented in the *American Journal of Hospice and Palliative Medicine*, spirituality was identified as a key need in an empirically developed conceptual model of the needs of children with life-limiting conditions (Donnelly, Huff, Lindsey, McMahon, & Schumacher, 2005).

Pediatric oncologist Kate Faulkner (1997) offered some general suggestions related to caring for a dying child; these include being flexible in one's approach, being sensitive to the use of nonverbal communication, respecting the child's desire for privacy, and being "explicit and literal" in responding to questions about death (p. 69). These maxims are most appropriate for the provision of spiritual care. Regardless of a dying child's age and religious tradition, a nurse needs to employ the art as well as the science of nursing in approaching such difficult topics as spirituality and death. Perhaps the best advice is to let the child take the lead, through questions or comments; the nurse can then attempt to cross over, as it were, to the child's world, to that place where the dying child may feel alone. Thus the nurse can become friend and advocate, as well as spiritual caregiver.

Teresa, a baccalaureate-prepared pediatric oncology nurse, described the difficulty and the rewards of such nursing advocacy:

> In peds oncology, the most stressful time is around a child's death, and it's the most rewarding time also. It's a gifted experience to be with that child and family. It's a lot like being a midwife to send the child to God; but it hurts so much to lose them when you've become their friend and the family's friend. But it's a spiritual experience for the nurse and for the child. Sometimes you pray with them, sometimes you sing hymns with them, and then again, maybe you just hold them.

Teresa, a Christian, explained that, for her, if the dying child was from a religious family, it was sometimes easier to know how to give spiritual care. "I mean, you know there are certain prayers or rituals for a Christian or for a Jewish child." Teresa related a recent experience with a dying eight-year-old who did not believe in God and who asked her what would happen after death. She said, "I told him it would be like walking in a beautiful woods, a beautiful forest where there are all kinds of trees and flowers and birds, and everything will be really peaceful. And, that he will be happy and not ever be sick again."

Pam, a master's-prepared pediatric nurse, also described the rewards of providing spiritual care for dying children:

> I was raised Southern Baptist and that is generally my preference, although I also consider myself a born-again Christian. I would never impose my beliefs on anyone, especially a child, but I feel that I can discuss spiritual needs and assess children's needs, especially for the dying child. I have prayed with children, but sometimes maybe it's just listening and a hug. And in some instances I would call a chaplain . . . I have found the chaplains to be very good—excellent, in fact. It's just that sometimes you are the one who is there, who the child knows and will talk to. This is a special gift for you; it's real rewarding. I think spiritual care is definitely in the pediatric nurse's job description.

Certainly not to be neglected in the case of a dying child are the spiritual needs of the family, those of both parents and healthy siblings. As in caring for the child, a nurse will need to call on all of his or her own spiritual strength and experience in order to journey with a family during the predeath and death experience. Cook (1982) suggested, first, that one accept that the family members are probably "not totally rational" during this time (p. 125). Second, Cook advised that the family be encouraged to "continue to function as a family," and that family communication be fostered (p. 125). A parent of a dying child may express seemingly undue anger over a small "glitch" in the provision of hospital or hospice nursing care; this is related to the terrible frustration associated with the loss of parental control in protecting one's child. Nonjudgmental, caring support expressed by a nurse during such an outburst may go far in alleviating the parent's anxiety. The family may also experience internal disorganization during the terminal illness and death of a child. With the ill child receiving so much attention, well siblings can experience feelings of neglect and rejection. Well siblings may also feel guilty about being healthy while a brother or sister is suffering from catastrophic illness. A supportive nurse who welcomes the verbalization of fears and anxieties on the part of all members of the family can facilitate communication between parents and well children.

Camille, a pediatric oncology nurse with more than 22 years of experience, spoke articulately about the spiritual care and spiritual needs of the family of a dying child:

> I think especially that nurses have to be careful not to be overzealous and impulsive with sharing their own spirituality, like saying, "this is God's will." The parents may be angry at God and not ready to hear that. Families accepting a terminally ill child is something they have to work through at their own pace; you don't want somebody anticipating that for you. Part of the art of nursing, the art of being human, is to determine where a person is spiritually. You want to embrace their needs and provide them empathy, but not overwhelm them . . . You have to remember also that not everyone believes that there is a Divine Force guiding our lives, and so illness of a child can be totally overwhelming. You just have to try and be where that parent is at the time.

The first part of this chapter focused on the spiritual and religious needs of the ill child and the ill adolescent—in acute illness, in chronic illness, during hospitalization, and in the dying process. The discussion concluded with a reminder that in caring for an ill or dying child, one must not forget the spiritual needs of the family. The remainder of the chapter concerns the spiritual needs of the family of the ill adult, as well as those of the family of the ill child.

▶ Spiritual Needs of the Family

The family is an important resource in the provision of spiritual care, not only for the sick child but for the ill adult as well. There are a number of understandings of the term *family* in contemporary society. Generally, the concept evokes an image of the basic nuclear family composed of two legally married parents and one or more offspring. Friedmann (1992) defined family as "two or more persons who are joined together by bonds of sharing and emotional closeness, who identify themselves as being part of the family" (p. 9). Today, however, there is a growing emergence of the single-parent family; for the single, unmarried individual, a number of persons belonging to such associations as church or friendship groups may be loosely described as family. It is important for nurses to also consider families' cultural needs when interacting with them. Such culturally sensitive caring can provide "spiritual support for family members" who may be involved in patient care and/or support, both while the patient is hospitalized and "after the patient returns home" (Neils, 2010, p. 235).

Families may be open, allowing members individuality and flexibility in role behavior, or closed and more rigid in terms of behavioral expectations (Dossey, 1988, p. 308). As social systems, families are said to have structure and function, including assigned roles, interactional patterns, and histories, each of which needs to be acknowledged in the planning of care (Turk & Kerns, 1985, p. 3). Some key functions of the modern family involve providing affection, companionship, security, a sense of purpose, socialization, and moral values (Reeder, Martin, & Koniak-Griffin, 1997, p. 46);

additionally, the provision of shelter and material support and the maintaining of morale fall within the purview of family responsibilities (LeMone & Burke, 1996, p. 37). The family also plays an important role in managing its members' health: primary prevention in supporting a healthy lifestyle, secondary prevention related to decisions to treat illness symptoms, and tertiary prevention manifested by family support of a member's compliance with a prescribed therapeutic regimen (Danielson, Hamel-Bissell, & Winstead-Fry, 1993, p. 11).

A plan for spiritual assessment and spiritual intervention for families was devised by Tanyi (2006); the unique spiritual needs of families of children with disabilities or special needs was highlighted by Speraw (2006). Speraw reported that parents or caregivers of ill children did not perceive nurses as being aware of or interested in their family spiritual needs (p. 213).

The Family, Illness, and Spirituality

Because healthy families generally function as units, it is important to minister to the spiritual needs of the entire family when one member is ill or in need of support (Clinebell, 1991). Families faced with serious short-term or chronic long-term illness of one of the members can benefit greatly from spiritual support provided by friends, church members, or pastoral care providers both from within or outside the health-care system. Emeth and Greenhut (1991) noted that remaining connected with God or with spiritual beliefs "can be difficult in a health crisis" and observed that often one needs to "rely on the faith of others, to get through a difficult period" (p. 210). Thus, the nurse should welcome a family's presence as a resource in the provision of spiritual support; including family members in a religious ritual or prayer service may help them feel comfortable in sharing in the spiritual support and care of the ill person (Peterson & Potter, 1997, p. 452). Research has identified prayer and belief in God as being the most important coping strategies for a family dealing with illness (Friedmann, 1992, p. 331).

The family's particular spiritual or religious tradition and experience will, of course, direct the kind and degree of spiritual care and support that will prove helpful during an illness experience. For the family not of a religious tradition, spiritual care may consist simply of the presence and concern demonstrated by those providing the intervention. For the family whose members are or have been actively involved in a church or faith group, the religious prayers and practices of the community can be extremely comforting. A Jewish family may appreciate reading the Psalms or other passages found in the Jewish canon of Scripture; for the Muslim family, a passage from the Holy Qur'an can provide support and comfort; and for the Christian family, the Gospel messages of Jesus often provide hope and sustenance during times of illness.

The New or Expanding Family: Spiritual Needs in Childbirth and the Postnatal Experience

For the new or expanding family the childbirth experience can be a time of significant emotional stress, especially for the mother-to-be. Certain factors such as cultural background, social support, and maternal confidence may ameliorate the stress and pain associated with the birthing experience (Reeder, Martin, & Koniak-Griffin, 1997, p. 532). Spiritual support may also help in reducing anxiety and facilitating the labor and delivery process. Three maternal–child nurses explored the "provision of spiritual care" by nurses on a maternal–infant unit (Dunn, Handley, & Dunkin, 2009). The study findings revealed important associations between the nurses' personal spirituality and spiritual well-being and the provision of spiritual care on the maternal–infant unit (p. 19).

The childbirth experience itself may incorporate aspects of the family's spiritual or religious tradition. Callister (1995) recounted the story of an Orthodox Jewish mother who gave thanks to God at the time of delivering a first-born son because of the belief that she is now "fulfilling the measure of her creation in obedience to Rabbinical law," and of a Mormon (Church of Jesus Christ of Latter Day Saints) mother who requested a blessing from her husband in the delivery room as she was about to give birth (p. 327). Callister (1995) asserted that nurses should provide the childbearing woman with an experience that respects the spiritual dimensions of her life (p. 330).

A maternal–child health (MCH) nurse may diagnose spiritual distress in a new mother in the case of death of the neonate (Corrine, Bailey, Valentin, Morantus, & Shirley, 1992, p. 141) or following delivery of an infant with a disorder such as a congenital or genetic anomaly. Moderately severe neonatal conditions such as cleft lip and palate, talipes equinovarus (club foot), or hip dysplasia may be more or less distressing, depending on parental experience and expectations. More serious congenital or genetic anomalies, such as trisomy 21 (Down syndrome) or spina bifida, may be exceedingly traumatic for parents and siblings. Disorders such as anencephaly or Tay-Sachs disease have a devastating impact on the family. Obviously, the occurrence of any illness or anomaly in a newborn poses difficult spiritual and ethical questions for the family. Hardee (1994) raised the rhetorical question "Should severely impaired or handicapped newborns be allowed to die?" Findings from conversations with 10 intensive care nursery (ICN) nurses revealed three themes of concern in response to the question: the suffering of the newborn, the nurse's stress in caring for a suffering newborn, and the nurse's feelings of inadequacy in terms of ethical knowledge to confront such dilemmas (p. 28). Ultimately, response to this question will be guided by the nurse's personal spiritual and/or religious belief system.

In the provision of spiritual care to parents faced with a critically or terminally ill newborn, some suggested interventions are to attempt to include the entire extended family in the experience in order to engender support and affirmation for the parent or parents, to assist the family in facing the reality of the situation rather than retreating into denial or fantasy, and to try to create some meaningful and positive interaction with the newborn (Kline, 1991, pp. 89–91).

Spiritual Needs of the Family in Acute Illness

Families of acutely ill patients can be found both at home and in the hospital. Because of the unexpected and often sudden onset of an acute illness, or of an acute exacerbation of a chronic condition, families may be neglected and left to fend for themselves regardless of the setting. In a home care situation, where the family is more directly involved in a therapeutic regimen, spiritual support of extended family members and friends can be available and accessible; in the hospital a more formal type of spiritual care may be required. In the hospital setting, however, many families feel constrained by the institution's restrictions and schedules (Katonah, 1991). Most hospital and clinic waiting rooms abound with anxious family members in need of spiritual support. Some needs identified by the families of acutely ill persons include the desire for competent care, pain management, compassion, and extended family support in coping with the impact of the illness on their lives (Durand, 1993, p. xii). Additional needs perceived by the families of hospitalized acutely ill patients are information about changes in a patient's condition and honest answers to questions (Leavitt, 1989). Lynn-McHale and Smith (1993) described religion as an "additional support for families experiencing crisis" and considered addressing a family's spiritual and religious concerns as facilitating coping in an acute illness experience (p. 318).

Maria, the mother of Anna, a 13-year-old suffering from advanced Ewing's sarcoma with metastasis, spoke at length about the importance of spirituality in terms of personal faith and religious practices such as prayer and hymn singing for herself and for Anna:

> We are a very Christian family. I was saved when I was about 21 and ever since I have lived my life for Jesus. Anna has witnessed for Jesus too. I couldn't get through this without my faith. You know Anna has Ewing's, one of the worst cancers you can get, and now she's relapsed so we just have to take each day at a time, each hour really! But we are putting the treatment in Jesus' hands; we are praying about it . . . Anna has really gotten involved with the Church Youth; she has witnessed with them. They are a real support to her now. They come and pray with her . . . I try to keep Anna up spiritually. Yesterday she had a "bone marrow" and we sang hymns and prayed through it to keep her spirits up. She's got a lot of faith; it's what gives her so much courage.

The Family in the Intensive Care Unit

Clark and Heindenreich (1995) identified spiritual well-being for the acutely ill patient experiencing intensive care as encompassing the support of caregivers, family members and friends, and religion and faith beliefs. The family of an acutely ill patient hospitalized in an intensive care unit (ICU) may spend long hours in waiting rooms, sometimes rarely leaving the hospital setting. This is a time when the arrival of a chaplain or nurse willing to provide spiritual care is generally welcomed unequivocally. Families need to verbalize their anxieties to someone with a caring heart as they attempt to face the severity of a loved one's illness (Niklas & Stefanics, 1975, p. 81). Families of ICU patients often express feelings of "helplessness" and "isolation" (Stromberg, 1992, p. 134) due to restricted visiting hours in a unit; the nurse or chaplain who is able to spend even a brief period of time with the family can become a bridge between the professional/technical aspects of the intensive care environment and the caring dimensions of the health-care facility. Ultimately, spiritual support is reported to be a key dimension of family care in the ICU (Rukholm, Bailey, & Coutu-Wakulczyk, 1991).

Some spiritual care interventions for the family in a critical care setting might include giving information about the patient, environment, and staff, to the degree possible; encouraging the family members to verbalize their anxieties and concerns; suggesting some coping strategies for attempting to keep up with physical needs such as nutrition and sleep; and reinforcing the fact that the family's anxiety is normal in such a situation, with the suggestion of some possible coping strategies to reduce stress (Gillman, Gable-Rodriguez, Sutherland, & Whitacre, 1996, p. 15). The ICU nurse might also include patients' families in bedside discussions whenever acceptable and attempt to include family needs when developing a plan of care (Chesla & Stannard, 1997).

Karen, an ICU head nurse, explained how she had learned the importance of allowing critically ill patients' families to express their stressful emotions:

> My first experience with a family having a really hard time, I said something to the doctor like, "this patient is dying and the family is really upset. Could we have something to help calm them down a little bit?" Well, he got all over my case, and he said "They don't need sedation; they need ventilation." At first I couldn't figure it out, and then I thought, you know, he's right. So, if a family wants to scream and yell and lay on the floor or do whatever they need to do to let it out, let them do it. Let them express that anger and pain in whatever way they have to, at least for the time being. That's part of spiritual care as far as I'm concerned.

Spiritual Needs of the Family in Chronic Illness

Chronic illness may have periods of acute exacerbation, requiring intense medical care and perhaps even hospitalization. Because of the long-term nature of chronic illness, families may become very fatigued and frustrated in the process of providing care. The family of a chronically ill person must continually be alert to changes in the health of their loved one; thus, these families need "ongoing support from friends, health care providers and communities" (Gilliss, Rose, Hallburg, & Martinson, 1989, p. 289). One example is that of the family raising a child with a disability. Following a study of families of a child with a disability (CWD), it was recommended that nurses working with CWD families acknowledge the importance of the parents' spirituality and encourage "parents' religiosity and spirituality in a sensitive and respectful manner" (Parker, Mandleco, Roper, Freeborn, & Dyches, 2011, p. 82).

The syndromes identified as HIV infection and acquired immunodeficiency syndrome (AIDS) are, with the advent of more effective therapeutic regimens, now being described as chronic illnesses, although acute exacerbations of HIV-related cancer or opportunistic infections still occur and may be considered life threatening. Smith (1988) asserted that "AIDS is a family syndrome," which has an impact not only on the person infected with the virus, but also on all of the family members and friends with whom he or she "shares important relationships" (p. 135). The spiritual needs of the families of those living with HIV and AIDS may be complicated by the need for privacy related to the stigma some still associate with the conditions. Stigma and secrecy can isolate a family from usual support systems such as extended family members, friends, and church members (Perelli, 1991, p. 41). One mother commented, however, that in caring for her son, she was forced to tell certain people that he had AIDS, "because I needed their support, as did he, through prayers and physical help" (AIDS Ministry Program, the Archdiocese of Saint Paul and Minneapolis, 1991, p. 40). Despite all of the physical and psychosocial patient considerations associated with an HIV diagnosis, the family is also grieving and needs spiritual or religious support to assist in their own coping (Amos, 1988).

Cancer is another illness syndrome identified as a chronic condition with potentially life-threatening manifestations as well. Danielson, Hamel-Bissell, and Winstead-Fry (1993) believe that a family member's diagnosis of cancer can be "one of the most spiritually disabling events" that a family will ever experience (p. 357). Often, following such a diagnosis, both the patient's and the family's lives are disrupted because of a treatment regimen involving surgery and possible chemotherapy.

The family needs significant support to facilitate coping with the myriad illness-related life changes (Sproull, 1992, p. 125).

In a study of 101 cancer patients and 45 parents of children with cancer, Spilka, Spangler, and Nelson (1983) discovered that spiritual and religious support was more important than psychological counseling; some activities appreciated were prayer, religious or spiritual reading, discussing church-related issues, spiritual counseling, and simply the presence of the spiritual caregiver (pp. 101–102). Raleigh (1992), in a study comparing 45 cancer patients and 45 patients with other chronic illnesses, found that overall the most important sources of hope were family, friends, and religion.

The significance of spirituality among 17 family caregivers of chronic dementia patients was revealed in nursing research conducted by Kaye and Robinson (1994). The investigators learned that the caregiver wives engaged in religious practices such as prayer and spiritual direction in coping with their spouses' illnesses and their own caring activities (p. 218). Based on their findings, the investigators recommended that nurses work with local churches that provide networks for such caregivers (p. 218).

Spiritual Needs of the Family Coping with a Terminal Illness

Here, a brief discussion of family needs in the predeath phase is presented; two case examples are drawn from the author's research with family members of persons in the later stages of AIDS.

In exploring the concept of nurse–family spiritual relationships among 11 hospice nurses and 12 bereaved families, Stiles (1990) identified five behaviors ascribed to nurses: being, doing, knowing, receiving and giving, and welcoming a stranger (p. 235). A nurse's way of being is sitting with and listening to the family; doing includes explaining, reassuring, and comforting; knowing involves sensitivity to the dying process; receiving and giving describes quality time spent between nurse and patient; and welcoming a stranger means inviting the patient's family to help prepare for the death (pp. 237–243). Wright (1997) asserted that listening to and being present to witness a terminally ill patient's and family's suffering is "the soul" of clinical nursing with families (p. 3). A veteran of 20 years of clinical work with families, Wright (1997) maintained that concern about a family's religious and spiritual beliefs has been one of the "most neglected" topics in family care. Yet, she asserted "the experience of suffering becomes transposed to one of spirituality as family members try to make meaning out of their suffering and distress" (p. 5).

Palliative care providers advise that "spiritual assessments should be conducted for all parents as differing support services may be needed. The palliative care team should ensure that parents' spirituality is being incorporated, as appropriate, into their children's routine care" (Knapp et al., 2011, p. 437).

Julia, the mother of 39-year-old Jonathan who was suffering from *Pneumocystis carinii* pneumonia as well as cytomegalovirus retinitis and other complications of advanced AIDS, spoke about the importance of spiritual care for herself and for her son:

> I can't tell everybody about this, but my pastor and some of the church members have been really kind and supportive; that helps so much. You

really need God and the church at a time like this. Jonathan needs the support of prayers too. I've asked the pastor to pray. That's all we can do now but it's so comforting.

And Nora, whose 42-year-old son Matthew was also experiencing symptoms of advanced AIDS, asserted:

It's only God and people's prayers that's getting me through this; they are holding me up. People have been sending prayers in cards and with phone calls. My wonderful priest is praying all the time. I don't know how I could survive without this spiritual support.

Nora admitted that sometimes she became angry with God over Matt's illness and questioned why, but she concluded, "Even when I was screaming at God, because you know, why, and why, and why? Even when I was angry with Him, I knew that God was crying with me" (O'Brien, 1992, p. 67).

Children and families have unique and important spiritual needs in dealing with illness and disability. For the young child as well as for the teen, the support of personal faith and religious practice can significantly mediate the suffering involved with an illness experience. Families of sick children and families of adults who are ill also need and benefit from spiritual care. Although the patient as the center of attention often receives much spiritual support and care, the patient's family members may be neglected or forgotten. Nurses have a prime opportunity to minister spiritually to children and to family members, especially during critical or terminal illness. The nurse must employ art and creativity in attempting to provide spiritual intervention for this fragile population.

▶ References

AIDS Ministry Program, the Archdiocese of Saint Paul and Minneapolis. (1991). *For those we love: A spiritual perspective on AIDS* (2nd ed.). Cleveland, OH: The Pilgrim Press.

American Nurses Association and the Society of Pediatric Nurses. (1996). *Statement of the scope and standards of pediatric clinical practice* (pp. 25–35). Washington, DC: American Nurses Publishing.

Amos, W. E. (1988). *When AIDS comes to church.* Philadelphia, PA: The Westminister Press.

Arnold, J. (1992). The voices on pediatrics: Walking with children and parents. In L. E. Holst (Ed.), *Hospital ministry: The role of the chaplain today* (pp. 93–106). New York, NY: Crossroad.

Ashwill, J. W., Droske, S. C., & Imhof, S. (1997). Introduction to pediatric nursing. In J. W. Ashwill & S. C. Droske (Eds.), *Nursing care of children: Principles and practice* (pp. 2–23). Philadelphia, PA: W. B. Saunders.

Ashwill, J. W., & Volz, D. (1997). The ill child in the hospital and other care settings. In J. W. Ashwill & S. C. Droske (Eds.), *Nursing care of children: Principles and practice* (pp. 346–371). Philadelphia, PA: W. B. Saunders.

Bull, A., & Gillies, M. (2007). Spiritual needs of children with complex healthcare needs in the hospital. *Paediatric Nursing, 19*(9), 34–38.

Burkhardt, M. A. (1991). Spirituality and children: Nursing considerations. *Journal of Holistic Nursing, 9*(2), 31–40.

Caldeira, S., & Hall, J. (2012). Spiritual leadership and spiritual care in neonatology. *Journal of Nursing Management, 20*(8), 1069–1075.

Callister, L. C. (1995). Cultural meanings of childbirth. *Journal of Obstetrics, Gynecology, and Maternity Nursing, 24*(4), 327–331.

Carretto, C. (1978). *Summoned by love.* Maryknoll, NY: Orbis Books.

Chesla, C. A., & Stannard, D. (1997). Breakdown in the nursing care of families in the ICU. *American Journal of Critical Care, 6*(1), 64–71.

Cichon, K. K. (1995). Life with Noah: Growing toward wholeness through parenting a handicapped child. *The Journal of Christian Healing, 17*(4), 18–25.

Clark, C., & Heindenreich, T. (1995). Spiritual care for the critically ill. *American Journal of Critical Care, 4*(1), 77–81.

Clinebell, H. (1991). *Basic types of pastoral care and counseling.* Nashville, TN: Abington Press.

Coles, R. (1990). *The spiritual life of children.* Boston, MA: Houghton Mifflin.

Cook, M. (1982). Ministering to dying children and their families. In J. A. Shelly (Ed.), *The spiritual needs of children* (pp. 117–129). Downers Grove, IL: InterVarsity Press.

Corrine, L., Bailey, V., Valentin, M., Morantus, E., & Shirley, L. (1992). The unheard voices of women: Spiritual interventions in maternal-child health. *American Journal of Maternal Child Nursing, 17*(3), 141–145.

Danielson, C. B., Hamel-Bissell, B., & Winstead-Fry, P. (1993). *Families, health & illness: Perspectives on coping and intervention.* St. Louis, MO: C. V. Mosby.

Donnelly, J., Huff, S., Lindsey, M., McMahon, K., & Schumacher, J. (2005). The needs of children with life-limiting conditions: A healthcare-provider-based model. *American Journal of Hospice and Palliative Care Medicine, 22*(4), 259–267.

Dossey, B. M. (1988). Relationships: Learning the patterns and processes. In B. M. Dossey, L. Keegan, C. E. Guzzetta, & L. G. Kolkmeier (Eds.), *Holistic nursing: A handbook for practice* (pp. 305–330). Rockville, MD: Aspen.

Dunn, L., Handley, M., & Dunkin, J. (2009). The provision of spiritual care by registered nurses on a maternal-infant unit. *Journal of Holistic Nursing, 27*(1), 19–28.

Durand, B. A. (1993). Preface: Determination of need. In S. L. Feetham, S. B. Meister, J. M. Bell, & C. L. Gillis (Eds.), *The nursing of families* (pp. ix–xiii). Newburg Park, CA: Sage.

Elkins, M., & Cavendish, R. (2004). Developing a plan for pediatric spiritual care. *Holistic Nursing Practice, 18*(4), 179–185.

Emeth, E. V., & Greenhut, J. H. (1991). *The wholeness handbook: Care of body, mind and spirit for optimal health.* New York, NY: Continuum.

Faulkner, K. W. (1997). Talking about death with a dying child. *American Journal of Nursing, 97*(6), 64–69.

Fowler, J. (1981). *Stages of faith: The psychology of human development and the quest for meaning.* San Francisco, CA: Harper San Francisco.

Friedmann, M. M. (1992). *Family nursing: Theory and practice.* (3rd ed.). Norwalk, CT: Appleton & Lange.

Fulton, R. A., & Moore, C. M. (1995). Spiritual care of the school age child with a chronic condition. *Journal of Pediatric Nursing, 10*(4), 224–231.

Gilliss, C. L., Rose, D., Hallburg, J. C., & Martinson, I. M. (1989). The family and chronic illness. In C. L. Gilliss, B. M. Highley, B. M. Roberts, & I. M. Martinson (Eds.), *Toward a science of family nursing* (pp. 287–299). New York, NY: Addison-Wesley.

Gillman, J., Gable-Rodriguez, J., Sutherland, M., & Whitacre, J. H. (1996). Pastoral care in a critical care setting. *Critical Care Nursing Quarterly, 19*(1), 10–20.

Handzo, G. F. (1990). Talking about faith with children. *Journal of Christian Nursing, 7*(4), 17–20.

Hardee, L. B. (1994). When a newborn cannot survive: What nurses really believe. *Journal of Christian Nursing, 11*(1), 26–28, 47.

Hardgrove, C., & Roberts, B. M. (1989). The family with a hospitalized child. In C. L. Gilliss, B. M. Highley, B. M. Roberts, & I. M. Martinson (Eds.), *Toward a science of family nursing* (pp. 148–161). New York, NY: Addison-Wesley.

Heller, D. (1985). The children's God. *Psychology Today, 19*(1), 11–17.

Hendricks-Ferguson, V. (2008). Hope and spiritual well-being in adolescents with cancer. *Western Journal of Nursing Research, 30*(3), 385–401.

Holiday, B. (1989). The family with a chronically ill child: An interactional perspective. In C. L. Gilliss, B. M. Highley, B. M. Roberts, & I. M. Martinson (Eds.), *Toward a science of family nursing* (pp. 300–311). New York, NY: Addison-Wesley.

Hufton, E. (2006). Parting gifts: The spiritual needs of children. *Journal of Child Health, 10*(3), 240–250.

Jerome, A. (2011). Comforting children and families who grieve. *School Psychology International, 32,* 194–209.

Johnson, S. B. (1985). The family and the child with chronic illness. In D. C. Turk & R. D. Kerns (Eds.), *Health, illness and families: A life-span perspective* (pp. 110–154). New York, NY: John Wiley & Sons.

Kamper, R., VanCleve, L., & Savedra, M. (2010). Children with advanced cancer: Responses to a spiritual quality of life interview. *Journal for Specialists in Pediatric Nursing, 15*(4), 301–306.

Katonah, J. (1991). Hospitalization: A rite of passage. In L. E. Holst (Ed.), *Hospital ministry: The role of the chaplain today* (pp. 55–67). New York, NY: Crossroad.

Kaye, J., & Robinson, K. M. (1994). Spirituality among caregivers. *Image: Journal of Nursing Scholarship, 26*(3), 218–221.

Kenny, G. (1999). Children's nursing: Assessing children's spirituality, what is the way forward? *British Journal of Nursing, 8*(1), 28; 30–32.

Kline, S. J. (1991). The voices on obstetrics: Participants and partners. In L. E. Holst (Ed.), *Hospital ministry: The role of the chaplain today* (pp. 79–91). New York, NY: Crossroad.

Knapp, C., Madden, V., Wang, H., Curtis, C., Sloyer, P., & Shenkman, E. (2011). Spirituality of parents of children in palliative care. *Journal of Palliative Medicine, 14*(4), 437–443.

Kohlberg, L. (1984). *The psychology of moral development.* San Francisco, CA: Harper & Row.

Leavitt, M. B. (1989). Transition to illness: The family in the hospital. In C. L. Gilliss, B. M. Highley, B. M. Roberts, & I. M. Martinson (Eds.), *Toward a science of family nursing* (pp. 161–186). New York, NY: Addison-Wesley.

LeMone, P., & Burke, K. M. (1996). *Medical–surgical nursing: Critical thinking in client care.* New York, NY: Addison-Wesley.

Lynn-McHale, D. J., & Smith, A. (1993). Comprehensive assessment of families of the critically ill. In G. D. Wegner & R. J. Alexander (Eds.), *Readings in family nursing* (pp. 309–328). Philadelphia, PA: J. B. Lippincott.

Marlow, D. R., & Redding, B. A. (1988). *Textbook of pediatric nursing* (6th ed.). Philadelphia, PA: W. B. Saunders.

Martin, G. T. (1997). The child with a chronic or terminal illness. In J. W. Ashwill & S. C. Droske (Eds.), *Nursing care of children: Principles and practice* (pp. 394–417). Philadelphia, PA: W. B. Saunders.

McSherry, W., & Smith, J. (2006). How do children express their spiritual needs? *Pediatric Nursing, 19*(3), 17–20.

Melamed, B. G., & Bush, J. P. (1985). Family factors in children with acute illness. In D. C. Turk & R. D. Kerns (Eds.), *Health, illness and families: A life-span perspective* (pp. 183–219). New York, NY: John Wiley & Sons.

Moran, M. (1997). Growth and development. In J. W. Ashwill & S. C. Droske (Eds.), *Nursing care of children: Principles and practice* (pp. 26–49). Philadelphia, PA: W. B. Saunders.

Mueller, C. (2010). Spirituality in children: Understanding and developing interventions. *Pediatric Nursing, 36*(4), 197–204.

Neils, P. (2010). The influence of Nightingale rounding by the liaison nurse on surgical patient families with attention to differing cultural needs. *Journal of Holistic Nursing, 28*(4), 235–243.

Niklas, G. R., & Stefanics, C. (1975). *Ministry to the hospitalized.* New York, NY: Paulist Press.

O'Brien, M. E. (1992). *Living with HIV: Experiment in courage.* Westport, CT: Auburn House.

O'Brien, M. E. (1995). The AIDS challenge: *Breaking through the boundaries.* Westport, CT: Auburn House.

Parker, J., Mandleco, B., Roper, S., Freeborn, D., & Dyches, T. (2011). Religiosity, spirituality and marital relationships of parents raising a typically developing child or a child with a disability. *Journal of Family Nursing, 17*(1), 82–104.

Pearson, H. (2010). Managing the emotional aspects of end of life care for children and young people. *Paediatric Nursing, 22*(7), 31–35.

Peterson, C. L. (2013). Spiritual care of the child with cancer at the end of life: A concept analysis. *Journal of Advanced Nursing, 70*(6), 1243–1253.

Perelli, R. (1991). *Ministry to persons with AIDS: A family systems approach.* Minneapolis, MN: Augsburg.

Peterson, V., & Potter, P. A. (1997). Spiritual health. In P. A. Potter & A. G. Perry (Eds.), *Fundamentals of nursing: Concepts, process and practice* (pp. 440–456). St. Louis, MO: C. V. Mosby.

Quinlivan, M. (2014). Supporting the delivery of effective pastoral care. *British Journal of School Nursing, 9*(8), 405–406.

Raleigh, E. D. (1992). Sources of hope in chronic illness. *Oncology Nursing Forum, 19*(2), 443–448.

Reeder, S. J., Martin, L. L., & Koniak-Griffin, D. (1997). *Maternity nursing: Family, newborn and women's health care* (18th ed.). Philadelphia, PA: J. B. Lippincott.

Roger of Taizé. (1990). *His love is a fire.* Collegeville, MN: The Liturgical Press.

Rukholm, E. E., Bailey, P. H., & Coutu-Wakulczyk, G. (1991). Family needs and anxieties in the ICU. *The Canadian Journal of Nursing Research, 23*(3), 67–81.

Shelly, J. A. (Ed.). (1982). Jesus and the children: A mandate to care. In *The spiritual needs of children* (pp. 11–16). Downers Grove, IL: InterVarsity Press.

Smith, W. J. (1988). *AIDS, living and dying with hope: Issues in pastoral care.* New York, NY: Paulist Press.

Sommer, D. R. (1989). The spiritual needs of dying children. *Issues in Comprehensive Pediatric Nursing, 12*(1), 225–233.

Spector, R. E., & Spertac, A. M. (1990). Social and cultural influences on the child. In S. R. Mott, S. R. James, & A. M. Spertac (Eds.), *Nursing care of children and families* (2nd ed., pp. 53–75). New York, NY: Addison-Wesley.

Speraw, S. (2006). Spiritual experiences of parents and caregivers who have children with disabilities or special needs. *Issues in Mental Health Nursing, 27*, 213–230.

Spilka, B., Spangler, J. D., & Nelson, C. B. (1983). Spiritual support in life threatening illness. *Journal of Religion and Health, 22*(2), 98–104.

Sproull, A. (1992). The voices on cancer care: A lens unfocused and narrowed. In L. E. Holst (Ed.), *Hospital ministry: The role of the chaplain today.* New York, NY: Crossroad.

Spur, S., Berry, L., & Walker, K. (2013). The meanings older adults attach to spirituality. *Journal for Specialists in Pediatric Nursing, 18*(3), 221–232.

Stiles, M. K. (1990). The shining stranger: Nurse–family spiritual relationships. *Cancer Nursing, 13*(4), 235–245.

Stromberg, R. (1992). The voices on coronary care: A confrontation with vulnerability. In L. E. Holst (Ed.), *Hospital ministry: The role of the chaplain today.* New York, NY: Crossroad.

Tanyi, R. A. (2006). Spirituality and family nursing: Spiritual assessment and interventions for families. *Journal of Advanced Nursing, 53*(3), 287–294.

Turk, D. C., & Kerns, R. D. (Eds.). (1985). The family in health and illness. In *Health, illness and families: A life-span perspective* (pp. 1–22). New York, NY: John Wiley & Sons.

Van Heukelem, J. (1982). Assessing the spiritual needs of children and their families. In J. A. Shelly (Ed.), *The spiritual needs of children* (pp. 87–97). Downers Grove, IL: InterVarsity Press.

Van Heukelem-Still, J. (1984). How to assess spiritual needs of children and their families. *Journal of Christian Nursing, 1*(1), 4–6.

Winkelstein, M. (1989). Spirituality and the death of a child. In V. B. Carson (Ed.), *Spiritual dimensions of nursing practice* (pp. 217–253). Philadelphia, PA: W. B. Saunders.

Wong, D. L. (1997). *Whaley & Wong's essentials of pediatric nursing* (5th ed.). St. Louis, MO: C. V. Mosby.

Wright, L. M. (1997). Spirituality and suffering: The soul of clinical work with families. *Journal of Family Nursing, 3*(1), 3–14.

Young, C., & Koopsen, C. (2011). *Spirituality, health, and healing: An integrative approach.* Sudbury, MA: Jones & Bartlett Learning.

CHAPTER 8

Spiritual Needs of the Older Adult

There is no such notion as retirement in terms of the purpose of God . . . God calls us to live life with Him as co-creators, co-workers in the reshaping and renewing of human history . . . and that calling is never completed until the day He calls us to live with Him.

Jitsuo Morikawa, 1974, as cited in Seymour, 1995

I treat patients as if they were part of my family. Especially the geriatric folks. People deserve to be treated with dignity and respect and care. Believing that nursing is a vocation impacts that. I just treat everyone with the understanding that they are spiritual beings, and we are all children of God. I have a theory that when we help one another we are helping each other.

Alice, Charge Nurse on a Geriatric Unit

This chapter documents the spiritual needs of the frail or ill older adult. Data identifying spiritual needs were obtained through both structured and unstructured interviews and interactions with three groups of older persons living with illness; the study populations included chronically ill elders who are active, homebound elders, and elders residing in a nursing home. The elders experienced a multiplicity of illness conditions including congestive heart disease, hypertension, arteriosclerosis, arthritis, diabetes, and Alzheimer's disease. Interview data were also elicited from caregivers of the frail elderly. Nursing research has documented the importance of nurses providing spiritual care to elders living both in the community (Castellaw, Wicks, & Martin, 1999) and in nursing homes (Hicks, 1999).

Currently the spiritual needs and spiritual care of older adults are receiving significant attention in the nursing literature. One study exploring the relationship of dignity to spirituality in elders revealed that "spiritual care underpins dignity through uplifting the spirit and (allowing the person to) feel alive and be valued" (Rykkje & Raholm, 2014, p. 17). Among the most fragile older adults are frequently those residing in nursing homes or continuing care retirement communities. For these elders the relationship between transcendence and spiritual well-being has been found to be significant (Haughen, Rannestad, Hammervold, Garasen, & Espnes, 2013). It is suggested that "facilitating patients' self-transcendence, both interpersonally and intrapersonally may increase spiritual well-being among cognitively intact nursing home patients' overall satisfaction" (Haughen et al., 2013, p. 66). Some defining characteristics of pastoral care for older adults in residential care include: "a trusting relationship, spiritual support, emotional support and practical support" (Wilkes, Cioffi, Fleming, & LeMiere, 2011, p. 213).

Perhaps the most challenging elder residential population for whom spiritual care is needed is the group experiencing dementia symptoms. Some current suggestions for spiritual care for dementia residents include: "integrating spiritual care into general care, described as physical touch and responsive intuition . . . being present and sensitive in communication . . . and meeting residents' religious needs" (Odbehr, Kvigne, Hauge, & Danbolt, 2015, p. 1). Other spiritual care intervention for dementia patients suggested are: "reflective practice and meaningful engagement with the person with dementia so as to facilitate shared understanding," "supporting the spiritual and religious beliefs of the person," and employing "an individualized or person-centered approach to care" (Daly & Fahey-McCarthy, 2014, p. 787). Also important are such activities as facilitating a patient's attendance at church services and supporting them in private prayer (Higgins, 2013, p. 25). The concepts of both spirituality and religiosity need to be considered in providing care for one suffering from dementia (Jolley & Moreland, 2011).

▶ The Older Adult

Who are the elderly? Who are those individuals whom society labels "seniors," or "older adults"? Definitions based on chronological age are changing as a result of the increasing longevity and functional ability of contemporary men and women. In a study to determine the preferred group descriptor of older Americans, the terms *mature, older,* and *senior* were the most frequently chosen adjectives; *aged* and *old* were the most disliked terms (Finley, 1989, p. 6). Past demographic profiles have identified persons as older adults if they had passed the age of 65. Individuals between 65 and 74 years of age were described as "young old"; those over 74 were identified as the "older elderly." In 1997, however, Roen suggested that the "young old" subgroup "may soon include people as old as 84" (p. 348).

Today, popular thinking seems to embrace the concept that, barring serious physical or emotional challenges, the majority of older adults are both cognitively and physiologically about 10 years younger than their chronological age indicates. Thus, a 21st-century 75-year-old is comparable to a 65-year-old of the past century. The theoretical understanding for this perception is based on two characteristics of contemporary society, first, the general publics' increased interest in and concern with healthy nutrition (for example the avoidance of high-cholesterol foods); second, the fact that today's elders are more active both physically and cognitively, which has the potential to keep both body and mind functioning better and longer than in the past.

Older adults are the most rapidly growing segment of the population. In 1991, the U.S. census identified 31 million Americans older than age 65; Holland and McCurren (1997) estimated that the number will increase "to approximately 33.5 million by the year 2005" (p. 81). Twenty percent of the U.S. population will be older than 65 by the year 2020; this group is anticipated to account for 70 percent of those who need "primary, acute, home and long-term nursing care" (Rice, Beck, & Stevenson, 1997, p. 27).

Tournier (1983) described the movement from adulthood to older age as one of the great turning points in life. Admittedly, certain potentially negative physiologic and psychosocial changes accompany the aging process. Although each person ages differently, some common characteristics are physical changes in hair, skin, and teeth; impaired vision and hearing; lessened appetite; skeletal changes related to arthritis or osteoporosis; and lowered energy levels, among others. As a result of these physiologic modifications, the older adult may experience social isolation, financial concern associated with the inability to work, and anxiety and depression related to worry about future health and health-care issues. Despite this rather bleak chronology of negative factors associated with the aging process, Taylor, Lillis, and LeMone (1997) believe that the older adult can continue to carry out the usual activities of middle age as long as the pace is modified and rest periods are included (p. 59).

Heriot (1995) warned that for too long our society has viewed aging in depressing terms rather than seeking out the positive developmental processes that can occur despite the negative physical changes (p. 349). Some developmental tasks for the elder include the creation of a new self-image as an older person, learning to adjust to and find meaning in life despite physical impairments or decreasing energy levels, adapting to a simpler lifestyle necessitated by lowered or fixed income, and seeking to promote and maintain a high quality of life as an older adult (Lueckenotte, 1997, p. 573). It is possible for the older adult to move past his or her physical deficits and "find a sense of identity and worth in relationships, and in intellectual, artistic and spiritual pursuits" (Maltby, 1990, p. 101). As well as enjoying relationships with family and friends, some other strategies for aging well are cultivating a positive attitude toward life, choosing activities one enjoys, and maintaining a health regimen of diet and exercise (Hogstel, 1995).

More and more older adults, especially in the younger-old category, are remaining in the workforce or initiating second or third careers; many are also involved in full-time volunteer activities. Chronological age, of itself, should not be considered a disqualifier for maintaining a responsible place in society (Stagg, 1981, p. 11). Ultimately, Finch (1993) posited, the aging process may become a time of peace and joy during which the elder, no longer struggling with the challenges of career or ego, may be able to enjoy the beauties of loved ones and of nature in "wise tranquility" (p. 11). Wisdom is a spiritual gift that the older adult has to give to the world, a gift much needed in contemporary society.

▶ The Spirituality of Aging

Even to your old age, I am, even when you turn gray I will carry you; I will carry you and will save you.

—**Isaiah** 46:4

Spiritual writers Henri Nouwen and Walter Gaffney (1990), in their book *Aging: The Fulfillment of Life*, described the aging process poignantly as a human experience "which overarches the human community as a rainbow of promises" (p. 19). Aging, the authors believe, "can lead us to discover more and more of life's treasures . . . aging is not a reason for despair but a basis for hope, not a slow decaying but a gradual maturing, not a fate to be undergone but a challenge to be embraced" (p. 20). Seymour (1995) also advanced the concept of viewing the aging process in a spiritual light, asserting that as one's physical strength weakens, the spiritual dimension of life may intensify. Supportive of that position is a quotation cited by Seymour from a 150-year-old volume, *Happy Talk towards the End of Life*. "Is your eyesight dimmer? Then the world is seen by you in cathedral light. Is your hearing duller? Then it is just as though you were always where loud voices and footsteps ought not to be heard . . . Yes, for twilight and silence . . . old age makes us like daily dwellers in the house of the Lord" (p. 100). Spiritual issues in later life are "often driven" by such paradoxes, suggest Young and Koopsen (2011) in discussing the "unique spiritual challenges of aging" (p. 315).

Scholars of aging disagree as to whether the older adult becomes more or less involved in both spiritual and religious issues (Bianchi, 1995; Burt, 1992). Admittedly, some of the physical and psychosocial deficits of older age may hinder one's religiosity or religious practice; however, personal spirituality often deepens (Seymour, 1995). If an older person is relatively well, research has shown that religious practice may increase (Ainlay & Smith, 1984; Hunsberger, 1985; Markides, 1983). Membership in a church "is claimed by 73% of women and 63% of men older than 50 years, although fewer attend regularly" (Roen, 1997, p. 356); older adults tend to view the practice of religion as more important than do younger adults (Peterson & Potter, 1997). A church or synagogue may provide social networks for an older adult, as well as delineating a structure within which to live out one's spiritual beliefs. Some church groups may even facilitate health care for the older adult through the support of a parish nurse.

David Moberg (1990) worried, however, that while many religious or faith communities have been concerned about meeting the physical needs of their elders, they may have neglected ministering to spiritual needs (p. 18). Spiritual needs in the older adult are manifestations of the spiritual development associated with the aging process. As Bianchi (1995) pointed out, creatively dealing with the fact of one's mortality is a "major life task" (p. 59), as well as a major faith task. The task can become central to finding meaning in life for an older adult. Boettcher (1985) believed that as an elder's physical and psychosocial world begins to shrink, "an inner expansion of awareness and spirit can develop" (p. 29).

In order to provide spiritual care to an older adult, it is important for the caregiver to have some understanding of the developmental faith tasks of aging (Maltby, 1990). One useful paradigm is that of James Fowler's (1981) stages of faith development. To explain the late adult era, the final two of Fowler's stages are appropriate: conjunctive faith, stage 5, and movement toward stage 6, universalizing faith. Stage 5, or conjunctive faith (midlife and beyond), is a time of attempting to look beyond rational explanations and seeing their limitations. In this stage, the older adult may look back on earlier religious beliefs and traditions, which may have been discarded, and begin to reincorporate them into current attitudes and practice. Fowler (1981) called this a "reclaiming or reworking of one's past" (p. 197). He noted also that this is a time of "opening to the voices of one's deeper self," of one's "social unconscious" (p. 198). Previous prejudices toward people or religions can now be rejected and a new openness created. Despite this movement toward an attitude of justice for all, the individual in stage 5 may remain somewhat torn between preserving his or her own tradition and needs and a "more universal" caring (Koenig, 1994, p. 92).

Fowler's (1981) sixth stage, universalizing faith, occurring in the final years of life, is identified as "exceedingly rare." "The persons best described by it have generated faith compositions . . . inclusive of all being" (p. 200). Persons in the sixth faith stage possess "enlarged visions of universal community," and generally tend to violate "usual criteria for normalcy" (p. 200). These persons are unequivocally committed to a vision involving justice and peace and are willing to sacrifice their lives in the cause (Koenig, 1994, p. 93). This final stage is similar to what has been labeled "mature religious faith," a time when one directs one's concerns away from self and toward the larger society (Koenig, 1994; Maitland, 1991; Payne, 1990).

Promoting spiritual well-being for an older adult may involve such activities as active listening (including presence, touch, and reminiscence) and spiritual support (forgiveness, hope, and prayer) (Gaskamp, Sutter, & Meraviglia, 2006, pp. 9–10); support for an individual's religion and spirituality (McFadden & Kozberg, 2008); and the interventions of spiritual assessment and spiritual care, as well as palliative care if appropriate (MacKinlay, 2008).

▶ Spirituality and Religious Practice in Older Adults

As an outgrowth of and support for one's spiritual development, religious practices may be very important to the quality of life of an older adult. The religious or faith tradition of the elder will direct the nature of specific practices. Studies of religiosity among elders have, however, identified certain practices common to a number of religious denominations. Some of these include prayer and meditation, church membership, participation in religious worship services, study of religious doctrine, and spiritual reading. Halstead (1995) also identified the use of religiously oriented videos, music recordings, and television programs as helpful to elders in practicing their religion (p. 416).

In a study of religious practice among 380 elders, Mull, Cox, and Sullivan (1987) found that 94 percent reported religion to be important in terms of their health and well-being. The well elders highly valued attendance at church or synagogue. For those who had greater physical disability, private religious practices such as prayer and watching religious TV programs became more important (p. 151). Religious practice can be seen as giving life to spiritual beliefs, providing an important spiritual support network for the older adult, and helping an ill elder to transcend physical or emotional suffering by internalizing a transcendent vision in terms of the meaning of life (Hall, 1985).

Religious and/or spiritual practices carried out by older adults have also been found to be associated with positive self-care agency, that is, self-caring activities. A study of 235 seniors concluded that "the older adults who reported routine practice of spiritual growth behaviors also reported having positive self-concepts and took the initiative and responsibility for self-care" (Callaghan, 2006, p. 49). Study implications for nursing included "incorporating spiritual assessments and interventions in caring for older adults" (p. 50). From research such as this, as well as from the extant literature on spirituality, aging, and nursing, a number of issues were identified "for translating evidence into practice" (Hudson, 2008, p. 145). Hudson identified the issues in terms of seven key themes, which include:

1. Spirituality, concept development and models
2. Spirituality and chronic illness
3. Promoting spiritual health and well-being
4. Spirituality and dying
5. Cross-cultural and multifaith issues
6. Spiritual assessment
7. Ethics (Hudson, 2008, pp. 146–148)

Hudson recommended that nurses "carefully consider the place of spirituality within a holistic framework of care for the older person" (p. 149).

As well as general concern for the spirituality and spiritual practice needs of the older adult, it is noted that current "changes from monocultural to multicultural societies challenge nurses to know how to provide culturally and faith appropriate care" (MacKinlay, 2008, p. 151). Like Hudson, MacKinlay also suggests concern about ethical issues: "Ethical perspectives of older people must be carefully addressed in nursing as frail and vulnerable older people struggle with issues of compromised autonomy" (p. 151).

A common religious practice universally identified with most Western and Eastern religions is that of prayer. Despite diminishing physical health, persons of all religious beliefs tend to pray more during their senior years than at any other time in their lives (Finley, 1989). Prayer is a practice with many faces. For a well elder, prayer may involve social interaction when engaged in during group worship services. For an ill or frail elder, private prayer or meditation can help alleviate feelings of loneliness or anxiety. For the confused or cognitively impaired older adult, traditional prayers learned in one's youth can sometimes be remembered and provide comfort. This is reflected in the comments of a chaplain with more than seven years of experience in ministering to nursing home residents. In justifying the inclusion of confused elders in religious rites, the chaplain asserted:

> Even patients who are pretty much out of contact, they are still able to make the sign of the cross; they are still able to say prayers they learned when they were three or four years old. It [religion] is one of the things that goes last, as far as the memory is concerned; well, at least some basic tenets that they hang on to because they were so deeply ingrained. (O'Brien, 1989, p. 144)

Establishing a schedule for times of prayer during the day can be helpful for the newly retired person who may be somewhat "at loose ends"; the person can look forward to this time "not as a duty but as a time of joy and relaxation" (Coupland, 1985, p. 44). Spiritual writer Robert Wicks (1997) suggested that older adults might choose to engage in several types of prayer during the day, including both formal and informal prayers ("conversations with God"), religious reflections, "spiritual letter-writing," and creating of one's own parables (p. 22). Some comforting Psalms that an elder might pray are Psalm 23, "The Lord is my shepherd"; Psalm 25, prayer for guidance; Psalm 34, God as protector; Psalm 62, trust in God; Psalm 71, prayer in old age; and Psalm 121, God's support in trials (Hynes, 1989, p. 49).

▶ Spirituality and Physical Diminishment

Every age has its own beauty. Why be afraid of physical decline when the years bring deeper insight and greater gentleness of action?

—Roger of Taizé, as cited in Finch, 1993, p. 23

When an elder's physical capacities are no longer functional at the level an individual may wish, a sense of inner comfort and peace may still be derived from spiritual beliefs and behaviors. Spiritual and religious practices such as meditation or silent prayer, or having a loving attitude toward others, may be part of a life plan even for the older old person afflicted with a multiplicity of physical deficits. In a study including 31 in-depth interviews with older adults whose health ranged from good to terminal illness, Hungelmann, Kenkel-Rossi, Klassen, and Stollenwerk (1985) found the concept of "harmonious interconnectedness" of relationships to constitute spiritual well-being. The core categories of spiritual well-being identified were "ultimate other," reflecting such concepts as belief and trust in God and religious practice; "other/nature," consisting of expressions of mutual love and forgiveness, and accepting and giving help; and "self," relating to accepting and valuing oneself (p. 150). The investigators reported that, for this population of elders, spiritual well-being represented a "state of peace and harmony . . . linked to past experiences and future hopes and goals" (p. 151).

A nursing diagnosis of alteration in spiritual well-being or spiritual distress in an ill elder may be related to the individual's anger or frustration over an illness or disability. Chaplain Mary Brian Durkin (1992), who ministers to patients on a rehabilitation unit, noted that a disabled patient's suffering was often associated with a negative attitude toward his or her condition. For such a patient the provision of spiritual counseling and support can be a critical element in coping with illness and disability. Sister Mary Byrne (1985) asserted that for some ill elders "spiritual support is their greatest need"; she pointed out that emotional support is not adequate if an older person's problem is of a spiritual nature (pp. 30, 32).

▶ Spirituality and Cognitive Diminishment

Many older adults experience some degree of cognitive impairment as they progress through the aging process. Rice, Beck, and Stevenson (1997) reported cognitive impairment or senile dementia of the Alzheimer type (SDAT) in an "estimated 10.3% of those over 65," and that "the incidence may be as high as 48% in persons over 85 years of age" (p. 29). The authors posited that approximately 75 percent of nursing home residents have some cognitive impairment (p. 29).

The latter statistic was supported during the author's conduct of an exploratory case study of a 230-bed nursing home, labeled "Bethany Manor" (O'Brien, 1989). Because of the large number of Bethany Manor residents manifesting dementia symptoms, an attempt was made, through qualitative interview, to gain at least minimal understanding of their spiritual, physical, and emotional needs. Five dominant themes describing attitude and behavior were derived from data elicited in interviews with a subsample of 24 moderately cognitively impaired residents. These concepts included conformity, related to the residents' desire to please, especially the nursing home staff; privacy, which meant "minding one's own business" and limiting social interactions in the nursing home; activity, relating to activities of daily living in the nursing home, as well as visiting with staff and family; externality, a theme describing the fact that, according to their comments, some residents seemed to "live" in the worlds of family and friends outside of the nursing home; and reminiscence, or telling stories of one's life, even as far back as childhood (O'Brien, 1989, pp. 37–39). Some hints as to a resident's spirituality did emerge in the data, for example, remarks about God, prayer, or attendance at church as a child. One woman commented, "When you look at the handicaps all the people here have, I say God's been good to me" (p. 39); another long-term resident asserted, "I have been brought up as a Christian and my belief is a great support to me now" (p. 47).

As pointed out by Sharon Mooney (2006), "The effect of Alzheimer's disease on spirituality, or on a person's relationship with God, is an area that has not been studied extensively" (p. 9). Thus, Mooney has explored "ways to help dementia patients remember God"; one suggestion was the use of "rituals" associated with a patient's faith tradition. Mooney explained, "For the present generation of older adults with progressive dementia, the importance of rituals as a means of enhancing some degree of orientation to reality, calming emotions and decreasing agitated physical behavior should not be underestimated" by nurses caring for these patients (p. 9).

It is understood that Alzheimer's disease "can create an overwhelming set of circumstances for those diagnosed and for those giving care . . . [and] under such circumstances, many diagnosed individuals and their families cope by drawing on spiritual and religious beliefs and practices" (Stuckey, Post, Ollerton, FallCreek, & Whitehouse, 2002, p. 199). Stuckey et al. assert that "even when persons with dementia are stripped of memory, it is still possible, and perhaps even more likely, to reach them in religious and spiritual pathways" (p. 206). This conclusion is supported by the work of Beuscher and Beck (2008), who conducted a literature review on spirituality and coping with Alzheimer's disease. Their "findings suggest that persons with early-stage Alzheimer's disease draw from their spirituality and faith to find meaning and courage in facing the challenges of cognitive losses" (p. 88). Beuscher and Beck conclude that for nurses, gaining an "understanding of how older persons with Alzheimer's disease cope with their memory loss is critical to the development of evidence-based interventions to minimize the stress of living with the disease" (p. 88).

One of the established nursing interventions for elders with cognitive diminishment is that of reminiscence. The process was studied among a group of 116 older adults with dementia living in long-term care facilities (MacKinlay & Trevitt, 2010). The nurse investigators collected qualitative data, generated prior to and after reminiscence group sessions, to evaluate the success of the project. Study findings revealed that "new relationships were developed among group members that improved life" for the study participants (p. 394). MacKinlay and Trevitt suggested that "spiritual reminiscence offers nursing staff a way of knowing those with dementia in a deeper and more meaningful way" (p. 394).

▶ Spiritual Concerns of the Older Adult

Two key spiritual concerns identified by older adults are loneliness and uncertainty of the future.

Loneliness

Loneliness can be a significant problem for the older adult (Fischer, 1995; Lotito, 1993; Normille, 1992). This is related to the onset of both physical and psychosocial deficits. Such deficits may cause the older person to become distanced from a faith or worship group. Restriction in ambulation can hinder an elder's religious practice in terms of attendance at church or synagogue worship services; impairment in sight and hearing may cause an elder to be sensitive about participating in faith group activities where such a limitation might be noticed. Elders may also retreat from church activities as a result of fatigue or depression associated with the aging process. For the elder not of a religious tradition, loneliness may relate to isolation from former work and friendship or volunteer groups, such as clubs and charitable organizations.

An older adult may take a number of steps to alleviate loneliness, such as making a conscious effort to get out, if able physically. Many churches today have special programs and groups for elders only; these can be social or may involve volunteer activities (Finley, 1989). Also, a number of community programs encourage the participation of the elderly who are mobile. For the homebound elder, church groups and some hospitals have projects such as Senior Connection, through which the ill older person can stay connected by phone to others in the area.

Although loneliness is a phenomenon experienced at some time and to some degree by virtually everyone, the loneliness of the older adult is unique in that it often grows out of loss (Valentine, 1994). An elder's loneliness can be the result of multiple losses: physical (isolation related to disabling health deficit), emotional (deaths of family and friends), social (loss of work-related relationships), financial (inability to travel or participate in social activities due to a fixed income), or spiritual (loss of ability to participate in religious worship services).

Although steps can be taken to alleviate an elder's loneliness, spiritual literature on the concept advises that "aloneness need not be a negative experience": "On the contrary, the emptiness of feeling alone can open one's heart, and make one more perceptive of the presence of God" (Deeken, 1986, p. 41). After a life filled with activity, work, family, and social activities, seniors may find that their aloneness provides a time of peace and quiet joy. For those elders, rather than bringing loneliness, the period of retirement from active work is welcomed as a spiritual journey, a preparation for the transition to eternal life.

Uncertainty of the Future

For the older adult, especially one experiencing illness, uncertainty of the future can be the source of much anxiety. The elder may have already witnessed the lingering illnesses and deaths of relatives or friends, each loss raising anew the specter of one's own mortality. Central concerns for the older adult generally are focused on economics (financial security or lack of security in the later stages of life) and autonomy (being able to care for oneself in illness or having some control over the kind of care received). Associated fears are those related to the possibility of future loneliness and cognitive impairment. The comments of a 77-year-old nursing home resident reflect such uncertainty. "I just don't know about the future. You work hard all your life, but in the end you never know. It's a worry, I'll tell you that for sure."

Some older adults, however, especially those with a spiritual or religious perspective on life, express little fear of the future. An 83-year-old nursing home resident described her present life as satisfactory. "I'm at peace and I hope to die here. I have reached a good age. God has been good to me. The things that could make me wonder about things, worry me, are lost. Death doesn't frighten me" (O'Brien, 1989, p. 45).

▶ Spiritual Needs of the Older Adult

Hammer (1990) identified the spiritual needs of the older adult as relating to the carrying out of religious practices such as grace before meals, Scripture reading, and prayer; for the older or frail elderly, some contact with a former church or faith group is important (pp. 3–4). Forbis (1988) advanced a broader understanding of spiritual need among older adults, identifying such activities as listening to music, reading poetry, and verbalizing fears and anxieties, as well as prayer and spiritual reading (p. 159). Forbis warned that an ill elder who had strong religious beliefs may be fearful of expressing doubts or anxieties to family or friends; such an individual may, however, share these concerns with a nurse who does not have the same expectations as significant others (p. 158).

A key spiritual need of the older adult, regardless of whether the elder identifies with a particular religious tradition, is the ability to find meaning in the aging process (Blazer, 1991). Although this can be the most difficult task of aging in the face of multiple physical, psychological, social, and financial losses, it is also the most challenging dimension of an elder's spiritual journey. Closely linked to this faith task of aging is the need to confront the prospect of death and the dying process. Although those who adhere to a religious tradition generally fear death less than those with no particular religious belief, the prospect of coping with the dying process causes anxiety in most older adults (Berggren-Thomas & Griggs, 1995). In the face of terminal illness, specific spiritual needs for trust, hope, and forgiveness most frequently manifest in an older adult. Related to these needs is the desire for reminiscence, which may help the elder to put present anxieties into the perspective of an entire lifetime.

Trust

Trust, a concept that can be defined as being related to a sense of security in one's future, can be greatly tested during the later stages of the aging process. Fear of the unknown associated not only with death and the dying process but also with the concept of an afterlife poses a great threat to trust in the older adult (Swift & Rench, 1991). The religious elder who has lived according to the tenets of his or her tradition may more easily maintain trust by reflecting on the rewards identified for the faithful. An older adult who does not subscribe to any particular religious belief system will need to draw on personal philosophical beliefs about the meaning of life and one's own contribution to society for support.

Hope

Hope, or the expectation of a positive outcome in the future, is closely linked to trust, especially for the elder from a religious background. Hope is strengthened by an older adult's adherence to strong religious and moral values (Fischer, 1988; Lenarz, 1988; Lotito, 1993). Hope may be more difficult for an ill elder who no longer feels in control of his or her life or future activities. Through a qualitative study to explore the meaning of hope among 12 older adults, Gaskins and Forte (1995) identified hope-related themes related to such factors as health, relationships, material resources, positive emotions, giving service, and reminiscing (p. 19). The most significant and frequently identified theme, however, was that of spirituality. "All of the [study] participants spoke of the important role spirituality played as a source of hope" (p. 19). The authors admitted that all elders in the study identified with a faith tradition, and thus the spirituality theme was often associated with religious practice and belief; hope was, for others, however, described as "having a moral creed for living one's life" (p. 20). And in a study of hope among 94 chronically ill elders residing in a long-term care facility, Beckerman and Northrop (1996) found the most important sources of hope to be faith, relationships, self-esteem, and the ability to give to others. Hope engenders in an elder the spirit to find meaning and joy in life and to maintain a positive sense of self-worth amid diminishing physical and psychological capacities.

Forgiveness

Perhaps the most frequently identified spiritual need for the older adult, especially in the face of serious or terminal illness, is the desire to give and to receive forgiveness. It is rare to find any person, especially one who has lived to elder years, who is not able to acknowledge some attitude or behavior for which he or she would wish forgiveness. The individual from whom the elder desires forgiveness may not be aware of the elder's need; the concern may totally reside in the heart and conscience of the one seeking forgiveness. The other important dimension of the concept relates to an older person's need to extend forgiveness to a person who in the elder's perception has done harm. To give and receive forgiveness are tasks not easily accomplished. Both, noted Fischer (1995), involve "a long and complex process of healing" (p. 127). Much emotional baggage related to old hurts, both given and received, may be deeply ingrained in the elder's persona; they are not easily let go of (Finley, 1989). It is important to remember, also, that desiring to forgive or accept forgiveness does not erase the memories; what forgiveness may accomplish is to "humanize" and incorporate a memory into an elder's current "self-understanding" (Maitland, 1991, p. 160). Healing occurs as the forgiving or forgiven elder reframes his or her self-image and is able to make peace with the past (Bozarth, 1995).

Reminiscence

Another need for the older adult, and one closely linked to giving or receiving forgiveness, is the need for reminiscence. As an individual reviews his or her life story, the need for forgiveness may emerge. There are also many other positive aspects to the act of reminiscence. First, an elder may be strengthened in dealing with present concerns and anxieties by remembering and reidentifying past coping skills used in dealing with stressful experiences. An elder may come to recognize that he or she has "endured beyond [the] ability to endure" (Seymour, 1995, p. 104). This can be a very beneficial memory in terms of facing the unknown future. The process of reviewing past life accomplishments can also serve to suggest what tasks an elder might still undertake, and what legacies can be left (Erikson, 1995, p. 14). In this way, reminiscence may serve as the catalyst for initiating a new career in later life or for helping the older adult to complete some partially finished tasks or activities. Additionally, an elder who reminisces as a social activity with family or friends can offer hard-earned wisdom as a gift to loved ones.

▶ Spiritual Needs in Long-Term Care

Long-term health care for the elderly involves providing "comprehensive, continuous care for older adults in diverse settings" (Collins, Butler, Guelder, & Palmer, 1997, p. 59). These settings include the elder's home or the home of relatives, retirement communities, assisted care facilities, and skilled care nursing homes. The care populations consist of active elders with chronic illness, the homebound elderly, and elders in need of skilled nursing home care. In discussing the need to "revolutionize" long-term care, Patricia Emery (2006), a nursing home director, commented, "Only two populations in this country still face routine and/or permanent institutionalization—convicted felons and the elderly" (p. 16). Some of the positive suggestions for change identified by Emery are "to explore placing control back in their (the elderly) hands" and "allowing them to participate in the decision making processes of life" (p. 22). This can be accomplished, Emery adds, "by providing a home, a sanctuary, a healing environment, where elders experience life and growth" (p. 22).

In a nursing study to explore the relationship between spiritual well-being and positive quality of life, the author conducted both structured and open-ended (conversational) interviews with three populations of older adults: mobile elders living with chronic illness, homebound elders, and nursing home residents (O'Brien, 1997). All study participants were over the age of 65 years. The sample group consisted of 38 mobile elders, 4 older adults who were homebound, and 10 nursing home residents. Data elicited from all three groups reflected a strong association between spiritual well-being, evaluated by a Spiritual Assessment Scale (O'Brien, 1997)—which measures personal faith, religious practice, and spiritual contentment/distress—and quality of life, evaluated in terms of hope (Miller Hope Scale, Miller & Powers, 1988; adapted 1997) and life satisfaction (Life Satisfaction Index-Z, Wood, Wylie, & Sheafor, 1969).

Qualitative data generated through open-ended, conversational interviews (Spirituality and Religiousness Interview Guide, O'Brien, 1997) also demonstrated the presence of hopefulness and life satisfaction among elders with a high degree of personal faith, involvement in religious practice, and lack of spiritual distress, that is, a strong sense of spiritual well-being. Data reflecting spiritual and religious characteristics of chronically ill elders—active elders living with chronic illness, homebound elders, and nursing home residents—are discussed relative to each subcategory.

Active Elders Living with Chronic Illness

Census data for 1989 revealed that 70 percent of men and 77 percent of women over 65 had one or more chronic illness; 81 percent of the men and 90 percent of the women were chronically ill by the age of 80 (Sapp & Bliesmer, 1995, p. 4). In an ethnographic study of spirituality among 12 chronically ill elders ranging in age from 65 to 89 years, Young (1993) identified recurrent themes of "hope, comfort, strength and well-being" as related to spiritual beliefs. The concept of hope was associated with trust in the existence of an afterlife, comfort and strength were derived from an elder's belief in God, and well-being was related to the sense of God's love and care provided both in the present and after death (p. 299). Koenig (1994), who also explored the spiritual needs of physically ill elders, described specific concerns such as the need for meaning and hope, the need for belief in transcendence, the need for spiritual support, the need to carry out religious practices, the need for a feeling of self-worth, the need for love, the need to trust in God, and the need to give to others (pp. 284–291). Ill elders, Koenig asserted, need to be not only prepared for death and the dying process, but also supported "in the life they have remaining" (p. 294).

In the author's study of spiritual well-being and quality of life (O'Brien, 1997) among 38 active (nonhomebound) chronically ill elders, participants ranged in age from 67 to 96 years; 30 were female and 8 were male. Thirty-five persons were white and three were African American. Fifty percent of the group had some college education. Twenty-three of the elders were Roman Catholic, 14 were Protestant, and one was Jewish. Seventy-eight percent of the chronically ill elders attended church at least once a week. Chronic illness conditions included such diagnoses as rheumatoid arthritis, hypertension, cardiomyopathy, asthma, osteoporosis, peptic ulcer, and diabetes mellitus. A number of the study participants also reported multiple diagnoses such as congestive heart failure, arthritis, and hearing loss; hypertension, arthritis, and glaucoma; and hypothyroidism and coronary artery disease.

Although, as noted, the association between spiritual well-being and positive quality of life was strong overall, certain individual scale items revealed interesting findings. Hope, as a concept, was rated high among the group; however, seven of the study participants disagreed with Miller Hope Scale item 4 ("I have energy to do what is important to me"), and over half of the group, 22 (57.8 percent), agreed moderately rather than strongly with the statement. And, although most elders responded negatively to the Life Satisfaction Index-Z item 3 ("This is the dreariest time in my life"), 16 respondents or 42 percent of the group also disagreed with Life Satisfaction Index-Z item 5 ("These are the best years of my life"). One 72-year-old woman penciled in the comment, "These are not the best years of my life, but they're good!" Several respondents commented on item 14 in the Spiritual Assessment Scale ("I am helped to communicate with God by spiritual reading or thinking about religious things"). For example, an 84-year-old woman admitted that because of failing eyesight, reading had become a problem.

The author's analysis of qualitative data elicited in interviews with the 38 chronically ill elders revealed five dominant themes reflecting spiritual well-being among the group: trust, comfort, joy, acceptance, and peace. Trust was associated with the constancy of God's protection, especially during difficult times. Comfort was defined as a sense of well-being received from prayer and spiritual reading, especially the reading of Scripture. Joy was seen as deriving from personal faith beliefs, religious practices, and the support of one's church. Acceptance was related to patience in the face of pain and suffering and faith that God would provide needed support. Peace was achieved in facing death; this was frequently associated with an elder's perception of having lived a "good life," as he or she understood the concept.

Trust

Mrs. Daly, an 88-year-old Roman Catholic diagnosed with congestive heart disease and arthritis, expressed great confidence in God. "I can always count on God to help me in my times of need. My trust in Him affects my whole life; he gives me strength to take part in senior citizen's programs. My belief in God makes me feel great, knowing that He is there watching over me every day, giving me time to spend with my daughter and my grandchildren. I'm healthy and happy. God is very good to me."

Mrs. Kelly, an 81-year-old Catholic who was somewhat more ill with cardiovascular disease, also verbalized trust in God. "I feel as though all my life God has been standing by me. He has always watched over me and helped me get through the pain." Mrs. Kelly added, "But more importantly God showed me how to find love."

Comfort

Mrs. Ann Johnson, an 89-year-old Baptist diagnosed with heart disease and arthritis, described the comfort she received from religion and religious practices. "I pray and am at peace. God and I have a relationship that comforts me. I talk to Him when I am lonely or in need or thankful. My trust in God is part of my everyday life . . . My faith in God got me involved in my church and the people in my church are the bright spot in my life, so I guess God has been a great comfort in my life."

Sixty-five-year-old Miss Smith, a Christian suffering from rheumatoid arthritis, reported comfort from spiritual reading. "I read from a religious book, *My Daily Bread*, which I find very comforting, especially in times of illness or sadness in my life. It keeps me remembering that God will never send me crosses heavier than I can bear."

Joy

Mrs. Davis, a 65-year-old Presbyterian with cardiac disease, described the joy her spirituality and religious practice brought to her life. "I know that I am in God's hands; He is looking out for me and that is a joy. Another thing that brings me a lot of happiness is that I attend Sunday school and church every Sunday. I have been with the same people in Sunday school for almost 29 years. These friends are very dear to me and we help each other in rough times; they are my church support."

Sixty-seven-year-old Mrs. Flaherty, a Catholic suffering from cardiomyopathy, reported, "My joy is from my love of God, which affects my everyday relationships with people. Although I can lose my temper sometimes, I try to be true to my faith and be loving and share the joy with people in my life."

Acceptance

Mr. Anderson, a 70-year-old diagnosed with a brain tumor, spoke about the importance of his Lutheran beliefs and practices in helping him accept his illness. "I know God cares for us in times of sickness. I pray and talk to Him and know that He hears me. He may not always answer the prayers the way I would like Him to do, but He knows what is best for me. I am at peace in my relationship with God. I trust in His Son, Jesus Christ, and know Him as my Lord and Savior. He has given me an inner peace to accept whatever happens, whatever my illness situation may be." Mr. Anderson explained that his church, the Evangelical Lutheran Church of America (ELCA), provided much support. "It gives me strength to deal with my illness. We are a community of believers, and God gives us the assurance that He is with us in time of need, and that He will heal us." Mr. Anderson concluded, "He is a caring and healing God. We are in His hands. Who could ask for anything more?"

Roman Catholic Mrs. Doherty, an 86-year-old suffering from arthritis, observed, "I feel at great peace in my relationship with God. I have been able to accept pain and put difficult times in perspective because I feel that God allows things to happen for a reason. I just trust that God will be watching over me no matter what happens. So in that way I can accept whatever happens."

Peace

Miss Mahoney, a 75-year-old Catholic and a cancer survivor also suffering from congestive heart failure, described the meaning of peace in her life. "I truly am at peace right now. I completely feel at peace in my relationship with God; I always have. There are hard times when you are struggling, but that does not take away your peace, your faith in God. I am at peace about death too; I'm not afraid to die. I know that God will be with me then, as always."

Seventy-eight-year-old Mrs. Pearson, diagnosed with coronary artery disease, explained that as a member of the Baha'i faith, her peace was related to having lived well. "I don't exactly have a relationship with God as in the sense of a 'relationship.' Baha'i's believe that God is all around us. But I do feel at peace with God, because I have led a good life. I honor God every day."

The Homebound Elderly

Chronically ill elders who are homebound or nonmobile and living in assisted care facilities may have significant spiritual needs related to the physical and psychosocial sequelae of their conditions. The physical and emotional pain associated with being homebound requires a depth of faith and spirituality (Burghardt, 1991), as well as spiritual maturity, which Birren (1990) interpreted as the elder's ability to focus on transcendent spiritual values, while still appreciating religious experiences of the past (p. 42).

In studying 26 Protestant, Catholic, and Jewish homebound elders, Brennan (1994) found that personal spirituality was described as giving "meaning and purpose to life" (p. 96). Brennan's study participants understood the difference between the concepts of religion and spirituality, yet perceived them to be interrelated; many described using prayer as a coping mechanism. A specific need expressed by more than half of the study group was the "desire to be able to discuss their spiritual beliefs and feelings with others, especially in times of crisis" (p. 96).

Four homebound elders interviewed for a study of spiritual well-being and quality of life (O'Brien, 1997) ranged from 75 to 91 years of age; all were female and were wheelchair or walker restricted. Three of the women were white and one was African American. Two members of the homebound subgroup were Roman Catholic, one was Mennonite, and the other was a member of the Church of Christ; all were unable to attend worship services because of physical disability. Their illness conditions included rheumatoid arthritis, diabetes and postpolio syndrome, hypertension and cardiovascular disease, and congestive heart failure and hypertension. Quantitative measures for this group revealed a strong relationship between spiritual well-being and positive quality of life.

Qualitative data elicited from the homebound elders reflected one unifying theme that might be described as confident prayer; that is, all four study participants spoke about the depth of their faith and trust in God related to their prayer practices and the prayers of their families and church members. Mrs. Allen, an 83-year-old Mennonite diagnosed with diabetes and postpolio syndrome, described herself as almost totally disabled, yet she displayed a strong faith. "I pray to God daily; He's on my mind all the time. I rely on God and on my church in hard times. God is very accessible. I'm very much at peace in my relationship with God." The remarks of 91-year-old Mrs. McCarthy, a Catholic with multiple diagnoses of congestive heart failure, coronary artery disease, and hypertension, who lives in an assisted care setting, reflected a similar theme. "I believe in God who watches out for me in times of sickness and health. I feel at peace with God; I pray to Him every day and I know He will take me when He is ready." Mrs. McCarthy added, "When I'm sick I also count on the prayers of my family and my church."

Mrs. Clark, an 82-year-old homebound member of the Church of Christ who was diagnosed with diabetes and hypertension, reported that although she could not get out to attend church services, she prayed all the time. "I pray and I know that God is taking care of me in all my trials and tribulations, and I will come out better in the end. I believe that no matter what happens God will be with me. You can trust God all the time." Mrs. Clark also commented on the importance of the prayer support of others. "My family members are all of the same religion and they pray for me, and we pray for each other. Being a Christian has helped keep us together, to keep God in the middle of everything."

Mrs. O'Connell, a 75-year-old Catholic who is wheelchair bound because of arthritis, described the peace she received from prayer. "I do feel at peace when I pray; it affects all the activities of my day. It gives me a positive attitude about things. I pray every day and trust in God and the Blessed Mother to get me through."

Nursing Home Residents

The term *nursing home* is broadly understood as describing a facility that "provides twenty-four hour skilled nursing care at an intermediate [i.e., nonhospital] level" (Simmons & Peters, 1996, p. 7). Data obtained in 1984 identified 19,100 nursing homes with approximately 1.6 million beds; this statistic reflected "a 22% increase over the previous ten years" (Millsap, 1995, p. 99). Presently almost 20 percent of older old adults (over 80) reside in nursing homes, and by the year 2030, the number is expected to triple (Koenig, 1994, p. 353). Mechanisms suggested to enhance the spiritual well-being of elders in institutional settings include "appreciation for the spiritual dimension of life," "spiritual care," "vitality of the spirit" of the setting, "spiritual health of the staff," and "presence of . . . clergy" (Minnix, 2008, pp. 66–67). A study of perception of the meaning and value of spirituality among five residents of a long-term care facility revealed such themes as "meaning," "coping," "positive outlook," "reliance," "comfort and consolation," and "hope for recovery" (Schwartz & Cottrell, 2007, p. 43).

Some characteristics of a contemporary nursing home population include average age in the 80s; most widowed or single; women in 3:1 proportion to men; many having some degree of dementia and/or arthritis or cardiovascular disease; many experiencing impaired vision or hearing, or both; and most requiring assistance with activities of daily living (Holland & McCurren, 1997, p. 97). Data from an urban nursing home with approximately 230 residents revealed a population physical profile heavily laden with such diagnoses as arteriosclerotic heart disease, diabetes mellitus, hip fracture, osteoporosis, arthritis, Parkinson's disease, Alzheimer's disease, and senile dementia (O'Brien, 1989, pp. 22–23).

The multiplicity of health deficits experienced by current nursing home residents requires skill and ingenuity in care planning, including that of spiritual ministry. Malcolm (1987) believed that nurses must work at developing "creative spiritual care" for elderly nursing home residents; she suggested that although usual care plans place symptoms of dementia under a psychosocial need heading, these aspects of an elder's personality may also be "interwoven with the spiritual" (p. 25).

Some religious rituals appropriate for the responsive nursing home resident include Baptism (for one who has never experienced the sacrament earlier in life), Communion (according to the resident's religious tradition), Anointing of the Sick, and celebrations of religious feast days (Simmons & Peters, 1996, pp. 76–83). For the seriously physically or cognitively impaired resident, Simmons and Peters noted that these rituals may be adapted and modified to meet the elder's condition. Many nursing homes are formally affiliated with a particular religious denomination, so the worship services and rites of that tradition may be central to the home's activities; however, arrangements are generally made for religious ministry to residents of different traditions.

The 10 nursing home residents who participated in the author's study of spiritual well-being and quality of life (O'Brien, 1997) ranged in age from 71 to 98 years; 8 were female and 2 were male. Eight of the nursing home residents were African American and two were white; three of the group were married. Group members had been living in the nursing home from 4 months to 5 years; all were wheelchair bound. Five of the nursing home residents were Roman Catholic, two were Baptist, one was Seventh-day Adventist, one was Pentecostal, and one was a Jehovah's Witness. Their collective diagnoses included peripheral vascular disease, bilateral knee replacements, cerebral vascular accident, rheumatoid arthritis, congestive heart disease, diabetes, blindness, right-sided paralysis, and fractured hip.

Quantitative data demonstrated a strong relationship between spiritual well-being and positive quality of life among the group. Interestingly, all of the nursing home residents agreed with the Miller Hope Scale item 4 ("I have energy to do what is important to me"). One might speculate that this group of wheelchair-bound nursing home residents had modified their expectations in terms of those activities for which they perceived energy to be required.

Three dominant themes were derived from qualitative data elicited in interviews with the nursing home group: faith in God and religious beliefs despite illness and disability, and acceptance of nursing home life; devotion, relating especially to private religious practices such as prayer and Scripture reading; and spiritual contentment, or a sense of peace in relation to where the elder is on his or her spiritual journey.

Faith

Mrs. Jackson, an 81-year-old Baptist resident who had experienced bilateral knee replacements, described a powerful faith. "I do believe in God; He gives me strength to do everything I need to do. He has blessed me so in my life; I am able to go on because of Him. Sometimes the road is rough; not everything is smooth. Sometimes it's hard to be in a nursing home. There are some bumps and some knocks but Jesus will be right beside you." Mrs. Jackson added, "I don't ever feel far away from God regardless of what happens. I read the Twenty-third Psalm in the Bible, you know, 'Yea, though I walk through the valley of the shadow of death, I will fear no evil for Thou art with me.' It just makes you forget anything that might have happened."

The remarks of Mrs. Earhardt, a 76-year-old Seventh-day Adventist resident with peripheral vascular disease, also reflected a strong faith. "I have faith in God, a relationship with God, and when I get stressed out or something happens to me, the Lord always makes a way for that to ease over. Then the stress leaves me and the breath of God comes back in me. My faith is everything to me; if the effect of God didn't work in me, I couldn't make it. There is no way that I could make it without the

Lord. I might as well just hang it up and forget it." Mrs. Earhardt concluded, "Faith in God means everything. If you don't have faith in God, you don't have faith in anybody. There is no one I look up to but Jesus. If you believe in His word, He will answer you."

A male nursing home resident, Mr. Martin, an 82-year-old bilateral amputee and member of a pentecostal church, the Church of God in Christ, explained his faith. "Faith is having a personal relationship with Jesus. I believe that to be a child of God, you have to be born again of the Spirit. You can go to Jesus and tell Him anything and He will listen to you. And according to His will, He will grant you what you ask."

Devotion

Mrs. Meehan, an 87-year-old Catholic resident who was recovering from a stroke, described her religious devotion. "I try to stay very close to God through my prayers and church services. Many times I have talked to God; I talk with my God every day, a lot of times a day. I also go to Mass here in the chapel every day and I have a spiritual advisor who I talk to. And I have my rosary too that I say for my family who have gone to God, and for my friends."

An 88-year-old Jehovah's Witness resident, Mrs. Jensen, also recovering from a stroke, spoke especially about the importance of Scripture reading. "I'm at peace with God because I believe deeply in Him through the Bible. I read the Bible every day and I've come through with flying colors. Scripture gives comfort in Jesus. I am a Jehovah's Witness and we believe deeply in Jesus Christ. Jehovah is our great God. I find him in my Bible."

Spiritual Contentment

Seventy-two-year-old Mrs. Annie Smith, a Baptist nursing home resident with hypertension and stroke sequelae, described the contentment brought about by her spiritual and religious beliefs. "I believe in God and in His Son Jesus who care for me in times of trials and tribulations. God is such a consolation to me. And I am content and very confident that I will be taken care of in any matter. I think I've lived according to His commandments and I feel that God directs me in things I have done in my life, so I'm at peace." Mrs. Smith concluded, "I am in constant prayer with God, and I pray day and night or anytime that I feel I need to."

Mrs. Loughlin, a 98-year-old with multiple cardiovascular conditions and a Catholic, also reflected spiritual contentment in her remarks. "I'm at peace at this time in my life. I can't go to church anymore, but I get to the chapel here. I say my rosary in the evening for all my relatives and I pray for the people here. Most of my life God has answered all of my prayers. He is the power and the glory and the strength of my life. And I don't ever feel far away from Him, so I'm very happy here." Mrs. Loughlin concluded, "I thank God for all the lovely privileges I've had in my life; my home, and my family, and some of the beauty of the world. I realize that if it is God's will that I live a little longer then it's OK, but if it is not, then He will take me home to Glory."

Overall findings from the author's study of spirituality and quality of life among three groups of elders—active elders living with a chronic illness, home-bound elders, and nursing home residents—revealed the presence of spiritual values including faith, hope, trust (confidence), joy, acceptance, peace (contentment), and devotion (commitment to prayer for self and others) among the study participants. These study data documenting the spiritual and religious beliefs and practices, as well as the needs, of ill elders are supportive of James Fowler's (1981) final faith stages in which the older adult seeks a deepening of his or her own spiritual life as well as expressing concern over the needs of the larger society.

Continuing Care Retirement Community Residents

In today's world of long-term care, one hears the term *CCRC* (which stands for continuing care retirement community) used even more frequently than *nursing home*, although in fact the modern CCRC generally contains one or several dimensions of the older style nursing home.

The CCRC concept has become popular in the past several decades of long-term care. CCRCs differ significantly in terms of contracts, housing options, services, and costs. Generally, however, a CCRC is expected to be a long-term care facility providing three levels of living options for an older adult: independent living (in a room, apartment, or even a small cottage home); assisted care (single room with meals served in a communal dining room); and skilled nursing care (single- or double-room occupancy). Some CCRCs have separate facilities for dementia patients.

The advantage of the CCRC for many elders is the fact that they can enter the facility on a more independent level and then stay in the same CCRC as physical and/ or cognitive needs require more assistance or care. Contracts vary significantly among CCRCs, as do costs. Some facilities provide a life-care contract, guaranteeing that the individual will be cared for until death; for such a contract, the cost of the entrance or admission fee is generally significant. CCRCs also usually require that a potential resident come with Medicare A, B, and D (drug coverage), as well as a health-care supplemental plan such one of those recommended by the Association for Retired Persons (AARP). Some contracts provide services and care for a specified period of time; others include a fee-for-service contract. The latter CCRC usually only requires a minimal entrance fee; however, if assisted or skilled care is later needed, monthly costs will escalate notably.

An important concern for many potential CCRC residents is the presence or lack thereof of spiritual and religious support at the facility. Currently most large CCRCs have a department of "pastoral care" and a chapel to meet the needs of residents from a variety of faith traditions. The sponsorship or the administration of the facility may or may not be associated with a particular religious community or church.

It is only during the past decade that the nursing and health-care literature has begun to address the needs and concerns of the CCRC resident. Generally, the CCRC literatures addresses such issues as home technology, "including the influence of primary care providers" (Courtney, Demiris, Rantz, & Skubic, 2008, p. 195); networking or "social interaction with other people living at the retirement community" or CCRC (Schafer, 2011, p. 795); factors associated with exercise among CCRC residents (Resnick & D'Adamo, 2010); and patient education in a CCRC (Wendel, Durso, Zabel, Loman, & Remsburg, 2003). Interestingly, the concepts of spirituality and religion in the CCRC are seldom addressed. In one paper on the topic of the "therapeutic landscape" and residential transition to a CCRC, Cutchin, Marshall, and Aldrich (2010) did include the fact that symbolism "embedded in the interior and exterior of the buildings on a CCRC campus is typically meant to affirm cultural values of the generation living there as well as provide a sense of who the residents view themselves" to be (p. 120); no examples such as religious symbolism, however, were identified. The authors do present a table comparing pre- and post-move activity of CCRC residents, which includes an item revealing a change in attendance at religious services, but the concept is not explored in depth.

In a qualitative exploration of life in a CCRC entitled "But I Am Not Moving," the investigator conducted interviews with 35 residents primarily focused on the topic of transitions or moving across the three levels of the studied facility's care. Analysis of the data revealed three key themes related to CCRC transitioning that were labeled autonomy, fatalism, and social disengagement (Shippee, 2009, p. 421). The theme of autonomy included such concepts as "being told to move" and "threats to privacy" (pp. 421–422); fatalism included such concepts as "death" and "irreversibility of the move" (p. 423); and social disengagement included the "nature of social interaction" (p. 425). The topics of spirituality and/or religion might only be considered as implicitly addressed in relation to such concepts as fatalism and death.

I spent seven months volunteering in the pastoral care department of a large, 600-bed CCRC. The facility was rich with symbolism in terms of its founders' religious and spiritual orientation. Both the exterior and interior of the buildings were embellished with religious statuary and art reflective of the institutions' spiritual commitment to care for elders. The presence of a department of pastoral care, several chaplains, and three chapels on the campus also reflected the spiritual nature of the CCRC and provided worship opportunities for residents from a variety of faith communities. Daily pastoral care visits were made to all residents and a number of special celebrations were conducted on religious holidays. The pastoral care dimension of caring at this CCRC was described by residents in independent living, assisted living, and the nursing center as being central to their life satisfaction at the facility and also as having been a key factor in their choice of this particular CCRC for their personal retirement.

▶ Spirituality and Quality of Later Life

The quality of life for an older adult depends greatly on the personal spirituality supporting the elder's perception of his or her current life stage. As has been demonstrated in this chapter, some of the physiologic and psychosocial literature presents a rather bleak picture of life and functional ability for an elder; the older a person becomes, the more forbidding the image seems to be. On the other hand, spiritual and religious writing has affirmed the journey of aging as encompassing a time of peace and fulfillment; a "time to be eagerly awaited and warmly embraced" (Sapp, 1987, p. 133). The truth, for most older adults, probably lies somewhere between these two extremes. Certainly there is a greater risk of physical deficit as one ages. Oppenheimer (1991) believed, however, that "realism does not require that we should anticipate all these ills" (p. 43). Some future problems may be prevented by heeding health/illness-related precautions. And, if unexpected health deficits occur, the use of established coping skills, especially those of a spiritual or religious nature, can greatly mediate the negative impact of the condition. As Oppenheimer concluded, some future suffering can be "circumvented"; other suffering needs to be "faced."

In nursing research to explore the meaning of quality of life among residents of a long-term care facility, Aller and Van Ess Coeling (1995) identified three themes descriptive of the concept; these include "ability to communicate with others," "ability to care for self," and "ability to help others" (p. 23). The latter theme also reflects well Fowler's (1981) final stages of faith development, conjunctive faith and universalizing faith, in which an older individual's social conscience takes precedence over the needs of self; the desire to reach out to others becomes primary. As one of Aller and Van Ess Coeling's (1995) elder study respondents commented, "Quality of life, to me, is not only self-betterment, but the betterment of others (p. 23).

A study of 71 elders residing in a nursing home revealed that quality of later life was decidedly subjective. An 88-year-old resident in relatively good physical and mental health admitted that she did not want to do "much of anything" at this point in her life. "I made up my mind I am at the end of my rope. You do sort of get that notion. I have felt I really don't have any incentive to live" (O'Brien, 1989, p. 44). An 83-year-old woman, however, compared her quality of life to that of more seriously disabled residents. "You feel sorry for them. Of course, you say to yourself: 'There but for the Grace of God, go I!' I wake up in the morning and say, 'Thank God, I've got another day.' I mean it" (p. 44).

Contemporary elder adults are living longer and functioning better than ever before. Although obviously some physiologic and psychosocial deficits accompany the aging process, a strong personal faith and participation in religious practices can greatly enhance an elder's quality of life. Chronically ill older adults living in a nursing care facility, as well as those living at home, may enjoy significant spiritual well-being in their later years. The aging adult may take comfort in the wisdom of Brother Roger of Taizé who observed:

> Every age has its own beauty. Why be afraid of physical decline when the years bring deeper insight and greater gentleness of action. (As cited in Finch, 1993, p. 23)

While some older adults are able to maintain a significant degree of physical and psychological health well into their later decades of life—even to the 80th and 90th years—others are struck by illness and disability as aging occurs. For some, the disease processes are diagnosed as progressive and ultimately terminal, thus placing the individual in an end-of-life status—some well before their anticipated time of death.

▶ References

Ainlay, S. C., & Smith, D. R. (1984). Aging and religious participation. *Journal of Gerontology, 39*(3), 357–363.

Aller, L., & Van Ess Coeling, H. (1995). Quality of life: Its meaning to the long-term care resident. *Journal of Gerontological Nursing, 21*(2), 20–25.

Beckerman, A., & Northrop, C. (1996). Hope, chronic illness and the elderly. *Journal of Gerontological Nursing, 22*(5), 19–25.

Berggren-Thomas, P., & Griggs, M. J. (1995). Spirituality in aging: Spiritual needs or spiritual journey. *Journal of Gerontological Nursing, 21*(3), 5–10.

Beuscher, L., & Beck, C. (2008). A literature review of spirituality in coping with early-stage Alzheimer's disease. *Journal of Clinical Nursing, 17*(5), 88–97.

Bianchi, E. C. (1995). *Aging as a spiritual journey*. New York, NY: Crossroad.

Birren, J. E. (1990). Spiritual maturity in psychological development. In J. Seeber (Ed.), *Spiritual maturity in the later years* (pp. 41–53). New York, NY: The Haworth Press.

Blazer, D. (1991). Spirituality and aging well. *Generations, 15*(1), 61–65.

Boettcher, E. (1985). Linking the aged to support systems. *Journal of Gerontological Nursing*, 11(3), 27–33.

Bozarth, A. R. (1995). *Lifelines: Threads of grace through seasons of change*. Kansas City, MO: Sheed & Ward.

Brennan, Sr. M. R. (1994). *Spirituality in the homebound elderly* (Unpublished doctoral dissertation). The Catholic University of America. Ann Arbor, MI.

Burghardt, W. J. (1991). Aging, suffering and dying: A Christian perspective. In L. S. Cahill & D. Mieth (Eds.), *Aging* (pp. 65–71). London, UK: Conciliam.

Burt, D. X. (1992). *But when you are older: Reflections on coming of age*. Collegeville, MN: The Liturgical Press.

Byrne, Sr. M. (1985). A zest for life. *Journal of Gerontological Nursing, 11*(4), 30–33.

Callaghan, D. (2006). The influence of growth on spiritual self-care agency in an older population. *Journal of Gerontological Nursing, 32*(9), 43–51.

Castellaw, L. S., Wicks, M. N., & Martin, J. C. (1999). Spirituality in white older women with arthritis. *Graduate Research Nursing, 1*(1), 1–9.

Collins, C. E., Butler, F. R., Guelder, S. H., & Palmer, M. H. (1997). Models for community-based long-term care for the elderly in a changing health system. *Nursing Outlook, 45*(2), 59–63.

Coupland, S. (1985). *Beginning to pray in old age*. Cambridge, MA: Cowley.

Courtney, K., Demiris, G., Rantz, M., & Skubic, M. (2008). Needing smart home technologies: The perspectives of older adults in continuing care retirement communities. *Informatics in Primary Care, 16*, 195–201.

Cutchin, M., Marshall, V., & Aldrich, R. (2010). Moving to a continuing care retirement community: Occupations in the therapeutic landscape process. *Journal of Cross Cultural Gerontology, 25*, 117–132.

Daly, L., & Fahey-McCarthy, E. (2014). Attending to the spiritual in dementia care. *British Journal of Nursing, 23*(14), 787–791.

Deeken, A. (1986). *Growing old and how to cope with it*. San Francisco, CA: Ignatius Press.

Durkin, M. B. (1992). A community of caring. *Health Progress, 73*(8), 48–53.

Emery, P. (2006). Building a new culture of aging: Revolutionizing long-term care. *Journal of Christian Nursing, 23*(1), 16–24.

Erickson, R. M. (1995). *Late have I loved thee: Stories of religious conversion and commitment in later life*. New York, NY: Paulist Press.

Finch, A. (Ed.). (1993). *Journey to the light: Spirituality as we mature*. New Rochelle, NY: New City Press.

Finley, J. (1989). *The treasured age: Spirituality for seniors*. New York, NY: Alba House.

Fischer, K. (1988). Hope never ends: God's promise to the elderly. *Journal of Christian Nursing, 5*(4), 32–35.

Fischer, K. (1995). *Autumn gospel: Women in the second half of life*. New York, NY: Paulist Press.

Forbis, P. A. (1988). Meeting patients' spiritual needs. *Geriatric Nursing, 9*(3), 158–159.

Fowler, J. W. (1981). *Stages of faith: The psychology of human development and the quest for meaning*. San Francisco, CA: Harper.

Gaskamp, C., Sutter, R., & Meraviglia, M. (2006). Evidence-based guideline: Promoting spirituality in the older adult. *Journal of Gerontological Nursing, 32*(11), 8–13.

Gaskins, S., & Forte, L. (1995). The meaning of hope: Implications for nursing practice and research. *Journal of Gerontological Nursing, 21*(3), 17–24.

Hall, C. M. (1985). Religion and aging. *Journal of Religion and Health, 24*(1), 70–78.

Halstead, H. L. (1995). Spirituality in the elderly. In M. Stanley & P. G. Beare (Eds.), *Gerontological nursing* (pp. 415–425). Philadelphia, PA: F. A. Davis.

Hammer, M. L. (1990). Spiritual needs: A forgotten dimension of care. *Journal of Gerontological Nursing, 16*(12), 3–4.

Haugen, G., Rannestad, T., Hammervold, R., Garasen, H., & Espnes, G. (2013). The relationship between self-transcendence and spiritual well-being in cognitively intact nursing home patients. *International Journal of Older People Nursing, 9*(1), 65–78.

Heriot, C. J. (1995). Developmental tasks and development in the later years of life. In M. Stanley & P. G. Beare (Eds.), *Gerontological nursing* (pp. 349–356). Philadelphia, PA: F. A. Davis.

Hicks, T. J. (1999). Spirituality and the elderly: Nursing implications with nursing home residents. *Geriatric Nursing, 20*(3), 144–146.

Higgens, P. (2013). Meeting the religious needs of residents with dementia. *Nursing Older People, 25*(9), 25–29.

Hogstel, M. O. (1995). Mental health wellness strategies for successful aging. In M. Stanley & P. G. Beare (Eds.), *Gerontological nursing* (pp. 17–27). Philadelphia, PA: F. A. Davis.

Holland, B. E., & McCurren, C. (1997). Aging. In J. M. Black & E. Matassarin-Jacobs (Eds.), *Medical–surgical nursing: Clinical management for continuity of care* (5th ed., pp. 81–104). Philadelphia, PA: W. B. Saunders.

Hudson, R. (2008). Application to practice guidelines. *International Journal of Older People Nursing, 3*, 145–150.

Hungelmann, J., Kenkel-Rossi, E., Klassen, L., & Stollenwerk, R. M. (1985). Spiritual well-being in older adults: Harmonious interconnectedness. *Journal of Religion and Health, 24*(2), 147–153.

Hunsberger, B. (1985). Religion, age, life satisfaction, and perceived sources of religiousness: A study of older persons. *Journal of Gerontology, 40*(5), 615–620.

Hynes, M. (1989). *The ministry to the aging.* Collegeville, MN: The Liturgical Press.

Jolley, D., & Moreland, N. (2011). Dementia care: Spiritual and faith perspectives. *Nursing and Residential Care, 13*(8), 388–391.

Koenig, H. G. (1994). *Aging and God: Spiritual pathways to mental health in midlife and later years.* New York, NY: The Haworth Press.

Lenarz, M. A. (1988). In the dark: A nurse struggles to give hope to the elderly. *Journal of Christian Nursing, 5*(4), 30–32.

Lotito, F. A. (1993). *Wisdom, age and grace: An inspirational guide to staying young at heart.* New York, NY: Paulist Press.

Lueckenotte, A. G. (1997). Older adult. In P. A. Potter & A. G. Perry (Eds.), *Fundamentals of nursing: Concepts, process and practice* (pp. 568–593). St. Louis, MO: C. V. Mosby.

MacKinlay, E. (2008). Practice development in aged care nursing of older people: The perspective of ageing and spiritual care. *International Journal of Older People Nursing, 3*, 151–158.

MacKinlay, E., & Trevitt, C. (2010). Living in aged care: Using spiritual reminiscence to enhance meaning in life for those with dementia. *International Journal of Mental Health Nursing, 19*, 394–401.

Maitland, D. J. (1991). *Aging as counterculture: A vocation for the later years.* New York, NY: The Pilgrim Press.

Malcolm, J. (1987). Creative spiritual care for the elderly. *Journal of Christian Nursing, 4*(1), 24–26.

Maltby, T. (1990). Pastoral care of the aging. In H. Hayes & C. J. van der Poel (Eds.), *Health care ministry: A handbook for chaplains* (pp. 98–104). New York, NY: Paulist Press.

Markides, K. S. (1983). Aging, religiosity, and adjustment: A longitudinal analysis. *Journal of Gerontology, 38*(5), 621–625.

McFadden, S., & Kozberg, C. (2008). Religious and spiritual supports for late-life meaning. *Generations, 32*(2), 6–11.

Miller, J., & Powers, M. (1988). Development of an instrument to measure hope. *Nursing Research, 37*(1), 6–10.

Millsap, P. (1995). Nurses' role with the elderly in the long-term care setting. In M. Stanley & P. G. Beare (Eds.), *Gerontological nursing* (pp. 98–106). Philadelphia, PA: F. A. Davis.

Minnix, L. (2008). Maintaining spirituality in institutional settings. *Generations, 32*(2), 65–67.

Moberg, D. O. (1990). Spiritual maturity and wholeness in later years. In J. Seeber (Ed.), *Spiritual maturity in the later years* (pp. 5–24). New York, NY: The Haworth Press.

Mooney, S. F. (2006). When memory fails: Helping dementia patients remember God. *Journal of Christian Nursing, 23*(1), 6–14.

Morikawa, J. (1974, September). American Baptist news service, Division of communications. *Aging without apology: Living the senior years with integrity and faith.* Valley Forge, PA: Judson Press.

Mull, C. S., Cox, C. L., & Sullivan, J. L. (1987). Religion's role in the health and well-being of well elders. *Public Health Nursing, 4*(3), 151–159.

Normille, P. (1992). *Visiting the sick.* Cincinnati, OH: St. Anthony Messenger Press.

Nouwen, H. J., & Gaffney, W. J. (1990). *Aging: The fulfillment of life.* New York, NY: Doubleday.

O'Brien, M. E. (1989). *Anatomy of a nursing home: A new view of resident life.* Owings Mills, MD: National Health Publishing.

O'Brien, M. E. (1997). *Spiritual well-being and quality of life in chronically ill elders* (Unpublished study funded by Research Grant-in-Aid). The Catholic University of America, Washington, DC.

Odbehr, L., Kvigne, K., Hauge, S., & Danbolt, L. (2015). Spiritual care to persons with dementia in nursing homes: A qualitative study of nurses and care workers' experiences. *BMC Nursing, 14*(70), 1–9.

Oppenheimer, H. (1991). Reflections on the experience of aging. In L. S. Cahill & D. Mieth (Eds.), *Aging* (pp. 39–45). London, UK: Conciliam.

Payne, B. (1990). Spiritual maturity and meaning-filled relationships. In J. Seeber (Ed.), *Spiritual maturity in the later years* (pp. 25–39). New York, NY: The Haworth Press.

Peterson, V., & Potter, P. A. (1997). Spiritual health. In P. A. Potter & A. G. Perry (Eds.), *Fundamentals of nursing: Concepts, process and practice* (pp. 440–455). St. Louis, MO: C. V. Mosby.

Resnick, B., & D'Adamo, C. (2010). Factors associated with exercise among older adults in a continuing care retirement community. *Rehabilitation Nursing, 36*(2), 47–53; 82.

Rice, V. H., Beck, C., & Stevenson, J. S. (1997). Ethical issues relative to autonomy and personal control in independent and cognitively impaired elders. *Nursing Outlook, 45*(1), 27–34.

Roen, O. T. (1997). Senior health. In J. H. Swanson & M. A. Nies (Eds.), *Community health nursing: Promoting the health of aggregates* (2nd ed., pp. 347–386). Philadelphia, PA: W. B. Saunders.

Rykkje, L., & Raholm, M. (2014). Understanding older peoples' experiences of dignity and its significance for caring: A hermeneutical study. *International Journal of Human Caring, 18*(1), 17–26.

Sapp, M., & Bliesmer, M. (1995). A health promotion/protection approach to meeting elders' health care needs. In M. Stanley & P. G. Beare (Eds.), *Gerontological nursing* (pp. 3–12). Philadelphia, PA: F. A. Davis.

Sapp, S. (1987). *Full of years: Aging and the elderly in the Bible and today.* Nashville, TN: Abington Press.

Schafer, M. (2011). Health and network centrality in a continuing care retirement community. *Journal of Gerontology, 66*(6), 795–803.

Schwartz, L., & Cottrell, R. P. (2007). The value of spirituality as perceived by elders in long-term care. *Physical & Occupational Therapy in Geriatrics, 26*(1), 43–62.

Seymour, R. E. (1995). *Aging without apology: Living the senior years with integrity and faith.* Valley Forge, PA: Judson Press.

Shippee, T. (2009). "But I am not moving": Residents' perspectives on transitions within a continuing care retirement community. *The Gerontologist, 49*(3), 418–427.

Simmons, H. C., & Peters, M. A. (1996). *With God's oldest friends: Pastoral visiting in the nursing home*. New York, NY: Paulist Press.

Stagg, F. (1981). *The Bible speaks on aging*. Nashville, TN: Broadman Press.

Stuckey, J., Post, S., Ollerton, S., FallCreek, S., & Whitehouse, P. (2002). Alzheimer's disease, religion and ethics of respect for spirituality: A community dialogue. *Alzheimer's Care Quarterly, 3*(3), 199–207.

Swift, H. C., & Rench, C. E. (1991). *Life, fulfillment and joy in the sunset years*. Huntington, IN: Our Sunday Visitor Publications.

Taylor, C., Lillis, C., & LeMone, P. (1997). *Fundamentals of nursing: The art and science of nursing care* (3rd ed.). Philadelphia, PA: J. B. Lippincott.

Tournier, P. (1983). *Learn to grow old*. Louisville, KY: Westminister/John Knox Press.

Valentine, M. H. (1994). *Aging in the Lord*. New York, NY: Paulist Press.

Wendel, I., Durso, S., Zable, B., Loman, K., & Remsburg, R. (2003). Group diabetes patient education: A model for use in a continuing care retirement community. *Journal of Gerontological Nursing, 29*(2), 37–44.

Wicks, R. J. (1997). *After 50: Spiritually embracing your own wisdom years*. New York, NY: Paulist Press.

Wilkes, L., Cioffi, J., Fleming, A., & LeMiere, J. (2011). Defining pastoral care for older people in residential care. *Contemporary Nurse, 37*(2), 213–221.

Wood, V., Wylie, M., & Sheafor, B. (1969). An analysis of a short self-report measure of life satisfaction: Correlation with later judgments. *Journal of Gerontology, 24*(2), 465–469.

Young, C. (1993). Spirituality and the chronically ill Christian elderly. *Geriatric Nursing, 14*(6), 298–303.

Young, C., & Koopsen, C. (2011). *Spirituality, health, and healing: An integrative approach*. Sudbury, MA: Jones & Bartlett Learning.

CHAPTER 9

Spiritual Needs in Death and Bereavement

By faith that Abraham obeyed when he was called to set out for a place . . . that was an inheritance given to him, and he set out not knowing where he was going.

Hebrews 11:8

Dying is part of the life cycle. Some of us will be lucky enough to know when we are going to die and be able to do so in a peaceful way surrounded by our friends and families. As far as critically ill and dying patients are concerned, you have to plan. They want spiritual comfort, they want information, they want to trust in having alleviation of pain, they want to die with the best sense of dignity they can, and that is something that I feel that nurses can facilitate.

Joanne, Charge Nurse at a Medical Outpatient Clinic

In this chapter, the spiritual needs of the dying are explored. Also identified are the family's spiritual needs related both to the death and to the bereavement experience. The author obtained empirical data through observation and informal interviews with dying patients and their families, as well as with their professional nursing caregivers.

Recent nursing literature is increasingly paying significant attention to spiritual needs and concerns in death and dying. Discussed are such topics as: "dying care interventions in the intensive care unit" (Kisvetrova, Skoloudik, Joanovic, Koneca, & Miksova, 2016, p. 139); "what constitutes a good or bad death?" (Ko, Kwak, & Nelson-Becker, 2015, p. 422); assisting patients' spiritual path in palliative care (Giske & Cone, 2015); hospice nurses' perspectives and experiences with spiritual care (Tiew, Kwee, Creedy, & Chan, 2013); understanding dying as a transition (Renz, Mao, Bueche, Cerny, & Strasser, 2013); and professionals coping with pediatric death and dying (Forster & Hafiz, 2015).

As an important addition to the concept of theory development in nursing, a middle-range theory of psychological adaptation to death and dying was offered by nurse theorist Marjorie Dobratz (2011). Dobratz's model, which is linked to the adaptation theory of Callistra Roy, includes findings from a number of studies on end-of-life psychological adaptation and provides assumptions and testable hypotheses (p. 370).

Current literature on family bereavement, discussed later in this chapter, also highlights the importance of spiritual and religious beliefs in facilitating long-term adaptation for loved ones (Draper, Holloway, & Adamson, 2013; Black, Santanello, & Rubinstein, 2014).

▶ The Spirituality of Death and Dying

Death is defined physiologically as occurring "when an individual has sustained either (1) irreversible cessation of circulatory and respiratory functions, or (2) irreversible cessation of all functions of the entire brain, including the brain stem" (President's Commission for the Study of Ethical Problems in Medicine, 1981, p. 1). From a theological perspective, death is conceptualized as "the final point of a human person's individual history . . . the decisive act of human freedom in which the person can either accept or reject the mystery of God and thereby put the final seal on his or her personal history and destiny" (Hayes, 1993, pp. 272–273). The spiritual understanding of death is undergirded by an individual's religious belief, that is, faith tradition. In Judaism, attitudes toward death vary both within and among specific traditions: Orthodox, Conservative, Reform, and Reconstructionist. In general, however, Judaism places great value on life as God's gift; there may be uncertainty about the existence of an afterlife (Grollman, 1993; Neuberger, 1994). Christian spirituality views death and dying in terms of the Gospel message of Jesus. Jesus' death provides a model for His followers who accept their sufferings in hope of the eternal reward He promised. For Jesus, death was not an ending but the beginning of eternal life with His Father (Kinast, 1993). Similarly, the Islamic perception of death incorporates the belief that an eternal life is part of God's plan (Esposito, 1990); the death of a loved one is considered only a "temporary separation" (Neuberger, 1994, p. 36).

The study of death and of the dying process teaches us much about the prevailing culture's attitude toward living (Moller, 1990). Historically, a number of theories of death and dying have been advanced; perhaps the best known is Kübler-Ross's (1969), which describes the stages of denial, anger, bargaining, depression, and acceptance. Angelucci and Lawrence (1995) developed a more contemporary nursing schema: "Health Promotion During the Dying Experience." This model includes cognitive-perceptual factors, such as perceived control and perceived benefits of preparing for dying; modifying factors, such as demographics, cultural influences, and social support; and health-promoting behaviors (p. 405). An important dimension of nursing support included in Angelucci and Lawrence's model is concern for meeting the patient's spiritual needs. This is seen as a significant element in promoting quality of life for the dying person (p. 412).

In discussing the "spirituality of dying," Chaplain Sharon Burns (1991) pointed out that to provide holistic care for a terminal patient, medicine and religion must work together. Chaplain Burns views spirituality as the "life principle" of a person's being and asserted that when the body is ill or dying, the spirit must be affected. An important facet of dealing with the spiritual dimension of dying is the introduction of reminiscence and reconciliation, that is, of allowing the patient to review his or her life and to accept the past as well as the present and future (Burns, 1991, p. 50). In this way, the dying person can integrate spiritual beliefs about the meaning and purpose of life with personal experiences and find comfort and consolation in legacies to be left.

In a similar vein, Derrickson (1996) described the spiritual work of the dying process as including the tasks of remembering, reassessing, reconciling, and reuniting. Remembering relates to reminiscence or a life review through which one can recognize the goodness of life, reassessing is the act of redefining personal worth, reconciliation means healing damaged or broken relationships, and reuniting refers to combining the material and spiritual elements of the person and the world (pp. 14–21). As well as engaging in a life review, some other specific tasks that comprise the "work" of dying are conversing with family and friends, which provides the opportunity to say what needs to be said, and giving and receiving forgiveness when needed (Kalina, 1993, pp. 36–38).

Kalina (1993) also identified spiritual signs that death is imminent, such as detachment from material goods; less tolerance for the mundane in conversation and preference for more times of silence; detachment from concern about appearance; and finally, detachment from relationships as the person recognizes that the end is near (pp. 45–46).

How a person dies can reveal a great deal about how he or she lived. So also, the spirituality manifested in death and in the dying process reflects the personal spirituality of the dying person. For a dying individual who adheres to the tenets of a religious denomination that professes belief in an afterlife, the dying process can represent a joyful transition to a better state, a place where the good acts of one's life are rewarded and sins are absolved. For the person who believes that existence of both body and spirit cease with physical death, the dying process may represent a fearful experience, especially if the individual has not fulfilled desired life goals and ambitions. Spiritual care will need to be carefully planned so as to be relevant to the prevailing spiritual and religious beliefs of the dying patient and his or her family. Many deaths occur in the hospital, nursing home, or hospice setting. With changes in the contemporary health-care system, however, more and more terminally ill individuals will die at home. Thus, the provision of spiritual support for patient and family may fall to the home health-care or parish nurse, as well as to hospital, hospice, or nursing home nursing staff.

▶ Spiritual Needs in the Dying Process

The dying process is unique to each person; a multiplicity of demographic, physical, psychosocial, and spiritual values may influence and mediate the experience. Such factors as age, gender, marital status, religious tradition, socioeconomic status, diagnosis, coping skills, social support, and spiritual belief, especially as related to the meaning of life and death, can influence one's management of the dying process. Despite the uniqueness of the individual, however, some universal needs are identified for most dying persons. These include the need for relief from loneliness and isolation, the need to feel useful, the need to express anger, the need for comfort in anxiety and fear, and the need to alleviate depression and find meaning in the experience (Kemp, 1995, pp. 11–16). Kenneth Doka (1993b) posited three broadly circumscribed spiritual goals of the dying person: "(1) to identify the meaning of one's life, (2) to die appropriately, and (3) to find hope that extends beyond the grave" (p. 146). The search for the meaning of life represents an attempt to bring together the dying individual's experiences, activities, and hoped for goals and outcomes; dying appropriately refers to dying in the manner that the individual finds most acceptable; and finding hope that extends beyond the grave relates to the dying person's peace and trust in his or her concept of an afterlife (pp. 146–148). If a dying person is unable to find purpose and meaning in life, he or she may experience guilt from the perception of aspirations unfulfilled (Featherstone, 1997). Other spiritual needs of the dying person identified in the nursing literature include the need for forgiveness and love (Conrad, 1985), for self-acceptance, and for positive relationships with others, including, for some, relationship with God or a deity (Highfield, 1992).

Although the physical and psychosocial needs of the dying may be more readily identified by overt emotional or physical symptoms, spiritual needs can be more difficult to assess. Because one's spiritual and religious beliefs are personal, symptoms of spiritual distress may not be openly displayed and thus may be neglected in the planning of care for a dying patient (Charlton, 1992). Such lack of attention to spiritual needs is not acceptable, however, for nurses attempting to provide holistic care during the dying process (Stepnick & Perry, 1992).

Dealing with spiritual needs of the dying, identified as a central task of caring for the terminally ill, is not easy (Katz & Sidell, 1994). The spiritual needs of a dying person with no formal religious affiliation can be particularly problematic; the individual may "agonize over life and death issues . . . asking 'why me?' questions" (p. 120). However, a religious person facing death may also raise such questions depending on his or her spiritual maturity and experience. Frequently these concerns arise when the dying person is young and has not yet achieved his or her desired life goals. For the nurse caring for such a dying patient, therapeutic intervention may include dealing with the major spiritual issue of anger at God and/or organized religion.

In a study of 40 patients, 20 dying of lung cancer and 20 of heart failure, qualitative interviews elicited data reflecting both spiritual need and spiritual well-being (Murray, Kendall, Boyd, Worth, & Benton, 2004). Some of the spiritual needs identified included "expressions of frustration, fear, hurt, doubt or despair, feeling isolated and unsupported, feeling useless . . . and feeling of losing control" (p. 41). Some signs of spiritual well-being were "having hope, goals and ambitions, social life and place in community retained, feeling valued, coping with and sharing emotions, being able to practice religion and finding meaning" (p. 41). Ultimately the authors concluded that "patients with life-threatening illness, even if still on 'active treatment' need help to cope with the prospect of dying, well before the terminal stage" (p. 44).

Tim, a 37-year-old terminal cancer patient, explained the importance of resolving spiritual issues prior to his impending death. "I guess it's like they say about 'no atheists in foxholes.' Well I'm in more than a foxhole. I need to get things together with myself and God before I go. I'm praying, and a pastor's been coming by to see me. I guess you don't think about all this until it gets near the end, but it's time now; it's definitely time."

▶ Spiritual Support in Death and Dying

Dying patients and their families cope with impending death in a variety of ways, depending on such factors as the age of the patient, the severity of the illness, the patient's religious beliefs, and cultural norms and values. One of the most frequently observed dilemmas is the fluctuation between acceptance and denial of the immediacy of death. Helping dying patients and families to manage the tension between these two attitudes is a key role of the spiritual caregiver (Joesten, 1992). One of the best ways of providing spiritual support in this situation is to allow the patient and family to verbalize their feelings; for a dying person "one of the greatest spiritual gifts" a nurse can give is to listen (Burns, 1991, p. 51).

Nursing literature subscribing to the concept of holistic care points out repeatedly that nurses must include spiritual support as part of the therapeutic regimen for the dying client (Conrad, 1985; Hittle, 1994; Taylor & Amenta, 1994). Some researchers have suggested also that if a nurse is to master the ability to assess and meet the spiritual needs of dying patients, he or she must engage in a personal spiritual journey in the process (MacDonald, Sandmaier, & Fainsinger, 1993; Praill, 1995; Price, Stevens, & LaBarre, 1995). It is impossible for a nurse to undertake the work of therapeutic spiritual support of patients without some understanding and acceptance of his or her own beliefs and attitudes about such issues as spirituality, religion, end-of-life decisions, and the existence or nonexistence of an afterlife. Olson (1997) believes that the "nurse's own spirituality will be reflected in the choice of interventions selected" (p. 132). This may be correct to a degree. The situation can be problematic, however, if nurse and patient have serious divergence in spiritual or religious beliefs and behaviors. The nurse must be comfortable and secure enough in his or her own spirituality and/or religious beliefs to remain open to differing spiritual or religious attitudes and needs on the part of the dying patient.

Some broad areas of spiritual nursing care for dying persons include assisting the patient to find meaning in life, hope, a relationship to God, forgiveness or acceptance, and transcendence (Kemp, 1995, p. 45). Five specific spiritual interventions for dying patients that fall within the purview of the nurse are praying, facilitating the presence of loved ones, allowing the dying person time to share, assisting in the completion of unfinished tasks, and assuring that the dying person has been given "permission" to die (Olson, 1997, p. 133). Nurses caring for dying patients should also attempt to identify the presence of spiritual pain, which may be manifested in terms of "the past (painful memories, regret, failure, guilt); the present (isolation, unfairness, anger); the future (fear, hopelessness)" (Eisdon, 1995, p. 641). Hospice research has documented the fact that spiritual care of dying patients falls within the scope of nursing practice (Hermann, 2001). Assessment of spiritual needs may be complex in end-of-life care (Sheldon, 2000); however, the provision of spiritual care in death and dying has been shown to enhance nurses' personal spirituality (Highfield, Taylor, & Amenta, 2000). A nursing theory recommended to support the provision of spiritual care for the terminally ill is the humanistic theory of Paterson and Zderad (Vassallo, 2001).

Young and Koopsen (2011) point out that dying "is a spiritual event of enormous importance"; "dying," they add, "is a profound process of spiritual transformation" (p. 245). For many, Young and Koopsen comment, dying involves one's attention being turned away "from the outer distractions in the world and turned inward toward a greater peace and comfort in spiritual fulfillment" (p. 245). This contention is supported by the perceptions of 38 hospice patients (Pevey, Jones, & Yarber, 2008), as well as by the research on death attitudes conducted by Dezutter et al. (2009).

Stepnick and Perry (1992) offered a plan to guide nurses in providing effective spiritual care to dying patients, employing a model of the transitional phases of dying. They believe that, although patients may have different beliefs and levels of spiritual maturity, they share some common characteristics and needs as death approaches (p. 18).

Based on Kübler-Ross's (1969) phases of denial, anger, bargaining, depression, and acceptance, some suggested nursing strategies include listening and assuring trust, being nonjudgmental about anger, being sensitive to the pain of the bargaining stage, keeping communication open, and preparing the dying patient for what to expect in terms of the end stages of illness (pp. 19–23).

It is an accepted fact that "nurses regularly encounter death in the care of [their] patients" (Schulling, 2012, p. 55); and death is "not an easy subject as it often feels like failure for family and healthcare professionals" (Rushing, 2012, p. 113). Nurse Arlene Reynolds (2009) thus poses the question, "How can I respond to dying patients?" (p. 197). Reynolds's response involved spiritual care and talking with a patient about his or her spirituality. She concluded that "Sometimes we tend to be overly concerned with the tasks of nursing, and miss moments to make an eternal difference for patients" (p. 197).

In attempting to make such an "eternal difference," however, how do nurses themselves cope with their patients' death and dying? "Where do nurses go for help?" (Peterson et al., 2010, p. 432). After conducting qualitative interviews with 15 nurses, all of whom had cared for dying patients, Peterson et al. concluded that the nurses relied on two sources of support, internal and external: "Internally, nurses found that evaluating the death and relying on professional distance helped them cope. Externally, the nurses looked to peers, religious resources and the patients and families themselves for comfort" (p. 435).

Brian, a master's-prepared psychiatric–mental health nurse, spoke about how he drew on his own spiritual journey in caring for dying patients:

> I hope that I always carry the motto of my former religious community [of nursing brothers], "Christ impels me," to my work with dying patients. Now I haven't done a good job of that every day of my life, I assure you; I'm an "earthen vessel" too. But nursing, for me, is a vocation; and I have always felt very privileged to work with patients in the last chapter of their lives on earth. It's such a rewarding experience. It's a tremendous privilege of being there, of ministering to the dying person.
>
> There was this patient and I was holding one of her hands and her daughter was holding the other, and it was like we were saying: "It's OK, you can let go." And then her daughter asked me to say a prayer, and I just sort of incorporated some ideas, like "you are surrounded by people who love you, and whenever you're ready to go, you can go to God. He's waiting for you." . . .
>
> When the patient dies, you think of what that person has given to you, and how their spirit will live on in you, and that's very special, very gifting.

Maggie, a hospice nurse, spoke about the importance of using touch to calm the anxieties of her patients entering the death experience:

> I will frequently reach out and touch a dying person physically; it's so important when they're scared. I don't think people are afraid to die; they are afraid of the process of dying. It's the loneliness, the isolation, the abandonment, the fear of people not wanting to touch them or care for them . . . What is most fearful is the unknown in the dying process. Are they going to be in pain; are they going to feel loved; is their family going to be there? And then, what happens after? I think we nurses are good about giving physical attention

to dying patients, and even psychosocial, but we're afraid to talk about the spiritual, about the fact that maybe they feel abandoned or forsaken by God. As caregivers, I think we shy away from that. But I've learned that it's really important that people are supported in whatever they feel comes after life, and in their concept of God.

Palliative Care

The World Health Organization (1990) defined palliative care as "the active total care, by a multi professional team, of patients whose disease is not responsive to curative treatment. Control of pain, of other symptoms, and of psychological, social and spiritual problems is paramount. The goal of palliative care is achievement of the best quality of life for patients and their families" (p. 1). Palliation essentially relates to the acts of relieving suffering and restoring peace to those who cannot be cured (Doyle, 1984). Palliative care focuses on immediate quality rather than length of life (Olson, 1997) and integrates physical, psychosocial, and spiritual care in its therapeutic plan (Katz & Sidell, 1994). Palliative care may be carried out in a variety of settings: a hospital, a nursing home, a hospice, or a patient's home. In addition to providing symptom relief and support of positive quality of life, palliative care as an emerging subspecialty of health care also includes promoting the dying person's independence as much as possible, facilitating communication between collaborating care agencies, supporting families and staff during the bereavement period, and influencing care through education and research in the area (James & MacLeod, 1993, p. 6).

Spiritual or religious beliefs may influence both the choice and the practice of palliative care for a dying person (Hamel & Lysaught, 1994). Hamel and Lysaught explained that in palliative care patients' religious beliefs may affect decisions about death and dying by "(a) helping to shape [their] worldviews, (b) giving form to their particular beliefs, (c) giving rise to moral principles and rules, and (d) shaping community character and dispositions" (p. 61). For the dying person whose life history has been consistent with the worldview, beliefs, and moral principles central to his or her religious tradition, a sense of peace and security related to end-of-life decisions will usually be demonstrated; the support of the individual's religious community is also generally evident. In such a case the palliative care interventions should be consistent with the religious tradition of the dying patient. The caregiver should attempt to "build on" the existing beliefs of the patient and support the faith tradition that has provided comfort and sustenance in the past (Murray & Lyall, 1994).

Several authors have addressed the positive relationship between spirituality and quality of life for persons experiencing palliative care (Vivat, 2008; Crang & Muncey, 2008), as well as noting the importance of spiritual support being provided by the health-care practitioner (Narayanasamy, 2007).

Hospice Care

The concept of palliative care was initiated primarily in concert with the hospice movement in Europe and the United States. The first modern nursing hospice of note, St. Christopher's, was founded in Sydenham, England, in 1967, under the direction of Dame Cicely Saunders, MD. The goal of St. Christopher's founder was to provide compassionate and loving care for those who were dying (Saunders, 1981, 1983).

During the medieval period a hospice was considered a place of hospitality for pilgrims on a journey, a stopping off place for travelers. The modern nursing hospice may also be described as a "way station" or "place of transit"; here, however, individuals are helped "to live fully in an atmosphere of loving kindness and grace" as they experience the process of natural death (Stoddard, 1978, p. 10). The goal of providing care and a place for the "weary traveler" to find "rest and safety" has not really changed from medieval times (Cohen, 1979). Most patients are indeed battle scarred and weary by the time they arrive at the hospice seeking relief. The central philosophy of hospice care emphasizes the fact that the outcome will be death, not prolongation of life; thus the care focus is in "comfort not cure" (Kirschling & Pittman, 1989, p. 1).

Hospice care in the United States is generally considered to have begun with the Hospice of New Haven project associated with Yale University, initiated in the mid-1970s. Nurses caring for those with terminal illness, especially nurses whose personal spirituality espoused the Judeo-Christian tradition, eagerly received the hospice message of compassionate care; for those caregivers the hospice concept was a direct reflection of the Scriptural admonitions to provide loving and sensitive care to those who are ill and in need of comfort. In hospice care, the nurse has the opportunity of reflecting a concept that Chaplain Trevor Hoy (1983) believes "lies at the heart" of spiritual care of the dying, and which is expressed in the Twenty-third Psalm: "Yea, though I walk through the valley of the shadow of death, I will fear no evil; for thou art with me" (p. 177). Hoy's position was supported by that of hospice chaplain Ted Harvey (1996) who described the two central concerns of spiritual care for the dying as relating to the patient's emotional well-being and his or her relationship with God (p. 41).

The more modern hospice concept refers to either a facility or a program that supports the dying person's spiritual and religious beliefs and goals (Franco, 1985, p. 80). Related to the complexities of the ever changing health-care system in this country, hospice chaplain Richard Grey (1996) suggested that the hospice mission and identity will continually need clarification. To that end, Grey proposed a psychospiritual care paradigm within which all hospice personnel can situate their particular activities, yet share in the common element of compassionate care. The National Hospice Organization Standards and Accreditation Committee developed a set of hospice service guidelines, which include policies related to admissions and discharge; levels of care; staffing, including a chaplain to provide spiritual care; services; and treatment (The National Hospice Organization, 1996b). A Hospice Code of Ethics has also been created, the first precept being "to remain sensitive to and be appreciative of the ethnic, cultural, religious and life style diversity of clients and their families" (The National Hospice Organization, 1996a, p. 76).

Five palliative care physicians conducted an open-ended qualitative study to assess hospice patients' attitudes toward the discussion of religious and/or spiritual topics with their doctors. From the study data, four dominant themes emerged: "1) treating the whole person, 2) treating with sensitivity, 3) favorable attitudes toward religious or spiritual discussions with doctors, and 4) no preaching" (Hart, Kohlwes, Deyo, Rhodes, & Bowen, 2003, p. 160). The physicians concluded that they were not expected to be "spiritual advisors" for their patients but that many patients did feel positive about speaking about spiritual issues with their doctors (p. 160).

Several nursing studies have explored the prevalence of spiritual care in the hospice setting. Millison and Dudley (1992), in surveying 117 hospice directors in three states, found that many nonclergy hospice personnel were providing spiritual care by listening to patients, teaching meditation or guided imagery, and referring patients to clergy. These authors also found that hospice personnel are a spiritual group, and that those who identified themselves as more spiritual "found greater satisfaction in their hospice work" (p. 63). In a chart review of home visits to 37 hospice care patients, Reese and Brown (1997) discovered that spirituality and death anxiety were the most commonly discussed topics between patients and caregivers.

Laurie, a hospice nurse for five years, spoke about the concepts of death anxiety, spirituality, and caring, as experienced with some of her patients:

> The patients are afraid when they are in the dying process, of what the end will be like; some use their faith to help but even still they can be afraid of the unknown. That's when I think the nurse's caring is so important. Caring is hard to define. I think it's the ability to show compassion, to be able to touch someone. To just sit and listen, especially to their spiritual concerns and feelings and not to be critical or judgmental, to be with the flow of the moment. Time is such a commodity for people who are dying; it's so important to listen to people who are dying. That's spiritual caring I think.

▶ Religious Practices Associated with Death and Dying

For a dying person, religious practices can provide an important dimension of spiritual support and comfort. Even if an individual has become alienated from a religious denomination or church, a terminal illness may be the catalyst for return to the practice of one's faith. This was clearly reflected in the comments of a 47-year-old male patient in the advanced stages of cancer. "I hadn't gone to my church for years; I don't know why. I just stopped going. But lately I've started up again, and I've been reading the Bible. When I die I want to have a church burial and be buried in a Christian cemetery; that's a big thing with my family."

Although the nurse caring for dying patients cannot be knowledgeable about the death-related beliefs and practices of all religious faiths, some familiarity with those of the major Western and Eastern traditions may provide a starting point for the provision of spiritual support. Having some idea of the theological positions and religious practices of different groups may assist the nurse in developing a relationship with a dying person and an empathetic and caring attitude (Head, 1994, p. 310). Anglican priest David Head (1994) believes that such knowledge on the part of a care provider will allow a dying patient to express spiritual or religious concerns more freely, without fear of being misunderstood (pp. 311–312). Ultimately, the best nursing approach to providing spiritual care to a dying person is to request information about religious beliefs and practices directly from the patient or family.

Western Traditions: Judaism, Christianity, and Islam

Judaism

Attitudes toward death for the Jewish patient may vary according to identification with a particular subgroup of Judaism: Orthodox, Conservative, Reform, or Reconstructionist. A Jewish person's approach to the dying process will also be influenced by his or her belief or nonbelief in the existence of an afterlife. Some Jews, especially those of the Orthodox tradition, do not subscribe to the concept of eternal life; they may, however, believe that faithful Jews will be resurrected when the Messiah comes. Some believe that one's good deeds in this life live on in the memories of family and friends. In Judaism, life is highly valued as a gift of God; all efforts to continue a productive life are supported. Thus, facing death may represent an ending of something precious. As Rabbi Julia Neuberger (1994) explained, "It is not so much uncertainty about the afterlife which causes a problem, but the emphasis put on the here and now" (p. 13).

A Jewish person who is dying, especially an Orthodox Jew, will generally receive visits from friends and synagogue members, because the duty to visit the sick is considered a mitzvah or good deed in Judaism. Some contemporary synagogues have established formalized groups called Bikkur Cholim societies, whose express purpose is to visit and minister to those who are ill; Bikkur Cholim members receive training from their synagogues in how to work with the sick. These individuals may also be present at a Jewish person's death and will offer prayers or readings from the Psalms, if desired by the patient or family.

After death occurs, synagogue members from the Jewish Burial Society may come to prepare the body of an Orthodox patient; no action should be taken by hospital or hospice personnel until it is determined whether this will occur. It is also customary that, after death, a Jewish person be buried within 24 hours; an exception may be made for the Sabbath. The formal ritual prayer of mourning, the kaddish, may be recited by a rabbi or family member; cremation and autopsy are avoided. After the burial has taken place, the important task of mourning is initiated. This involves friends and relatives of the deceased visiting at the family's home, or sitting shiva for the next seven days. This mourning period provides the grieving family with the support and care of those close to them and to the deceased person during the time immediately following death. Following shiva, 30 days of mourning, shloshim, continues; during this time the family may resume usual activities but avoids formal entertainment (Grollman, 1993).

Christianity

Three major subgroups within the Christian tradition are the Eastern Orthodox Churches, Roman Catholicism, and Protestantism; in addition, a number of other faith groups are identified as followers of Christ. Virtually all Christian traditions believe in eternal life, as promised in the Gospel message of Jesus. Thus, for the devout Christian, although the dying process can raise anxieties in terms of possible pain and suffering, death itself is viewed as a positive transition to a life with God and to one's eternal reward. Protestantism, which relies on the concept of salvation, trusts that faith will bring the believer into a better world (Klass, 1993). Older adult Christians sometimes express a desire for God to come and "take them home."

As death approaches, the majority of Christian patients and their families welcome a visit from a priest or minister; the pastoral visitor may be from the family's church or can be a hospital or hospice chaplain. These ministers will generally pray and read a Scripture passage with the dying person and their family. Eastern Orthodox Christians, Roman Catholics, and some Episcopalians may request an anointing or the "Sacrament of the Sick" prior to death; they may also wish to make a confession of sins and receive the sacraments of Penance and of Holy Eucharist (Holy Communion).

A priest or family member may cross the arms of the Eastern Orthodox patient after death, situating the fingers to represent a cross.

After death occurs, most Christians will have a period of "viewing" of the body, sometimes called a "wake"; this ritual, which provides the opportunity for friends and family to call, takes place from one to three days after the death, in either the family home or a funeral home. A priest or minister may offer prayers periodically during the viewing. Christian burial services vary according to denomination. Eastern Orthodox, Roman Catholic, and some Episcopalian (Anglo-Catholic) Christians attend a funeral Mass of Requiem for the deceased prior to interment in a church cemetery. Although Mass is still the norm for the Catholic funeral, emphasis is now placed on life rather than death, and the central theme is resurrection; the priest celebrant wears white rather than black vestments. This changed focus, from grieving the death to hope in God's love and trust in the resurrection, indicates "a more healthy biblicism and pastoral practice" (Miller, 1993, p. 42). Other Christians participate in funeral or memorial services of their denominations; some families prefer a private service conducted by a minister in the home. The latter may be desired if cremation is chosen and no formal trip to the cemetery is planned.

Private memorial services are also the norm for the deceased who did not adhere to any conventional religious tradition. As Irion (1993) pointed out, a dying "secularist" also has a spiritual need to find meaning and purpose in life and in death (p. 94). The secular humanist usually places a high value on life and life accomplishments; these may be remembered and honored at a nonreligious memorial service.

Islam

The devout Muslim, like the Christian, views death as representing a spiritual transition to eternal life with Allah (Renard, 1993). Although a terminally ill Muslim may fear the dying process related to possible suffering, the concept of death itself is accepted as the will of Allah. Thus, excessive grieving of death by a Muslim may be considered inappropriate and represent a contradiction of Allah's plan. The death of a loved one should be viewed as only a temporary loss (Neuberger, 1994, p. 36). Islam, like Christianity, holds a belief in "resurrection of the body, final judgement and assignment to heaven or hell" (Kemp, 1995, p. 58).

As death approaches, family members or a Muslim minister, an imam, may read a passage from the Holy Qur'an to comfort the patient and family. The dying Muslim may wish to face Mecca, in the East, and ask forgiveness of Allah for sins. After death occurs, members of the family frequently wish to prepare the body through ritual washing and wrapping in a white cloth. After the body is prepared, the deceased may be laid out in a position facing Mecca.

Burial rites for a Muslim patient can vary, but generally interment takes place in a Muslim cemetery 24 hours after death.

Eastern Traditions: Hinduism, Buddhism, and Confucianism

Hinduism

Hinduism consists of a number of related Indian religious traditions, all of which are centuries old. Although a pantheon of lesser gods is associated with Hinduism, as demonstrated in Indian temples and holy places, most devout Hindus believe in the existence of one supreme being or deity. The many less powerful gods and goddesses are considered to be forms or derivatives of the one deity, with power and interest in specific areas of one's life.

The concept of reincarnation or rebirth influences the dying Hindu's attitude toward death; death itself is viewed as a union with God. How one has lived in this world is influential in how one might return in the next life; this concept is referred to as karma.

Hindu patients often prefer to die at home where they can be more certain of the presence of a priest (Green, 1989a). A Brahmin priest, who performs the death rites, may tie a string or cord around the dying person's neck or wrist, which should not be removed; prayers are also chanted by the priest. Following a Hindu's death, the funeral is usually carried out within 24 hours, and cremation is the traditional ritual.

Buddhism

Buddhism, founded by Gautama Siddhartha, differs from most other major religious traditions in that the Buddhist does not accept the existence of God or of a Supreme Being; Buddhists do, however, acknowledge the presence of a multiplicity of individual gods who are involved and interested in the lives of the Buddhist. Devout Buddhists live according to the "eightfold path" of right belief, right intent, right speech, right conduct, right endeavor, right mindfulness, right effort, and right meditation (Kemp, 1995, p. 60). The ultimate goal of the Buddhist is to reach the interior state of Nirvana or inner peace and happiness; this is achieved after having lived according to the eightfold path.

The Buddhist's attitude toward death is also influenced by belief in the concept of rebirth; death is accepted as a transition and as part of the cycle of life. A Buddhist monk may chant prayers at the death of a devout Buddhist in order to provide peace of mind at the point of death (Green, 1989b). An important dimension of the dying process for a Buddhist is to remain conscious in order to be able to think right and wholesome thoughts (Kemp, 1995). The deceased is generally cremated after death.

Confucianism

Confucianism is the tradition founded by the ancient Chinese scholar and philosopher, Confucius. Confucianism places great emphasis on respecting the memories and the contributions of one's ancestors. Elaborate death and burial rituals allow the bereaved to formally express grief and bring "continuity with the past and with tradition" (Ryan, 1993, p. 85). Ryan (1993) reported that in the Confucian tradition a person is taught to live life in such a way that after death good memories of the deceased may be honored (p. 86). The fate of the deceased in an afterlife depends on the quality of his or her natural life; it is also important that the deceased be properly honored by relatives after death. This relates to a strong belief in a "continuity of life after death" (Neuberger, 1994, p. 48).

The Confucianist's funeral may be an elaborate ritual, its complexity reflecting the status of the deceased. A carefully crafted coffin may be purchased by the family prior to death so that the dying person will know that he or she will be well honored at the burial rites.

▶ Spirituality and the Rite of Burial

The burial rite provides important spiritual support for the family and friends of a deceased person. The planning of one's own funeral or memorial service may provide comfort for the dying person. In contemporary society, as chronically ill persons live longer and are able to anticipate death, they often become involved in the planning of their burial rites. During the early period of the acquired immunodeficiency syndrome (AIDS) epidemic in this country, with many gay men not only anticipating their own approaching deaths but also experiencing the deaths and burial rites of friends, planning the memorial service became a central activity of the dying process. As one 45-year-old man suffering from advanced Kaposi's sarcoma humorously commented, "I've put so much into the plans for my memorial service, it's beginning to resemble the coronation of a king." Despite the humor of the patient's remark, he nevertheless admitted that creating the memorial service plans was very comforting, observing, "This way I don't have to worry about my family having to deal with this when they are grieving my death."

As Rando (1988) pointed out, burial rites help families confront the death of a loved one and begin the grieving process (p. 261). The funeral provides an opportunity for meeting the spiritual, psychological, and social needs of the bereaved (Raether, 1993, p. 214). Some specific therapeutic benefits of the bereavement ritual include confirming the reality of death; acknowledging the loss; providing an opportunity to express feelings; remembering and validating the life of the deceased; accepting the changed relationship with the deceased; supporting family and friends; and, in the case of religiously oriented funerals, placing the meaning of life and death in a religious/philosophical context (Rando, 1988, pp. 266–269).

Burial rites can also be helpful to nurse caregivers who wish to formally terminate relationships with patients who have died. In one clinical research facility, nurses worked extensively with dying children, most of whom returned home to a different geographical location for death and burial; thus, staff requested that the hospital chaplain periodically conduct pediatric memorial services to provide nursing staff the opportunity for formal farewells to the deceased children.

In evaluating the concepts of death, burial, and bereavement, Margaret Holloway (2006) explored the often heard phrase, "Death is the great leveler." Holloway agrees that the thought represents the "acknowledgement that in death our common humanity is affirmed" (p. 834). Holloway goes on, however, to offer the option of a transcultural spirituality of death and bereavement, which means "the challenge . . . is not so much to find a common model . . . as to seek out the means to access the strengths and resources in each other's tradition which affirm our common humanity" (p. 838).

▶ Spirituality and the Bereavement Experience

The body of literature dealing with the postdeath period includes the terms *bereavement*, *grief*, and *mourning*; these are sometimes used interchangeably, all being understood as describing the physical and psychosocial experience of loss following the death of a loved one. Rando (1988) defined *grief* as "the process of experiencing the psychological, social and physical reactions to [one's] perception of loss" (p. 11). *Mourning*, derived from the Greek "to care," is described as "an emotion that results from the universal experience of loss" (Davidson, 1984, p. 6). And Sanders (1989), in her book *Grief: The Mourning After*, distinguishes between the three concepts: bereavement is conceptualized as the overall experience one faces after a loss, grief is viewed as representing the physical and psychosocial reactions an individual experiences while in the state of bereavement, and mourning describes the culturally prescribed behaviors carried out after a death (p. 10).

Historically, the study of the bereavement experience, including the aspects of grief and mourning, began with the work of Eric Lindemann in 1944. His classic study of 101 bereaved survivors of Boston's "Coconut Grove" fire provided the benchmark for our contemporary understanding of the grieving process. Lindemann described the acute reaction to the death of a loved one as including such somatic responses as "a feeling of tightness in the throat; choking with shortness of breath; need for sighing; an empty feeling in the abdomen; lack of muscular power; and an intense subjective distress described as tension or mental pain" (p. 141).

Later scholars of bereavement such as Bowlby (1961) and Parkes (1972) viewed the grief reaction as being of longer duration and consisting of such phases as acute grief, chronic grief, conflicted grief or complicated grief, and prolonged or delayed grief. Writing in 1983, Colin Murray Parkes and Robert Weiss asserted that when grief was uncomplicated, recovery was generally accomplished within one year after the loss; this time period has been extended significantly in recent years, although the one-year anniversary may represent a milestone in the healing process for some mourners.

Extant research also supports the importance of a number of potentially mediating variables related to the bereavement experience: the meaning of the bereavement to the mourner; the relationship between the deceased and the bereaved; the physical, social, material, and psychological resources of the bereaved person; and the spiritual and religious beliefs of the family (Rando, 1988; Sanders, 1989). Sanders's (1989) model, labeled the "Integrative Theory of Bereavement," included the earlier noted variables as well as the external mediator of religious practice. The work of identifying and meeting the spiritual or religious needs of bereaved persons is central to supporting positive coping with grief and loss.

Manifestations of an uncomplicated grief reaction are generally divided into four categories: physical, cognitive, emotional, and behavioral. Some of these as described by Worden (1982) include physical reactions such as stomach emptiness, shortness of breath, tightness in chest and throat, and fatigue; cognitive reactions of disbelief and mental confusion; emotional responses of sadness, guilt, anger, loneliness, numbness, and yearning for the deceased; and behavioral disruptions such as insomnia, loss of appetite, social isolation, crying, and restlessness (pp. 20–23). Worden described the four tasks of mourning during the bereavement experience as accepting "the reality of the loss," experiencing "the pain of the grief," adjusting "to an environment in which the deceased is missing," and reinvesting "emotional energy . . . in another relationship" (pp. 11–15). Rando (1988) suggested specifically that the bereaved person should not isolate himself or herself, accept the support of significant others, obtain information about what to expect in the grieving process, realize that grief may be expressed in a variety of ways, allow himself or herself to cry and to talk about the deceased, and trust that the pain will decrease after a time (pp. 242–248). It is pointed out that "each, person's journey through the grief process is profoundly unique . . . and is experienced spiritually, behaviorally, physically, and cognitively" (Young & Koopsen, 2011, p. 266), and that one's religion and/or spiritual philosophy of life influences his or her attitude toward grief and bereavement (Becker et al., 2007; Lees, 2008; Wortman & Park, 2008).

It is well known that for many dying persons, spirituality and/or religion play(s) an important role in the coping process; the influence of spirituality and religion on bereavement is less well documented. A systematic review of the extant research on spirituality and bereavement revealed that "ninety-four percent show some positive effects of religious/spiritual beliefs on bereavement" (Becker et al., 2007, p. 207). The study authors admit, however, that there was a great "heterogeneity regarding included populations and outcome measurements" (p. 207).

Bereaved persons need and will often accept spiritual support from the family's pastoral care provider, rabbi, minister, priest, or, in some cases, a nurse if he or she is skilled in bereavement counseling and support. Other significant persons who may provide spiritual support for the bereaved are church or faith group members who also understand the grieving person's or family's spiritual and theological perspective on the loss. Whether spiritual care is provided by the pastor, nurse, or church member, intervention should focus on supporting two major tasks of the bereaved individual: letting go of the deceased person and becoming reinvested in current life activities. The spiritual caregiver's challenge in grief and bereavement is to balance the activities of strengthening and disputing; the caregiver must "know when to comfort and support and when to challenge and confront" (Joesten, 1992, p. 144). Joesten observed that an important dimension of spiritual intervention for bereaved persons is the presence of a caring other who is willing to be there and share in the grief and the pain (p. 145); he asserted that the spiritual caregiver assists the bereaved most by being someone who offers hope and honesty amid the darkness of the experience (p. 148).

Finally, it is important to remember, as noted by Young and Koopsen (2005), that for those dealing with loss, "individuals in the early stages of spiritual development may need more external support and communication, while more spiritually developed individuals may use rituals, rites and symbols for comfort" (p. 192).

Death of a Child

There is perhaps no loss so grievous for any person as the loss of a child. Most parents are devastated when one of their children dies, regardless of the age of the child. The common understanding of family, in virtually all societies, is that a child will survive his or her parents. Although family members attempt to find meaning and purpose in the life of the deceased offspring, the task is more difficult in the death of an infant or a very young child. The bereaved parents are often left with great frustration related to unfulfilled dreams and expectations. As Sanders (1989) observed, children represent a parent's legacy for the future; they are to be the bearers of the family tradition (p. 163). A parent may also experience guilt that he or she was somehow not able to protect the child from illness and death.

Sanders (1989) identified some parental responses to bereavement: despair, related to the ability to go on living following a child's death; confusion, related to the parent being unable to accept the reality of the death; guilt that the parent was not able to be responsible for the child's welfare; and anger, associated with the inability to prevent the child's death (pp. 165–169). Death of a child may also affect a marriage if the usual ways of interacting between the spouses are disrupted by the loss (Rando, 1988, p. 170). Many relationships end in separation or divorce as a result of the terminal illness and death of the couple's child.

Parents may find comfort in religious and spiritual beliefs, especially if they were able to integrate these into coping with the child's illness prior to the death experience. A nurse should not, however, attempt to impose such beliefs on a parent or parents with words such as "This must have been God's will," because the bereaved may still need to express feelings of anguish or anger over their loss (Amenta, 1995, p. 206). The nurse can, however, provide the spiritual care of presence by being available to the parents with a loving and listening heart.

A significant amount of research has been done on the impact of the death of a child on surviving parents. One example is exploring parental grief and depression after the death of a child from cancer. In this study, the investigators found that while a "minority" of 58 parents actually met their criteria for parental grief and depression, "almost half of the sample was experiencing significant separation distress associated with persistent longing and yearning for their child" (McCarthy et al., 2010, p. 1321). And in a study of 31 parents whose child had died from cancer it was found that fathers coped by being more "task focused," while mothers were more "child focused" (Alam, Barrera, D'Agostino, Nicholas, & Schneiderman, 2012, p. 1). The researchers concluded that the findings emphasized "the need for tailoring bereavement support services in the family" (p. 2). Finally, a study of the lived experience of six mothers who had experienced the unexpected death of a child revealed a number of helpful coping behaviors employed by the study participants; these included "positive beliefs, faith beliefs, everlasting love, pleasant remembrances, social engagement, and staying connected" (Parker & Dunn, 2011, p. 221). Parker and Dunn observed that "by exploring, through interviews, the lives of mothers who have experienced the loss of a child, healthcare providers may become more aware of the needs of those who grieve" (p. 232).

Death of a Spouse

The death of one's life partner is a traumatic event, regardless of the number of years a couple has been together. The death of a spouse is recognized as emotionally overwhelming and is generally considered one of the most devastating human losses possible (Osterweis, Solomon, & Green, 1984, p. 71). Raphael (1983) posited that conjugal bereavement is one of the most disruptive and potentially stressful experiences that an adult can experience and may affect the essential meaning of the survivor's existence (p. 177). A particular difficulty for the surviving spouse is identity transition; that is, the change in self-image in beginning to view oneself as a single person rather than as one-half of a couple. In the case of a small number of bereaved partners, the inability to identify as a single person has generated feelings of helplessness so severe as to result in suicide (Raphael, 1983).

Some bereaved spouses experience physical symptoms of their grief. Parkes, Benjamin, and Fitzgerald (1969) coined the metaphor of the "broken heart" based on their findings that some widower deaths within six months of bereavement were due to heart disease related to the loss of one's spouse. An important mediator of such mortality and morbidity is the presence of spiritual and social support for the bereaved spouse. Shuchter's (1986) study of 70 bereaved spouses revealed that interaction with significant others helped the bereaved by providing emotional support and caring, and by giving the surviving spouse an opportunity to become involved in the concerns of others (p. 110).

Sanders (1989) found the practice of religion, particularly church attendance, to be a mainstay among bereaved spouses (p. 194). Nurses may have the occasion to provide spiritual care to bereaved spouses who stay in touch after the death of their partner in a hospital setting. If face-to-face interaction is not possible, a written note of condolence from a loved one's nurse can be very meaningful. During the dying process in a health-care facility, staff nurses often become important significant others for the family of the ill person. Any expression of care and concern after the death, such as a letter or a phone call, will convey a deeply appreciated message of spiritual support.

Death of a Parent

The death of a parent frequently represents a loss of security on the part of the bereaved child or children. Although a surviving child may be chronologically an adult at the time of parental death, the loss of love and caring can be great. Even adult children who have undertaken complete support of a frail parent feel keenly the pain of a mother's or a father's death. The nature of the former parent–child relationship is, of course, a mediating variable in the bereavement experience of the offspring. Sanders (1989) believed, however, that even if a parent–child relationship has not been exemplary, a significant bond exists, which is traumatic when broken (p. 202).

The nurse assisting at the death of a parent, even an elderly parent, must be sensitive to the deep spiritual meaning of the parent–child bond. The grief associated with this death experience can be powerful and deep for surviving offspring of any age. Awareness of the significance of this loss will guide the nurse in his or her efforts to provide spiritual support for the grief experience of an adult child as well as that of a bereaved young child or teen.

▶ Spiritual Care in Bereavement: The Healing Process

Clearly, the nurse seeking to provide spiritual care to a bereaved person will need to have some knowledge of the individual's spiritual and/or religious beliefs and practices related to loss and grieving. Respect for the religious attitudes and practices of the bereaved must be clearly communicated by one attempting to provide care and support (Doka, 1993a, p. 191). If a bereaved individual appears to have dysfunctional beliefs related to a particular religious tradition, referral to a clergyperson of the person's denomination or the use of religious books may be helpful (Doka, 1993a). Clinebell (1991) suggested that a caregiver attempting to facilitate the work of the grieving process may want to employ a ministry of caring and presence, responsive listening, counseling as the bereaved attempts to rebuild his or her life, facilitating of spiritual growth, and supporting the bereaved in reaching out to others with similar losses (p. 221). Although the funeral provides an important opportunity for the emotional expression of grief, Clinebell pointed out that it may take many months for the bereaved person to come to terms with a loss, and continued spiritual support is needed during that time. Some postfuneral questions that might encourage the expression of emotions are, "What have you been feeling since the funeral?" "What sort of memories keep coming back?" "How often have you let yourself cry?" "Have you had trouble keeping going?" and "Would you tell me more about the way he/she died?" (p. 224).

In order for healing to be completed, the bereaved person must be able to let go of the deceased. Although this may have appeared to occur at the time of death, when a family member verbally gives a dying person permission to give up, the emotional attachment may remain with the survivor. Many bereaved persons express significant distress at coming to a point at which they have difficulty remembering what the deceased looked like, or even at letting several hours pass without thinking about the deceased. Ruskay (1996) proposed an approach to bereavement care in which the griever is encouraged to incorporate the loss into daily activities and plans; the bereaved person is counseled to incorporate some of the deceased person's interests, for example, gardening, into their lives, thus adding a positive dimension to the grieving process (p. 5).

In discussing bereavement care, Bouton (1996) distinguished between the goals of grief counseling and bereavement care. Grief counseling is envisioned as facilitating the work of grieving to achieve a successful outcome by helping the bereaved person face the reality of the loss; cope with physical, psychological, and spiritual grief reactions; and reinvest himself or herself into life activities. Bereavement care is conceptualized as identifying and resolving the pain and conflict resulting from the loss that may block completion of the grieving process (p. 17).

Additionally, spiritual and religious beliefs are important considerations in the provision of bereavement care. Religious beliefs may be instrumental in defining right or acceptable attitudes and behavior in relation to the bereavement experience (Koenig, 1994, p. 405). Cullinan (1993) conceptualized spiritual care of the bereaved as a "sacred art." While acknowledging the existence of a multiplicity of theories related to the relationships among spirituality, religiosity, and bereavement, Cullinan (1993) viewed spirituality as undergirded and influenced by the individual's faith development, cultural background, and religious or denominational affiliation and practice (p. 197). Such an adaptive type of psychospiritual approach to care, Cullinan argued, will help the bereaved person to cope with the loss in a more positive and healthy way (p. 197).

Personal spirituality and religiosity or religious practice are important mediating variables in coping with death and bereavement. Dying persons' and their families' spiritual and religious beliefs about such concepts as the meaning of life and death, the existence of an afterlife, and the purpose of suffering can influence profoundly how the dying process is experienced. The nurse, sensitive to the spiritual and religious beliefs of a dying patient and his or her family, may be able to provide therapeutic spiritual support and intervention that will mediate the pain associated with the death and bereavement experiences.

▶ References

Alam, R., Barrera, M., D'Agostino, N., Nicholas, D., & Schneiderman, G. (2012). Bereavement experiences of mothers and fathers over time after the death of a child due to cancer. *Death Studies, 36*, 1–22.

Amenta, M. O. (1995). Loss, death and dying. In D. D. Ignatavicus, M. L. Workman, & M. A. Mishler (Eds.), *Medical–surgical nursing: A nursing process approach* (pp. 95–212). Philadelphia, PA: W. B. Saunders.

Angelucci, D., & Lawrence, M. (1995). Death and dying. In M. Stanley & P. G. Beare (Eds.), *Gerontological nursing* (pp. 400–414). Philadelphia, PA: F. A. Davis.

Becker, G., Xander, C. J., Blum, H. E., Lutterbach, J., Momm, F., Gysels, M., . . . Higginson, I. J. (2007). Do religious or spiritual beliefs influence bereavement? A systematic review. *Palliative Medicine, 21*, 207–217.

Black, H. K., Santanello, H. R., & Rubinstein, R. L. (2014). A pragmatic belief system in family meaning-making after death. *Death Studies, 38*(8), 522–530.

Bouton, B. L. (1996). The interdisciplinary bereavement team: Defining and directing appropriate bereavement care. *The Hospice Journal, 11*(4), 15–24.

Bowlby, J. (1961). Processes of mourning. *International Journal of Psychoanalysis, 42*(8), 317–340.

Burns, S. (1991). The spirituality of dying. *Health Progress, 72*(7), 48–52.

Charlton, R. G. (1992). Spiritual need of the dying and bereaved: Views from the United Kingdom and New Zealand. *Journal of Palliative Care, 8*(4), 38–40.

Clinebell, H. (1991). *Basic types of pastoral care and counseling.* Nashville, TN: Abingdon Press.

Cohen, K. P. (1979). *Hospice: Prescription for terminal care.* Germantown, MD: Aspen Systems.

Conrad, N. L. (1985). Spiritual support for the dying. *Nursing Clinics of North America, 20*(2), 415–426.

Cullinan, A. (1993). Bereavement and the sacred art of spiritual care. In K. J. Doka (Ed.), *Death and spirituality* (pp. 195–205). Amityville, NY: Baywood.

Crang, C., & Muncey, T. (2008). Quality of life in palliative care: Being at ease in the here and now. *International Journal of Palliative Nursing, 14*(2), 92–97.

Davidson, G. W. (1984). *Understanding mourning: A guide for those who grieve.* Minneapolis, MN: Augsburg.

Derrickson, B. S. (1996). The spiritual work of the dying: A framework and case studies. *The Hospice Journal, 11*(2), 11–30.

Dezutter, J., Soenens, B., Luyckx, K., Bruyneel, S., Vansteenkiste, M., Duriez, B., & Hutsebaut, D. (2009). The role of religion in death attitudes: Distinguishing between religious belief and style of processing religious contents. *Death Studies, 33*, 73–92.

Dobratz, M. C. (2011). Toward development of a middle-range theory of psychological adaptation in death and dying. *Nursing Science Quarterly, 24*(4), 370–376.

Doka, K. J. (Ed.). (1993a). The spiritual crisis of bereavement. In *Death and spirituality* (pp. 185–194). Amityville, NY: Baywood.

Doka, K. J. (Ed.). (1993b). The spiritual needs of the dying. In *Death and spirituality* (pp. 143–150). Amityville, NY: Baywood.

Doyle, D. (1984). *Palliative care: The management of far-advanced illness.* Philadelphia, PA: The Charles Press.

Draper, P., Holloway, M., & Adamson, S. (2013). A qualitative study of recently bereaved people's beliefs about death: Implications for bereavement care. *Journal of Clinical Nursing, 23*(9/10), 1300–1308.

Eisdon, R. (1995). Spiritual pain in dying people: The nurse's role. *Professional Nurse, 10*(10), 641–643.

Esposito, J. L. (1990). Islam. In J. A. Komonchak, M. Collins, & D. A. Lane (Eds.), *The new dictionary of theology* (pp. 527–529). Collegeville, MN: The Liturgical Press.

Featherstone, S. M. (1997). Coping with loss, death and grieving. In P. A. Potter & A. G. Perry (Eds.), *Foundations of nursing: Concepts, process and practice* (pp. 457–476). St. Louis, MO: C. V. Mosby.

Forster, E., & Hafiz, A. (2015). Paediatric death and dying: Exploring coping strategies of health care professionals and perceptions of support provision. *International Journal of Palliative Nursing, 21*(6), 294–301.

Franco, V. W. (1985). The hospice: Humane care for the dying. *Journal of Religion and Health, 24*(1), 79–89.

Giske, T., & Cone, P. H. (2015). Discerning the health path: How nurses assist patient spirituality in diverse health care settings. *Journal of Clinical Nursing, 24*(19/20), 2926–2935.

Green, J. (1989a). Death with dignity: Hinduism. *Nursing Times, 85*(6), 50–51.

Green, J. (1989b). Death with dignity: Buddhism. *Nursing Times, 85*(9), 40–41.

Grey, R. (1996). The psycho-spiritual care matrix: A new paradigm for hospice caregiving. *American Journal of Hospice and Palliative Care, 13*(4), 19–25.

Grollman, E. A. (1993). Death in Jewish thought. In K. J. Doka (Ed.), *Death and spirituality* (pp. 21–32). Amityville, NY: Baywood.

Hamel, R. P., & Lysaught, M. T. (1994). Choosing palliative care: Do religious beliefs make a difference? *Journal of Palliative Care, 10*(3), 61–66.

Hart, A., Kohlwes, R., Deyo, R., Rhodes, L., & Bowen, D. (2003). Hospice patients' attitudes regarding spiritual discussions with their doctors. *American Journal of Hospice and Palliative Care, 20*(2), 135–139; 160.

Harvey, T. (1996). Who is the chaplain anyway?: Philosophy and integration of hospice chaplaincy. *American Journal of Hospice and Palliative Care, 13*(5), 41–43.

Hayes, Z. (1993). Death. In J. A. Komonchak, M. Collins, & D. A. Lane (Eds.), *The new dictionary of theology.* Collegeville, MN: The Liturgical Press.

Head, D. (1994). Religious approaches to dying. In I. B. Corless, B. B. Germino, & M. Pittman (Eds.), *Dying, death and bereavement: Theoretical perspectives and other ways of knowing.* Sudbury, MA: Jones & Bartlett Learning.

Hermann, C. P. (2001). Spiritual needs of dying patients: A qualitative study. *Oncology Nursing Forum, 28*(1), 67–72.

Highfield, M. F. (1992). Spiritual health of oncology patients: Nurse and patient perspectives. *Cancer Nursing, 15*(1), 1–8.

Highfield, M. E. F., Taylor, E. J., & Amenta, M. O. (2000). Preparation to care: The spiritual care education of oncology and hospice nurses. *Journal of Hospice and Palliative Nursing, 2*(2), 53–63.

Hittle, J. M. (1994). Death and spirituality: A nurse's perspective. *American Journal of Hospice and Palliative Care, 11*(5), 23–24.

Holloway, M. (2006). Death the great leveler? Toward a transcultural spirituality of dying and bereavement. *Journal of Clinical Nursing, 15*(7), 833–839.

Hoy, T. (1983). Hospice chaplaincy in the caregiving team. In C. A. Corr & D. M. Corr (Eds.), *Hospice care: Principles and practice* (pp. 177–196). New York, NY: Faber & Faber.

Irion, P. E. (1993). Spiritual issues in death and dying for those who do not have conventional religious belief. In K. J. Doka (Ed.), *Death and spirituality* (pp. 93–112). Amityville, NY: Baywood.

James, C. R., & MacLeod, R. D. (1993). The problematic nature of education in palliative care. *Journal of Palliative Care, 9*(4), 5–10.

Joesten, L. B. (1992). The voices of the dying and the bereaved: A bridge between loss and growth. In L. E. Holst (Ed.), *Hospital ministry: The role of the chaplain today* (pp. 139–150). New York, NY: Crossroad.

Kalina, K. (1993). *Midwife for souls: Spiritual care for the dying.* Boston, MA: St. Paul Books and Media.

Katz, J., & Sidell, M. (1994). *Easeful death: Caring for dying and bereaved people.* London, UK: Hodder & Stoughton.

Kemp, C. (1995). *Terminal illness: A guide to nursing care.* Philadelphia, PA: J. B. Lippincott.

Kinast, R. L. (1993). Death and dying. In M. Downey (Ed.), *The new dictionary of Catholic spirituality* (pp. 252–256). Collegeville, MN: The Liturgical Press.

Kirschling, J. M., & Pittman, J. F. (1989). Measurement of spiritual well-being: A hospice caregiver sample. *The Hospice Journal, 5*(2), 1–11.

Kisvetrova, H., Skoloudik, D., Joanovic, E., Konecna, J., & Miksova, Z. (2016). Dying care interventions in the intensive care unit. *Journal of Nursing Scholarship, 48*(2), 139–146.

Klass, D. (1993). Spirituality, Protestantism and death. In K. J. Doka (Ed.), *Death and spirituality* (pp. 51–74). Amityville, NY: Baywood.

Ko, E., Kwak, J., & Nelson-Becker, H. (2015). What constitutes a good and bad death? Perspectives of homeless older adults. *Death Studies, 39*(7), 422–432.

Koenig, H. G. (1994). *Aging and God: Spiritual pathways to mental health in midlife and later years.* New York, NY: The Haworth Press.

Kübler-Ross, E. (1969). *On death and dying.* New York, NY: Macmillan.

Lees, J. (2008). A spiritual perspective on loss and bereavement. *International Journal for Human Caring, 12*(2), 90–94.

Lindemann, E. (1944). Symptomatology and management of acute grief. *American Journal of Psychiatry, 101*(1), 141–148.

MacDonald, S. M., Sandmaier, R., & Fainsinger, R. L. (1993). Objective evaluation of spiritual care: A case report. *Journal of Palliative Care, 9*(2), 47–49.

McCarthy, M., Clarke, N., Ting, C., Conroy, R., Anderson, V., & Heath, J. (2010). Prevalence and predictors of parental grief and depression after the death of a child from cancer. *Journal of Palliative Medicine, 13*(11), 1321–1326.

Miller, E. J. (1993). A Roman Catholic view of death. In K. J. Doka (Ed.), *Death and spirituality* (pp. 33–50). Amityville, NY: Baywood.

Millison, M. B., & Dudley, J. R. (1992). Providing spiritual support: A job for all hospice professionals. *The Hospice Journal, 8*(4), 49–66.

Moller, D. W. (1990). *On death without dignity: The human impact of technical dying.* Amityville, NY: Baywood.

Murray, D., & Lyall, D. (1994). Pastoral care. In D. Doyle (Ed.), *Palliative care: The management of far-advanced illness* (pp. 414–427). Philadelphia, PA: The Charles Press.

Murray, S., Kendall, M., Boyd, K., Worth, A., & Benton, T. F. (2004). Exploring the spiritual needs of people dying of lung cancer or heart failure: A prospective qualitative interview study of patients and their carers. *Palliative Medicine, 18*, 39–45.

Narayanasamy, A. (2007). Palliative care and spirituality. *Indian Journal of Palliative Care, 13*(2), 32–41.

The National Hospice Organization. (1996a). Hospice code of ethics. *The Hospice Journal, 11*(2), 75–81.

The National Hospice Organization. (1996b). Hospice services guidelines and definitions. *The Hospice Journal, 11*(2), 65–73.

Neuberger, J. (1994). *Caring for dying people of different faiths* (2nd ed.). St. Louis, MO: C. V. Mosby.

Olson, M. (1997). *Healing the dying.* New York, NY: Delmar.

Osterweis, A., Solomon, F., & Green, M. (1984). *Bereavement reactions: Consequences and care.* Washington, DC: National Academy Press.

Parker, B., & Dunn, K. (2011). The continued lived experience of the unexpected death of a child. *Omega, 63*(3), 221–233.

Parkes, C. (1972). *Bereavement. Studies of grief in adult life.* New York, NY: International University Press.

Parkes, C. M., Benjamin, B., & Fitzgerald, R. (1969). Broken hearts: A statistical study of increased mortality among widowers. *British Medical Journal, 1*(1), 7400–7443.

Parkes, C. M., & Weiss, R. (1983). *Recovery from bereavement.* New York, NY: Basic Books.

Peterson, J., Johnson, M., Halversen, B., Apmann, L., Chang, P. C., Kershek, S., . . . & Pincon, D. (2010). Where do nurses go for help? A qualitative study of coping with death and dying. *International Journal of Palliative Nursing, 16*(9), 432, 434–438.

Pevey, C. F., Jones, T. J., & Yarber, A. (2008). How religion comforts the dying: A qualitative inquiry. *Omega, 58*(1), 41–59.

Praill, D. (1995). Approaches to spiritual care. *Nursing Times, 91*(34), 54–57.

President's Commission for the Study of Ethical Problems in Medicine and Biomedical and Behavioral Research. (1981). *Defining death* (Pub. No. 81-600150). Washington, DC: US Government Printing Office.

Price, J. L., Stevens, H. O., & LaBarre, M. C. (1995). Spiritual caregiving in nursing practice. *Journal of Psychosocial Nursing, 33*(12), 5–9.

Raether, H. C. (1993). Rituals, beliefs and grief. In K. J. Doka (Ed.), *Death and spirituality* (pp. 207–215). Amityville, NY: Baywood.

Rando, T. A. (1988). *Grieving: How to go on living when someone you love dies.* Lexington, MA: Lexington Books.

Raphael, B. C. (1983). *The anatomy of bereavement.* New York, NY: Basic Books.

Reese, D. J., & Brown, D. R. (1997). Psychosocial and spiritual care in hospice: Differences between nursing, social work, and clergy. *The Hospice Journal, 12*(1), 29–41.

Renard, J. (1993). Islamic spirituality. In M. Downey (Ed.), *The new dictionary of Catholic spirituality* (pp. 555–559). Collegeville, MN: The Liturgical Press.

Renz, M., Mao, M. S., Bueche, D., Cerny, T., & Strasser, K. (2013). Dying is a transition. *American Journal of Hospice and Palliative Medicine, 30*(3), 283–290.

Reynolds, A. (2009). How can I respond to dying patients? *Journal of Christian Nursing, 26*(4), 197–198.

Rushing, D. (2012). "Am I going to die, Aunt Deborah?" *Journal of Christian Nursing, 29*(2), 113–116.

Ruskay, S. (1996). Saying hello again: A new approach to bereavement counseling. *The Hospice Journal, 11*(4), 5–14.

Ryan, D. (1993). Death: Eastern perspectives. In K. J. Doka (Ed.), *Death and spirituality* (pp. 75–92). Amityville, NY: Baywood.

Sanders, C. M. (1989). *Grief: The mourning after: Dealing with adult bereavement.* New York, NY: John Wiley & Sons.

Saunders, C. (1981). The founding philosophy. In C. Saunders, D. H. Summers, & N. Teller (Eds.), *Hospice: The living idea* (p. 4). Philadelphia, PA: W. B. Saunders.

Saunders, C. (1983). The last stages of life. In C. A. Corr & D. M. Corr (Eds.), *Hospice care: Principles and practice* (pp. 5–11). New York, NY: Springer.

Schulling, S. (2012). God's dominion over death. *Journal of Christian Nursing, 29*(1), 52–56.

Sheldon, J. E. (2000). Spirituality as a part of nursing. *Journal of Hospice and Palliative Nursing, 2*(3), 101–108.

Shuchter, J. (1986). *Dimensions of grief: Adjusting to the death of a spouse.* San Francisco, CA: Jossey-Bass.

Stepnick, A., & Perry, T. (1992). Preventing spiritual distress in the dying client. *Journal of Psychosocial Nursing, 30*(1), 17–24.

Stoddard, S. (1978). *The hospice movement: A better way of caring for the dying.* Briarcliff Manor, NY: Stein and Day.

Taylor, E. J., & Amenta, M. (1994). Midwifery to the soul while the body dies: Spiritual care among hospice nurses. *American Journal of Hospice and Palliative Care, 11*(6), 28–35.

Tiew, L. H., Kwee, J. H., Creedy, D. K., & Chan, M. F. (2013). Hospice nurses' perspectives of spirituality. *Journal of Clinical Nursing, 22*(19/20), 2923–2933.

Vassallo, B. M. (2001). The spiritual aspects of dying at home. *Holistic Nursing Practice, 15*(2), 17–29.

Vivat, B. (2008). Measures of spiritual issues for palliative care patients: A literature review. *Palliative Medicine, 22*, 859–868.

Worden, J. W. (1982). *Grief counseling and grief therapy: A handbook for the mental health practitioner.* New York, NY: Springer.

World Health Organization. (1990). *Cancer pain relief and palliative care: Technical report series 804.* Geneva, Switzerland: Author.

Wortman, J. H., & Park, C. L. (2008). Religion and spirituality in adjustment following bereavement: An integrative review. *Death Studies, 32*, 703–736.

Young, C., & Koopsen, C. (2005). *Spirituality and health and healing.* Thorofare, NJ: Slack Incorporated.

Young, C., & Koopsen, C. (2011). *Spirituality, health, and healing: An integrative approach.* Sudbury, MA: Jones & Bartlett Learning.

CHAPTER 10

Parish/Faith Community Nursing: Caregiving within the Church Community

The role of parish nurses is basically a reaching out for more whole person ways of ministering to people who are hurting.

Granger Westberg, 1999

The parishioners that I minister to are mostly older and with a lot of health problems physically; some are cognitively impaired as well. But they all love to have the parish nurse come, as a representative of the church, to minister to them. I help them with any health problems or questions. Sometimes I pray with them or read the Bible if they want or sometimes just listen. Older folks love to reminisce about the past. Talking about the good things that happened in the past validates their lives and helps them accept where they are now in the journey of life.

Elizabeth, Parish Nurse

A parish nurse related the following anecdote: At a conference for religious pastors of urban churches, a presentation was given on the topic of parish nursing. Although the parish nurse presenter was described as well prepared and articulate, most of the clergy audience came away admitting that they still "did not know what parish nursing really was." This is a very telling story and reflects the lack of understanding of many contemporary nurses and pastors related to the place of the subfield of parish nursing within the larger profession. This chapter explores the philosophy of parish nursing, including the scope and standards of practice, and the historical background, models, educational preparation, spirituality, parish nursing research, and the present day art and practice of parish nursing. In addition to literature review in the area, empirical examples of parish nursing are presented in data elicited through interviews with contemporary practitioners and recipients of parish nursing.

▶ Parish Nursing/Faith Community Nursing

In the nursing literature on church-related health care, one currently finds both labels: "parish nursing" and "faith community nursing." This is related to the fact that the title changed in some quarters during the past decade.

A Professional Title Change

Before proceeding to discussions of the philosophy, scope and standards of practice, history, and models of parish nursing, it is necessary to address the relatively recent title change for the profession adopted by some—that is, from parish nursing to faith community nursing. Over the past decade, certain practitioners in the field have started informally using the label *faith community nursing*. This title was formally adopted by a number of parish nurses in 2005 with the publication of the American Nurses Association's (ANA) *Faith Community Nursing: Scope and Standards of Practice* (the second edition of this work was published in 2012 by the ANA and the Health Ministries Association [HMA]).

Historically *parish nursing* was the original label adopted for nurses, mostly volunteers, who worked with congregational health issues following the 1970s and 1980s vision of the Reverend Dr. Granger Westberg, the acknowledged founder of the parish nursing concept. This earlier title is reflected in the original publication of the *Scope and Standards of Parish Nursing Practice*. The title formally changed, however, with the publication of the 2005 *Scope and Standards of Practice*: "In the 2005 revision of the ANA *Scope and Standards of Practice,* the term faith community nurse was adopted to be inclusive of the titles of parish nurse, congregational nurse, health ministry nurse, crescent nurse, or health and wellness nurse (ANA and HMA, 2005)" (Gustafson, 2008, p. 1033).

A number of contemporary parish nursing publications use the newer title, highlighting the concept of the faith community rather than the parish. Some examples are: "The Emerging Role of Faith Community Nurses in Prevention and Management of Chronic Diseases" (McGinnis & Zoske, 2008); "State of Research for Faith Community Nursing 2009" (Dyess, Chase, & Newline, 2010); "Services Delivered by Faith-Community Nurses to Individuals with Elevated Blood Pressure" (Monay, Mangione, Sorrell-Thompson, & Baig, 2010); "A Documentation Approach for Faith Community Nursing" (Miller & Carson, 2010); and "Clergy Knowledge and Attitudes Concerning Faith Community Nursing: Toward a Three-Dimensional Scale" (Thompson, 2010).

Some article titles use a combination of the terms *faith community* and *parish*, such as: "Faith Community Nursing/Parish Nursing in a Frontier State" (Peterson, 2011). In a commentary entitled "Nursing in the Church," a master's-prepared nurse with the titles "faith community nurse–health ministry educator" and "parish nurse consultant," admits that currently "parish/faith community nursing is experiencing growing pains" (Hinton, 2012, p. 141).

And, finally, a number of nursing journal articles still employ the earlier classic usage, *parish nursing*, to describe the content, including "Exploring Parish Nurses' Perspective of Parish Nurse Training" (Ziebarth & Miller, 2010); "Parish Nurse-Initiated Interdisciplinary Mobile Health Care Delivery Project" (Mayernik, Resnick, Skomo, & Mandock 2010); and "A Congregation and Parish Nurse Meet an Angel" (Bond, 2011).

Although the more common descriptor found in the contemporary nursing literature seems to be *faith community nursing*, parish nurses Deborah Patterson and Mary Slutz (2011) have argued for retention of the title parish nurse to describe nursing that is based in a Christian congregation. In the article "Faith Community/ Parish Nursing: What's in a Name?" Patterson and Slutz point out that "retaining the language 'parish nurse' promotes a broader understanding of the purpose of this specialty practice, not only as inreach or outreach on behalf of a church or health system, but as a focused and integrated 'parish' ministry" (p. 31). While Patterson and Slutz agree that the title faith community nursing is "appropriate to describe this broad specialty practice across all faiths, the title 'Parish Nurse' should not be abandoned by those working in the context of Christian faith communities" (p. 32). The authors observe that the term *faith community nursing* "does not go far enough to convey the outreach that as Christians [they] are called to ministries of service" (p. 32). Ultimately, Patterson and Slutz concluded that "For a Christian calling, Parish Nurse is an honored title that any registered nurse educated in the specialty and serving a Christian faith community should be honored to hold" (p. 33).

In a recent article entitled "A Renewed Look at Faith Community Nursing," the author reiterates the fact that the terms *parish nursing* and *faith community nursing* continue to be used interchangeably and "have the same meaning" (Schroepfer, 2016, p. 63). The current definition of *faith community nursing*, as identified in 2012 by the American Nurses Association and the Health Ministries Association, is cited by Schroepfer (2016) as: "the specialized practice of professional nursing that focuses on the intentional care of the spirit as part of the process of promoting holistic health and preventing or minimizing illness in the faith community" (p. 63). The greatest strength of faith community nursing is described as "the consistency and trust built between parishioners and the faith community" (p. 65).

Currently the American Nurses Association Credentialing Center (ANCC) offers "Faith Community Nursing" board certification; the offering of certification began in August 2014. Eligibility criteria for the "Faith Community Nursing" certi- fication include: "current active R.N. license; equivalent of 2 years full time practice as a registered nurse; minimum of 1000 practice hours in specialty area of 'Faith Community Nursing' within the last 3 years; a minimum of 30 hours of continuing education in 'Faith Community Nursing' within the last 3 years; and two professional development categories such as academic credits, presentations, publications" and others (Breisch, 2016, p. 13).

Parish or faith community nursing, is presently viewed as a unique resource for the community as "it seeks to support mainstream healthcare providers by en- couraging faith groups to employ or appoint part-time registered nurses . . . to help improve public and community health in their local areas" (Wordsworth, Moore, & Woodhouse, 2016, p. 66). The number of parish/faith community nursing programs has increased dramatically since the discipline's formal beginning in 1964; there are now "thousands of FCN nurses serving populations around the world" (Shores, 2014, p. 299). One example in the United States is the parish nurse serving parish- ioners at St. Bartholomew's Church in Nashville, Tennessee, by providing a variety of health-care programs such as blood pressure screening and nutritional education (Donnelly, 2014). Findings from a study of patients of parish nurses revealed that patient/parishioners, as well as resolving health challenges, reported: "changes in spiritual identity" and "an enhanced understanding of who they were in God/Christ" (Van Dover & Pfeiffer, 2011, p. 1824).

▶ Parish Nursing Defined

The Philosophy of Parish Nursing

Essentially, the philosophy of parish nursing is grounded in the relationship between spirituality or faith beliefs and the conduct of caring for the sick. This might be described best in the following paradigm of "Beatitudes for Parish Nurses," which combines the Scriptural beatitudes identified by Jesus in His Sermon on the Mount (Matthew 5:3–10) with the primary roles identified for contemporary parish nurses: health counselor, health educator (health promoter), health referral agent, health advocate, health visitor, integrator of faith and health, and coordinator of support and volunteer groups.

Beatitudes for Parish Nurses

Blessed are parish nurses who care for the poor, for theirs is

The kingdom of heaven.

Blessed are parish nurses who mourn for parishioners lost, for they will

Be comforted.

Blessed are parish nurses who visit the isolated and the elderly,

For they will inherit the land.

Blessed are parish nurses who advocate for marginalized clients,

For they will be satisfied.

Blessed are parish nurses who minister to those in pain and suffering,

For they will be shown mercy.

Blessed are parish nurses who bring peace to patients who are anxious

And afraid, for they will be called children of God.

Blessed are parish nurses who suffer misunderstanding for the sake of

Their ministry, for they will see God.

Blessed are parish nurses who comfort and care in the Lord's Name, for

Their reward will be great in heaven.

The former director of the International Parish Nurse Resource Center, Ann Solari-Twadell (1999), suggests that the best way to answer the question "What is parish nursing?" is to study the philosophy of the discipline (p. 3). Solari-Twadell notes that in calling the nurse to care for the "whole person," parish nursing includes and, in fact, highlights the individual's "spiritual dimension": "The pastoral dimensions of nursing care are emphasized, with particular attention to the spiritual maturity of the nurse. This begins to distinguish the practice from the traditional community health nurse and to set the parameters for the role" (pp. 3–4). Two key points of Solari-Twadell's identified philosophy are that "parish nursing holds the spiritual dimension to be central to the practice," and "the focus of practice is the faith community and its ministry" (p. 15). The philosophy of parish nursing has been described as the guiding principle to "promote the health of a faith community by working with the pastor and staff to integrate theological, sociological and physiologic perspectives of health and healing into the word, sacrament and service of the congregation" (Lovinus, 1996, p. 7). The parish nurse serves as "a role model for the relationship between one's faith and health" (Solari-Twadell & Westberg, 1991, p. 24).

The parish nurse is considered by most parish nurse educators to be a registered nurse with well-developed clinical and interpersonal skills, a strong personal religious faith, and a desire or felt call to serve the needs of a parish or faith community. A parish nursing philosophy builds on the existing philosophy of caring and commitment already espoused by the nurse as a professional ethic. One parish nurse described her ministry as a vocation. "Nursing in a faith community is a calling, an absolute caring for people and a deep sense of personal faith" (Palmer, 2001, p. 17). Parish nurses are generally noted for their roles as educators and health promoters within a congregation. "They provide information on healthy life styles and ways to prevent illness" (Dunkle, 2000, p. 316); they also, however, tend to patients' "psychosocial and spiritual needs" (p. 316). It is pointed out that parish nurses practice within a specific "cultural community": "in a place of worship where the focus is on meeting spiritual needs; the nurses work with the community leaders as their professional partners" (Trofino et al., 2000, p. 60). As a final point in examining the philosophy of parish nursing, it is important to emphasize that the role or title of parish nurse does not limit one to working with any "particular faith community or religious denomination"; it has, therefore, been suggested by some that the label be changed from parish nursing to "health ministry" or "congregational nursing" ("Parish Nursing," 2000, pp. 8–9).

Scope and Standards of Practice

Between 1996 and 1998, a document identifying the scope and standards of parish nursing practice was developed by the Practice and Education Committee of the HMA. The HMA is a professional organization that represents parish nurses and other health ministers. The scope and standards document was acknowledged by the ANA, Congress of Nursing Practice, in Spring 1998. The introduction to the document states that "Parish nursing promotes health and healing within faith communities" (American Nurses Association, 1998, p. 1). The purpose of the scope and standards document is to "describe the evolving specialty of parish nursing and to provide parish nurses, the nursing profession, and other healthcare providers, employers, insurers, and their clients with the unique scope and competent standards of care and professional performance expected of a parish nurse" (p. 3). The parish nurse scope and standards are based on the ANA's 1991 *Standards of Clinical Nursing Practice* (p. 4). The definition of *parish nurse*, as articulated formally in the scope and standards of practice is, "The most common title given to a registered professional nurse who serves as a member of the ministry staff of a faith community to promote health as wholeness of the faith community, its family and individual members, and the community it serves through the independent practice of nursing as defined by the nurse practice act in the jurisdiction in which he or she practices and the standards of practice set forth in this document" (p. 7).

Some of the parish nurse's roles, as identified in the initial scope and standards of practice, include collecting client health data (health assessment); diagnosing, based on the data; identifying desired health outcomes; health care and promotion planning; implementing interventions; and evaluating client responses (ANA, 1998, pp. 9–14). The nurse also participates in such activities as quality assessment, performance appraisal, education, collegial sharing, ethical decision making, collaboration with the community, research, and resource utilization (pp. 15–22).

As previously mentioned, a second document describing parish nurses' scope and standards of practice was published by the ANA in 2005 under the title *Faith Community Nursing: Scope and Standards of Practice*. Related to the current and ongoing changes in the health-care system, the ANA (2012), in collaboration with the HMA, recently published a second edition of this document. It was reported that "twenty-one practicing RNs who represent the specialty . . . contributed to this edition" (Bennett, 2011, p. 9). The current publication "builds on the 2005 and 1998 editions, as well as *ANA's Nursing: Scope and Standards of Practice,* 2nd Edition" (p. 9).

The second edition of *Faith Community Nursing: Scope and Standards of Practice* "describes the specialty practice of faith community nursing for the nursing profession, faith community nurses, other healthcare providers, spiritual leaders, employers, insurers, health care consumers, families, and members of faith communities" (ANA, 2012, p. 1). In defining faith community nursing, the ANA document points out that the faith community nurse (FCN) "is knowledgeable in two primary areas: professional nursing and spiritual care" (p. 5). The "goals of the FCN are the protection, promotion and optimization of health and abilities; the prevention of illness and injury; and the alleviation of suffering in the context of the values, beliefs and practices of a faith community, such as a church, congregation, parish, synagogue, temple, mosque or faith based community agency" (p. 5).

▶ A Brief History of Parish Nursing

The contemporary concept of parish nursing is usually attributed to Lutheran pastor Granger Westberg, as an outgrowth of his holistic health center project of the mid-1980s. This experimental program of care was supported by the Kellogg Foundation and the University of Illinois College of Medicine (Westberg, 1990). Although Pastor Westberg is appropriately acknowledged as the founder of the current parish nursing movement in the United States, one should also recognize the health-care activities of the early Christian Church, as well as the European models of parish nursing, such as the 19th-century German Christian Deaconesses, the Gemein-deschwestern (Zerson, 1994, p. 20). The earliest deacons and deaconesses of the fledgling Christian community established immediately after the death of Christ considered care of the sick in their homes to be one of the primary ministries of the Church. Following those early centuries and throughout the Middle Ages, men and women felt their calling to minister to the ill and the infirm to be a vocation from God. St. Vincent de Paul, the great minister to the sick in 17th-century France, established "societies of women of the Church who banded themselves together with some simple rules to tend the sick and the poor of the immediate neighborhood. They called themselves the 'servants of the poor'" (Woodgate, 1946, p. 43). These women could surely be considered forebears of contemporary parish nurses.

In the mid-20th century, an article was published in a religious nursing journal entitled "In the Parish" (Cummings, 1960). The nurse author begins the piece by relating the fact that in recent issues of the journal she had read about nurses "in hospitals, in clinics, in schools and in homes" but, she lamented, "Alas, I was not included, for in the parish, is my job" (Cummings, 1960, p. 26). Nurse Cummings describes her role as a parish health counselor in a parish of about 3,500 families and asserts that, at this time, her Church believes that their multidisciplinary health program is "the only one of its kind in the United States" (p. 26). This innovative parish nursing program was focused on such things as care of the chronically ill elders in the parish, education for home care of the ill, referral to community agencies, volunteers service, and home visiting. Nurse Cummings's role as a parish health counselor reads very much like that of the parish nurse of today. Some other parish nursing activities described in the 20th-century nursing literature included a Christian Church–affiliated "volunteer nursing program" to provide care for the ill and infirm in their homes (Martin & Lacoutre, 1953) and an "organized plan for visiting individuals who are ill and lonely" sponsored by a Church Diocesan Council of Nurses ("Council Projects," 1956, p. 42).

In the era of the late 1970s and early 1980s, Pastor Granger Westberg's interest in and support of the concept of holistic health care, including the subfield of parish nursing, began to capture the attention of some members of the larger nursing community. With his support, a parish nursing program was sponsored by Lutheran General Hospital in Park Ridge, Illinois; parish nursing was also initiated at several parishes in the area. As the ministry developed, the International Parish Nurse Resource Center (IPNRC) was created in 1986 under the aegis of Advocate Lutheran General Hospital. Together with a committee of nurse consultants from across the country, the staff of the IPNRC developed a model curriculum for parish nursing education. The IPNRC also began to sponsor annual Westberg Symposiums to provide a forum for parish nurses from across the country to come together to discuss the emerging subfield and its practice. In an October 2001 letter addressed to the "Friends of the International Parish Nurse Resource Center," however, it was announced that the IPNRC would no longer be an agency of Advocate Health Care, the umbrella organization providing support for this parish nursing education effort. It was anticipated that the Westberg Symposiums and some other activities formerly conducted by the IPNRC would continue to be supported in other arenas.

Another previously mentioned parish nursing association, the volunteer membership group called the Health Ministries Association (HMA), was derived from the emerging parish nursing interest of the 1970s and 1980s. The HMA, collaborating author of the *Scope and Standards of Nursing Practice*, is an association for those who serve in health ministry. The group "serves as the professional specialty organization for parish nurses and as such has been accepted by the American Nurses Association for membership in the Nursing Organization Liaison Forum (NOLF)" (FAQ About HMA & Parish Nursing, 2001, p. 1).

As the new millennium dawned, it was estimated that "200 institutions in the United States offered parish nurse education"; no curriculum has been endorsed by the ANA ("The ANA does not endorse curriculum"); "there is no process in place for parish nurses to become certified"; and "parish nursing" has been "designated a specialty practice by ANA," which means that "a parish nurse cannot practice without a license" in his or her state (Story, 2001, p. 3). It was also noted that it will probably take a number of years, and "a minimum of $80,000" before ANA certification exams can be offered (p. 3).

▶ Early Models of Parish Nursing

Four early models of parish nursing have been defined: congregation-based volunteer (CBV), congregation-based paid (CBP), institution-based volunteer (IBV), and institution-based paid (IBP) (Kuhn, 1997, p. 26). The terms *congregational nurse practitioner (CNP)* and *congregational care nurse (CCN)* have also begun to be used to describe the role of the nurse working primarily within a parish or faith community (Souther, 1997). A parish nurse may be employed by a church to work as a member of a ministerial team and provide some nursing services to parishioners; a hospital or other health-care institution may also employ a parish nurse in partnership with a local parish, as a way of bringing health promotion into the community. Wilson (1997) described the parish nurse as "a community health nurse who also becomes God's representative of love, caring and healing on earth" (p. 13). The parish nurse does not compete with the public health nurse, but rather works in concert with other nurses in the community (Schank, Weis, & Matheus, 1996).

Lynda Whitney Miller (1997) developed a contemporary parish nursing model undergirded by the theological perspective of evangelical Christianity. The Miller Model of Parish Nursing contains four major components: "person/parishioner"; "health"; "nurse/parish nurse"; and "community/parish" (p. 18). Miller's goal is to provide Christian nurses with a theoretical base to support the practice of parish nursing (p. 17). A separate parish nursing model called the "Circle of Christian Caring" was created by Dr. Margie Maddox (2001). In her model, Dr. Maddox incorporated a number of activities already in place when she began to serve as parish nurse at a large Presbyterian church. Dr. Maddox noted that as she "worked with the services in which the church was already engaged, the model began to emerge" (p. 11). The Circle of Christian Caring model focuses on the parish nurse roles of health educator, health counselor, referral resource/client advocate, and facilitator of groups and/or processes (pp. 12–13).

Parish Nursing Education

Related to the early emerging models of parish nursing were a variety of educational programs that prepared one for the field of parish nursing. These educational offerings ranged from weekend or weeklong continuing education unit (CEU) programs, which may have awarded from 3 to 6 CEUs, to academic courses in parish nursing, which awarded 3 to 6 credits for the overall program. There were also several post-baccalaureate and graduate programs that focus on the topic of nursing in a faith community. These programs were sponsored primarily by health-care institutions, colleges and universities, seminaries, or other church-related associations. In some instances, community interfaith groups of churches collaboratively put together parish nurse education programs to prepare nurses to serve in their various faith communities. The multiplicity of parish nurse preparation programs were, as noted earlier, conducted in a variety of ways; some of these included "one day to weeklong orientations, continuing education workshops, seminars, distance learning, and ongoing coursework over weeks and months, as well as credit-bearing coursework in BSN, MSN and M.Div. programs offered over the course of a semester or, for some, over several years" (McDermott, Solari-Twadell, & Matheus, 1999, p. 271).

Three examples of early parish nurse programs are:

- A weeklong continuing education program, sponsored by a Christian nursing group, following which the participants were awarded 3 CEUs and were "commissioned" as parish nurses. Requirements for the course included having a state nursing license, some clinical nursing experience, and the desire to work with a faith community.
- A parish nurse preparation program, sponsored by a college and awarding the participants 3 CEUs, which held classes on six alternating Saturdays. This program required that the RNs have at least three years of experience and be partnered with a faith community. The course ended with a "dedication ceremony."
- A university-affiliated program that covered nine days and awarded the participants 5.4 CEUs. As well as including the usual topics described in the following paragraphs, this longer program included participation in several interfaith services and provided student on-site observations and clinical experiences with parish nurses in the community.

Some basic components of most early parish nursing programs included such topics as a theology of health and healing; the nurse's role in spiritual care; history, philosophy, and models of parish nursing; ethical issues in parish nursing; assessment of the individual, the family, and the congregation; documentation and accountability; the functions of the parish nurse, such as health counseling, health education, health referral, coordination of volunteers and support groups, patient advocacy, and integration of faith and health; working with a congregation; health promotion; dealing with grief and loss; and legal considerations in the conduct of parish nursing. Some programs also included classes focusing on such activities as prayer and worship leadership, research, grant writing, service among underprivileged people, and working with a ministerial team.

▶ The Spirituality of Parish Nursing

Although nurses from a variety of religious denominations are currently engaged in parish nursing, it is the nurse's personal spirituality and spiritual vocation to serve the ill that inspire and support the ministry. For Christian nurses, Jesus' blessing, related by the evangelist Matthew "I was ill and you cared for me" (25:36) provides both the catalyst and the reward for their caring for the sick within a faith community. Most parish nurses, many of whom serve on a volunteer basis, carry out their nursing within their own faith communities. This is usually desirable for both nurse and congregation, because the parish nurse is thus familiar with the spiritual and religious beliefs of the congregation and of the pastor. In the future, however, if parish nursing becomes "professionalized" to a greater degree, and if acceptable to a faith community, parish nurses may be hired to work with a church not of their own denomination. This kind of partnering does exist to some degree, in contemporary hospital-based parish nursing programs in which staff parish nurses provide consultation and support to developing church programs from a variety of religious traditions.

Perhaps one of the most critical elements in beginning a parish nursing program with a faith community is to listen to the needs and desires of the pastor and the parishioners. Lloyd and Ludwig-Beymer (1999) in discussing a concept they call VOC or "voice of the customer," note that "parishioners, whom we may think of as clients, patients, or in other terms, must be listened to. Clients are the ones who define quality and set the expectations of performance" (pp. 108–109). A director of a large community-based health ministry program observed that when approached about the initiation of a parish ministry program in their churches, most pastors raise three immediate questions: "How much of my time will this involve?"; "How much money is it going to cost me?"; and "Can I be sued?" The goal is to be able to provide negative answers to all three questions to allay the pastors' anxieties about the burden of establishing a parish nursing program for their congregation.

In this era of continued change within the U.S. health-care system, including such factors as short hospital stays, same-day surgeries, and early discharges, parish nursing, or nursing provided to those in their homes by members of a local faith community, may be critical to a patient's recovery, and perhaps even to his or her survival. No longer are patients, especially older patients or those who live alone, allowed the luxury of remaining in the hospital until they are able to fully function on their own. Health insurance policies rarely cover such extended stays, even if a patient's recovery may be at risk. It is expected that many of the former hospital nursing care services will now be provided by relatives or friends in a home care setting. This makes the role of the contemporary parish nurse vitally important to recovering patients who have no extended family networks and who may depend on their churches for caring support in times of crisis or significant need. It is suggested that individuals of all ages can benefit from the "personal caring and attention offered by a parish nursing model" (Stewart, 2000, p. 116).

The role of the parish nurse, as bridge between the patient and the faith community, incorporates the important activity of discussing spirituality with ill parishioners, a behavior that some clinical nurses admit to finding difficult (Wiebe, 2008). This is a dimension of spiritual care essential to the role of the contemporary parish nurse (Wordsworth, 2007).

One of the first things a parish nurse may find helpful in beginning to work with a faith community, especially a church to which the concept of parish nursing is new, is to do a "needs assessment" of the parish. There are a variety of needs assessment schemas being developed; however, the assessment must take into account certain factors that vary in parishes, such as the mean age of the parishioners, the range of socioeconomic levels in the church, the parish size, and the availability of volunteers to assist with the development of a parish health ministry. Parish nurses report that a critical factor in beginning a new effort with a faith community is the support of the pastor; as noted previously, he or she may have concerns about the time, financial, and/or legal burdens that the establishment of any new program may bring to the church. If, however, the potential parish nurse or health ministry team can predict that the program will be a benefit, rather than a burden, to the church, most pastors will be enthusiastic in their support of the effort.

An example of a professional parish needs assessment is that conducted by the University of Massachusetts, Amherst School of Nursing, at the request of a large urban parish. The school was also asked to assess a newly hired parish nurse. The assessment's aims were to "determine the health status of parishioners; identify their perceived health needs and perceived barriers in meeting those needs; and to assist the church and parish nurse in developing a health program for their faith community" (Swinney, Anson-Wonkka, Maki, & Corneau, 2001, p. 40). The assessment team concluded that the health needs of this faith community were similar to those identified in the goals of "Healthy People 2000," that is, "increased life span in a healthy state, reduced health disparities . . . and access to preventive care" (p. 43). In another study of the health needs and preferences of an individual faith community, in which 67 church members, 6 parish nurses, and the pastor participated, 80 percent of the services desired were educational, including education about such factors as health screening, disease, staying well, spiritual health, and emotional health (Mayhugh & Martens, 2001, p. 15). Some other parish nursing preferences of the faith community studied by Mayhugh and Martens were consultation about health problems, visiting (hospital, home, and nursing home), and coordination and training of volunteers (p. 15).

Although existing church-based parish nursing programs are still new to many faith communities, the number and scope of these ministries is expanding rapidly. In some churches, programs may be limited to such activities as monthly blood-pressure screenings, with occasional health educational programs for the congregation and infrequent home or hospital visiting by members of an "on-call" volunteer team; there may or may not be a parish nurse leading the effort. In other parishes, well-developed parish health ministry programs exist, under the leadership of a paid part-time or full-time parish or congregational nurse.

Depending on the interest and sophistication, in terms of health-care experience, on the part of a pastor and congregation, a church may require that their parish nurse have specific training in parish nursing; be a nurse practitioner; have a number of years of experience in nursing; or simply be a registered nurse who has a commitment and desire to work with a faith community. For example, one church in a moderately sized urban area advertised for a part-time parish nurse who would be a licensed RN in the state with at least three years of experience in nursing; the church also wanted the candidate to have completed a parish nursing preparation course, although the parameters of that course were not specified. It was noted that the nurse's role would include health promotion, disease prevention, education, counseling, advocacy, health screening, and referral. The parish nurse's hours could be "flexible."

Some congregations employing either paid or volunteer parish nurses try to schedule "office hours" at the parish, for example, Wednesdays and Fridays, 9 to noon, so that parishioners can come for private consultation or education. In such a situation, the parish nurse will usually have "on call" hours also. Some of the activities associated with existing parish nursing or health ministry programs, in addition to parish nurse office hours and monthly blood-pressure screening, include exercise classes (especially for seniors), cardiopulmonary resuscitation (CPR) classes, foot care classes, nutritional education classes, diabetes education classes, prenatal classes, bike safety classes for children, self–breast exam classes, substance abuse classes for parents and teens, healthy aging classes, family fitness classes, and classes preparing church volunteers for such ministries as hospital and nursing home visiting, homebound visiting, and respite family care.

The parish nurse may also do some home and hospital visiting as time permits; the nurse's most important role, however, is to serve as the health ministry team leader and coordinator of nonmedical health ministry volunteers. The parish nurse is an advocate for the ill parishioners of a faith community and a source of referral to needed and appropriate community health services.

▶ Parish Nursing Research

In an exploratory study of the parish nursing role, 48 practicing parish nurses identified ways in which they incorporated spiritual care into their activities, including prayer, if acceptable to the client; a caring and compassionate attitude; discussing illness-related spiritual concerns; and conducting or participating in rituals such as healing services and the distribution of Communion (Kuhn, 1997, p. 27). A nursing study of 40 parish nurses, who identified 1,800 client interactions, revealed that although approximately one-half of the nurses' activities dealt with physical problems, the other half related to spiritual–psychosocial issues (Rydholm, 1997). This latter finding is supported by the comments of parish nurse Linda Miles (1997), who asserted that in all of her nursing she included the spiritual dimension of care. "Spiritual nurturing contributes to improved life satisfaction and quality of life, improved health, reduced functional disability, and lower levels of depression" (p. 24).

A number of case study articles describing innovative experiences in parish nursing have been presented in the literature. For example, Dr. Margie Maddox (2003), in "Clinical Experience in Parish Nursing," described a newly created student clinical course in parish nursing; and Gretchen Quenstedt-Moe (2003), in "Parish Nursing and Home Care: A Blended Role?" explored parish nurses adopting a primary role of home visiting that she viewed as helping "fill the gaps left by the fragmented health care system" and that can "help parishioners to find meaningful connections that involve their needs, the parish nurse and God" (p. 30).

In looking at parish nursing as meeting the spiritual needs of elders at or near the end of their lives, a qualitative study of 15 end-of-life older adults revealed the importance of the parish nurse's spiritual care interventions: "1) Sharing of prayer and scripture; 2) Spiritual presence (listening with the heart); and 3) Pastoral counseling (including facilitating participation in religious rituals)" (O'Brien, 2006, p. 30).

The Gift of Faith in Chronic Illness

The author conducted an exploratory pilot study of the impact of parish nursing on persons who were unable to practice their faith because of illness and disability. The aim of the study was to test the effectiveness of a model of parish nursing/health ministry on spiritual well-being, hope, and life satisfaction among persons marginalized from their churches, and to explore the relationship between spiritual well-being and quality of life (measured in terms of hope and life satisfaction) for chronically ill persons. For a study participant distanced from his or her church, or desirous of additional spiritual support, pastoral care intervention was carried out in the hope of increasing spiritual well-being and positive quality of life. Following an initial individual spiritual needs assessment, pastoral care interventions were tailored by the parish nurse for each study participant.

The sample group consisted of six chronically ill individuals: four men and two women whose ages ranged from 45 to 92, with a mean of 74 years. Three patients were married, two were widowed, and one was single. Five individuals were college graduates and one completed high school; one person lived alone, one resided in a nursing home, and four lived with spouses or adult children. Three of the study patients were Protestant (Protestant, Church of God, and United Church of Christ), two were Roman Catholic, and one patient was Jewish. In terms of church attendance, the group reported attending services from once a month (or even daily when possible) to two to three times a year. Church attendance was quite variable depending on illness symptoms and remission and exacerbation of disease conditions. Patients' diagnoses included glaucoma and lupus, cancer, renal failure (dialysis), myasthenia gravis, type II diabetes and hypertension, substance abuse, and stroke. The study group reported degrees of disability as being from minimal to complete; this again varied with exacerbation of illness symptoms.

The initial needs assessment was carried out using three quantitative tools and one qualitative tool: the Spiritual Well-Being Scale (O'Brien, 1999); the Miller Hope Scale (Miller & Powers, 1988; abbreviated with permission of the author); the Life Satisfaction Index-Z (Wood, Wylie, & Sheafor, 1969); and the Spiritual Well-Being Interview Guide (O'Brien, 1999). Following the collection of baseline data, three or more pastoral visits were planned by the parish nurse, with the nursing interventions geared to the health considerations of the study participant. As well as listening to, counseling, and praying with patients, small devotional items such as prayer books, Bibles, religious pictures, or other items requested by a patient were provided to assist in facilitating the practice of his or her faith. At a final pastoral care visit, study participants were again evaluated in terms of spiritual well-being and quality of life.

The sample population was identified through referrals from a local pastor and from a neighborhood parish, neither of whom had staff engaged in parish nursing, and through several informal referrals. All six individuals approached to participate in the study agreed with enthusiasm; appropriate informed consent procedures were carried out prior to initiation of the research.

The initial exploration of the impact of parish nursing on a group of chronically ill persons revealed that all benefited from the pastoral care interventions of the parish nurse. The quantitative measurement tools identified a number of spiritual needs and concerns amenable to pastoral counseling, such as "uncertainty that God might not take care of one's needs"; "getting angry" at God for "letting bad things happen" to oneself or to persons one cares about; frustration about not being able to attend church because of disability; fear of having done some things "for which God might not forgive"; and "uncertainty" about being at peace with God and with God's care. There were, however, a number of positive changes documented in response to these items following the parish nurse's intervention. One example is the case of a 45-year-old man, suffering from several chronic illnesses, who asserted that the parish nurse's visits had helped him a great deal. In his initial assessment, the patient agreed that there were "some things for which [he feared] God may not forgive [him]"; following the parish nursing intervention the study participant disagreed with the item, that is, he no longer was living with the fear that God would not forgive him for perceived transgressions.

The patient's spiritual well-being measures also changed positively on a number of other items following nursing intervention. For example, at baseline interview (Time 1 [T1]), he responded that he was "uncertain" about whether he was at peace with God but at follow up (Time 2 [T2]), he agreed that he was at peace. At T1 he admitted "uncertainty" about three other items: receiving strength and comfort from spiritual beliefs, believing God is interested in activities of his life, and spiritual beliefs supporting a positive image of himself and others as members of God's family, but at T2 the patient responded affirmatively to all three items. At T1, the study participant disagreed that he found "any satisfaction in religiously motivated activities" but at T2 he strongly agreed. At T1, he agreed to having "pain associated with spiritual beliefs," but at T2 he strongly disagreed. Finally, at T1 the study participant admitted to sometimes feeling "far away" from God, but at T2 he disagreed with having any such perception.

It is important to note that this patient also reflected a number of positive changes in terms of hope and life satisfaction following the parish nurse's intervention, including being positive about most aspects of life, being able to set goals, being positive about the future, being valued for who he was, looking forward to doing things he enjoyed, trying to do things important to him, things seeming better, being as happy as when younger, things being as interesting and being as satisfied with life as before his illness, and feeling that he had gotten most of the important things and what he had expected out of life.

In his responses to the qualitative study questions, this study participant also reported a very positive response to the interactions he had had with the parish nurse. The patient had asked for a devotional item that was unfamiliar to the parish nurse and to the study's principal investigator. It was called (he thought) a "prayer box" to help organize his prayers. The patient, who self-identified as Protestant, did not belong to any particular church but did have a strong belief in the existence of God. Through the use of a religious articles catalog, the research team located a small wooden box labeled a "God box"; the box came with a guide for use; it was suggested that the user write out thoughts, concerns, or prayers and place them in the box as one might make entries into a journal. The study participant reported at a follow-up interview that he was delighted with his prayer box. "I use that, I have something in it right now, in the box. The 'God box' I found extremely comforting. I put some real issues that I'm facing and the fact that I was trying to take my will back and get in [God's] way. I wrote it all down on a piece of paper, all my concerns and issues and fears, and then at the end I said 'God I'm putting this in Your hands.' Almost a ceremonial kind of thing. I put it in the box and I prayed over it and then put the box away and walked away."

The patient concluded, "It helped me to be able to put [my concerns and fears] someplace else; to, like, take it out of my head and put it there [in the 'God box']."

Comments of other study participants following the parish nurse's interactions reflected similar positive outcomes, such as "I am at peace with God"; "I don't know how people survive without a trust and faith in God"; "That [practice of faith] is what keeps me going"; "Without your religion, you would be nowhere"; and "God will not let us have more than we can bear without His help; what a peace that gives you."

A participant in a separate study exploring the functions of parish nursing, Angela, a parish nurse for the past five years, described her understanding of the parish nursing role:

> I think being a parish nurse is being a "be-er," rather than a "do-er." We are there to listen, to be a facilitator, to assess and refer. We're not getting into the doctor's or the community health nurse's turf. Here's an example: You see somebody who's had a headache for weeks and they can't sleep and they have been to the doctor. I look at the spiritual dimension. Maybe there's some spiritual problem that is causing the headaches and the not sleeping; something else may be going on. Maybe they need to talk with the pastor. The parish nurse goes into a house and sees that maybe the dishes are not done, or the steps are starting to crack. Maybe there is someone in the church who can help with that. Or you can see that your client is getting confused

and leaving the stove on; maybe you need to do a referral to the VNA. A lot of us work with volunteers also; you can teach them to take blood pressures and vital signs. I do that, as a representative of my church; and arranging for transportation for people who maybe need to go to a doctor or dentist.

Finally, Angela explained how spirituality was incorporated into her parish nursing interventions:

> Spirituality is all encompassing. Sometimes, these people, it's all they need. They need somebody to listen and to say "let's talk about this." Then you can assess their needs and minister to them if they need that; counseling or referral or whatever comes up. Sometimes it is just that something is wrecking their spiritual equilibrium; something is attacking their spiritual base. It might be guilt or anxiety about something they feel they did wrong. Sometimes it's easier for a person to talk to a nurse before they go to the pastor . . . I think parish nursing is caring; it is a caring ministry. It's spiritual care, and it's health promotion and it's illness prevention. If we could get people to a healthier life style, a more spiritual life style, then they wouldn't get into trouble and need secondary and tertiary care.

This chapter has explored briefly the basic dimensions of parish nursing, including the discipline's professional title change adopted by some practitioners; philosophy, scope, and standards of practice; the history of parish nursing; early models of parish nursing and parish nursing education; working with a faith community; and parish nursing research. Parish nursing is presently a developing subfield within the larger nursing community, but interest in the area is growing rapidly. New parish nursing education programs continue to be developed by colleges and universities and by church-related organizations. It is hoped that eventually there will be ANA certification for parish nurses. Until this comes about, however, professional nurses who feel called by God to serve within a faith community continue to support and enhance the parish nursing role through their vision and their dedication. The concept of parish nursing is very new and it is also very old; contemporary parish nurses have embraced their ministry with the caring and commitment of the first-century deacons and deaconesses and with the wisdom and understanding of present-day nursing knowledge. Parish nursing, however it develops in the coming decades, is definitely here to stay.

▶ References

American Nurses Association (1998). *Scope and standards of parish nursing practice.* Washington, DC: American Nurses Publishing.

American Nurses Association. (2012). *Faith community nursing: Scope and standards of practice* (2nd ed.). Silver Spring, MD: Author.

Bennett, F. (2011). ANA, HMA to co-publish Faith Community Nursing: Scope and Standards of Practice. *The American Nurse, 43*(6), 9.

Bond, A. (2011). A congregation and parish nurse meet an angel. *Parish Nurse Perspectives, 10*(4), 6–7.

Breisch, A. J. (2016). ANCC offers certification in faith community nursing. *Tar Heel Nurse, 78*(1), 13.

Council projects: Plan for friendly visiting. (1956). *The Catholic Nurse, 5*(1), 42–44.

Cummings, A. L. (1960). In the parish. *The Catholic Nurse, 8*(3), 26–29.

Donnelly, M. E. (2014). Faith community nursing: Health care in the church. *The Tennessee Nurse, 77*(1), 9.

Dunkle, R. E. (2000). Parish nurses help patients, body and soul. In R. Hunt (Ed.), *Readings in community based nursing* (pp. 316–320). Philadelphia, PA: Lippincott.

Dyess, S., Chase, S., & Newlin, K. (2010). State of research for faith community nursing 2009. *Journal of Religion and Health, 49*, 188–199.

FAQ about HMA & parish nursing. (2001). Connections, *The Health Ministries Association Information & Contacts, 1*(2), 1.

Gustafson, C. (2008). The nurse in parish nursing. In M. Stanhope & J. Lancaster (Eds.), *Public Health Nursing* (pp. 1033–1054). St. Louis: Mosby.

Hinton, S. (2012). Nursing in the Church. *Journal of Christian Nursing, 29*(3), 141.

Kuhn, J. (1997). A profile of parish nurses. *Journal of Christian Nursing, 14*(1), 26–28.

Lloyd, R., & Ludwig-Beymer, P. (1999). Listening to faith communities. In P. Solari-Twadell & M. McDermott (Eds.), *Parish nursing: Promoting whole person health within faith communities* (pp. 107–121). Thousand Oaks, CA: Sage Publications.

Lovinus, B. (1996). A healer in the midst of the congregation. *Journal of Christian Healing, 18*(4), 3–18.

Maddox, M. (2001). Circle of Christian caring: A model for parish nursing practice. *Journal of Christian Nursing, 18*(3), 11–13.

Maddox, M. (2003). Clinical experience in parish nursing. *Journal of Christian Nursing, 20*(2), 18–20.

Martin, G., & Lacoutre, C. (1953). Volunteer nursing. *The Catholic Nurse, 2*(2), 13–14.

Mayernik, D., Resnick, L., Skomo, M., & Mandock, K. (2010). Parish nurse-initiated interdisciplinary mobile health care delivery project. *Journal of Obstetric, Gynecologic and Neonatal Nursing, 39*(2), 227–234.

Mayhugh, L. J., & Martens, K. H. (2001). What's a parish nurse to do: Congregational expectations. *Journal of Christian Nursing, 18*(3), 14–16.

McDermott, M., Solari-Twadell, P., & Matheus, R. (1999). Educational preparation. In P. Solari-Twadell & M. McDermott (Eds.), *Parish nursing: Promoting whole person health within faith communities* (pp. 269–276). Thousand Oaks, CA: Sage Publications.

McGinnis, S., & Zoske, F. (2008). The emerging role of faith community nurses in prevention and management of chronic diseases. *Policy Politics Nursing Practice, 9*, 173–180.

Miles, L. (1997). Getting started: Parish nursing in a rural community. *Journal of Christian Nursing, 14*(1), 22–24.

Miller, J., & Powers, M. (1988). Development of an instrument to measure hope. *Nursing Research, 37*(1), 6–10.

Miller, L. W. (1997). Nursing through the lens of faith: A conceptual model. *Journal of Christian Nursing, 14*(1), 17–20.

Miller, S., & Carson, S. (2010). A documentation approach for faith community nursing. *Creative Nursing, 16*(3), 122–131.

Monay, V., Mangione, C., Sorrell-Thompson, A., & Baig, A. (2010). Services delivered by faith-community nurses to individuals with elevated blood pressure. *Public Health Nursing, 26*(6), 537–543.

O'Brien, M. E. (1999). *Spirituality in nursing: Standing on holy ground.* Sudbury, MA: Jones & Bartlett Learning.

O'Brien, M. E. (2001). *The nurse's calling: A Christian spirituality of caring for the sick.* Mahwah, NJ: Paulist Press.

O'Brien, M. E. (2006). Parish nursing: Meeting spiritual needs of elders near the end of life. *Journal of Christian Nursing, 23*(1), 28–33.

Palmer, J. (2001). Parish nursing: Connecting faith and health. *Reflections on Nursing Leadership, 27*(1), 17–19; 45–46.

Parish nursing: Building on the spiritual dimensions of nursing. (2001). *Pennsylvania Nurse, 55*(6), 8–9.

Patterson, D., & Slutz, M. (2011). Faith community/parish nursing: What's in a name? *Journal of Christian Nursing, 28*(1), 31–33.

Peterson, C. (2011). Faith community nursing/parish nursing in a frontier state. *Parish Nursing Perspective, 10*(2), 17.

Quenstedt-Moe, G. (2003). Parish nursing & home care: A blended role? *Journal of Christian Nursing, 20*(3), 26–30.

Rydholm, L. (1997). Patient focused care in parish nursing. *Holistic Nursing Practice, 11*(3), 47–60.

Schank, M. J., Weis, D., & Matheus, R. (1996). Parish nursing: Ministry of healing. *Geriatric Nursing, 17*(1), 11–13.

Schroepfer, E. (2016). A renewed look at faith community nursing. *MEDSURG Nursing, 25*(1), 62–66.

Shores, C. I. (2014). Spiritual interventions and the impact of a faith community nursing program. *Issues in Mental Health Nursing, 35*(4), 299–305.

Solari-Twadell, P. (1999). The emerging practice of parish nursing. In P. Solari-Twadell & M. McDermott (Eds.), *Parish nursing: Promoting whole person health within faith communities* (pp. 3–24). Thousand Oaks, CA: Sage Publications.

Solari-Twadell, P., & Westberg, G. (1991). Body, mind and soul: The parish nurse offers physical, emotional and spiritual care. *Health Progress, 72*(7), 24–28.

Souther, B. (1997). Congregational nurse practitioner: An idea whose time has come. *Journal of Christian Nursing, 14*(1), 32–34.

Stewart, L. E. (2000). Parish nursing: Renewing a long tradition of caring. *Gastroenterology Nursing, 23*(3), 116–120.

Story, C. (2001, April). Carol's corner. *Puget Sound Parish Nurse Ministries, 3*, 1.

Swinney, J., Anson-Wonkka, C., Maki, E., & Corneau, J. (2001). Community assessment: A church community and the parish nurse. *Public Health Nursing, 18*(1), 40–44.

Thompson, P. (2010). Clergy knowledge and attitudes concerning faith community nursing: Toward a three-dimensional scale. *Public Health Nursing, 27*(1), 71–78.

Trofino, J., Hughes, C., O'Brien, B., Mack, J., Marrinan, M., & Hay, K. (2000). Primary care parish nursing: Academic, service and parish partnership. *Nursing Administration Quarterly, 25*(1), 59–74.

Van Dover, L., & Pfeiffer, J. (2011). Patients of parish nurses experience renewed spiritual identity: A grounded theory study. *Journal of Advanced Nursing, 68*(8), 1824–1834.

Westberg, G. (1990). *The parish nurse: Providing a minister of health for your congregation*. Minneapolis, MN: Augsburg.

Westberg, G. (1999). A personal historical perspective on whole person health and the congregation. In P. Solari-Twadell & M. McDermott (Eds.), *Parish nursing: Promoting whole person health within faith communities* (pp. 35–41). Thousand Oaks, CA: Sage Publications.

Wiebe, G. (2008). Why is it so hard to talk about spirituality? *Newsletter of the Parish Nurse Interest Group of the Registered Nurses Association of Ontario, Spring*, 8.

Wilson, R. P. (1997). What does a parish nurse do? *Journal of Christian Nursing, 14*(1), 13–16.

Wood, V., Wylie, M., & Sheafor, B. (1969). An analysis of a short self-report measure of life satisfaction. *Journal of Gerontology, 24*(2), 465–469.

Woodgate, M. V. (1946). *St. Louise de Marillac*. London, England: B. Herdor Book Company.

Wordsworth, H., Moore, R., & Woodhouse, D. (2016). Parish nursing: A unique resource for the community and district nurses. *British Journal of Community Nursing, 21*(2), 66–74.

Wordsworth, H. (2007). Reclaim the spirit. *Nursing Standard, 22*(10), 22.

Zerson, D. (1994). Parish nursing: 20th century fad? *Journal of Christian Nursing, 11*(2), 19–22.

Ziebarth, D., & Miller, C. (2010). Exploring parish nurses' perspectives of parish nurse training. *Nursing 2010, 41*(6), 273–280.